Minding the Gap Between Restorative Justice, Therapeutic Jurisprudence, and Global Indigenous Wisdom

Marta Vides Saade
Ramapo College of New Jersey, USA

Debarati Halder
Parul Institute of Law, Parul University, India

A volume in the Advances in Public Policy and Administration (APPA) Book Series

LIBRARY
GRANT MacEWAN
UNIVERSITY

Published in the United States of America by
  IGI Global
  Information Science Reference (an imprint of IGI Global)
  701 E. Chocolate Avenue
  Hershey PA, USA 17033
  Tel: 717-533-8845
  Fax: 717-533-8661
  E-mail: cust@igi-global.com
  Web site: http://www.igi-global.com

Library of Congress Cataloging-in-Publication Data

Names: Vides Saade, Marta, 1957- editor. | Halder, Debarati, 1975- editor.
Title: Minding the gap between restorative justice, therapeutic
  jurisprudence, and global indigenous wisdom / Marta Vides Saade, and
  Debarati Halder, editor.
Description: Hershey, PA : Information Science Reference, [2023] | Includes
  bibliographical references and index. | Summary: "The intent of this
  book is to bridge the gap in which differences create challenges or
  obstacles to either restorative justice , therapeutic jurisprudence , or
  both, and recommends approaches that would move that gap to a place of
  transformation that is not merely illusory"-- Provided by publisher.
Identifiers: LCCN 2022020101 (print) | LCCN 2022020102 (ebook) | ISBN
  9781668441121 (hardcover) | ISBN 9781668441138 (paperback) | ISBN
  9781668441145 (ebook)
Subjects: LCSH: Restorative justice. | Therapeutic jurisprudence. |
  Ethnophilosophy.
Classification: LCC HV8688 .M565 2023 (print) | LCC HV8688 (ebook) | DDC
  364.6/8--dc23/eng/20220606
LC record available at https://lccn.loc.gov/2022020101
LC ebook record available at https://lccn.loc.gov/2022020102

This book is published in the IGI Global book series Advances in Public Policy and Administration
(APPA) (ISSN: 2475-6644; eISSN: 2475-6652)

British Cataloguing in Publication Data
A Cataloguing in Publication record for this book is available from the British Library.

All work contributed to this book is new, previously-unpublished material.
The views expressed in this book are those of the authors, but not necessarily of the publisher.

For electronic access to this publication, please contact: eresources@igi-global.com.

Advances in Public Policy and Administration (APPA) Book Series

ISSN:2475-6644
EISSN:2475-6652

MISSION

Proper management of the public sphere is necessary in order to maintain order in modern society. Research developments in the field of public policy and administration can assist in uncovering the latest tools, practices, and methodologies for governing societies around the world.

The **Advances in Public Policy and Administration (APPA) Book Series** aims to publish scholarly publications focused on topics pertaining to the governance of the public domain. APPA's focus on timely topics relating to government, public funding, politics, public safety, policy, and law enforcement is particularly relevant to academicians, government officials, and upper-level students seeking the most up-to-date research in their field.

COVERAGE

- Government
- Law Enforcement
- Political Economy
- Politics
- Public Administration
- Public Funding
- Public Policy
- Resource Allocation
- Urban Planning

IGI Global is currently accepting manuscripts for publication within this series. To submit a proposal for a volume in this series, please contact our Acquisition Editors at Acquisitions@igi-global.com or visit: http://www.igi-global.com/publish/.

Titles in this Series

For a list of additional titles in this series, please visit: http://www.igi-global.com/book-series/]

Societal Transformations and Resilience in Times of Crisis
Ghazala Shoukat (University of Sindh, Pakistan) and Muhammad Nawaz Tunio (Alpen Adria University, Autria)
Information Science Reference • © 2023 • 320pp • H/C (ISBN: 9781668453261) • US $215.00

African Policy Innovation and the Political Economy of Public-Private Policy Partnerships
Fred Olayele (Sprott School of Business, Carleton University, Cnada)
Information Science Reference • © 2022 • 297pp • H/C (ISBN: 9781799873839) • US $215.00

Interdisciplinary Approaches to the Future of Africa and Policy Development
Icarbord Tshabangu (Leeds Trinity University, UK)
Information Science Reference • © 2022 • 375pp • H/C (ISBN: 9781799887713) • US $215.00

Direct Democracy Practices at the Local Level
Christophe Emmanuel Premat (Stockholm University, Sweden)
Information Science Reference • © 2022 • 325pp • H/C (ISBN: 9781799873044) • US $215.00

Handbook of Research on Interdisciplinary Studies on Healthcare, Culture, and the Environment
Mika Markus Merviö (Kibi International University, Japan)
Information Science Reference • © 2022 • 365pp • H/C (ISBN: 9781799889960) • US $270.00

Challenges and Barriers to the European Union Expansion to the Balkan Region
Bruno Ferreira Costa (University of Beira Interior, Portugal)
Information Science Reference • © 2022 • 372pp • H/C (ISBN: 9781799890553) • US $215.00

701 East Chocolate Avenue, Hershey, PA 17033, USA
Tel: 717-533-8845 x100 • Fax: 717-533-8661
E-Mail: cust@igi-global.com • www.igi-global.com

This book is dedicated the ancestors who are always with us,
to the ancient Grandmothers and Grandfathers who purify us,
to the two-legged, four-legged, winged, finned, rooted, and flowing,
to the Elders who walk among us and teach us,
and for the ancestors yet to come.

Noxtin Nomecayotzin – All My Relations
Vasudhaiva Kutumbakam – The World is One Family

Editorial Advisory Board

Table of Contents

Section 1
Indigenous Wisdom: Africa and the Diaspora

    Seth Tweneboah, University of Education, Winneba, Ghana
    Anthony Richards, Wild Caribbean, Barbados

    Johnson Oluwole Ayodele, Lead City University, Nigeria
    Jane Roli Adebusuyi, Lead City University, Nigeria

    Angelo Kevin Brown, Arkansas State University, USA

Detailed Table of Contents

Section 1
Indigenous Wisdom: Africa and the Diaspora

Chapter 1
    Seth Tweneboah, University of Education, Winneba, Ghana
    Anthony Richards, Wild Caribbean, Barbados

This chapter explores the role of traditional methods of social control that deploy the power of the deities as a missing dimension of justice delivery. The authors present the rituals associated with deploying the traditional mechanism of control as both reconciliatory and therapeutic. Drawing on both historical and contemporaneous instances from Ghana and the Caribbean, the chapter contends that the continuous reliance on African spirit-based justice delivery method betrays not only the insufficiencies in the Western superimposed adversarial legal system but also a tacit and open rejection of this imported system. The chapter interrogates the prospects and pitfalls of indigenous Africa and its diasporan conflict resolution mechanism.

Chapter 2

Johnson Oluwole Ayodele, Lead City University, Nigeria
Jane Roli Adebusuyi, Lead City University, Nigeria

The Yoruba people have unwritten normative, proverb-driven traditional jurisprudence to resolve all emerging disputes. Regrettably, colonialism suddenly emerged to compel the Yoruba people to drop their restorative treatment of the primary justice stakeholders and replace it with the castigatory European justice paradigm. This chapter studies the inclusive character of the traditional justice system of the Yoruba of southwestern Nigeria. It collected secondary data from the internet and archival sources. Data analysis indicates that including the victims, offenders, and the community in conflict management enhances the Yoruba traditional conflict resolution skills. To creatively halt the miscarriage of justice in postcolonial Yorubaland, policymakers should transform the justice systems to ground solutions for disputes in local realities. Also, both justice systems should replace competition with cooptation and embrace a symbiotic restorative response to dispute resolution for the deepening of Yoruba jurisprudence.

Chapter 3

Angelo Kevin Brown, Arkansas State University, USA

The indigenous peoples of Southern Africa have a tradition of using restorative justice practices. The region has used restorative justice practices primarily until European colonization had enforced a Western criminal justice and legal system. During and after colonization, Southern Africa has continued to use traditional methods for public safety and resolving conflicts in communities. This led to governments having a dual system in which nonserious violations are usually handled in the traditional courts, and the more serious crimes are handled in the formal criminal courts.

Section 2
Indigenous Wisdom: Middle East

Chapter 4

Mehrdad Rayejian Asli, The Institution for Research and Development
in Humanities (SAMT), Iran

Despite the recognition of the concept of 'restorative justice' in the Persian literature of criminal sciences during recent decades, Iran has a long history of traditional customs and heritages with restorative function that their origins could be found in both pre-Islamic and post-Islamic historical eras. However, the restorative practices have entailed contradictory outcomes of reception and censure. The sympathizers believe that they are a specific means for interaction and relations between tribes, clans, and ethnic groups, or mechanisms of social control. But the opponents criticize such practices due to their potential detrimental consequences particularly in some cases of forced marriage. Notwithstanding these considerations and concerns, one approach to this issue alongside the subject of the present book is to inquire the capacities of restorative practices within domestic customs and traditions of Iranian society. In addition, the legislative manifestations of restorative practices within the Iranian legal system and challenges of the related legislation deserve to be discussed.

Section 3
Indigenous Wisdom: India

Chapter 5

Beulah Shekhar, National Forensic Sciences University (NFSU), India
Ranjani Castro, Karunya Institute of Technology and Sciences, India
Hitesh Goyal, National Forensic Sciences University (NFSU), India

The research will conceive restorative justice and therapeutic jurisprudence as two sides of the same coin, and one is the result of the other as a major development in criminological thinking. Notwithstanding, roots in a variety of indigenous cultures, including spirituality and holistic healing traditions and strives to re-connect offenders with their surroundings and communities. The objective of this research is to explore the experiences of victims and offenders involved in restorative justice practices, concerning increase in their general well-being, self-esteem, and satisfaction of the process and decrease in their feeling of shame, guilt, stress, regret, and anger. Restorative justice mechanisms enhance therapeutic jurisprudence through restoration, resilience, reconciliation, reintegration, rehabilitation, reformation, and resocialization among victims and offenders. Another objective is to understand from practitioners whether restorative practices facilitate conflict resolution and discuss the alternate conflict resolution model for restorative justice and therapeutic jurisprudence.

Chapter 6
*Swikar Lama, Sardar Patel University of Police, Security, and Criminal
Justice, Jodhpur, India*

Restorative justice is a type of alternative dispute resolution, but not all ADR (Alternative Dispute Resolution) procedures constitute restorative justice. This chapter examines community-based alternative dispute resolution systems, attempting to distinguish the similarities and differences between ADRS (Alternative Dispute Resolution Systems) and restorative justice procedures. It examines whether these community-based ADRs adhere to restorative justice principles such as victim empowerment, deliberate effort by those involved in decision-making to reduce stigmatization and punishment of the offender, emphasis on strengthening or repairing interpersonal relationships, and so on. It also looks into whether formal restorative justice processes could imbibe some of the good features of these community-based ADRs.

Chapter 7
Debarati Halder, Parul Institute of Law, Parul University, India

Therapeutic jurisprudence (TJ) emphasizes the law's healing touch to cure the socio-legal evils that may hamper the wellbeing of people at large. The chapter deals with extramarital affairs, breach of trust in marriages, and the role of TJ in restitution of justice for spouses, especially female spouses who may be pushed to trauma, extreme depression, frustration, and anger due to extramarital affairs by unfaithful husbands with special reference to India. In ancient Hindu Codes and customary laws, extramarital affairs by husbands did not find specific mention as offensive behavior in marriage. This has led the contemporary laws to not acknowledge extramarital affairs as offences in marriage. But in the ancient times, women in India had rights to seek restitution of justice from family elders and community elders. This alternative dispute resolution mechanism provided much needed healing touch. The chapter researches on the hidden role of TJ in the ancient and contemporary laws in India dealing with victimization of women by way of extramarital affairs by husbands.

Section 4
Indigenous Wisdom: Native American and First Nation

Chapter 8

*Rosemary White Shield, Council of State Governments Justice Center,
    USA
Rod Robinson, Center for Strength Based Practices, USA*

Many aspects of global Indigenous wisdom teach us that true justice is a spiritual force that allows for the ebb and flow of balance to enter and sustain human reality. Within this form of justice is the organic movement of healing and restoration for the continuation of life. Indigenous perspectives on the concept and practice of restorative justice are often expressed as a process that acts to open a pathway for justice intended to restore balance and to engage the healing process for individuals, families, communities, and creation. The chapter presents the kinship system model as a non-linear structure within an indigenous paradigm to reference principles of restorative justice, therapeutic jurisprudence, and Indigenous wisdom through a non-colonial process of discernment, understanding, and ways of knowing.

Foreword:
Revitalizing and Using Indigenous Ways of Wisdom

Each day in Native North America, we see the devastation that Western colonization has done to Indigenous cultures, spirituality, languages, lands, traditional governments, and ways of life. America's Indigenous peoples rank at the bottom in every socio-economic category. North America's Indigenous peoples suffer from poor health, the lowest life expectancy, poor educational achievement, social problems such as suicide, alcoholism, and drug abuse, the highest unemployment rate, and lack of sustainable economic development on lands designated as reservations and reserves. Driven by racism and beliefs that Indigenous peoples were uncivilized, heathens, and inferior, the European colonizers and their successor settler-nations confiscated lands and exploited abundant natural resources while removing Indigenous peoples from ancestral lands and destroying traditional governments and ways of life. Western governmental structures, laws, adversarial courts, and jails replaced traditional governments and laws and methods of maintaining social order that had taken centuries to develop. The authors in this book show that colonialism's destruction of Indigenous peoples' traditional ways of life is not confined to North America but is common throughout much of the Indigenous world. What, then, should the world's Indigenous peoples do to address and overcome these challenges and problems so that they can move into the future on their own terms.

Indigenous peoples were doing just fine before Western laws, institutions, methods, and ways of life were imposed on them. The path, then, to modern self-determination and improved quality of life for Indigenous peoples partially lies in their own ancient knowledge, spiritual traditions, concepts of balance and harmony, ways of kinship, consensual problem-solving, holistic healing traditions, and traditional governing and dispute resolution practices. Bringing Indigenous knowledge to bear on modern disputes (and other social and economic problems) requires revitalizing and reconstructing doctrines, principles, rules, customs, practices, and morals that may have fallen into disuse due to colonization or suppression.

Certain ancient knowledge may have been forgotten, but remnants of others may be recoverable and reconstructed for modern application. Drs. Tweneboah and Richards suggest that ancient African rituals, suppressed by colonialism and now dormant, could be reanimated and used for reconciliation and therapeutic jurisprudence in the Caribbean area because they are ancestral methods of social control. Drs. Ayodele and Adebusuyi tell us that colonialism overwhelmed Yoruba traditional proverb-driven jurisprudence so that it was abandoned in favor of Western justice paradigms. They recommend restoration of this ancient method so that justice can be realized through the participation of victims, offenders, and their communities. Experience shows that disputants and their families honor and respect outcomes when they participate in finding solutions to the underlying cause of the dispute.

Whether the process is called restorative justice or therapeutic jurisprudence, the end result should be to positively reconnect the offender with the community, as Dr. Shekhar, Ms. Castro, and Mr. Goyal state. The focus, however, should not be entirely on the offender because the victim has greater interests at stake. These scholars posit that Indigenous peoples' ways of resolving disputes should leave both victim and offender with less feelings of shame, guilt, stress, regret, and anger. Positive feelings of well-being, better self-esteem, and satisfaction with the process should be the results. Worthy of note is that some of the elements of restorative justice and therapeutic jurisprudence are used in Native American traditional dispute resolution methods (peacemaking).

A dual system where Indigenous justice methods interface with or operate alongside formal Western-style courts works too as the Diné (Navajo people), who live in the southwestern United States, have experienced. Some Indigenous peoples favor culturally and spiritually derived methods over Western imposed laws and courts. Indigenous restorative justice practices provide alternatives to the colonizer's courts in Southern Africa as Dr. Brown explains. When Indigenous communities relearn and use their centuries-old justice methods, Indigenous traditional justice regains strength, vitality, acceptability, and efficiency and can eventually supersede imposed Western laws and formal courts.

Is restorative justice a form of alternative dispute resolution (ADR)? Dr. Lama analyzes this issue and concludes that restorative justice is a type of ADR but not all ADR procedures comprise restorative justice. There are of course similarities and differences between ADR and restorative justice, as Dr. Lama states, but the overall emphasis should be on victim empowerment, reduced punishment of the offender, less stigmatization of the offender, strengthening or repairing interpersonal relationships among victim and offender and their community, and so on. These outcomes are also desired attributes of many Indigenous peoples' dispute resolution systems world-wide, including those practiced in the Americas.

Indigenous peoples' traditional ways and methods sometimes conflict with commonly accepted modern ways and methods, particularly as they impinge universal human rights. Dr. Halder addresses this issue in the context of extra marital affairs committed by husbands. How should wives be protected in marriage if old customary laws and modern laws do not address a husband's marital misdeeds? A husband's extra marital affair may have negative effects on the mental health of the wife. What remedies should be available to the wife? Dr. Halder suggests that husbands' extra marital affairs should be criminalized and prosecuted as cruelty to wife so that women are protected in marriages, including toxic marriages.

Along the same lines, Dr. Rayejian Asli addresses the issue of conflicts between continuing old customs and modern ways within the context of customary forced marriages which can be detrimental to the well-being of a woman. Dr. Rayejian Asli explains that when a murder is committed, the offender's family forces a female relative to marry into the victim's family as compensatory restorative ritual and practice. Dr. Rayejian Asli's research also explains that certain customs can influence modern criminal legislation and policies to benefit society. Conflicts between old customs and universal human rights and commonly accepted modern ways present difficult questions that will pit people who sympathize with the custom against opponents who will argue that the custom is outdated and harmful and should be retired. Questions about harmful customs and what should be done with them must be discussed and answered with the participation of all segments of the affected society. The state or nation always has final authority to enact laws that protect its citizens.

Indigenous peoples' cultures, languages, connection with place, concepts of property, and ways of life are usually grounded in long-held spiritual or religious beliefs, or whatever term the Indigenous group uses. Dr. White Shield and Mr. Robinson explain that justice, as conceptualized by Indigenous peoples, is usually embedded in spirituality (or religious beliefs); thus, spiritual force drives the processes of restorative justice and therapeutic jurisprudence when Indigenous peoples engage in dispute resolution. The purposes of traditional dispute resolution, from the perspective of most Indigenous peoples, are to heal the disputants and their families (mentally, physically, and spiritually) and communities. The ultimate goals are to restore balance, harmony, and peace consistent with the Indigenous group's worldview so that society can continue to move forward. Kinship, such as relationships with family and clan, is central and vital to most Indigenous peoples' problem-solving methods, including peacemaking, a traditional Native American system of dispute resolution. Dr. White Shield and Mr. Robinson explain that Indigenous peoples utilize the Kinship System Model, a non-linear structure within an Indigenous paradigm, to ensure that healing happens through restorative justice and therapeutic jurisprudence so that balance, harmony, and peace are achieved as essential elements of human reality.

In the pages that follow, scholars from various areas of the globe explain how restorative justice and therapeutic jurisprudence can utilize Indigenous peoples' longstanding methods, customs, traditions, and spiritual concepts to resolve disputes. Although the authors focus their discussions on dispute resolution, the same traditional methods, customs, traditions, and spiritual concepts can be applied beyond dispute resolution to areas such as health, social, and economic problems. Customary concepts can contribute to building safe and thriving Indigenous communities. Indigenous peoples and their allies must share and learn from each other to overcome or alleviate the negative effects of imposed Western laws, institutions, and ways of life. Indigenous peoples can move into the future using their own longstanding traditional methods, norms, customs, and institutions. This is just a way of saying that Indigenous peoples can become self-determining peoples on their own terms.

Raymond D. Austin
Northern Arizona University, USA

Raymond D. Austin *is a faculty member with the Applied Indigenous Studies Department at Northern Arizona University, Flagstaff, Arizona. Previous to his NAU appointment, Dr. Austin taught at the University of Arizona College of Law in Tucson, Arizona. Dr. Austin is Diné (Navajo) from the Navajo Nation. Dr. Austin's book, Navajo Courts and Navajo Common Law, A Tradition of Tribal Self-Governance (University of Minnesota Press, 2009), is the only book available on use of American Indian customary law in the courts of Native nations in the United States. Dr. Austin has written articles on Navajo law and courts for law journals and has given dozens of invited lectures.*

Foreword:
Fruitful Provocations

Back in 1997 as part of a University of Washington Law School symposium, "Indian Law Into the Twenty-First Century," I published what I hoped would be a provocative article. Titled "Overextended Borrowing: Tribal Peacemaking Applied in Non-Indian Disputes," the article challenged a claim that was being advanced by the United States Attorney General, a Justice of the United States Supreme Court, and the President of the American Bar Association, all of them echoing the same point around that same time (Goldberg, 1997). Their claim – that federal and state courts could benefit from incorporating Native American peacemaking into their justice systems – struck me as facile and even romanticizing. Their critique of the adversarial U.S. justice system certainly had merit. But their suggestion that Native American peacemaking could be inserted as a cure for those failings was far more questionable. As a non-Indigenous person who had been researching and teaching about federal Indian law and Native Nations' legal systems for 25 years at that time, I knew enough to doubt the ease of transposing processes steeped in distinctive belief and kinship systems into institutions grounded in wholly different world views and social organization. The differences or "gap" between Native American and Anglo-American cultures, including how those differences played out in the different justice systems, had been well-articulated by many others.

The chapters in this fascinating volume expand in rich detail upon the contrasts stressed in "Overextended Borrowing." First, they look far beyond Indigenous North America, attending to Indigenous and longstanding justice systems in Africa, Asia, the Middle East, and the Caribbean. This wider geographic sweep draws in an array of systems, underscoring both their diverse means of achieving conflict resolution or "peacemaking," as well as the shared ways in which they depart from dominant, colonially derived forms of secular, adversarial justice. Second, they dive deeply into the world views, sources of knowledge, and social arrangements underpinning each system, portraying the specific teachings, spiritual beliefs, and human connections that give each one its sustenance. In some cases, as in the explication of African and Caribbean imprecation, this elaboration helps dispel negative characterizations from outsiders and underscores the restorative or therapeutic nature of the process. A full appreciation of the particularities of these Indigenous justice systems should help erase misconceptions about the ease of incorporating Indigenous peacemaking into very differently constituted Western adversarial systems. Third, by presenting Indigenous perspectives and centering Indigenous ways of knowing, the chapters supply a more grounded approach to the intersections, conflicts, and potential synergies that arise when disparate Indigenous and adversarial justice systems coexist. Suppression of Indigenous justice by colonial regimes is one unavoidable theme. But the enduring idea of justice as a form of healing and of restoring harmonious interpersonal and community relations also emerges powerfully from the accounts of Indigenous systems in this volume. Creative, well-considered ideas for collaboration and integration with more secular, adversarial systems emerge from these explorations, such as those presented in the chapter on justice for Yoruba people in Nigeria.

A prime aspiration of scholarly work is to provoke new investigations and frameworks for thinking. Not only has this volume fulfilled the ambitions of "Overextended Borrowing," it has advanced its own excellent provocations for future research.

Carole E. Goldberg
UCLA, USA

Carole E. Goldberg *is Distinguished Research Professor of Law and the Jonathan D. Varat Distinguished Professor of Law Emerita at UCLA. She has previously served as UCLA's Vice Chancellor, Academic Personnel, Associate Dean of the UCLA School of Law, Chair of UCLA's Academic Senate, and the Oneida Indian Nation Visiting Professor of Law at Harvard Law School. She also serves as Chief Justice of the Court of Appeals of the Hualapai Tribe and Chief Justice of the Court of Appeals of the Pechanga Band of Indians. From 2011 – 2014 she was one of President Barack Obama's appointees to the Indian Law and Order Commission. Professor Goldberg has written widely about federal Indian law and tribal law. She is co-author of a casebook, American Indian Law: Native Nations and the Federal System (7th ed., 2015), and co-editor and co-author of Cohen's Handbook of Federal Indian Law (1982, 2005, and 2012 editions). Her recent books include Defying the Odds: The Tule River Tribe's Struggle for Sovereignty in Three Centuries (Yale University Press, 2010, with Gelya Frank), Captured Justice: Native Nations and Public Law 280 (Carolina Academic Press, 2012 and 2020, with Duane Champagne), and A Coalition of Lineages: The Fernandeño Tataviam Band of Mission Indians (University of Arizona Press, 2021, with Duane Champagne). In 2013 she received the Lawrence Baca Lifetime Achievement Award from the Federal Bar Association's Indian Law Section.*

REFERENCE

Goldberg, C. E. (1997). Overextended borrowing: Tribal peacemaking applied in non-Indian disputes. *Washington Law Review*, 72, 1003–1020.

Preface

OVERVIEW

The title of this volume was inspired by the work of Kathleen Daly whose analysis of data about restorative justice from the South Australia Juvenile Justice (SAJJ) project led her to caution that practitioners and theorists must "mind the gap" in which differences create challenges or obstacles to restorative justice. As she tells it, her reflection started as American amusement with an unfamiliar British term in a London tube referring to the space between the platform and train floor. The timing coincided with the controversies about "gap studies' in socio-legal research, and Richard Abel's (Abel 1980) idea that there are inadvertent consequences or symbolic meaning in the gap between ideals and practice, "image and reality" (p. 810). Dr. Daly's own analysis and discussion was related to the restorative conferencing process used in the SAJJ process. She noted a preference and ease for achieving "fairness" over "restorativeness." Some of this is due to the seemingly more certain solutions in the mainstream justice system compared to the uncertainty in a wrong-doer's apology. And, while she cautions us that while "the nirvana story of restorative justice helps us to imagine what is possible . . . it should not be used as the benchmark for what is practical and achievable." Why not? Because that nirvana story assumes people are ready and able to resolve disputes, that apologies are genuine, and that there is a gap in the "older and newer" understandings of justice that are difficult to traverse. (Daly, 2003) (p. 234)

The intent of this book is to "mind the gap" in which such differences create challenges or obstacles to either restorative justice or therapeutic jurisprudence, or both. Dr. Daly was referring to the gap between a rights-based criminal justice system, and a restorative system that aims to repair harm when she wrote about "older and newer" understandings. She cautioned that to mind the gap would move that gap to a place of transformation that is not merely illusory, or "the nirvana story."

The scholars and practitioners here point to understandings of justice and processes by which to achieve these that are even older, and not only pre-existed rights-based systems, but had the resilience to continue despite historical events that would have seemed to replace them with the dominant system of a new regime, even when these new regimes did impact the influence of these ideas. That is another gap to be minded. This volume privileges those resilient voices to begin a conversation to traverse that gap.

UNDERSTANDING WHAT WE MEAN: THE CONTEXT IN THE WORLD TODAY

In general terms, the contemporary conversations, of theory and practice, restorative justice is about healing the parties, while therapeutic jurisprudence is about creating a legal process that is healing. There is some overlap. In the dominant rights-based systems, these ideas are viewed as alternative practices. In the indigenous understanding, healing the parties through processes that do not harm them is the traditional way and primary.

For heuristic purposes that allow comparison and contrast, the method suggested by Norval Morris of considering the defining, limiting, or guiding principles for a practice, provides the possibility of precision (Morris 1976). A defining principle is one that expresses the norm, or norms that would be determinative. A limiting principle provides a limit, or limits, that cannot be exceeded. A guiding principle expresses a general value, or values, that should be respected unless other values sufficiently strongly justify rejection.

In the Mainstream

In the dominant rights-based system Kant's universal principles are interpreted as principles defined by perfect obligations that are universal and reciprocal, limited by the requirement that a person refrain from treating another person as a means to an end, and guided by what is owed to a person. Onora O'Neill's constructivist interpretation of Kant has offered that his formula of the maxim that one should act so as to will that your action should become a universal law would also include imperfect obligations or incomplete obligations. That means that a rational person would also will that universal principles include something more than mere restraint from using persons as means to an end. If humanity is an end in itself, then persons have an obligation to act positively to further the agency of others. What this means is that instead of a wronged person asking, "What is owed to me?" or a wrongdoer asking "What consequence is owed to me?" they would ask "What ought I to do, given my action (inaction) impinges on others, and may destroy or erode their capacities for action?" Her view is that human beings are not merely distinct rational beings but also vulnerable and needy human beings. Her ideas resonate with those of Amartya

Sen who distinguishes between individual capacities as traits of character and the capability to exercise these effectively. Imperfect obligations that could determine action in the interstitial spaces would define ethical action and by extension define justice, limited by the requirement that direct or indirect indifference to the care of others is rejected, and guided by the vulnerable nature of human persons that required a deliberative response to a particular person (Vides Saade, 2006, pp. 913-919). And yet, while there exist some sources within the philosophical history of mainstream law and justice for a more comprehensive approach to justice, the dominant, mainstream system of justice has a strong preference of rights based on perfect and reciprocal obligations.

This means that the defining principle is retribution primarily through deterrence or incapacitation, limited by desert – meaning deservedness. The guiding principle is protection of society from the wrongdoer. The rehabilitative ideal that is sometimes articulated although not often implemented is insufficient in that its defining principle is the achievement of rehabilitation of the wrongdoer, primarily through incapacitation limited by what is necessary for rehabilitation. This ideal has failed due to lack of necessary services provided for the rehabilitation of the wrongdoer on their own. Here, the guiding principle is restoration of order in the society. In either case, this results in a view that restorative justice and therapeutic jurisprudence are alternative responses to doing justice somehow less than and not as comprehensively effective as the dominant, mainstream system yet will be permitted if useful to that system.

Restorative Justice

There are various ways to describe restorative justice, and yet, the clearest explanation that allows for points of comparison and contrast are the classic three Big Ideas of restorative justice:

1. *The Principle of Repair: Justice requires we work to heal victims, offenders, and communities that have been harmed by crime.*
2. *The Principle of Stakeholder Participation: Victims, Offenders and Communities should have the opportunity for active involvement in the justice process as early and fully as possible.*
3. *The Principle of Transformation in community and government roles and relationships. We must rethink the relative roles and responsibilities of government and the community. In promoting justice, government is responsible for promoting a just order, and community for establishing a just peace.*
    (Van Ness & Strong, 2006; Schiff & Bazemore, 2002)

The first shift from the mainstream rights-based approach to justice was to focus on the person or persons who had been wronged, and away from the wrong-doer. This resulted in a myriad of victims' rights projects. This is a partial move and the writers in the following pages describe a similar history in some of their discussions. The fully restorative practices shifted again to include the community in the process resulting in various forms of conferencing that included wronged, wrong-doer, and the community that also experienced the wrong or to which the wrong-doer would be reintegrated. To the extent restorative justice is has transformational possibilities, that is often viewed as an event between the wronged person and the wrong doer. As to the community stakeholder, the transformational possibilities are many times viewed as primarily concerned with the reintegration of the wrong-doer, and not necessarily a call for social change of the community (Vides Saade, 2008).

Although the term had not yet been adopted, the contemporary revival can be traced to early victim-offender programs in the 1970s, and 1980s, consisted primarily of "post-sentence meetings between victims and offenders in Canada and the USA, and victim-offender mediation for youth justice cases in England, Scandinavia, and Western Europe (Daly and Immarigeon, 1998). When restorative justice, [sometimes termed interchangeably as transformative justice], began to be a widely used term in the early 1990s, it was offered mainly to admitted [already adjudicated] youth, not adult offenders. Sexual and partner or family violence were excluded." (Daly, 2022, Chapter 13). Some of the authors that follow point to a similar trajectory in which the purpose of adopting the restorative approach was viewed as a way to unclog the overload on mainstream court systems by disposing of minor cases. By the 1990s, restorative justice approaches with decision-making processed other than victim-offender mediation became established through the world in places as diverse as New Zealand, Australia, Singapore, the United Kingdom, Ireland, and South Africa, with examples drawn from aboriginal and original peoples of those regions. In Canada and the United States, the peacemaking processes of First Nation and indigenous peoples had considerable influence in the growth and development of these programs (Yazzie & Zion, 1996).

In restorative justice, the defining principle is transformation of all stakeholders, that means wrongdoer, wronged, and society represented by a particular community of stakeholders with possibilities limited by the good of the community. The guiding principle is restoration of balance and harmony.

The challenges to restorative justice emerged in early writings as that of pouring new wine from ancient vines into new wineskins due to the various emerging visions. The concerns focused on the consequences to familiar responses to crime when inserting the new restorative features. In the Christian biblical parable, pouring new wine into old wineskins would cause those to burst (Revised New Jerusalem Bible). At that time four likely consequences were articulated that all seemed possible to reconcile: the challenge to abolish criminal law, the challenge to rank multiple goals, the challenge to determine harm rationally, and the challenge to structure community-government cooperation (Van Ness, 1993). Over time these challenges took on additional dimensions and other challenges emerged.

What those who intended to use restorative justice as a means to an end did not know is that this kind of justice takes time, in fact significantly more time, and contains a higher level of uncertainty in the experience of the parties when it has no cultural, philosophical, or historical context. The perceived fairness of a polite process with established ground rules is easier to believe than the genuineness of the empathy and apology from a wrong doer (Daly, 2002, p. 234). And more, and why this volume was written, that:

Like butterfly collecting there is a tendency within much of restorative justice literature to extract examples (often drawn from around the world or across time) which are abstracted and removed from the cultural environment which sustains them (citations). Again, like the butterfly collector, the examples sought are "pretty" or "exotic" ones that seek to illustrate the case for restorative justice, rather than engage with the less attractive aspects of social arrangement and human relations. ~(Crawford 2002, p. 111)

What was forgotten was that the ancient vines were still producing grapes and the new generations of ancients who grew them were still producing new wine, that the old wineskins had not burst.

Therapeutic Jurisprudence

Like restorative justice, therapeutic jurisprudence generally promotes a less adversarial approach to provide a remedy for harm done by wrongdoing. While a restorative justice approach may be a form of therapeutic jurisprudence, the range of options in therapeutic jurisprudence includes much more. Sometimes, references to these approaches are conflated resulting in confusing analyses. Nevertheless, the origins, core doctrinal and theoretical foundations and historical trajectory of therapeutic jurisprudence is distinct. These approaches cannot be defined by what they are not.

Therapeutic jurisprudence is an interdisciplinary approach that in both practice and theory is best understood as one that is concerned with "the extent to which substantive rules, legal procedures, and the roles of lawyers and judges produce therapeutic or antitherapeutic consequences." (Wexler & Winnick 1991, p. 981). The approach is based on the insights shared by co-founding law professors David Wexler and Bruce Winick of the United States. As Professor David C. Yamada recounts in his comprehensive meta-level examination of therapeutic jurisprudence, the two scholars met fortuitously in 1975 while Professor Wexler was on sabbatical from his appointment at the University of Arizona Law School, and was assigned an office next to Professor Winick at the University of Miami Law School. The rest is history, the story of therapeutic jurisprudence (Yamada, 2021, pp. 667-668). Professor Wexler's work focused on the intersection of mental health and criminal justice, while Professor Winnick's work covered a range of topics and areas of law such as preventive law, criminal justice, mental health, legal practice and legal education (Yamada, 2021 p 669). Their respective body of work was interdisciplinary, and after Professor's Winick death, continues to be so for Professor Wexler. Since then, therapeutic jurisprudence has expanded into a global community of legal educators, legal practitioners, and practitioners from a range of disciplines. In 2017, the International Society for Therapeutic Jurisprudence (ISTJ) was organized. The field then experience a "growth spurt" and now includes writing related to law (Yamada, 2021, pp. 671-678) such as employment law, family law, education law, elder law, and gender law, as well as the original and more directly related work in problem-solving courts such as drug diversion in the criminal courts, mental health law, family dependency treatment courts, domestic violence ours, unified family courts, and tribal healing courts, the latter described as a "sub-category of work on problem-solving courts" (Yamada, 2021, p. 675-676, citations omitted).

Therapeutic jurisprudence has been most fully defined as:

> *[t]he study of the role as therapeutic agent. It is an interdisciplinary enterprise designed to produce scholarship that is particularly useful for law reform. therapeutic jurisprudence proposes the exploration of ways in which consistent with principles of justice and other constitutional values, the knowledge, theories, and insights of the mental health and related disciplines can help shape the development of the law. Therapeutic jurisprudence builds on the insight that the law itself can be seen to function as a kind of therapist or therapeutic agent. Legal rules, legal procedures, and the roles of legal actors (such as lawyers and judges) constitute social forces that, whether intended or not, often produce therapeutic or antitherapeutic consequences. Therapeutic jurisprudence calls for the study of these consequences with the tools of the social sciences to identify them and to ascertain whether the law's antitherapeutic effects can be reduced, and its therapeutic effects enhanced, without subordinating due process and other justice values. . . . Therapeutic jurisprudence suggests that, <u>other things being equal</u>, positive therapeutic effects are desirable and should generally be a proper aim of law, and that antitherapeutic effects are undesirable and should be avoided or minimized. ~(Winick, 1997, pp.185, 188-189)*

Later iterations would add human dignity to this definition, in the words of Michael Perlin it is the "core of the entire therapeutic jurisprudence enterprise," that it is not possible to write about therapeutic jurisprudence "without taking seriously the role of dignity in the legal process" (Perlin, 2017, 1135, 1137). Correspondingly, the element of compassion is frequently viewed as adding to the definition. This be based in the social sciences as psychology of compassion, understood as a "sensitivity to and concern for the suffering of others and a commitment to alleviating and preventing it. The "other" in the context of TJ is any person upon whom the law acts within the legal process" (Hopkins & Bartels, 2019, 107). Or in a philosophical sense as a

virtue, value or disposition to act . . . [Including two elements]

First is empathy – the capacity to sense that another is suffering, and to know what it might feel like to be subjected to that kind of suffering . . . . The second . . . is a felt need to try and alleviate that sensed suffering of others ~(Stobbs, 2020 p 81).

The features of this definition do create challenges in discerning what distinguishes therapeutic from other and the practical application of therapeutic jurisprudence, and how and who defines precisely what constitutes a therapeutic effect. The relationship between therapeutic purposes and the law is another feature that raises questions for theory and practice alike. Still, for purposes of reading the chapters that follow the defining principle is clearly the focus on the role of law and its potential for therapeutic consequences and minimizing harm to the parties, limited by the needs of due process and preservation of the rule of law, guided by the principle that this is a framework for analysis of law for best practices to reform the body of legal procedures using interdisciplinary approaches.

Professor Yamada invites interlocutors to this expanding and fresh conversation:

[W]hile transcending strict ideologies, geographic boundaries, and rigid doctrinal directives. TJ is grounded in a belief that our laws, legal systems, and legal institutions—and legal actors within them—should strive to affirm dignity and well-being, fueled by compassion and informed by insights about what makes us human. Those who find such values, understandings, and objectives for the law compelling and attractive may well find a home in this community of scholars and practitioners. ~(Yamada, 2021, 748-749)

The Voices of Indigeneity

The contributions that follow show how indigenous understandings of the definitions of what justice demands, what community means, what constitutes a therapeutic response, and how restorative reintegration might happen when traditional and historical features are defined on their own terms. These understandings begin with those possibilities for healing and transformation that pre-date the contemporary restorative justice movement or therapeutic jurisprudence school of thought. These authors examine how communities can also include constraining, exclusionary, and repressive influences, whether by tradition or by historical forces. The reader is asked to consider how they would describe the defining, limiting, and guiding principles in the particular contexts offered by the authors.

THE AUDIENCE

The contributions in this book represent a parsing of values, actions and practices in their lived culture and traditions. It is offered to practitioners, academic faculty, academic administrators, undergraduate and graduate students, grant-makers, indigenous elders and holders of tradition, and all those many others, both indigenous and mainstream, who are looking for the way to support those who live in two worlds – both traditional indigenous and mainstream government justice systems.

The intention of these writings is to provide a description of indigenous systems on their own terms, that means defined by the meaning that makes that world view, culture, tradition, and community primary. These understandings are not defined by metaphor, or by what they are not. They represent a distinct set of systems, not a subset of a mainstream system whether innovative or not, and always based in a particular world view, culture, tradition, and community. While these systems might inform mainstream changes wherever indigenous systems are found, these are not the same, and the attempt to adopt terms and processes that are not equivalent is overextended borrowing. A better understanding of the distinctivenss of these differences is what is offered here.

OVERVIEW OF THIS EDITED VOLUME

This edited work was gifted and honored by a Foreword from each of two respected thinkers on the issues presented here. They each took time to read the finished chapters and provide their own considered thoughts to the task intended here. An Introduction opens this edited volume. It is a meta-discussion of the methodological implications of this work, and the challenges and gifts of working from the interstitial spaces. This Preface introduced the context for this subject matter that is both a starting point for those readers new to the topics and a review and highlighting of points to be referenced for those experienced scholars. The Dedication and Acknowledgements express the gratitude towards all those who made this book possible. The Contributors introduce themselves in their own words.

The chapters are divided into four sections represented by eight chapters, and a Conclusion. These are Section 1, "Indigenous Wisdom: Africa and the Diaspora"; Section 2, "Indigenous Wisdom: Middle East"; Section 3, "Indigenous Wisdom: India"; and Section 4, "Indigenous Wisdom: Native American and First Nation." These are followed by a Conclusion that includes closing comments by contributors who were inspired to represent the metaphysical, epistemological, and ontological distinctiveness of their writing through stories, narratives and teachings in their truest form.

In Section 1, Chapters 1 through 3, examine Ghana and the Caribbean, Nigeria, and Southern Africa, respectively. In Chapter 1, Drs. Tweneboah and Richards point to the continued appeal to Akan deities when individuals seek justice in Ghana and in the communities of the Caribbean diaspora. Traditional mechanisms are seen as providing more timely relief and as both reconcilatory and therapeutic. This includes the practice of imprecation, that is of invoking the powers of Akan deities to harm the target, especially after the formal legal system has failed them. Imprecation and other controlled ritual practices, such as the broom trial by ordeal, allow an opportunity to provide a last resort option for reconciliation and healing as well as an initial reference point between parties signaling the seriousness of a conflict by the threat of imprecation. The imposition of colonizing systems has not diminished their influence. The resilience over time and distance of such religious and spiritual systems from Ghana, and neighboring African countries, to the Caribbean has allowed for some permissible integration of the practices when they save time, and yet not a full use within the mainstream court system. The insider view provided by the authors opens the conversation n redefining what it means for a process to be healing or therapeutic.

In Chapter 2, Drs. Ayodele and Adebusuyi recommend that retrieval of the traditional justice system (TJS) of Yorubaland in southwest Nigeria guided by accurate local knowledge, good networks of communication with the grassroots, and deep-rooted traditions to stablize governance. The authors view that TJS should be viewed as the primary justice system, while the formal State court system imposed in colonial times is the alternative. The advantages to the indigenous elder-driven TJS includes such traditional Yoruba practices of *Ayelala*, or incantations to deities, to help capture perpetrators, and other increased community involvement in re-settling formerly incarcerated offenders. Because neither system is a cure-all, the authors propose a hybrid system that is a synergy between the TJS and formal justice systems that would also provide signposts for cultural retrieval of TJS practices displaced by postcolonial systems.

The traditional practices in Southern Africa are the subject of Dr. Brown in Chapter 3. Dr. Brown examines the precolonial traditional practices in Southern Africa, Botswana, Eswatini, Namibia. These include Ubuntu philosophy, and those found in the indigenous communities of South Africa such as the Bantu agricultural community, hunter and gathering groups such as the San, and other herding groups like the Khoikhoi, and the large rural tribes such as the Zulu, Xhosa and Sotho. Many of these practices reemerged in the late 20th century and later as traditional practices were accepted by the contemporary government. Some of these practices continued and were preserved and continued due to the rural nature of where tribes were living, strong tribal ties, and distrust or lack of knowledge of the formal legal system. Customary traditional law has also been codified in South African law to form a hybrid system of Western and traditional practices, including community-based and collective reconcilation for the good of the community, especially regarding less serious crimes. In Botswana where customary traditional law is used for minor offenses, criticism arises over inequality in cases that greatly impact women, as well as lack of protection of suspects. In Lesotho, Eswatini (formerly Swaziland), and Namibia a dual legal system implementing both traditional law and customs as well as the Roman-Dutch influenced common law sytem is practiced. The author attributes the acceptance of hybrid systems to the influence of the South African Truth and Reconcilation Commission proceedings.

In Chapter 4, Dr. Rayejian Asli examines the restorative capacities within pre-Islamic and post-Islamic domestic customs and traditions, together with the legislative adoption of restorative practices witin the Iranian legal system. He selects two traditional rituals that have application between ethnic groups that could be described as restorative practices used to avoid bloodshed. These are: 'cease-blood' or 'peace-blood'[1] (*khoon-bass* or *khoon-solh*) and 'resolution' (*fasl*). Both are related primarily to domestic matters. "Peace-blood is an old Islamic custom for a decision by agreement. Resolution is a pre-Islamic tradition, and a marriage exchange has a key role. Both involve compensation, and have problematic elements that include the exchange of a woman and her dowry as compensation for a loss. These are sometimes preferred because the legal justice system is unavailable. More, Dispute Resolutions Councils have been established with an awareness of such traditional practices. Challenges include human rights considerations and justice system concerns, considerations of social and cultural context, and social solidarity, the difference between adoption of a restorative justice doctrine and its practical implementation.

In Chapter 5, Dr. Shekhar and her co-authors Ms. Castro and Mr. Goyal consider the relationship between restorative justice and therapeutic jurisprudence as developed in India. Their point of departure is that while all restorative justice is consistent with therapeutic jurisprudence not all therapeutic jurisprudence is restorative justice because the therapeutic reformation of law and legal process includes other practices.

They conducted a limited sample of victim-offender mixed-method research design which included both qualitative and quantitative methods for data collection and analysis. Their aim was to study whether restorative justice mechanisms enhance therapeutic jurisprudence through the seven key elements of restorative justice, that is, restoration, resilience, rehabilitation, reintegration, reformation, reconciliation, and resocialization among victims and offenders. They interviewed both victims and offenders. They found satisfaction with the process was high, and point to further study of traditional forms such as *panchayat* and *lok adalat*.

In Chapter 6, Dr. Lama begins with the idea that while restorative justice is a type of alternative dispute resolution system (ADRS), not all alternative dispute resolution systems constitute restorative justice. His work makes a close study of Nyaya Panchayats (Justice Assembly) and the more recent Mahila Panchayats (Women's Assembly), including attending various Samaj sessions, and convenient sampling of twenty women from ten Samaj (Women's Society), as practices that provide an understanding of community necessary for reintegration of the offender into society. He concludes that while while these community-based ADRS have some advantages for local resolution using a traditional format familiar to its users, and adhere to some restorative justice principles, they still need to implement various restorative justice mechanisms in order to instill its principles.

In Chapter 7, Dr. Halder observes that traditional Vedic texts considered marriage to be a sacred institution that united both bride and bridegoom and all the families of the parties to the marriage. Extramarital affairs were regarded as a moral sin with a narrow opportunity for restorative justice and therapeutic effects. Accordingly a woman who experienced a breach of trust in the marriage, such as an extramarital affair, would have family elders and community members to provide therapeutic support. Customary laws regulating marriage were influenced by British laws primarily regarding codes related to entering into the marriage relationship, or regarding extramarital affairs with only a narrow category of persons which may give rise to criminal responsibility. Dr. Halder argues that without recognition of breach of trust as an offense separate from existing criminal penalties for negligence in maintainng a wife and children, such a breach must be included in civil and criminal remedies for domestic violence in order for the wife to have sufficient therapeutic remedies for the physical, financial and psychological harm caused by mainstream court proceedings.

In Chapter 8, Dr. White Shield and Mr. Robinson present a Kinship System Model as an indigenous frame of reference for features for understanding feature of restorative justice and therapeutic jurisprudence. The Kinship System Model is an Indigenous paradigm that places Indigenous values and cultural values at the center. This paradigm originates in Indigenous ways of knowing, including the wisdom found in oral libraries, lived experience, embodied Law, and with Elders. The four aspects of Kinship System Model are: knowledge, synergistic participation, interpretation and expression. It includes principles of balance, healing and a relational worldview to guide the actualizing of justice, restoration, and healing for all concerned as tribally determined. The insight is that these principles are understood as not merely a way of doing justice but as a way of life.

CONCLUSION

This book seeks to avoid the dangerous of over-extended borrowing when examining the contributions of indigenous wisdom throughout the globe. As Dr. Carole Goldberg introduced in her discussion "Overextended Borrowing: Tribal Peacemaking Applied in Non-Indian Disputes," comparing what she termed Indian and non-Indian process, meaning Native American and United States mainstream process:

Cultural differences between Native and non-Indian cultures make the process of cross-cultural importation treacherous at best, and altogether futile at worst. This is true even if, as most borrowing proponents assume, alternatives to the prevailing U.S. legal system are desirable, and tribal peacemaking is working ewll within Indian Country. The operation of tribal peacemaking presupposes certain socio-cultural conditions, such as religious homogeneity and strong kinship networks, that cannot be replicated in most of contemporary non-Indian America. If the non-Indian legal system is to become less adversarial and more effective in resolving conflict, it will have to get that way because of features of non-Indian culture that lend themselves to such transformation, not because of romantic yearnings for a different way of life. ~(Goldberg, 1997, p. 1005)

In offering these these understandings of global indigenous systems drawing on indigenous wisdom, together with principles for comparing and contrasting these systems, this book offers insights to inspire the reader to find ways to honor both the indigenous and mainstream ways of approaching justice in a good way.

Marta Vides Saade
Ramapo College of New Jersey, USA
16 June 2022

REFERENCES

Abel, R. L. (1980). Redirecting Social Studies of Law. *Law & Society Review*, *14*(3), 805–827. doi:10.2307/3053198

Crawford, A. (2002). The State, Community, and Restorative Justice. In L. Walgrave (Ed.), *Restorative Justice and the Law*. Willan.

Daly, K. (2004). Mind the gap: restorative justice in theory and practice. In A. von Hirsch, J. Roberts, A.E. Bottoms, K. Roach, & M. Schiff (Eds.), Restorative Justice and Criminal Justice: Competing or Reconcilable Paradigms? (pp. 231-235). Hart Publishing Co.

Daly, K. (2022). *Remaking Justice after Sexual Violence Essays in Conventional, Restorative, and Innovative Justice* (E. Zinsstag & T. Camp, Eds.). Eleven International Publishing.

Daly, K., & Immarigeon, R. (1998). The past, present, and future of restorative justice: Some critical reflections. *Contemporary Justice Review*, *1*, 21–45.

Goldberg, C. E. (1997). Symposium "Overextended Borrowing: Tribal Peacemaking Applied in Non-Indian Disputes." *Wash. L. Rev., 72*(1003).

Hopkins, A., & Bartels, L. (2017). Paying attention to the Person: Compassion, Equality, and Therapeutic Jurisprudence. In The Methodology and Practice of Therapeutic Jurisprudence. Carolina Academic Press.

Morris, M. (1976). *Punishment, Desert and Rehabilitation. In Equal Justice Under the Law*. U.S. Department of Justice.

Perlin, M. L. (2017). "Have You Seen Dignity?": The Story of the Development of Therapeutic Jurisprudence. *Touro L. Rev.*, *24*(17), 20.

Revised New Jerusalem Bible (RNJB), 2019, 5 Luke 36-39.

Van Ness, D. (1993). New wine and old wineskins: Four challenges of restorative justice. Criminal Law Forum, 4(2), 251-276. doi:10.1007/BF01096074

Van Ness, D., & Strong, K. H. (2006). *Restoring Justice: An Introduction to Restorative Justice*. Anderson.

Vides Saade, M. (2006). Entertaining Angels con Pasión. *University of Detroit Mercy Law Review*, *83*, 5.

Vides Saade, M. (2008). Restorative Justice, Empowerment Theory and Transformative Spirituality: Searching for Authentic Strategies in China, Hong Kong, India, and Korea. In K. van Wormer (Ed.), *Restorative Justice Across the East and the West* (pp. 229–252). Casa Verde Publishing.

Wexler, D.B., & Winick, B.J. (1991). Therapeutic Jurisprudence as a New Approach to Mental Health Law Policy Analysis and Research. *U. Miami. L. Rev., 45*(979).

Winick, B. J. (1997). The Jurisprudence of Therapeutic Jurisprudence. *Psych., Pub. Pol'y. L*, 3, 184.

Yamada, D.C. (2021). Therapeutic Jurisprudence: Foundations, Expansion, and Assessment. *U. Miami L. Rev., 75*(660).

Yazzie, R., & Zion, J. (1996). Navajo Restorative Justice: The Law of Equality and Justice. In B. Galaway & J. Hudson (Eds.), *Restorative Justice: International Perspectives*. Criminal Justice Press.

ENDNOTE

[1] 'Blood stop' and 'blood peace' in other references (e.g., Osanloo, 2020, p. 11).

Acknowledgment

Thank you to those whose words through time and space inspired this book. Dr. Raymond Austin, Dr. Carole Goldberg, and Dr. Kathleen Daly. Special gratitude for your words in the Foreword matter in this volume, and for the title.

To each and all members of the Editorial Advisory Board for your unwavering professionalism, precision, and generous service in the double-blind peer review process. Thank you for your candid and encouraging words to the authors, and for the occasional recommendations for chapter contributors. For those who worked through sabbaticals, family-caregiving, natural disasters, at the start of your retirement plans, ceremonial obligations, completing your own writing or work, and other intervening events of life, there are no words. Without your timely work this book would not have made it to print.

To each and all of the contributing authors for your answer to the invitation and call to offer words at this time and place to share with a community of practitioners, scholars, students, and holders of indigenous traditions, thank you – for persisting with the strength, and creative authorship that made it possible for you to carry those traditions forward, and for coming to this time and place to leave your beautiful and valuable words.

To the publisher of this book for inviting an edited volume on how cultural worldview challenges restorative justice and therapeutic jurisprudence. The year from those initial conversations flew by. Special appreciation for those representatives who patiently and kindly opened paths to make the work possible even when challenges arose.

And, on behalf of everyone who worked on this project, heartfelt appreciation to all the named and unnamed family and community members who supported each and all of us, throughout the days and months of attention to this project. We are humbled by your trust.

Introduction

This Introduction is an invitation to the reader to consider a meta-discussion of the methodological implications of this work, and the challenges and gifts of working from the interstitial spaces.

In the Preface, readers will find a concise summary of what is meant by restorative justice, therapeutic jurisprudence, and how those concepts might be compared and contrasted to understandings in indigenous wisdom that bear a superficial resemblance to those ideas. Here is presented a discussion of the "how," and "why" questions.

In his recent article "From 'what works' to 'how it works' in research on restorative justice conference: the concept of readiness," Dr. Suzuki introduces the variable of a participant's attitudes and emotional dispositions to engage in restorative justice conferencing as a feature to be considered in research on the effectivenss of such a process. This idea might be instructive in framing some of the complexities when considering the gap between restorative justice, therapeutic jurisprudence and indigenous wisdom. For Suzuki readiness is defined as "participants' attitude, emotional dispositions towards and knowledge about restorative justice and the other parties prior to a face-to-face meeting." Suzuki applies his ideas to conventional statistical anlysis with a focus on negative outcomes such as "dissatisfaction, hostile attitudes towards the other party and perceived insincerity of apology" (Suzuki, 2020, p. 360). These are among the problemmatic issues mentioned by some of the authors in this volume. There are certainly others. For Suzuki, readiness has three dimensions: orientation, emotion, and knowledge. Orientation refers to the scope and limit of a particular participant's attitude toward achieving a restorative outcome. (Suzuki, 2020, p. 361, citations omitted) Orientation includes the extent to which the participants are influenced by other motives whether social or strategic. The authors in this volume point to such mixed motives on the part of participants, as well as the mainstream system acknowledgement of local, indigenous processes. Emotion refers to the emotionally charged nature of restorative justice processes, that for purposes of this Introduction might also be said of solutions offered by therapeutic jurisprudence. Problemmatic emotions include nervousness about the process, distress about the underlying event that resulted in the process – including psychological effects such as fear, as well as physical issues such as lack of sleep, headaches, and so on (Suzuki, p. 363-364, citations omitted). While these might dissipate sufficiently to make the process effective, some authors who follow point out that high emotions, sometimes condoned and other times encouraged, in local processes might be either contrary to the stated purpose of restorative or therapeutic sessions or make the possibilities offered by these processes inappropriate for one or all parties involved. And finally, knowledge as a dimension of readiness refers to the preparation and level of understanding that participants have about the purpose of the particular process (Suzuki, 2020, p. 364-365, citations omitted). As some of the authors writing about indigenous practices point out, the information and understanding of participants is sometimes limited by their access to a full range of justice options, as well as a mistrust of some of these options due to historical experience or difference in worldview. For the further research suggested by authors here, such an analysis could yield information that would include consideration of epistemological concerns raised by indigenous understandings.

Indigenous Methodology

This book aimed at providing insights and research *with* Indigenous people, not *on* or *about* them. The form of language influences ways of thinking and being. To the extent that research involves the wording of questions when doing quantitative inquiry, and narrative in qualitative inquiry, language is important. Many indigenous languages reflect a non-binary, holistic understanding and worldview. Binary language and choices limit categories to mainstream epistemology, that is a certain way of knowing, usually linear (Waters, 2004). One reason for the movement to recover indigenous languages is to find an understanding of particular indigenous beliefs and values. Yet this is a "layered endeavour" when living in both binary and non-binary worlds. Eliminating the "Western gaze" remains a challenge for any researcher who seeks to do research "with" indigenous people. "Indigenous methodologies, based as they are on Indigenous epistemologies, distinguish themselves from qualitative approaches embedded in Western history and intellectual tradition. However, Indigenous methododolgies coexist with qualitative research" (Kovach, 2021, p. 24-26).

According to Margaret Kovach, "[f]or a methodology to be correctly identified as an Indigenous methodology, it must be anchored in Indigenous epistemology, theory, ethics, story, and community" (Kovach 2021, p. 42). She recommends a Prologue, in any writing that would allow the writer to situate oneself within their particular community (Kovach, 2021, p. 144). In this volume, the Conclusion provides that opportunity to some extent. Trust and trustworthiness of information being conveyed is verified by the character of the person sharing the knowledge.

Citing the unpublished doctoral dissertation of Winona Stevenson (2000), Margaret Kovach writes:

From a Néhiyaw perspective, Winona Stevenson (2000) states that truth (validity) or tâpwê, is bound with the integrity of the person sharing knowledge. Stevenson makes the following suggestion to the Indigenous historian: "The tasks of tribal historians are to recover the past and to present it to the public in a form that meets the approval of the people whose histories and lives it represents" (p. 298). Our stories, our research, are our tâpwê. It is about standing behind one's words and recognizing collective protocol, about showing that one is accountable for one's words. The story is not separate from the teller or the audience. This is an ethical and axiological premise of Indigenous practice and often conflicts with the objective, decontextualized notion of truth and trustworthiness found within Western intellectual tradition.

While this is a challenge not limited to indigenous methodology, in fact it is the challenge posed by other formerly marginalized voices, the importance to indigenous research resides in the primacy of oral tradition as a source of knowledge. "Oracy, as a form of knowledge sharing, relies upon the spoken word associated with a simultaneous witnessing other. . . . The written expression of Indigenous knowledges does not supersede the oral tradition in Indigenous societies." Oracy includes reciprocity between speaker and listener, teacher and student, and community. Much is lost in translation by written reductions (Kovach, 2021, p. 30, 247-249). In an academic culture that privileges written product, it might be prudent to remember that much of what is considered sacred scriptural text, now reduced to somewhat established canons or interpretations by esteemed seers over time, were once stories, oracy preserved by memory. Empirical knowledge is gained through observations. Stories allow for the valuing of intangible knowledge such as the "inward knowing [that] exists in ceremony, through fasts, and is communicated through dreams and by sitting in circle" (Kovach 2021, p. 218, citations omitted).

In order to seek to understand across the gap of research methods and language, "strategic concessions " in the use of terminology and application of concepts are necessary on the part of both indigenous and mainstream interlocutors. (Kovach, 2021, p. 110, citing Smith, 2006). The authors in this volume made their best effort to navigate this gap and are to be commended.

What can be said about indigenous ways of knowing:

Experiential knowledge is organic and kinetic and embedded in the subjectivity of lived experience. As such, thought, feeling, and action are all respected. In the presence of a respect-based holism, dichotomies dissolve. Because being and doing are intricately related, we can say that Indigenous epistemologies are holistic, animate epistemologies that are axiological in nature (i.e., based on values, ethics, spirituality, and aesthetics). Indigenous theory flows from this epistemological assumption concerning Indigenous knowledge production. ~ (Kovach, 2021, p. 182)

Interstitial Spaces

When writing, identity in difference is the place of conscience. While Anne Waters considers that it may be the case that as Vine Deloria claims that for the American Indians "that identity manifestations, i.e., our ways of being in the world, may or may not be conscious awareness[,]" she makes a different inference. To the extent that "American Indian consciousness, and hence American Indian identity, is cognitively of, and interdependent with, our land base," [she focues on] what it means for inner/outer indentity, and for consciousness and worldview preservation" (Waters, 2004 p. 155). Her discussion uses her own story of living in the in-between, interstitial spaces and what she calls "creative cognitive dissonance."

At once,

the serious philosopher, searching for some semblance of meaning relevant to my being in the world, both a participant in an academic elite, and simultaneously a stubborn word warrior against that same elite seen as colonizer . . . I shift and become the lawyer, the careful word-crafter restrained from my passion for justice and fairness, admonishing my colleagues to join in the legal struggle for equality in a land not of my making or being . . . . I am at once with and also against all that I have become . . . a supporter of oral tradition, and also a writer of words on paper.... (Waters 2004, p 170)

She proposes a friendly relationship with relaxed interstitital meaning and shifting voices as ultimately a convergence of who she is becoming. If readers find themselves caught in the dissonance, they should not be surprised.

Here, the work of Maria Lugones on purity and separation offers a somewhat complementary interpretation. She begins with the example of cracking an egg and separating the white from the yoke. An exercise in purity. The next step would be to add water and oil to the yoke to make mayonnaise, an unstable emulsion. And, it curdles so the ingredients become separate, but not quite. They coalesce to different degrees so what results is yolky oil or oily yoke. She relates this to her background as *mestizja* – both indigenous and european, with the separation of the egg and yolk as control over creativity, and the impurity of the curdling as *mestizaje* defying control (Lugones, 1994, pp. 458-460). In the indigenous Nahuatl language, this word for this in-betweenness is *nepantla*. The "lover of purity, the impartial reasoner is outside history, outside culture . . . [and] occupies the privileged vantage point with others like him, all charaterized by the "possession" of reason (Lugones, 1994, p. 467). And yet, reality interrupts and fragments this purity, leaving the individual frustrated. Differences and heterogeniety may either be embraced or viewed as threatening. Likewise, "[c]urdling may be a haphazard technique of survival as an active subject, or it can become an art of resistance, metamorphosis, transformation." (Lugones, 1994, p. 478).

It seems that in the examination of the relationship between indigenous understanding, and the ideas of restorative justice, and therapeutic jurisprudence, both purity and impurity are needed. The reader may observe the choices made, the strategic concessions occuring by intention or default, or a bridging of the gaps yet to be made in the dynamic of the relationships.

Models

When considering how indigenous understandings are adopted or adapted to mainstream restorative justice and therapeutic jurisprudence, the models sometimes used in the construction of formal systems related to restorative justice might be helpful. The four as summarized by Daniel Van Ness are: the unified model, the dual-track model, the safety-net model, and the hybrid model. (Vides Saade, 2008, pp. 235-236, citations omitted). Applied to the processes described by the authors who follow, these may be described as follows. The unified model is one in which only the indigenous form of dispute resolution is available. For example, this might happen by default due to accessibility or lack of right to appeal local decisions, or in those situations where the mistrust of the mainstream system is so high that it is not considered whatsover except in its function as constraining local indigenous processes. The dual-track model is one which both indigenous and mainstream systems operate simultaneously with participants moving back and forth between them as necessary. This was sometimes seen in the chapter discussions when the indigenous community reluctantly participated in the mainstream system of justice and then followed it with their own process nevertheless. The safety-net model is similar to the dual-track model except that this model is definitive in its preference for the local, indigenous, process. The hybrid model is an approach that progresses from one system to another, depending on the effectiveness of the approach. This progression could be an orderly one, or could be chaotic as the parties seek the best result for themselves.

The original expression of these models as descriptive of possibilities the assumption was that a common worldview was held by the parties, or at least that the parties had acquiesced to the mainstream view of the dominant legal system. More, although these related to restorative justice the distinction between the process and outcomes was often conflated, and therapeutic outcomes described as restorative, while re-integration and community not made primary to restoration. Nevertheless, these provide another framework in the layers necessary for assessing the relationship between the gaps between indigenous wisdom, restorative justice, and therapeutic jurisprudence.

Readers, please take note of the complexities.

Marta Vides Saade
Ramapo College of New Jersey, USA
16 June 2022

REFERENCES

Lugones, M. (1994, Winter). Purity, Impurity, and Separation. *The University of Chicago Press Journal*, *19*(2), 458.

Smith, G. H. (2006). Interview with M. Kovach/Interviewer. In M. Kovach (Ed.), *Searching for arrowheads: An inquiry into approaches to Indigenous research using a tribal methodology with a* Nêhiẏaw Kiskêẏihtamowin *worldvie*. (pp. 156-168). University of Victoria.

Stevenson, W. L. (2000). *Decolonizing tribal histories* [Unpublished doctoral dissertation]. University of California, Berkeley.

Suzuki, M. (2020). From 'what works' to 'how it works' in research on restorative justice conference: the concept of readiness. *The International Journal of Restorative Justice, 3*(3), 356-373.

Van Ness, D. (2003). *Creating restorative systems. In L. Walgrave (Ed.), Restorative Justice and the Law*. Willan Publishing.

Vides Saade, M. (2008). Restorative Justice, Empowerment Theory and Transformative Spirituality: Searching for Authentic Strategies in China, Hong Kong, India, and Korea. In K. van Wormer (Ed.), *Restorative Justice Across the East and the West* (pp. 229–252). Casa Verde Publishing.

Waters, A. (Ed.). (2004). *Language Matters: Nondiscrete nonbinary dualism*. Blackwell.

Section 1
Indigenous Wisdom: Africa and the Diaspora

Chapter 1
Indigenous Conflict Resolution Mechanism as Reconciliatory and Therapeutic:
Lessons From Ghana and the Caribbean

Seth Tweneboah
University of Education, Winneba, Ghana

Anthony Richards
Wild Caribbean, Barbados

ABSTRACT

This chapter explores the role of traditional methods of social control that deploy the power of the deities as a missing dimension of justice delivery. The authors present the rituals associated with deploying the traditional mechanism of control as both reconciliatory and therapeutic. Drawing on both historical and contemporaneous instances from Ghana and the Caribbean, the chapter contends that the continuous reliance on African spirit-based justice delivery method betrays not only the insufficiencies in the Western superimposed adversarial legal system but also a tacit and open rejection of this imported system. The chapter interrogates the prospects and pitfalls of indigenous Africa and its diasporan conflict resolution mechanism.

DOI: 10.4018/978-1-6684-4112-1.ch001

INTRODUCTION

Despite the increasing incursions of state approaches to justice delivery, in Africa and its diasporan societies in the Caribbean, indigenous approaches that appeal to the power of the deities remain a fundamental means of seeking justice. On Sunday, January 2, 2022, for example, a video clip showing an aggrieved taxi driver, publicly identified as, Tamimu Yahaya, in the act of imprecating personnel of the Ghana Police Service gained prominence on social media (MyJoyOnline, 2022). The video shows Tamimu pouring libation with a bottle of hard liquor summoning the police to Ayensu, the river deity of his hometown. According to Tamimu, on that fateful day, he was driving to a nearby town when he was stopped by a police patrol team. The police, he said, accused him of possessing a dried substance believed to be Indian hemp in his car, leading to his unlawful assault and extortion. In summoning the police to the river deity, Tamimu complained that: "I don't have the time to go to the court. My court is the river in my town, Nana Ayensu" (MyJoyOnline, 2022).

As is expected, this episode received mixed reactions from the Ghanaian populace with many saluting the man for resorting to a "swift justice" delivery mechanism rather than the slow-paced state justice system. In a matter of days, what can be referred to as the Tamimu affair moved the top police hierarchy to act. Subsequent to the circulation of the video and the public discussions that ensued, on January 6, 2022, the police hierarchy ordered the immediate interdiction of the personnel of the police involved in order to pave way for further investigations to go on (Modernghana, 2022). Public imprecation in Ghana has been framed as a culture given that the practice is so pervasive in the public domain (Tweneboah, 2014). The entire episode as narrated above forces us to ponder on some questions and to also pay attention to an irrefutable gap in justice delivery. In Ghana, what role does imprecation play in resolving conflict in society? How have imprecatory and other indigenous African spiritual appeals been employed in the African diaspora especially in the Caribbean? Are there forms of continuity between indigenous African justice delivery mechanism and the spirit-directing approaches to justice of the anglophone Caribbean? To what extent is it possible to bridge the gaps between the state and non-state, particularly individual approaches to justice delivery? Are these forms of reconciliatory and therapeutic justice? To what extent is it possible to bridge the gap between Caribbean spirit-directing reconciliatory and therapeutic justice systems and state judicial apparatus?

Drawing on both historical and contemporaneous instances from Ghana and the Caribbean, this chapter interrogates the intricate link between state and non-state justice delivery systems, paying attention to the extent to which these intersect with people's spirituality. The chapter, therefore, examines the nature and scope of traditional methods of social control in societies that are constitutionally secular and religiously pluralistic. It contends that the continuous use of a conflict resolution mechanism that relies on the spiritual forces, reveals not only the insufficiencies in the Western superimposed adversarial legal system but also both a tacit and open rejection of this imported system. The chapter brings to the fore traditional West African and Caribbean conflict resolution mechanism as both reconciliatory and therapeutic. The concept and deployment of these mechanisms have indeed been deemed as widespread throughout the contemporary Ghanaian public sphere. Over the years, this phenomenon has received various negative connotations owing to, among other reasons, the influence of historical colonizers as well as imported religions such as Christianity and Islam. Despite the deep moral revulsion about the phenomenon, its continuous deployment evidences the significant role indigenous spirituality plays in conflict resolution and justice seeking in society.

From this perspective, this chapter explores the issue of traditional justice delivery in the form of imprecation and other ritual practices as a missing dimension of justice delivery. We present the ritual practices of these methods of justice delivery as both reconciliatory and therapeutic.

Focusing on the function of social control mechanism that rely on the deities, the chapter attempts to demonstrate an interplay between African spirituality and the contemporary justice system. The chapter is divided as follows: Section 1 introduces the entire discussion, highlighting the key questions of concern for viewing traditional West African and Caribbean conflict resolutions as both reconciliatory and therapeutic, and how they are approached. Section 2 gives a general framework within which the discussion thrives, justifying the selection of Ghana and Caribbean as reference points of the entire discussion. Section 3 examines the spirit-directing methods of social control in the form of imprecatory and other ritual practices, paying attention to their scope and nature. Section 4 discusses the unexamined significance of imprecatory practice and traditional justice delivery systems. It demonstrates the manner in which these serve not only as mechanism of resolving conflict in society, but also as both reconciliatory and therapeutic in nature and form. Section 5 attempts to bridge the gap between the state and non-state systems of justice delivery in Ghana and the Caribbean. Section 6 concludes the discussion, summarizing the key issues raised in the chapter.

FRAMING THE ISSUES

This chapter draws on both historical and contemporaneous instances from Ghana and Caribbean to examine the continuous reliance on spirit-directing conflict resolution and justice delivery that rely on the authority of the deities. The chapter focuses on how the resilient trust in the justice delivery authority of the deities that reveals not only the insufficiencies in the Western superimposed adversarial legal system but also a tacit and open rejection of imported legal system. We interrogate the prospects and pitfalls of indigenous African and its diasporan conflict resolution mechanism. The choice of these two settings is purposive particularly owing to their historical connection. The precedent of previous researchers pointing to possible Akan affinities in slave oaths gives purchase to our justification for selecting Ghana and the Caribbean (Gaspar, 1999; Bilby 1997; Palmié, 2013; Matory, 2005). The choice of these two societies is, thus, an attempt to demonstrate the kind of disjuncture and continuity that exist between these locations.

There have been debates revolving around the continuity of African tradition versus innovation in the Americas. Both sides of the debate recognized the agency of the enslaved but disagreed on the processes involved. Those who emphasized continuity, especially in the Caribbean (Brathwaite, 1972; Warner-Lewis, 1999) rejected the notion of a "social amnesia" created by the Middle Passage. They saw the crossing of the "Black Atlantic" as providing pathways of cultural transmission. They explored the roles of memory and resistance employing comparative studies to identify possible continuities formerly called "Africanisms" and "retentions."

The creativity school, on the other hand, was strongly influenced by Mintz's and Price's "An anthropological approach" which was highly skeptical of continuity (Mintz & Price, 1976). They assumed that Africans from diverse ethnicities, mutually unintelligible languages, thrown together on the plantation would face severe obstacles to reproducing institutions, especially without ritual specialists with religious and legal authority. They placed emphasis on the early establishment of new "creolized" forms of culture in the plantation setting through individual interactions with Europeans, and first contact between Africans from diverse regions. Thornton (1992) and others such as Gilroy (1993) breathed new life into the continuity argument by identifying broad zones of cultural continuity within West Africa and West Central Africa respectively which could have allowed for cohesiveness and reassembly on the plantation.

Continuity or Creativity within Justice Systems and Oaths?

A key question of interest in this chapter is whether there are forms of continuity or creativity in oath swearing Ghanaian indigenous justice delivery mechanism and the Caribbean spirit-directing approaches to justice. To be sure, attempts have been made to establish some links between Akan ancestral practices such as the swearing of oath and the Caribbean particularly among the Maroons of Jamaica and the Guianas (Bilby, 1997). A most crucial indigenous mechanism of justice delivery common among the Akan of West Africa is the *nsedie*, "assertive self-imprecatory oaths" (Agyekum, 1999, p. 366). *Nsedie* is the ritual of calling upon "some supernatural power to bear witness to what has been said and to impose a supernatural sanction should the statement be false" (Rattray, 1927, p. 215). Thus, if someone is suspected of committing an offence, they are made to call upon the wrath of a deity upon themselves or their accuser. The belief is that if they are innocent, their innocence will be proven (Parker, 2021, p. 44). However, if the suspect is guilty, they would not dare making the declaration else the supernatural power would inflict harm or punishment on the suspect. This usually took the form: "If I am guilty, may the harm fall on me." If I am not guilty, set me free."

This verbal oath was also underpinned by the ingestion of some sanctified substance, usually herbal concoction, hence the label "drinking the gods."

While the assertive self-imprecation is no longer a common practice in the Caribbean, around the time of Emancipation, there arose spirit-directing mechanisms of detecting persons suspected of theft. Also known as "drinking the deities," *nsedie* has been noted to have persisted in the Guianas and among the Jamaican Maroons. Especially among maroons, the belief in the legal and justice delivery authority of the spiritual forces has been well acknowledged. In the territory of the Aluku maroons, for example, Tata Odun was held as the most important and powerful spiritual entity after the Creator (Bilby, 1997; Konadu, 2010, p. 113). The ritual of *diigi sweli* which translates as drinking an oath among the Aluku Maroons of French Guiana has a genealogical resemblance, but also with the Akan practice of "drinking the gods." Kenneth Bilby draws the connection of this powerful deity to its West African roots suggesting that "Tata Odun is said to have come over from Africa along with the ancestors and to have led them safely through the forest to their present location" (Bilby, 1997, p. 174).

In Antigua, for example, it is reported that the oath the enslaved Africans employed took the form which shared some commonalities with the Akan *nsedie* (Gaspar, 1999). Like the Akan of Ghana (Rattray, 1927, p. 215), the enslaved of Antigua called upon "some supernatural power to witness what has been said and to impose a supernatural sanction should the statement be false"

In the case of imprecation in Jamaica today, the oath takes a form which we found to share some commonalities with the Akan *nsedie* formal for taking the oath.

By St Peter, By St Paul
By the living God of all.
If I am the one that stole [the missing property], let it choke me.

There seems to be an evident continuity here. This notwithstanding, we have made attempts to avoid essentializing the West African roots of these practices in the Caribbean. The introduction of ostensibly Christian elements in the form of the invocation of the names of saintly figures (rather than calling upon the African deities) is particularly evidence of creativity.[1]

IMPRECATION AND THE POTENTIAL FOR CONFLICT RESOLUTION

In Africa the relationship between religion and other realms of life is said to be interlinked (Mbiti 1989 pp. 1–5; Nukunya 2011; Palmié, 2013; Matory, 2005). Religion is said to permeate in all sectors of life so fully well that some posit that it is difficult to separate the physical and the spiritual realm. Among the Akan of Ghana, R.S. Rattray reports that there is a significant cross-fertilization of religion and traditional law. Writing on the law and constitution of the Asante (an Akan group) he records that owing to the religious basis of Asante legal norms, during his research, he very often had to pause and reflect on the religious basis of certain laws of the people (Rattray, 1929, p. 2). Religion, thus, provides a significant basis for justice delivery in society. A cardinal but largely ignored justice delivery mechanism in this society is imprecation, locally referred to as *duabɔ*. It is the invocation of vengeance or retribution from a superhuman power upon an adversary. Agyekum (1999) refers to it as "grievance imprecation". As a form of justice delivery system, it is largely regulated by a number of prohibitions. Indeed, it is mainly held as a taboo. As Agyekum explains:

The duabɔ taboo is purely a religious verbal taboo. It is the practice of the Akans in invoking supernatural powers in defence and in the execution of certain forms of justice. This has given rise to the origin of imprecation based on the desire of the imprecator to harm the target (Agyekum, 1999, p. 358).

In Akan religion and philosophy, as in many other religious traditions, the names of the deities must not be trivialized. Doing so amounts to defiling and blaspheming against the deities. Akan *duabɔ*, then, is regulated by certain prohibitive norms because the spiritual forces of nature (other than God) are believed to be irascible, and their punishments are swift and ruthless. Even so, the Akan believe that there are occasions that *duabɔ*, like all other Akan verbal taboos, is permissible, and indeed encouraged to demand justice (Agyekum, 1999, p. 374).

SPIRIT-DIRECTING RITUALS, THERAPEUTIC AND RECONCILIATORY JUSTICE

In spite of the many negative connotations associated with the traditional justice delivery system that deploys the power of the deities, the process has been identified to have some benefits akin to therapeutic mediation. Some scholars agree that healing is critical after a wrongful action that has resulted in either party feeling victimized (Bazelon, 2018). In this sense, an acknowledgement of one's error and the willingness to render an apology and reconcile with the other party potentially lessens every burden associated with emotional distress in the injured party. This then creates an atmosphere of repentance for the offending party. Despite the many negative connotations associated with *duabɔ* ritual, for example, in Akan justice delivery system, before any pacificatory rites to reverse the intended harms against the adversary, it is the primary duty of the shrine panel or its agents to resolve any disputes leading to the invocation of the intervention of the spiritual forces. To secure a fair, decisive, and authoritative resolution, a trial is often imperative. The trial process involves a laborious employment of logical reasoning, analogy, and probable inference. The proceeding also involves rigorous and interrogative and witty statements. It is believed that the catastrophic effect of the action occurs when the imprecatee, that is, the person on whom a curse has been cast, begins to experience nightmares and anxiety disorders, and become psychologically unsecured. As Agyekum explains, once the imprecatee realizes that his or her condition is caused by a supernatural force and runs to the deity and performs the necessary rituals, he or she will be assured of freedom (Agyekum, 1999, p. 364). The fines and sanctions involved at this stage become minimal.

Tweneboah (2021a) records a trial proceeding he witnessed at Tom Kramo shrine court in the Nkoranza Traditional Area of Ghana. The case, he writes, involves two friends, Akwasi, and Yaw. The former, pretty intoxicated, had imprecated the latter whom he accused of assault. When the matter was reported to the elders of Tom Kramo shrine, a panel was constituted to try the case. After a brief deliberation, listening to both parties, the court found Yaw's own evidence to be self-implicatory enough to warrant a decision. The trial panel reasoned that Yaw had unfairly assaulted his friend who had lost his coordination by reason of intoxication. It was the panel's averment that an intoxicated Akwasi did not have the full use of his faculty and therefore was not expected to be as sober and reasonable as the assaulter expected. The shrine court, thus, found the assault to be warrantless. An amount of 200 Ghana cedis was awarded as a compensation to Akwasi. What is curious here is that in his speech to thank the shrine panel, Akwasi made a very profound reconciliatory statement, pleading for clemency for his assaulter. Tweneboah narrates Akwasi's plea thus:

Nananom, pardon me to say that Yaw's punishment be mitigated for I cannot accept this compensation. Yaw and I have been friends since our infancy days. We have never harboured any ill-feelings between us. We drink and have much thoughts together. What happened on that day was an accident. I imprecated him out of the pain I was enduring and I needed something to save my head. Tomorrow if I am lying motionless, he will still be the one who will first come to my aid, perhaps he will even mash kenkey and push it into my throat. I cannot roast my tongue and eat and still feel the taste. Nananom I beg to reject the compensation (Tweneboah, 2021a, p. 7).

This plea for clemency as Tweneboah (2021a) notes is for purposes of the reconciliation and the preservation of relationships in society.

In recent past, a series of trending videos have appeared in Ghana and neighboring Cote D'Ivoire depicting instances of the *nsedie* oath-taking. These popular videos circulated on social media of a spirit-directed trial aimed at identifying a thief from among a group of male suspects. The divination or ordeal deployed what might be described as the credible threat of ritual strangulation using brooms composed of fibers from the oil palm tree to interrogate the suspects and then to identify, accuse and shame one of their number. The practice involved the accused being seated on a stool and broom fibers hanged around their neck while they recite the words of an oath or incantation. Suspects were made to sit on a small stool and repeating after ritual specialists some incantations, while palm brooms were passed about their neck (YouTube, 2017). Eventually, the brooms seemed to become entangled around the neck of one of the suspects, and the broom operator (traditional priest) may jerk him backwards off the stool. The choking suspect now appears contrite, and the assembled onlookers are satisfied. A particularly prominent case in January 2021 involved a music celebrity, DJ Deversaille in Cote D'Ivoire who was also accused of theft of a 50 thousand francs. In this episode, the accused was choked by the broom after taking the oath. Allegedly, he continued to deny guilt. His defiance produced bemused laughter from the onlookers, including the victim of the theft. He later released a song protesting his innocence., which has won him both admiration and derision.

While the broom ritual is prominent in Ghana and some other parts of West Africa, traces of similar trials have been identified in the Caribbean around the time of the 1834 Emancipation Act (Putman, 2012). Some cases were reported from the Danish Virgin Islands in 1815 (Putman p. 255) Trinidad in 1836 (Bridgens, 1836), Antigua in 1838 and Grenada in 1898 (Bell, 1889) respectively (see map). A version of such ritual practices has persisted in Jamaica into the present day.

Figure 1. Map of the Caribbean, showing territories where the broom(weed) divination was described (names underlined). From North to south: Jamaica, Virgin Islands, Antigua, Grenada, Trinidad.
Adapted from Kmusser, 9 April 2011. Creative Commons Attribution-Share Alike 3.0 all data from Vector Map. https://en.wikipedia.org/wiki/Caribbean#/media/File:Caribbean_general_map.png

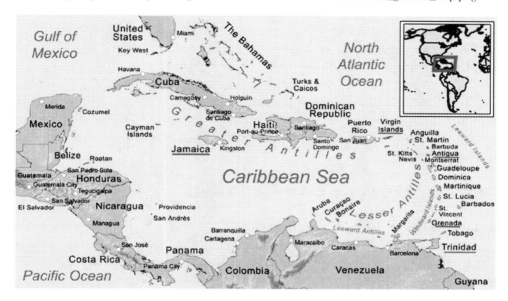

In describing this divinatory ritual, the African Caribbean Institute of Jamaica (ACIJ) indicated thus:

Broomweed[2] (Sida acuta Burm) …along with John Charles [Cordia globosa] may be specially woven together by a practitioner to form a necklace that is then placed around the neck of a person accused of lying. If nothing happens to the individual by 12pm then he is presumed innocent.

Interview with a Jamaican spiritualist (name withheld) conducted by one of the authors of this chapter suggests that this ritual practice is now uncommon and reserved for a "big case," such as the theft of valuable livestock. It is now deployed in circumstances where the accused continues to protest innocence, despite overwhelming evidence to the contrary. The last occasion on which the spiritualist performed such a trial was in 2019. This case involved the theft of a goat in Sligoville (St Catherine Parish, Jamaica). An eyewitness account implicated a cousin of the goat's owner as the one who had stolen the animal, but the accused denied it. The spiritualist asked three times, "John (name changed), is [it] you [who] take it?" John continued to deny taking the goat. According to the spiritualist, this denial "give me

9

franchise to use the broomweed proof." The suspect was then made to stand in the yard in full sun at around 11.45am. As the spiritualist incanted the words below, a broomweed necklace was looped around his neck and tied. He was warned that the necklace would choke him by 12.30 pm if he was indeed the thief.

By Saint Peter, by Saint Paul,
By the Living God of all,
If John is the thief let him be strangled by twelve-fifteen (12.15pm)

The practitioner explained that the aim of the ritual was to propel the accused toward the point of confession, and more importantly, to prove his guilt to the family and others involved, bringing a resolution. Here lies the potential for therapy and reconciliation.

Imprecatory Practices in the Caribbean

Some other imprecatory practices in the Caribbean do not provide much scope for reconciliation but are perhaps possibly therapeutic in nature and form. In 1931 on Cat Island (Bahamas), the African American anthropologist Zora Neale Hurston interviewed an obeahman who detailed how to eliminate an enemy:

Set your altar table with black and white candles. Put a mirror in the center and a white basin of water and a sharp knife or dagger. Read the scripture "Plead my cause, O God, with them that strive against me. Fight against them that fight against me." Then the looking glass will show you your enemy, known or unknown. When he appears, chop the water with the blade and it turns to blood in the basin. In two or three hours the enemy is dead (Hurston, 1931, p. 324).

In Afro-Caribbean spirituality candles are a means of attracting the spirits. Beeswax is considered more powerful than paraffin. In obeah rituals, which incidentally is common in Vodou, Santeria and other religions, they can be used alone or in combination with Psalms from the Bible and other ritual objects. A similar connection can be drawn to the *duabɔ* ritual of Ghana in which the basin of water and mirror might be interpreted as creating a portable substitute for a sacred river.

Traditionally, rural Jamaicans – whose access to state approaches to justice is low – have invested some plants with spiritual power that could be harnessed in cases of retribution. Martha Beckwith collected evidence of this in her 1929 seminal work. In her *Black Roadways*, Falconer, one of Beckwith's informants in the Santa Cruz Mountains of Jamaica described her remedy against thievery as follows:

Plant guinea yam[3] with a short stick..... and put a silver threepence[4] in the sod; when it sprouts, flog off the leaves. But do not let them fall on you, or your own body will swell. "Pain-cocoa"[5] and "China-cane" may be treated in the same fashion (Beckwith, 1929, p. 129).

Another plant believed to be used in this way is the sesame or wangla. It may be planted on the farm. If there is a theft, the sesame seeds are carefully collected and burnt. This act was believed to produce blisters that look like burnt sesame seeds on the skin of the thief.

Wangla should be planted in the provision ground and the seeds carefully gathered. There is the belief that if a thief robs the field and the owner can find a fresh footstep, he or she must take up the earth carefully in a leaf, measure it with a spoon, and put "fourthirds" [6]as much wangla seed with it and put the whole into a pot upon the fire. The name of the suspected thief is then called upon and if the suspicion is right, it is believed that as many "bumps" will appear on the thief's foot as there are seeds that 'pop' or "his skin will strip off (Beckwith 1929 p. 129)

Today, in Jamaica, the phrase "burn wangla for you" is used in jest, or at worst, as a threat. Nonetheless, a spiritual healer in Kingston complained that he has had to treat the skin disorders of clients who believed that they were victims of burning wangla.

The gaps between these practices and the state approaches to justice-seeking and delivery remain considerable. Recent attempts to repeal the Obeah Act of 1898 by the Jamaican Attorney General of Jamaica led to stiff opposition, particularly from the church (Paton 2019). Parliament instead amended the Obeah Act, providing new penalties, a complete about-face.

Broomweed Gallows in Jamaica

In both homeland Africa and its diaspora under British colonial rule, the practice of native African social justice systems was often ruled illegal and attracted severe sanctions such as fines, beatings, and imprisonment, even at a time when similar practices in European capitals would attract little more than only derision from the same ruling classes. Yet collective aspirations of Africans held to have been legitimated by the spiritual forces were ridiculed or held in contempt. The traditional mechanism of social control was conceived pejoratively to refer to credulous beliefs and practices of the African population. In a sense, it was held as belonging to the realm of the paranormal (Ellis, 1887, pp. 10–11). In West Africa and the Caribbean, the British, for instance, saw ritual practices of the indigenous faith especially the justice delivery system as a threat to the successful imposition of imperialist domination. As such campaigns to get shrines dedicated to the deities and other spiritual forces of nature destroyed, banned or removed in the colonies were variously launched by the colonial regime (Gray, 2000, 2001). The Colonial Annual Report for 1895 of the Gold Coast colony (independent Ghana) notes thus:

During the year steps were taken by the Government for the complete suppression of the worship of the Fetish Katawero. This Fetish, which was located in Akim Swaidru, was accredited with powers of life and death, and many a wealthy native fell a victim to its supposed powers, it being a rule that the property of persons stated by the priests to have died by order of the Fetish should be divided between the Fetish priests and the Head Chief of the country. The shrines of the Fetish were broken down, the sacred groves destroyed, and the people delivered from the tyranny of the rapacious priesthood.

Especially in the case of the black populations forcibly transported to the Americas, for fear that gatherings, and the attendant recognition of black leadership would threaten the order of the colonial rule, several legal measures were put in place.[7] Most records of "obeah" for example, detail encounter with law enforcement agencies, and academic treatments have little choice but to focus on this bounty. There is now a body of literature on the criminalization of obeah etc. which, though it may be critical of the authorities, still treats the African principally as the object of colonial legal processes (Handler & Bilby, 2012; Paton, 2015).

BRIDGING THE GAPS

The negative construction of African spiritual mechanisms of social control came to signify a sort of legal hindrance in both Africa and the Caribbean. In Jamaica, for instance, owing to its potency and wider appeal, the British colonizers increasingly framed the obeah practice as forms of criminal deception, malignant "witchcraft" or "sorcery" (Handler & Bilby, 2012). The persistence of these justice delivery practices, however, became the angle of vision through which imperialist Europe positioned itself in the colonies as a rational and anti-superstitious civilizing agent. In this section, therefore, we present the persistence of these practices as a weapon of the colonized and enslaved people's resistance.

For Handler and Bilby (2012), notwithstanding the negativity associated with spirit-directing methods of social control which are religion-based, obeah, for instance, has been found to be a useful spiritual phenomenon in solving a wide range of everyday problems. Paton presents obeah ritual practice as an essential spiritual healing technique. Its curative power lies in the fact that it is first framed as a sign of Africanness (Paton, 2015, p. 43).

Despite their imperfections, imprecatory practices and other forms of justice delivery that deploy the power of the deities continue to hold sway in society. It is within this context that we call for the need to strike a balance between these forms and other state approaches to justice delivery systems. Undeniably, recent attempts have been made to move towards a favorably non-litigious, non-adversarial mechanism of dispute resolution. There have also been attempts to adopt mutually integrated perspectives to the study and understanding of law and to improve legal outcomes (Atmasasmita, 2018; Pogodin & Krasnov, 2018; Wright, n.d.). In most jurisdictions, legal education is gradually moving towards the inclusion of integrative law into the curriculum of institutions as a means to bolster access to dispute resolution and to encourage an ultimate shift in conceptualizations and practice of law. Integrative law also pays heed to the wide-ranging consequence of conflict on individual lives and the society itself. It takes cognizance of the emotional and psychological, physical, and spiritual effects of conflict.

Proponents argue for a truly interdisciplinary approach that aims to connect diverse fields that potentially and in reality furnish us with a workable theory of normative behavior and social action (Cominelli, 2018; Wright, 2016). Proposals have been made on the need to strike a balance between adversarial methods and non-adversarial methods of legal problem-solving and assessing mediation. Even so, much continues to be desired when it comes to the acceptance of religious and cultural systems of traditional societies whose legal norms are deemed as low. The dominant legal positivist interpretation of the justice system advocates a shift in perspective with a deeply cognitivist fervor, neglecting the role religious resources play in the practical legal experience of people. Following HLA Hart, practical and analytical jurisprudence has been devoid of the religious and customary underpinnings or the collective societal aims or functions the law plays. Positivism is an invitation to reflect on non-cognitivism in ethics.

For many, non-state justice systems must not be encouraged because they impede avenues for asserting and defending individual legal rights. In Nigeria, for example, the courts have previously acknowledged that the reliance on what is referred to (derogatively) as the *juju* method, that is, traditional oath-swearing, was laudable when it comes to cost-effectiveness in terms of saving time, finances, and other logistics. But, at the same time, the court has also held that this method was fraught with a myriad of drawbacks (Oba, 2008). It is the contention of the court that one cannot, for example, put *juju* in the witness box for any purpose. Again, it has been contended that the activities, methods and procedure of oath-swearing fall under the realm of the supernatural, even though its effects may be eventually visible or experienced (Tweneboah, 2014, p. 7). Similarly, in resorting to *duabɔ*, unlike the formal courts, judgements or decisions of the deity involved are not subject to challenge or appeal. That is to say, there is no guarantee of a fair trial in matters of spiritual justice.

From the foregoing, it is imperative to conclude that there is a significant interplay of the justice delivery system. A close introspection of the various episodes of imprecatory and other practices reveals a very significant interplay of the justice system. It is also instructive to know the manner in which one might resort to these spiritual justice delivery systems and still go to court to demand justice and vice versa. Very often, aggrieved parties deploy imprecation, for example, after the formal legal system has failed them (Assmann, 1992, p. 162). Among the Akan of Ghana, for example, *duabɔ* is aptly termed as a spiritual norm of the last instance (Tweneboah, 2021b).

In Ghana, this is typically exemplified in the 2015 episode in which some irate youth of the Nkoranza municipality imprecated the Electoral Commission (EC) and voters in the area in order to prevent them from taking part in the district-level elections of that year (Emmanuel, 2015). Irate youth of the area boycotted the district level elections as a form of protest following the loss of their investment in some defunct microfinance companies. These microfinance companies took deposits from some residents with the promise of giving them huge returns, but the companies failed to return to them their investments. This situation is believed to have led to the loss of lives of some customers. What started as a simple investment issue soon took a national security dimension (Tweneboah, 2021b). The whole situation led to the frustration of residents of the area. After several failed attempts to appeal to state authorities to intervene, the customers resorted to spiritual justice as a form of seeking redress. In a televised press conference, the aggrieved customers imprecated the owners, the workers, and agents of the insolvent microfinance companies, as well as the Governor of the Bank of Ghana and other political actors whom they accused of being behind the locking up of their monies. It is for this reason they also warned officials of the EC not to step foot into the area to organize any elections there, accusing the EC of insensitivity to their plight.

On August 29, 2015, a notice and some ritual implements including slaughtered chicken and eggs were found at the premise of the EC. The notice, pictured below, was a stern warning to the EC cautioning it not to send any electoral materials to any polling station for voting. It warned that should the EC failed to hasten, its officials and workers risk the wrath of the deities of the area including the dreaded Tom Kramo and Sessiman Toa deities of the area. The group also threatened to burn election materials if the EC did not call off the exercise in the area. The situation compelled the EC to postpone elections in both Nkoranza North and South until April 2017.

Figure 2. A notice and ritual items of egg and chickens used to imprecate rituals at the EC office
Nkoranza (Gomda, 2015)

The situation above shows that the persistence of imprecation reflects a gap that has emerged and continues to increase between legal conditions set by the state for its people and the daily needs and practice of the people, the majority of whom lack access to state approaches to justice delivery.

Spirit-driven mechanisms of seeking justice are very often preferred by the masses because apart from being consistent with their religious and cultural values, the system is seen as providing speedy, less expensive, and expeditious justice. Like other forms of non-state justice systems, indigenous mechanisms of justice delivery that appeal to the power of the deities are often said to be "the guarantors of order and security as well as access to justice at the local level; they often have legitimacy the state justice system may lack" (USAID, 2019).

To explicate this, we revisit the Tamimu affair with which we began this chapter. In spiritually summoning the police for false accusation and extortion, Tamimu addressed his concern as:

If you are seeing me here [by the river side], it's not in a bad motive. This river is in my village. My name is Tamimu Yahaya. Yesterday January 2 [2022], I was driving from Asamankese to go and buy car tyre. I was stopped by the [police] patrol team. I complied. When they searched my car, they accused me of putting wee [Indian hemp] into my car boot.

Taminu recounted that he knew very well that he did not possess any such substance and saw the whole episode as a setup. Even though he denied any knowledge of the said substance, the police insisted that he was the one who put it there. Because of this, he narrated, one of the police hit him twice to force him to confess. According to Tamimu,

They gave me an instant fine of 500 Ghana cedis. The 500 Ghana cedis that they collected from me, I don't have time to go to court [demand it]. My court is the riverine deity in my town, Nana Ayensu; that is my court, Nana Ayensu. And so, I am handing over the matter to the river in my village to intercede for me. Nana Ayensu should intercede for me. Nana, I came in peace, Nana this is your grandchild Tamimu Yahaya standing before you.

Imprecation is, thus, deployed and is also sustained as a result of a breakdown of social convention and the trust associated with it. In this sense, as a mechanism for addressing everyday grievances in society, imprecation is still presented as a form of controlled ritual practice. In the Akan traditional society, for example, imprecation is held as a proscriptive behavior, and is therefore invoked as a last resort (Tweneboah, 2021b). It is an approach to justice that aims to prevent damages and restore society to the hitherto peaceful coexistence between parties. The key here is that unlike the combative and adversarial nature of the state justice system, imprecatory and other traditional methods of justice delivery seek to repair harm by providing an opportunity for the aggrieved party and the offender to come to peaceful terms with each other. By taking responsibility for the harm caused, the practice provides for an atmosphere of reconciliation and healing.

In attempting to bridge the gap, we emphasize that over the last few decades, there has been a positive public, even state, reception of the status of African derived ritual practices in the Caribbean. In places such as Anguilla (1980), Barbados (1998), Trinidad and Tobago (2000), and St Lucia (2004), there have been attempts at decriminalizing obeah, for instance (Handler & Bilby, 2012, p. xiii). These attempts reverberate the changing status and perception of African-derived religions in other parts of the Americas. Since the 1930s in Brazil, Candomblé, for example, has been given a wider recognition as a "national folk institution," attaining a national symbol (Matory, 2005, pp. 164, 166). In Cuba, following religious liberalization in 1991, as Stephan Palmié records, "Afro-Cuban religions are no longer the object of state-sponsored denunciation as ideological aberrations" (Palmié, 2013, p. 20). Rather, she writes, they have been hailed as "one of Cuba's most unique and powerful weapons in the international struggle against capitalist cultural hegemony and an enduring contribution to global culture" (Palmié, 2013, p. 20). In Haiti, the status of Vodou as "a religion in its own right that should in no way be confused with a superstitious practice" has become a subject of politicization (Ramsey, 2013).

At the same time, ironically, attempts are being made in Ghana, for example, where a bill has been tabled to outlaw certain practices that are seen as offensive to civilizing conduct. In November 2021, three Members of Ghana's Parliament introduced a Private Members Bill to amend the country's Criminal and Other Offences Act 1960 (Act 29) to prohibit the practice by any person as a witch doctor, or witchfinder. Among other key goals, the bill sought to proscribe the declaration, accusation, naming or labeling of another person as a witch; to prohibit a person from employing or soliciting anyone to accuse, name, label, indicate, or declare another person as a witch and provide for related matters. While this bill has been hailed as providing a voice to the many silenced elderly women who have lost their properties and even lives to accusations of witchcraft and other related beliefs, the motive behind specifically mentioning witchdoctors or witchfinders remains an enigma. Over the years, Christian (particularly Neo-Pentecostal/Charismatic) actors have been found guilty of inflaming witchcraft related passions in society. Many of their activities and teachings on witches and demons have led to the abuses of suspected witches in society (Onyinah, 2004; Tweneboah, 2015).

In Liberia and Sierra Leone, the legal system bundles a range of oath-taking ordeals under the term sassywood. These range from drinking a deadly "red water" poison to relatively harmless tasks such as separating two brooms laid one upon the other. The Liberian government formerly licensed sassywood practitioners. Some academics have supported the use of sassywood, in view of the failures of the legal system, especially in the wake of war (T. & Coyne, 2012). However, under pressure from human rights organizations, sassywood was banned in 2005. Studies have found that the populace does not see all these practices as equal. They argue that the legislation has served to diminish the power of chiefs to dispense justice, and paradoxically promotes lawlessness (Heaner, 2008).

In attempting to bridge the gap, it is imperative to note that the selective targeting of traditional religious functionaries contributes to the tacit state subordination of indigenous religious resources. As has been suggested elsewhere, in legally pluralistic societies such as Ghana and most of West Africa, a properly functioning plural legal society is not promoted by taking all functions of other traditions and investing them under one institution, each of which is only a source of plural normative orders. Rather, effective plural legal orders are built through an unbiased and equal provision of platform and opportunity to all institutions in society without unjustified legal impediments (Tweneboah, 2020, p. 164).

CONCLUSION

Recent episodes of people deploying the power of traditional West African and Caribbean deities to mediate tensions in both private and public arenas have necessitated a renewed interest in the prominence of religious imaginations in justice delivery scholarship. To be sure, after centuries of the rude superimposition of European approaches to justice delivery, the tendency to appeal to the power of the spiritual forces to mediate in society remains fundamental in African and its diasporan societies. The deities and other spiritual forces of nature play an especial role when it comes to conflict resolution and peaceful neighborliness. Ironically, notwithstanding the wide-ranging antipathy towards indigenous conflict resolution mechanism, the spirit-driven method of justice delivery system that relies on the power of the deities and other supernatural forces continually hold sway as a crucial means of settling disputes in both private spaces and in the public sphere.

From this perspective, this chapter has made a number of contributions. It has shown that in spite of the historical antipathy and uneasiness associated with traditional justice delivery system, recent homemade videos continue to provide traditional media houses and academia with unprecedented entry into an otherwise inaccessible regions and private spaces. It demonstrates that the manner in which European colonialism and enslavement of African population systemically sought to tacitly and openly privilege state centric approaches to justice delivery. It further demonstrates how the continuous deployment of the power of the deities in settling disputes and tensions in society signals the resilience of spirit-directing social control measures and reveals the insufficiencies in the Western superimposed adversarial legal system and an open rejection of this imported system. The chapter has presented indigenous Ghanaian and Caribbean delivery mechanism as having both therapeutic and reconciliatory value, which is an area which has been given scanty attention in the literature.

This startling degree of symmetry across space and time has rejuvenated our investigations into the origins, nature and meaning of indigenous systems of judicial inquiry during the period of Emancipation and in the years pivotal to the rise of freed peasantry between 1830 and 1940).

REFERENCES

Agyekum, K. (1999). The Pragmatics of Duabo "Grievance Imprecation" Taboo among the Akan. *Pragmatic*, *9*(3), 357–382.

Assmann, J. (1992). When Justice Fails: Jurisdiction and Imprecation in Ancient Egypt and the Near East. *The Journal of Egyptian Archaeology*, 78(1), 149–162. doi:10.1177/030751339207800108

Atmasasmita, R. (2018). *Integrative Law Theory, Reconstruction of Development Law Theory and Progressive Law Theory*. Genta Publishing.

Bazelon, L. (2018). *Rectify: The Power of Restorative Justice After Wrongful Conviction*. Beacon.

Beckwith, M. W. (1929). *Black Roadways: A Study of Jamaican Folk Life*. University of North Carolina Press.

Bell, H. H. J. (1889). *Obeah: Witchcraft in The West Indies*. Sampson Low.

Bilby, K. (1997). Swearing by the Past, Swearing to the Future: Sacred Oaths, Alliances, and Treaties among the Guianese and Jamaican Maroons. *Ethnohistory (Columbus, Ohio)*, 44(4), 655–689. doi:10.2307/482884

Brathwaite, K. (1972). *The Development of Creole Society in Jamaica, 1770-1820*. Clarendon Press.

Bridgens, R. (1836). *West India scenery with illustrations of Negro character, the process of making sugar, &c. From sketches taken during a voyage to and residence of seven years in, the island of Trinidad*. R. Jennings.

Cominelli, L. (2018). *Cognition of the Law: Toward a Cognitive Sociology of Law and Behavior*. Springer. doi:10.1007/978-3-319-89348-8

Ellis, A. B. (1887). *The Tshi-Speaking Peoples of Gold Coast of West Africa: Their Religion, Manners, Customs, Laws, Language, Etc.* Chapman and Hall.

Emmanuel, K. (2015, September 6). *Angry youth of Nkoranza community revoke curses on Central Bank*. Pulse.Com.Gh. https://www.pulse.com.gh/ece-frontpage/illegal-microfinance-angry-youth-of-nkoranza-community-revoke-curses-on-central-bank/nje9d0d

Gaspar, D. B. (1999). *Bondmen and Rebels: A Study of Master-Slave Relations in Antigua*. Duke University Press.

Gilroy, P. (1993). *The Black Atlantic: Modernity and Double Consciousness*. Harvard University Press.

Gomda, A. R. (2015, August 29). Juju Hits EC. *Daily Guide*. https://www.modernghana.com/news/639445/juju-hits-ec.html

Gray, N. (2000). *The Legal History of Witchcraft in Colonial Ghana: Akyem Abuakwa, 1913-1943* [Unpublished: Doctoral dissertation]. Columbia University.

Gray, N. (2001). Witches, Oracles, and Colonial Law: Evolving Anti-Witchcraft Practices in Ghana, 1927-1932. *The International Journal of African Historical Studies*, *34*(2), 339–363. doi:10.2307/3097485 PMID:18198526

Handler, J. S., & Bilby, K. M. (2012). *Enacting Power: The Criminization of Obeah in the Anglophone Caribbean 1760-2011*. University of the West Indies Press.

Heaner, G. (2008). Religion, law and human rights in post-conflict Liberia. *African Human Rights Law Journal*, *8*(2), 458–485.

Hurston, Z. N. (1931). Bahamian Obeah. *Journal of American Folklore*, 320–326.

Konadu, K. (2010). *The Akan Diaspora in the Americas*. Oxford University Press. doi:10.1093/acprof:oso/9780195390643.001.0001

Matory, J. L. (2005). *Black Atlantic Religion: Tradition, Transnationalism, and Matriarchy in the Afro-Brazilian Candomblé*. Princeton University Press.

Mbiti, J. S. (1989). *African Religions and Philosophy* (2nd ed.). Heinemann Education Botswana Publishers.

Mintz, S. W., & Price, R. (1976). *An Anthropological Approach to the Afro-American Past: A Caribbean Perspective*. Institute for the Study of Human Issues.

Modernghana. (2022, January 6). *Asamankese: Five policemen interdicted for allegedly assaulting and planting 'weed' on driver*. https://www.modernghana.com/news/1130045/asamankese-five-policemen-interdicted-for-alleged.html

MyJoyOnline. (2022, January 6). *Police interdict 5 officers over alleged extortion while on patrol duty*. MyJoyOnline.

Oba, A. A. (2008). Juju Oaths in Customary Law Arbitration and Their Legal Validity in Nigerian Courts. *Journal of African Law*, *52*(1), 139–158. doi:10.1017/S0021855308000065

Palmié, S. (2013). *The Cooking of History: How Not to Study Afro-Cuban Religion*. Chicago University Press. doi:10.7208/chicago/9780226019734.001.0001

Parker, J. (2021). *In My Time of Dying: A History of Death and the Dead in West Africa*. Princeton University Press.

Paton, D. (2015). *The Cultural Politics of Obeah: Religion, colonialism and modernity in the Caribbean world*. Cambridge University Press. doi:10.1017/CBO9781139198417

Pogodin, A. V., & Krasnov, E. V. (2018). Integrative Law Understanding as Basis for the Lawyer. *The Journal of Social Sciences Research*, *5*(5), 400–403. doi:10.32861/jssr.spi5.400.403

Putman, L. (2012). Rites of Power and Rumors of Race: The Circulation of Supernatural Knowledge in the Greater Caribbean, 1890–1940. In D. Paton & M. Forde (Eds.), *Obeah and Other Powers: The Politics of Caribbean Religion and Healing* (pp. 249–254). Duke University Press.

Ramsey, K. (2013). Vodouyizan Protest: An Amendment to the Constitution of Haiti. *Journal of Haitian Studies*, *19*(1), 272–281. doi:10.1353/jhs.2013.0019

Rattray, R. S. (1927). *Religion & Art in Ashanti*. Clarendon Press.

Rattray, R. S. (1929). *Ashanti Law and Constitution*. Oxford University Press.

T., L. P., & Coyne, C. J. (2012). Sassywood. *Journal of Comparative Economics*, *40*(4), 608–620.

Thornton, J. K. (1992). *Africa and Africans in the Making of the Atlantic World, 1400-1680*. Cambridge University Press.

Tweneboah, S. (2014). The Culture of Duabɔ (Imprecation), Legal Dysfunction and the Challenge of Human Rights Development in Ghana. *Human Rights Research*, *9*, 1–10.

Tweneboah, S. (2020). *Religion, Law, Politics and the State in Africa: Applying Legal Pluralism in Ghana*. Routledge.

Tweneboah, S. (2021a). Akan Deities as Agents of Conflict Resolution Mechanism in Ghana: Promises and Pitfalls. In E. T. Yin & N. F. Kofie (Eds.), *Advancing Civil Justice Reform and Conflict Resolution in Africa and Asia: Comparative Analyses and Case Studies*. IGI Global. doi:10.4018/978-1-7998-7898-8.ch001

Tweneboah, S. (2021b). Religion, Law, and Politics in Ghana: Duabɔ (Imprecation) as Spiritual Justice in the Public Sphere. *African Journal of Legal Studies*, *14*(2), 209–229. doi:10.1163/17087384-12340081

USAID. (2019). Non-State Justice System Programming: A Practitioners' Guide (AID-OAA-I-13-00034/7200AA18F00003). United States Agency for International Development.

Warner-Lewis, M. (1999). *Trinidad Yoruba: From Mother-Tongue to Memory*. University of the West Indies Press.

Wright, J. K. (2016). *Lawyers as Changemakers: The Global Integrative Law Movement*. ABA Book Publishing.

Wright, J. K. (n.d.). Integrative Law. *University of Western Australia Law Review, 46*(2), 237–252.

KEY TERMS AND DEFINITIONS

Broom (or Broomweed): This is a besom (or *praeɛ* in the Akan language) constructed from a bundle of palm fibres, usually without a pole for a handle.

Imprecation: Imprecation is an act of invoking evil, dreadful or woeful happenings or calamity upon a person against whom the words are uttered. It is act of invoking the wrath of a supernatural force to intervene in a dispute between parties.

*Nsedie***:** The act involving calling upon some supernatural powers to witness what has been said and to impose a supernatural sanction.

Obeah **(or Obeahman):** An ancestor-based tradition in the Caribbean believed to have been inherited from the Akan of Ghana. This religious practice and system of belief is said to be a set of hybrid or combination of various religious elements. Legally, in Jamaica, the Obeah Act of 1898 defines a person practicing obeah as any person who, to effect any fraudulent or unlawful purpose, or for gain, or for the purpose of frightening any person, uses or pretends to use any occult means, or pretends to possess any supernatural power or knowledge.

Sassywood: Sassywood is a form of trial by ordeal particularly prominent in Liberia in which an accused person is forced to ingest some poisonous substance often made of the bark of the *Erythrophleum suaveolens* tree.

ENDNOTES

[1] There is no evidence that these saints are "syncretized" with African deities as in Haitian Vodou and Cuban Santeria.

[2] Several small shrubs of the genus *Sida* (Malvaceae) with small yellow flowers that grow in waste places in tropical regions.

[3] Yam in the Caribbean and Africa should be distinguished from the sweet potato. The latter is often called yam in the USA.

[4] The sum of three pence, especially before decimalization (1971).

5   "Coco" in Jamaica refers to the cocoyam or taro (*Colocasia* sp). China Cane may refer to *Dieffenbachia,* best known as a houseplant. Contact with the bruised leaves of plants in this family (Araceae) may cause irritation of the mucous membranes and skin.

6   Four thirds or 130%, implying that the volume of wangla (sesame seed) should exceed that of soil.

7   Even in recent times, a large gathering of Caribbean people in London is treated by government and reported media as a public order issue, rather than as a celebration of the largest summer festival in Europe, or as a business issue (Lott-Lavigna, 2017).

Chapter 2
One Space for Two Justice Praxes in Nigeria:
The Yoruba Experience in Stakeholders' Restoration

Johnson Oluwole Ayodele
https://orcid.org/0000-0002-1297-4043
Lead City University, Nigeria

Jane Roli Adebusuyi
Lead City University, Nigeria

ABSTRACT

The Yoruba people have unwritten normative, proverb-driven traditional jurisprudence to resolve all emerging disputes. Regrettably, colonialism suddenly emerged to compel the Yoruba people to drop their restorative treatment of the primary justice stakeholders and replace it with the castigatory European justice paradigm. This chapter studies the inclusive character of the traditional justice system of the Yoruba of southwestern Nigeria. It collected secondary data from the internet and archival sources. Data analysis indicates that including the victims, offenders, and the community in conflict management enhances the Yoruba traditional conflict resolution skills. To creatively halt the miscarriage of justice in postcolonial Yorubaland, policymakers should transform the justice systems to ground solutions for disputes in local realities. Also, both justice systems should replace competition with cooptation and embrace a symbiotic restorative response to dispute resolution for the deepening of Yoruba jurisprudence.

DOI: 10.4018/978-1-6684-4112-1.ch002

INTRODUCTION

Nearly all the traditional peoples of the world have developed homegrown conduct-regulating values and grievance-redressing norms that took cognizance of restoration during their evolutionary processes. Usually, traditional people are socialized, in their everyday interactions, to comply with their community norms. While the indigenous justice system of the Yoruba people does not unendingly castigate the offender, using cultural blessings, it deters a future commission of the same or other offences. Offender sanctifications stimulate the disputants, before the gods, to accept the decisions of the peacemakers without keeping any grudges against each other. Dispute settlements are customary practices driven by proverbs, traditions, and norms considered to be customary law, the sum of the practices, norms, values, and standards of indigenous people in their local communities that guide their daily routine. A particular country can have a significant number of traditional justice systems within it, as different communities often have their customary law. The customary law may be oral or written, and decisions may or may not be recorded as jurisprudence. Before the advent of the colonial invasion of the Yoruba kingdom, tested systems of arbitration had been established. Therefore, the colonialists did not meet the Yoruba people in a state of anomie. The occasional civil and criminal issues that emerged were within the capacity of the existing structures of the local governance to creditably manage. Therefore, the widespread social order that the colonialists met on the ground surprised them.

In the context of history, the colonial epoch began in Nigeria in the 15th century with the slave trade. The British determined the geographical profile of Nigeria by controlling an area now known as Nigeria through a process that was completed in five successive phases. The first was the settlement of Lagos becoming a colony in 1861. The Royal Niger Company controlled central Nigeria from 1886 to 1900. This event was followed by the amalgamation of its territories into the new Protectorate of Southern Nigeria. In 1906, the Protectorate of Southern Nigeria merged with the Lagos Protectorate (Coleman, 1963, p. 41-44). Finally, the Southern Protectorates amalgamated with Northern Nigeria in 1914, although a certain degree of administrative distinction between the Southern and Northern Nigeria was maintained (Crowder 1978, p. 191). As a consequence of the amalgamation, the three main ethnolinguistic groups comprising of Hausa-Fulani in the north, the Yoruba in the southwest, and the Igbo in the southeast emerged. Thus, some 250 ethnic groups and minorities' interests coexist in one country. The country is somewhat less than half Muslim (mostly in the north) and about 45% Christian with a wide range of indigenous beliefs shared by many Nigerians (Lewis et al., 1998, p. 27-28). Instead of adopting indirect rule the way the British colonialists had done, they should have adopted an integrative approach that would have blended the British judicial values of laws and policies with those of the colonies' cultural norms and traditions for a coherent institutional development. However, this rule lasted until 1960, when Nigeria attained independence. The colonial incapacity to forge this justice unity accounts for the competition rather than cooptation that would have prepared the foundation for judicial integration that Nigeria lacks up till today.

Literature Review

Restorative justice (RJ) that reestablishes, compensates, reintegrates, and ensures community involvement in confronting crime, disputes, and distress-associated problems (Doolin, 2007) is not new to the black race. Even long before the arrival of the colonial masters, African communities had been resolving their disputes without external interference. It is in this context that the insistence of Ladan (2013) that restoration takes the forms of compensation, reparation, or apology to facilitate the mending of broken relationships becomes extremely enlightening. As it is today, the efficiency of RJ in the adopted Western criminal justice system as the experience has shown in South Africa is not anymore as efficacious as it once was (Louw & Wyk, 2016). Nonetheless, RJ has reemerged at the justice fore to remind the world that it has returned to the old ways of resolving disputes (Llwelyn & Howse, 2002). In confirmation of this claim, some other scholars have argued that RJ is deep-rooted in Africa, and certainly in many parts of the world, the names adopted notwithstanding (Mangena, 2011). Other equally significant philosophies of restorative justice comprise offender liability for wrongdoing, respect for all participants, and focusing the approach on victims (Umbreit & Armour, 2010).

The customs which characterized the first and second Comte's law of three stages are contextually analogous to the experiences of most traditional communities of the world. The similarity of the unwritten values that most African communities, especially the Yoruba people share with the earliest histories of the West in the context of the traditional justice system (TJS) can, therefore, be assumed. Thus, traditional institutions play incredible roles in accomplishing stable democracy in societies including Nigeria (Osifo, 2017). Is it not a paradox that these traditional institutions promoted the defense of the rights and interests of various community dwellers in pre-colonial Nigeria (Nweke, 2012; Isaac, 2018)? Unfortunately, these days, a traditional ruler remains in office at the pleasure of the political office holders who hire and fire (Osifo, 2017). As evident everywhere, the democratization of Nigeria has not significantly influenced the stability of the traditional institutions positively in Nigeria (Kalu & Falola, 2019). Credible institutions have all studied traditional justice systems and informal justice systems more comprehensively (UN Women, UNICEF & UNDP, 2013). The United Nations studied 10,000 men in Asia and the Pacific on gender-based violence in September 2013. Thus far, the study represents the largest cross-country comparable data set on the use of violence by men in Asia-Pacific to the present day. On the whole, it found that almost a half of the male respondents used physical and/or sexual violence against a female partner. This ranged from 26 to 80 percent across the study sites. Almost a quarter of the male respondents acknowledged perpetrating rape against a woman or girl. This ranged from 10 to 62 percent across the study sites (WHO, LSHTM, SAMRC, 2013).

Intimate partner and sexual violence give rise to issues having serious short- and long-term mental, physical, sexual, and reproductive health implications for women. These IPV induced health problems impose socioeconomic costs on women, their children, and societies, as a whole. IPV can lead to homicide and suicide; injuries; unintended pregnancies, gynecological complications, and sexually transmitted infections. The study conducted by WHO in 2013 on the health burden connected with violence against women, it found that women who had been victims of physical or sexual abuse were 1.5 times more likely to have a sexually transmitted infection and, in some regions, HIV. Women who went through IPV were 16% more likely to suffer a miscarriage and 41% more likely to have a pre-term birth (WHO, LSHTM, SAMRC, 2013).

Similarly, other scholars have studied some areas of the justice system focusing on different aspects. However, the effectiveness of the *orishas*, significant components of traditional justice, in compelling witnesses to confess the truth, making the law on perjury contextually unnecessary, and prevent wrongful conviction has not been exhaustively studied among the Yoruba people of southwestern Nigeria. The postcolonial Nigeria manifests only two dominant forms of justice systems – the informal and formal justice systems. All the seemingly numerous indigenous justice systems possess location-specific differences within the land area that account for the diversity of the values evolving from one large traditional environment having the collective solidarity as their focus. For instance, the concept of the god, Ṣàngó among the Yorubas, was believed to strike offenders with a 'thunderbolt' thereby meting out instant judgment (see Dierk, 2011; Johnson, 1921, p. 149-152). Therefore, he was mostly regarded as the god of justice. All of these are under one large umbrella of informality while the imported colonial justice belongs to another genre entirely. The essential difference between the two regimes may not be apparent to a non-African audience. It is not a complex challenge for Africans to differentiate between a system that is essentially foreign and that which is substantially native, the diversity in religion notwithstanding. In the sociocultural context of Nigeria both as a postcolonial society in a globalized 21st-century world, Nigerians are committed to the concern for decolonized moral and cultural independence. Therefore, the interaction between the restorative content of the traditional justice system gives a meaning to the possibility of integration between the formal and informal in the postcolonial Nigerian society. The restorative content of the traditional justice is a way of life in Africa generally and Nigeria in particular. Despite the delicate nuances that differentiate one from the other, a foreigner may not even recognize the very fine thread of diversity in the cultural characters of African communities.

Therefore, whether it is a precolonial, colonial, or postcolonial epoch, the influence of the justice system on the people during these different phases of African history would have been the same without foreign intervention. Because culture is dynamic, the African culture now takes cognizance of the changing global norms in the scheme of postcolonial interactions among the Yoruba people of southwestern Nigeria. This is one of the motivating assurances that the traditional and formal justice systems will synergize for the public good. Moreover, the choice of the Yoruba people of southwestern Nigeria for this social observation is appropriate because of their commitment to the traditional justice system without strikingly being derisive of the efficacy of the criminal justice system. The objective of this chapter is to show how the restorative contents of the traditional justice practices, irrespective of the simultaneous existence and provisions of the formal justice, prevent wrongful conviction, reestablish the victims, and offenders, and return communities to their pre-dispute social equilibrium in southwestern Nigeria. To achieve its objective, the study answers the following questions. (i). What are the strengths and inadequacies of the traditional justice system vis-à-vis the contemporary official legal system? (ii). Contextually, which justice system is logically alternative to the other in southwestern Nigeria – the formal or traditional justice? (iii). Which of the two justice systems is more restorative to the primary stakeholders of the justice systems in southwestern Nigeria? (iv). How can both justice systems work together to promote social order among the Yoruba people of southwestern Nigeria? How the nexus between the formal and informal justice systems that compelled *Amotekun* to stem the rising crime in southwestern Nigeria is the knowledge gap that this chapter hopes to bridge.

An Overview of Justice Architecture in the Yoruba Society

The Yoruba people occupy the southwestern part of Nigeria. Of the over 250 indigenous groups making up Nigeria, Yoruba is the second largest with 21% population according to July 2012 estimate (FBI Factbook, 2012). In Yorubaland, the ruler, chief priest, and elders typically decided on the improvement of the life of the community through oracular guidelines that shape the administration of government and judiciary (Tobi, 1996). Among the Yoruba people, the *Oba* (natural ruler) frequently sought the advice of the *babalawo* (Ifa priest) on how to improve the well-being of his people (Adegboye, 1983). Outside the cases of murder, incest, and the violation of the mysteries of secret societies, other matters were within the *bale's* competent jurisdiction (Fadipe, 1970). The Yoruba traditional or natural rulers provide a system of administration that is driven by accurate local knowledge,

political order, but it may not address deeply embedded inequities. It may provide procedural justice but deny substantive social justice. Indeed, both liberal and even illiberal regimes are governed by the rule of law" (p. 160). Mechanisms that facilitate protection from arbitrary justice are inherent in the customary procedure which enable tempers to cool with time to suitably present the cases to the elders or council for appropriate judicial trial. If in the pre-colonial epoch in Africa, "... an offence committed by an accused person was so grievous as to excite the crowd or the injured party into instant retaliation," the offender might escape summary justice (Elias, 1956, p. 215) by seeking asylum in a sacred shrine or the king's palace for the duration of the hearing of the case against him. "Once a supposed or even a criminal has sought the refuge of a sanctuary - be it ever so ramshackle as a flimsy grove of bare thatch, none of his pursuers dare touch him" (Elias, 1956, p. 215). This lifeline provision affords an alleged offender to avoid instant penalty until a proper judicial hearing is conducted and has been institutionalized by law and practice in most pre-colonial African societies. Africans devised these kinds of lifelines to serve as a protective valve from free and frequent "indulgence in a vendetta by the populace." (Elias, 1956, p. 215).

No matter how long such protection may last, among the Yoruba people, it is acknowledged generally that *elese kan ko ni lo lai j'iya* (meaning no offender shall go unpunished). Therefore, anyone who flouts any laid down principles, rules, and regulations are appropriately treated by the law of the land (Alli, 2001, p. 113). This commitment suggests maximum regard for the rule of law in Yoruba legal culture. because of the nature of investigation and cross-examination embedded in the legal culture (Olaoba, 2002, p. 81), "... no offender escapes punishment in Yoruba society... no one was made a scapegoat for the offence he has not committed; doing so amounts to incurring the wrath of the ancestors" (Olaoba, 2002, p. 83). A Yoruba legal maxim *Ika t'o ba se l'oba nge* (in his punitive expeditions, the king targets the criminal element). Consistent with the objectives of the present study, in this section, this chapter presents its arguments by starting with the essence and weaknesses of the traditional justice system. The chapter progresses to interrogate the TJS as the mainstream to which formal justice is logically alternative in southwestern Nigeria. It then presents the TJS as more restorative to the primary stakeholders of the justice system than the formal alternative in southwestern Nigeria. Then, it makes a strong case for the need to encourage the traditional and formal justice systems to work together for the furtherance of social order in southwestern Nigeria.

THE WEAKNESSES AND STRENGTHS OF THE YORUBA TRADITIONAL JUSTICE SYSTEM

This section presents the weaknesses and strengths of the traditional justice system. To make the compelling resources of the TJS come out more effectively, there is a need to conceptualize justice as well as discuss the principles of the Yoruba TJS before presenting its weaknesses and strengths. It is probably better to begin the examination of justice whether traditional or formal with the definition of justice itself. The International Council on Human Rights holds traditional justice systems as: … non-state norms and institutions that tend to draw moral authority more from contemporary or traditional cultural, or customary or religious beliefs, ideas, and practices, and less from the political authority of the state… (Wojkwoska & Cunningham, 2010, p. 59). The non-Africans have a lot to learn for it to capture the cultural realities of the Yoruba people because it is practically "impossible to describe and sometimes understand indigenous (customary) legal systems by using Western concepts" (Bunikowski & Dillon, 2017, p. 42). At this juncture, the non-African audience needs a bit of broader-based information to capture the realistic perspectives from which Africans look at themselves considering their conception of justice. It is obvious that some foreigners probably find it difficult to relate to the reality that some seemingly esoteric principles undergird the traditional justice system. First, widely accepted and understood social or cultural values, norms, beliefs, and processes drive community conflict resolution. This provokes legitimacy and a high compliance rate with the decisions of the justice system. Second, a high premium is placed on the primacy of truth, belief in ancestral authorities, superstitions, charms, sorcery, and witchcraft as making up considerable components of dispute resolution and prevention mechanisms in traditional African societies (Adeyinka & Lateef, 2014). Third, Africans cherish and firmly embed respect for elders, ancestors, parents, fellow people, and the environment in the mores, customs, taboos, and traditions.

For these reasons, the TJSs are "easy to get; use the native language; and naturally, their dealings are simple and do not necessitate the amenities of a lawyer. Their sanctions emphasize reconciliation, compensation, rehabilitation and restoration" (Wourji, 2012, p. 273). Therefore, TJS can be trusted by individuals who have been excluded from the formal justice system to access justice in Africa, reinforce the rule of law, and engender development among communities (Hunter, 2011). In many pre-colonial kingdoms, even today among the Yoruba people, checks and balances remain rooted in the traditional procedures of political and administrative governance (Edo, 2010). As a principle, legal equality insists that the law should be equally applicable to everyone irrespective of hierarchy. In Yoruba land, "every town, village or hamlet is under a responsible head, either a provincial king or *baale* (Mayor)" (Johnson, 1960, p. 75). The position of the king or *Oba* qualifies him to punish offenders because he is *"Igbakeji Orisa"* (the second in command to the deities) or *Kabiyesi* (an unquestionable authority). Although the king is supreme and exercises absolute power, within the ambits of the unwritten constitution. If the king does anything that is beyond the provisions of the unwritten constitution, Bashorun, the head of the *Oyomesi,* has the prerogative to move the rejection of a tyrannical king in which case His majesty has no alternative but to take poison and die (Johnson, 1960, p. 70). The consciousness of the power of the kingmakers prevents anarchy. The stern positions of the kingmakers supersede those exercised by the norms that hold judges in the formal system accountable. In sum, in traditional Yoruba jurisprudence, nobody is above the law. Thus, the rule of law is firmly entrenched in Africa's unwritten constitution.

In present-day Nigeria, it may be helpful to note that customary law is one of the sources of the Nigerian legal system, and generally, it is said to be unwritten as opposed to written English law (Ekhator, 2019; Oamen & Aigbokhan, 2018). Despite that much modern or the post-colonial customary law is unwritten in Nigeria and most parts of Africa, there has been a growing body of "treatises and court decisions setting down customary rules of law as the authors judge them to be. Therefore, it is now much easier to state the rule of customary law on a particular issue." (Ocran, 2006, p. 467; Oba, 2006, p. 97). Thus, western legal history methods can be used to analyze colonial and the post-colonial customary laws in Nigeria (Ibhawoh, 2013). For example, Ibhawoh analyzed case law arising from the Judicial Committee of the Privy Council, colonial regional appeal courts for West Africa and East Africa (Ibhawoh, 2013a, p. 4). Some scholars have also analyzed native courts and customary courts in the colonial and post-colonial eras in Nigeria (Kaplan, 1997; Ikponmwosa & Evbayiro, 2017; Oriakhogba & Fenemigho, 2019). However, it will be difficult to rely on the methods of western legal history for the analysis of pre-colonial laws in Africa. For this reason, most efforts to give independent historical capacity to precolonial laws in Africa have had to rely on the use of oral interviews, oral traditions (including proverbs) and analysis of secondary materials such as books, articles, and reports (Agbakoba & Nwauche, 2006). If Western military history scholarship increasingly relies on oral historical methodology (Morillo & Pavkovic, 2017), what then is the fuss about the Indigenous pre-colonial laws being mainly unwritten because many African kingdoms (including Yoruba) had no writing system or literate culture (Ocran, 2006; Ekhator, 2018)?

Therefore, the practice that like cases is sometimes not treated alike, is exemplified in Yorubaland with saying such as *bi a se ma pa omo awo; a ko gbudo p'ogberi be e,* (the elites should enjoy some unspoken privileges in the course of doing justice). Despite this seeming reckless anti-egalitarian conception of justice, the *ogboni* cult, one of the very potent instruments of actualizing this seemingly unjust privilege, intervenes whenever the traditional ruler becomes intolerably despotic to strip him of his royalty by requesting him to vacate the royal stool. This kind of erring traditional rulers complied by vacating their royal positions through the commission of suicide because *iku ya j'esin lo* (it is more decent to die as a king than face the ridicule of forcible removal). "African societies have always had a form of governance peculiar to them, and which operated following their traditions and belief systems" (Abioye, 2011, p. 23). In Africa, as it is among the Yoruba people, "a person lacking in moral worth, and integrity is less than a person. He is, at best, not better than a beast" (Igbafen, 2014, p.124). To the extent that communalism recognizes that community values supersede individual values, the welfare of the individual is inseparable from the welfare of the community. This is so because the individual is nonexistent in the absence of the community (Igbafen, 2014, p. 127). It is in this regard that in Yorubaland, whoever commits a crime faces the music no matter how highly placed. It is on this philosophy that the saying among Yoruba *orin o dara, eni orin aafin ni, se aafin ni orin buburu ye ni?* (An evil song should not emanate from the palace because of its sacredness).

The informal justice systems do not always provide a cure-all intervention for a social disorder just as the formal alternative is incapable of doing the same. Despite informal justice systems being extensively considered in many communities as the most acceptably credible means of achieving an outcome that satisfies the sense of local justice, situations sometimes exist that they fail to live up to this ideal expectation. Some traditional rulers and peacekeepers in customary justice systems were reported to have compromised by using their powers as instruments of oppression to deprive the people of their rights and benefits (Albert, Hérault, Awe, & Omitoogun, 2013). For example, they are assumed to have used their privileged positions to appropriate land and other valuable properties from disputing parties to further deepen their economic interests (Sangroula & Sangroula, 2016). Similarly, some traditional rulers typically claim a certain percentage (which is often shared with the elders) from the properties under dispute as a reward for settling disputes (Albert et al., 2013). It is against this background that objective critique of the local realities of justice is done in southwestern Nigeria. Whenever the extreme situation in which the traditional system becomes incompetent to handle the excesses of offenders occurs, the assumption that underlies such complexity would be construed to belong to the spiritual realm and such peculiar occurrence is the prerogative of the gods, deities. Therefore, an attempt to understand to describe the traditional legal system by using western concepts will lead to misleading conclusions (Bunikowski & Dillon, 2017).

However, despite the acclaimed merits of formal justice, to what extent has it assisted in transforming the deeply corrupt, hostile, and violent world into a place of calm where everyone can pursue and achieve his/her career without encountering frustrating racial discrimination? The fact that both justices are in active operation while Rahmon Adedoyin and his cohorts murdered Timothy Adegoke, a postgraduate student of the Obafemi Awolowo University at Ile Ife, in Osun State confirms the inherent incapacity of both systems operating independently. This failure advertises the need for both the formal and informal justice systems to partner to ensure community surveillance in the prevention and detection of crimes. Therefore, a constant evaluation, re-evaluation, and proactive response to the realities of the local population to cancel out mutual manifest shortcomings of both justice systems are appropriate at this juncture. This advocated partnership of the TJS with the formal justice system is timely because it can rid the Yoruba in particular and Nigeria in general of individual and systemic ineffectiveness, corruption, and repression (Abdul Karim, 2012). Traditional Yoruba communities have existed and governed themselves in ways different from the non-African approach before the advent of the colonialists. Their lifestyles including justice systems drove rewarding sociopolitical relationships. These resources bonded the Yoruba people in solidarity with one another. Empirical evidence exists to indicate that traditional legal orders have competent peacebuilding mechanisms (Werner, 2010; Adebayo et al., 2014). TJS can promote access to justice for the rural poor and the illiterate people with its flexible, voluntary, relationships fostering, and restorative justice proffering content that gives some level of autonomy to the parties in the process (Kariuki, 2014). In the events of disputes amongst Yoruba people or communities, disputants often turn to negotiations and, in other cases, to the institution of the council of elders or elderly men and women who act as third parties in the resolution of conflicts (Kariuki et al., 2016).

THE JUSTICE SYSTEM THAT IS ALTERNATIVE TO THE OTHER IN SOUTHWESTERN NIGERIA

This section presents data that show the conceptions and an unfair displacement of classical justice structures among the Yoruba people of southwestern Nigeria. This effort begins with the explanation of the historical reality to settle once and for all the subjective narratives about which genre of justice is the correct alternative to the other in Yorubaland. TJS of the Yoruba people predates "the contemporary criminal justice practices" (Bowd, 2009, p. 9) that accompanied their contact with the colonial administration. To distinguish between the mainstream classical justice system in the context of Yoruba jurisprudence and the one that came to forcibly unseat and deprive it of ascendancy, it is probably helpful to explain the logic undergirding the Yoruba question *Se ori lo siwaju de eewo ni tabi eewo lo siwaju de ori?* (Which exists before the other, the parasite or the host?). As yet, it is not anywhere stated in the literature that Europe discovered Yorubaland. Also, the colonialists did not settle in southwestern Nigeria before the Yoruba people later joined in treating the western mode of social justice as the classical genre. Therefore, making the formal justice option to seem the one that came to unseat the traditional alternative is counterintuitive in the extreme. The colonialists were never in doubt that they needed a legal system to maintain control of their subjects and settle disputes among them. Therefore, wherever the colonial metropoles started their systems of law and dispute resolution, they disregarded the pre-existing mechanisms of conflict resolution as primordial or appropriate for 'natives' only (Joireman, 2001). Somehow, virtually all of the metropoles saw the sharing of their seemingly advanced legal systems with their colonies as one of their goals, if not a duty. This kind of mindset provided a firm basis for the entire colonial enterprise in the Yoruba space of southwestern Nigeria. Little wonder then that during colonial epochs, Africans were compelled to accept foreign administrative and adjudication practices. Most African practices during this period were tagged barbaric and were filtered to conform to what is obtained in the colonial context of a 'civilized world.' (Osemwonwa, 2000, p. 14).

This decision dispossessed the Yoruba people of their traditional justice values as weapons of maintaining social justice in their domains. There is the need to explore the etymological origin of the phrase "alternative to" so that this chapter can present the narratives that will effectively dislodge the counterintuitive logic on which its ascendancy gained support from the minds of seekers of credible knowledge. Which of the two justice systems should be alternative to the other using a factual presentation of historical analysis driven by natural justice, equity, and good conscience? Is it the traditional justice or formal justice system? Auguste Comte propounded the law of three stages. This law suitably applies here. Comte assumed that all human societies essentially transit from the theological stage to the metaphysical, and finally to the positive stage. If the West went through these theoretical stages, an inference is possible here. Every local population across the world, for always, goes through its discreet consensus that throws up traditional structures of justice as their legitimate institutions for the expression of their understood justice in the course of cultural evolution. That some non-Africans have subtly presented the TJS as an alternative to the formal system has a clandestine way of making the former subservient to the latter. It should be remembered, however, that "For many people throughout the world their primary access to justice is through informal justice systems" (Wojkowska, 2006, p. 12). Making the justice structures that predated colonialism in Yoruba land serve as alternative institutions to the formal justice system does not possess an iota of superior knowledge for which the customary position could be compelled to bow.

In which context of the justice system did the formal justice system come first in southwestern Nigeria? The attainment of legal sophistication is not the focus of interest here. The acknowledgment of Commander Frederick Forbes, the then British Crown representative (Phillips, 1969). He objectively assessed the complexity of the political structure he met on the ground in Yorubaland. Forbes found the superlative administrative and political hierarchy as it symbolized governance in Yorubaland has "four presidents," and "840 principal rulers or "House of Lords", 2,800 secondary chiefs or "House of Commons", 140 principal military ones and 280 secondary ones in its system of government to make "Abeokuta and its system of government, the most extraordinary republic in the world" (Adeuyan, 2011, p. 18). This exceptional political organization of the Yoruba society has underscored the people's commitment to a deep sense of justice which prevailed until the European imperialists invaded their land in the second half of the nineteenth century through the Christian missionaries, British army of occupation, and the deployment of brute force (Aderibigbe, 1962; Atanda, 1967; Ayandele, 1967; Tamuno, 1962).

Some African scholars have inadvertently given in to the dishonest agenda of making the traditional justice system subservient to the formal justice on the continent of Africa. Imposing western justice norms on the local population of Yoruba people was itself an unprovoked breach of decorum. How can the justice system that had been shaping and regulating the lives of the Yoruba before their contact with the colonialists become an alternative to an unsolicited justice norm emerging from a culturally less enriched background? Regardless of how unsuitable the colonialists interpreted the native devices were to the justice needs of the local population, it is not their business to superimpose their culturally inconsistent values on the Yoruba people. Having done the absurd, they went ahead to slam the pejorative profile of being an alternative to a system they deliberately imported and imposed. This is inappropriate and therefore unacceptable. Western justice is rationally and objectively alternative to the traditional justice system. Therefore, any non-western scholar who supports the offensive reordering of the justice systems has a mind that requires to be appropriately decolonized. The reasons underlying the argument, using, or doing the first instead of the second requires to be intellectualized to correct the age-long error that is associated with the use of the phrase 'alternative to' in the context of the nexus between the traditional and formal justice systems in Yorubaland. It would be appropriate to heed the warning of Nwolise (2005) that a society that disregards the enlightening value of its past for its present and future, cannot be self-assured and self-sufficient; and will therefore experience a dearth of internally created drive and strength. In this regard, which of the two justice systems can we present as verifiably occupying the first position – the traditional or formal justice system?

Anchored on a Yoruba proverb which says *araba ni baba, eni a ba laba ni baba*, (whoever first sojourns in a place is the earliest settler), therefore, the first to exist in the area now recognized as Yorubaland automatically gained a classical status of ownership by settlement. It is against this philosophy that the justice structure of the Yoruba people who settled in that geographic setting before the colonial exploration acquires the status of original existence against which other subsequent structures should ideally be contrasted. Whenever the argument comes up that the traditional justice system is referred to as the alternative justice system, the inverted logic gains ascendancy. The assumption that nothing bore the semblance of justifiable justice before the advent of the colonialists in Yorubaland sustains the making the formal justice system seem the one against which the traditional system competes. The phrase 'alternative to' forecloses a possible construction of a nexus between the formal and informal justice system. To the extent that the justice that is being considered directly touches on the lives of the Yoruba people, then the question of the establishment of ownership here is not reckless.

This section presents data that show the conceptions and displacement of classical justice among the Yoruba people of southwestern Nigeria. This effort begins with the explanation of the historical reality to settle once and for all the subjective narratives about which genre of justice is the correct alternative to the other in Yorubaland. TJS of the Yoruba people predates "the contemporary criminal justice practices" (Bowd, 2009, p. 9) that emerged with their contact with the colonial administration. To distinguish between the mainstream classical justice system in the context of Yoruba jurisprudence and the one that came to forcibly unseat and deprive it of relevant ascendancy, it is probably helpful to explain the logic undergirding the Yoruba question *Se ori lo siwaju de eewo ni tabi eewo lo siwaju de ori?* (Which exists before the other, the parasite or the host?). The literature does not record it anywhere that Europe discovered Yorubaland, or the West settled in southwestern Nigeria before the Yoruba people. Therefore, treating the western mode of social justice as the classical genre among the Yoruba people is plainly counterintuitive.

This colonial imposition dispossessed the Yoruba people of their traditional justice values as weapons of maintaining social justice in their domains. There is the need to interrogate the historical basis of the phrase "alternative to" as a means to dislodge the counterintuitive logic on which the ascendancy of the western form of justice had gained support from the minds of seekers of credible knowledge. To present which of the two justice systems deserves to be alternative to the other will involve drawing from the wisdom of the law of three stages by Auguste Comte. Comte assumed that all human societies essentially transit from the theological stage to the metaphysical, and finally to the positive stage. If the West navigated these theoretical stages, an inference is possible here. Every local population across the world, always, explores its discreet consensus that throws up traditional structures of justice as their legitimate institutions for the expression of what they understood as justice in the course of their cultural evolution. That the colonizers have subtly presented the TJS as an alternative to the formal system has a clandestine way of making the former subservient to the latter. It should be remembered, however, that "For many people throughout the world their primary access to justice is through informal justice systems" (Wojkowska, 2006, p. 12). Therefore, making the justice structures that predated colonialism in Yoruba land serve as alternative institutions to the formal justice system that was empowered to overcome it does not possess an iota of superior knowledge for which the customary position could be compelled to bow.

THE MORE RESTORATIVE JUSTICE SYSTEM IN YORUBALAND

Traditional or Formal

This section presents the comparative information about the values of traditional and formal justice systems to establish, in the light of data, which of the systems is more restorative to the justice stakeholders in Yorubaland. Being the criterion against which the desirability of the two justice systems under examination can be objectively decided, this section follows a layout that starts by defining the concept of crime from the perspectives of both justice systems. It then defines restorative justice. It goes on to define and access the traditional justice performance using its putative demerits that caused the ascendancy of the formal justice system. Presenting the arguments through this framework will not only promote structure but also promises to facilitate the articulation of the central theme. This chapter, therefore, holds that a crime is the commission of any act that the legislative assembly of a state recognizes as an offence. A crime encroaches upon a moral code, normative pattern, religious doctrine, or legal right of another person(s). It is the judicial interpretation, police enforcement, and the rehabilitation efforts of the correctional facility that serve as the crowning glory of the action against crimes. Restorative justice (RJ) concentrates on what needs to be healed or reimbursed; learned in the wake of crime; and strengthened to avoid re-occurrence (Elliott, 2011). To establish whether the formal or informal justice system is more restorative to the stakeholders of the justice system, this chapter holds restorative justice as a process and effect-driven pursuit of a justice-based intervention providing soothing-therapeutic remedies for the reintegration of the victims, offenders, and communities, in the aftermath of a crime. The way the operators of the traditional and formal justice systems conceive and pursue the achievement of justice will determine which is more restorative than the other in the Yoruba southwest of Nigeria. It is its place-specific value of the informal justice systems that justify the reference to them as customary, informal, community-based, grassroots, indigenous, and local (Allen & Macdonald, 2013).

The African legal culture scowls at any act that upsets the "social equilibrium, deities, shrines, ancestors, kinship, elders, age-grade associations and the chiefs are some of the indigenous mechanisms of crime control in nearly all African societies" (Ani, 2012, p. 743). Therefore, the norms that the Yoruba people used to regulate their members' conduct before their contact with the colonialists were never from outside the Yorubaland. Before the advent of colonialism, the Yoruba people had lived organized lives. The model of justice that the Yoruba people adopted greatly differs from the retributive justice system that pervades most countries of the world in the 21st century. Rather than creating a more accountable, friendlier, and more integrated human community, the retributive model of justice legitimizes violence with its castigatory orientation. Members of an ordered society need to be protected from wrongful convictions. For example, a 2014 study conservatively estimates that 4.1% of inmates, in the United States, awaiting execution on death row are innocent (Gross, O'Brien, Hu & Kennedy, 2014). The formal criminal justice system of Nigeria is a western approach driven by three core components - the law enforcement (Police), judicial process (Courts), and correctional institutions (Prisons). In every phase of the criminal justice procedure, an accused offender passes from the investigation, through the trial, to the type and length of punishment if there is a conviction (Nwosu, 2011). There is no doubt that the formal justice system is committed to a rigid application of extreme punishment without taking cognizance of the factors that may have triggered the offence in the criminals (Shajobi-Ibikunle, 2014). Similarly, bribery and corruption commonly characterize formal justice, commodify justice, and transform it into instruments of intimidation and abuse (Salihu & Gholami, 2018). These vicious practices are opposed to the ideals of restorative justice. Several decades after independence and the adoption of formal justice, Ajayi and Buhari (2014) observe that Nigerians do not have faith and still generally consider the adversarial court system as external to them. The none-acceptance of the system among Yoruba people of south-western Nigeria manifests in the following common saying *Ákii dari kóótu sóré* meaning "we do not come back from the (formal) court for a dispute and remain friends" (Albert et al., 2013). Similarly, *Atebi atare Olorun ma je a rejo'* meaning "for good or ill, God will make the experience of a court case elude us' (Albert et al., 2013).

Therefore, completely different from the formal justice system and similar in some regard to the traditional justice system, the principle of restorative justice centers on the victim in the criminal justice system (Leyh, 2011). Restorative justice is a process whereby all the parties with a stake in a particular offense come together to collectively resolve how to deal with the aftermath of the offense and its implications for the future. In addition to using the ideals of restorative justice spelled out here, this chapter adopts the four Rs (reconciliation, restitution, reintegration, and restoration) which Abajuo (2016) identified as the main concepts of restorative justice ideal to serve as the explanatory planks to justify its position. The process of reconciliation involves participatory and interactive features to foster a high level of cross socialization between the core stakeholders of criminal justice to evaluate the intensity of their actions and reactions to one another and the health of their community. The mutual appreciation of each stakeholder's feeling about the disruptive impact of the crime heals wounds and facilitates recoveries to activate future interactions that will strengthen the post disposal bonding of the disputing parties (Nwosu, 2011). Moreover, the formal justice system has been marred by corruption and ethnoreligious intolerance that have infiltrated the rank and file of the Nigeria Police causing the circumvention of the dispensation of duties and justice to Nigerians (Afon & Badiora, 2016).

Most Nigerian prisons are congested, the inmates are malnourished, no worthwhile health services which necessitate recurring events of indiscipline, rape, and drug abuse that combine to weaken the institutional roles of the custodial facilities (Akinnawo & Akpunne, 2016; Nnam, 2016). The courts have become business centres where justice is commodified; politicians have politicized judicial service to the extent that the judges are confused, over-worked, and uncoordinated to give conflicting judicial verdicts (Salawu, 2016). These have reduced public confidence in the justice system (Imam, 2016; Michael, 2016). The formal justice system is lame and therefore cannot embark on any meaningful reconciliation agenda in the communities of Yoruba of southwestern Nigeria. The criminal justice system of Nigeria is currently bedeviled by several problems like delay in police investigations, overuse of prison sentences by the courts, non-adherence to the complainant, accused and prisoner rights, prisons congestions, and shortages of funds to the components of the system (Cooper-Knock & Owen, 2015; John & Musa, 2014; Badamasiuy & Bello, 2013). Nigeria has abused custodial punishment such that the Network of University Legal Aid Institutions has claimed that over 50 per cent of Nigeria's awaiting trial inmates are under the age of 30. In 2018, it had 75, 589 prisoners out of which 24, 450 are convicted while 51, 139 of them are awaiting trial. The figure includes 1, 509 women then in detention (The Network of University Legal Aid Institutions, 2018). Consequently, it has been estimated that over eighty percent of conflicts are resolved through informal justice systems in some countries (Danish Institute for Human Rights, 2012, p. 7).

In terms of reintegration, in most cases, the retributive justice releases badly rehabilitated products of the prisons to the community where they terrify and victimize other law-abiding members of their various communities. Therefore, for the formal justice system, reintegration failure is a foregone conclusion that will not fail to cause restoration collapse. Experience of recidivism has confirmed that the greater proportion of the products of the formal justice system in Nigeria did not benefit positively from practical correction initiatives. To the extent that ex-offenders do not feel a sense of being seen as usefully refined members of their communities, the traditional justice system has done comparatively better than its formal counterpart in this regard. Although restoration is one of the critical philosophies of contemporary custodial services, the fact of rising recidivism does not present the criminal justice system as having achieved any remarkable success in this regard. The organs of the criminal justice system determine the dispensation of justice in any state and society

(Bellessa, 2012). The major challenge facing these organs in Nigeria is the disturbing prison congestion which gains expression in brazen recidivism. As of October 2014, the total prison population in Nigeria stood at 57, 121. Out of this number, pretrial or remand detainees constitute 69.3%, nearly 70% of the population (International Center for Prison Studies, n.d.). As of September 2015, Kirikiri Medium Security Prison with a capacity to accommodate 1,700 inmates, held 2,631 inmates. Out of this number, only 198 (7.5%) were convicted and serving their jail terms, while the remaining 2, 433 (92.5%) were awaiting trial detainees (Office of the Comptroller of Kirikiri Medium Security Prison, 2015). These statistics simply point to the need for the present justice system to be overhauled. The sluggish pace at which Nigeria's criminal justice system operates financially chokes the victims and witnesses who suffer trauma as a result of the crime and are seeking quick closure (Cassell, 1994). Therefore, a criminal justice that is shackled by this suffocating pressure of prison overcrowding cannot rehabilitate efficiently how much less restore the intrinsic worth of the inmates that are progressively being damaged daily.

Restoration is imaginable in circumstances of confidence. The formal justice system appears to have uprooted the offenders from their communities and built an impenetrable wall of we/they dichotomy between the offenders and their victims. This way, the formal criminal justice system waters hostility that digs serious gorges of irreconcilable depths in the relationship between the offenders and the victims in Nigeria. Demonstrably, restorative justice has a positive effect in reducing the frequency and the severity of reoffending (Sherman, Strang, Mayo-Wilson, Woods, & Ariel, 2015; Umbreit, Coates, & Vos, 2008; Shapland, Robinson, & Sorsby, 2011; Strang, Sherman, Mayo-Wilson, Woods, & Ariel, 2013). However, formal justice has recidivism as one of its core regrettable outcomes in Yorubaland. Since recidivism is a critical by-product of the inadequacy of retributive justice in restoration in the study area, the traditional justice is closer, in performance to restorative justice than the formal criminal justice system. It should be noted, however, that restorative justice practices are established on philosophies that highlight the significance of proactively building constructive relationships and a sense of community to prevent and address wrongdoing and involve processes to repair relationships when harm has occurred (Berkowitz, 2016; The Advancement Project, 2014). Based on this thought, the points presented in this chapter add up to confirm that the TJS is closer to the implementation of the restorative ideal than the formal justice system.

Despite the importance and widespread global acceptance of the efficacy of these emerging principles and practices in promoting effective criminal justice administration, attempts in Nigeria to integrate these concepts into the criminal justice system have yielded limited results (Odoh, 2015). Sadly, the concept of restorative justice has not been functionally institutionalized in the Nigerian criminal justice system. Being a more liberal way of doing justice to advance both individual and community peace" (Ifemeje & Ozuru, 2021, p. 158). To the extent that restorative justice can work a lot better in the 21st century in Africa than court proceedings (Omale, 2006; Gabagambi, *2020*), especially in the cultural reconciliation of the offender to his/her society, a synergy between both formal and informal may be helpful to restore order in southwestern Nigeria. Sustainable restorative justice is a vibrant process of engaging, enabling, integrating, reintegrating, and transforming relationships and interactions (Kamara, 2019; Van Ness & Strong, 2015). Conclusively, "The principles of restorative RJ and traditional African mediatory practices share a similar vision about giving social healing to offenders, victims, and communities in the aftermath of victimization" (Ayodele, 2017, p. 44). Therefore, the traditional justice system transcends the formal alternative in the context of restorative offerings among the Yoruba people of south west Nigeria.

HOW BOTH JUSTICE SYSTEMS CAN WORK TOGETHER TO PROMOTE SOCIAL ORDER IN YORUBALAND

This section presents how a synergy between the traditional and formal justice systems can improve the state of public security among the Yoruba people of southwestern Nigeria. In Nigeria (and Sub-Saharan African countries), the policy of indirect rule introduced by the colonialists thoroughly modified the natural ways of life of the Yoruba people and completely replaced their existing structure of justice which saw the emergence of the formal court system as a method for settling disputes (Ajayi & Buhari, 2014). Having come to stay, the experience of the formal justice application all over Africa has shown that the system is not a flawless structure. Therefore, it faces various encounters that range from sluggish prosecution of criminal cases, prison overpopulation, soaring crime rate, and incurable recidivism. All these concerns have combined to promote an insecure and unjust society. Just as it was experienced in South Africa, if Nigeria embraces restorative justice that is driven by traditional and customary responses to crimes, in the overhaul of its criminal architecture (Skelton, 2013), Nigeria in general and Yorubaland in particular, may recapture its lost sense of justice. The traditional justice systems are home-grown, culturally appropriate, operate on minimal resources, and are easily acceptable by the communities they serve (Pimentel, 2010), they will continue to enjoy patronage among the Yoruba people of southwestern Nigeria.

Corroborating this assumption is the position of the participants of a 2014 study in Ogun state conducted to see the extent of the penal efficacy of *ayelala* in southwestern Nigeria. *Ayelala* typifies a deified ancestor (Aihiokhai, 2012), a human being who once lived an extra-ordinary and mysterious life on earth, became deified as a god at death (Omotoye, 2011), worshiped especially by Ikale people (Jemiriye &

Awosusi, 2007) and generally, ilaje people, a Yoruba subgroup in the South Eastern part of Yoruba land mainly inhabiting Ilaje and Ese Odo Local Government Areas of Ondo State (Ajetunmobi, 2012). *Ayelala* is famous for its effective punishment of criminals when invoked. Following the killing of congregants at an owo catholic church on Sunday by unknown gunment, Mrs Yemi Mahmood led a peaceful protest organized by the market women in Owo, chanting incantations in their local dialect as they placed the leaves and knives they each held, as insignia of traditional war and peace, on the floor as part of the ritual process. They did this to place an irreversible curse on the perpetrators of evil by invoking the god of Iron (*Ogùn*) to go after them and facilitate their being urgently tracked down. The following day, Ogunoye III (2022), the traditional ruler of Owo, announced the arrest of the alleged perpetrators of the attack. This is a classic example of how the formal and informal social control structures can partner to rid the contemporary Yorubaland of crime. Ojo (2014) conducted an opinion survey of Igbesa community people in Ogun State with 52 participants to investigate whether *Ayelala* should be incorporated into Nigeria's Criminal Justice and Political Systems. He found a consensus among 94% of the participants that the deity is very efficient in punishing offenders of law and order when invoked. But 54% favoured its inclusion implementation in the Criminal Justice System of Nigeria.

The way the formal justice system is presently crafted does not make it seek restorative justice. The Nigerian Correctional Services Act of 2019 was a big relief initially because it provides a leeway for collaborative operation between the formal and traditional justice systems to implement RJ measures in contemporary Nigeria. Operationally, not much has been achieved in terms of the translation of documented ideals into verifiable relief realities for inmates. It is, therefore, sufficient to add nations such as the United States, China, South Africa, Russia, and many others having similar challenges of prison overcrowding have used the resources of restorative justice to limit the worsening outcomes of retributive justice (Abrams, Umbreit, & Gordon, 2006). The literature is replete with instances of the resources which the traditional justice system can put behind the efficiency of the formal justice system if a formal synergy is encouraged. First, the TJS offers experimental and collective learning opportunities to the members of the community. The community members are both witnesses at the crime and solution scenes. They function as correctional service providers and monitor the progression of disputants' compliance with the terms of dispute resolution. The inclusion of all that took part in the traditional justice system often demonstrates the benefits they had derived from their participation. This fosters a sense of belonging and collective responsibility in the community. The crime resolution assignment is usually carried out on neutral community grounds which promotes accountability, fairness, and transparency of outcome. In this way, the restoration and empowerment of social norms, values, and belief systems occur in ways that make social ills unacceptable in the community. For the fact that the traditional justice processes do not impose any form of fee on the users, using the cultural resources is a matter of course and in the process, the people evolve a common sense of identity that enhances the pursuit of collective positive social and development agendas. Thus, since informal justice systems can be a reflection of the 'failure on the part of governments to take adequate comprehensive action' in responding to people's needs (Stewart, 2010), its conscious incorporation into the formal justice framework can usefully stimulate complementary efficiency.

CONCLUSION

This chapter has examined the two justice systems in southwestern Nigeria to determine a more suitable alternative to the other. It interrogates which of the two prominent justice systems is more restorative to the primary stakeholders in southwestern Nigeria. Finally, it demonstrated how both justice systems can work together to promote social justice among the Yoruba people of south west Nigeria. Globalization has welded the whole world into one small community in which cultural isolation is no longer potentially conceivable. Regardless of the fine points of the traditional justice system, western philosophy regarded pre-colonial Africa as pre-law, and therefore, contended that developing states required proper Western legal systems to cross the threshold of modernity. Here, caution is of the essence. To attain a global epistemic status in science, the theorists of Yoruba jurisprudence have to acknowledge the danger of an uncritical adoption and adaptation of foreign application of knowledge (Ake, 1986). Having done that, they would need to construct endogamous theorists of science and knowledge for development. It is sad, even against the clarion call for global tolerance of racial differences, that some foreign observers of African ways of life paid no due regard to the unusual strengths of the African tradition but focused suspiciously on its pockets of harmful inadequacies. Since "the traditional justice systems have historically functioned as an alternative or as a complement to the formal State court system" (United Nations, 2016, p. 1) the injustice of Africans being seen as incapable to construct credible histories about themselves gains a tragic ascendancy. Objectively, the formal justice system is an alternative method of resolving disputes in Yorubaland and not the other way round.

Functionally, restorative justice provides a very different framework for understanding and responding to crime. By performance, the TJS works more closely with the restorative paradigm than the formal justice system. Until the victims, offenders' families, and community opinion leaders are duly integrated into the conflict resolution framework, the Yoruba community will continue to grapple with endemic insecurity. Therefore, there may be no signals to signpost the need for the restructure of indigenous elder-driven socialization to use customary laws, traditions, and practices to navigate interactions with other community members. This could rewardingly occur through education, socialization, resocialization of offenders, and resettlement of the victims and society after victimization has unsettled them. Using the two systems as alternatives or in collaboration promises to make one approach overcome the shortcoming of the other (Assaye, Anteneh, Dinberu, & Ali, 2021). A broad inclusion in dispute resolution should be the core focus of the new non-racist justice order. Policymakers in public justice should forge a justice context where the emphasis consciously shifts from the western pejorative obsession with traditional justice and the non-western citizens' concentration on the retribution content of the formal justice system. In this new normal, there will be no recrimination.

The pursuit of social justice to bridge the gap between unfairness and social order in Yorubaland in particular and Nigeria, in general, will become meaningfully actualized in the context of the lived experiences of the Yoruba people. The Yoruba people will then properly provide the obvious and prudent sequence of justice alternatives to present a new realm of organized global justice platforms. This effort will produce mutually complementary justice interactions and strengthen the undergirding anchor of social order in southwestern Nigeria and beyond. In the light of data, this chapter suggests that rather than demonizing the deities, elders, and age-grade associations, these indigenous mechanisms of crime control should be strengthened to stem the sporadic outbreak of terrorism among the Yoruba people. The public policy should create a space for the interchange of ideas on relationship-building that will revitalize the traditional justice system. Knowledge of traditional norms and values should be intensified to redefine relationships and fine-tune lopsided power imbalances between formal and traditional justice systems. The Nigerian Correctional Service (NCS) Act (2019) should functionally institutionalize the restorative justice paradigm in the Nigerian criminal justice system.

REFERENCES

AbajuoR. M. (2016). An Appraisal of the Administration of Criminal Justice Act, 2015. https://ssrn.com/abstract=2665611

Abdul Karim, Y. (2012). Socio – Economic Effects of Judicial Corruption in Nigeria. *International Journal of Humanities and Social Science Invention*, *1*(1), 31–36.

Abioye, F. (2011). *The Rule of Law in English-speaking African Countries: The Case of Nigeria and South Africa* [PhD diss.]. University of Pretoria.

Abrams, L. S., Umbreit, M., & Gordon, A. (2006). Young Offenders Speak About Meeting Their Victims: Implications for Future Programs. *Contemporary Justice Review*, 2(3), 243–256. doi:10.1080/10282580600827835

Adebayo, A. G. (2014). Indigenous Conflict Management Strategies in West Africa: Beyond Right and Wrong. Lexington Books.

Adegboye, E. A. (Ed.). (1983). *Traditional Religion in West Africa*. Ibadan University Press.

Aderibigbe, A. B. (1962). The Ijebu Expedition, 1892: An Episode in the British Penetration of Nigeria Reconsidered. In *Historians in Tropical Africa*. Salisbury.

Adeuyan, J. O. (2011). *Contributions of Yoruba People in the Economic & Political Developments of Nigeria*. AuthorHouse.

Adewale, S. A. (1994). Crime and African Traditional Religion. Orita, 25(1-2), 54.

Adeyinka, A. & Lateef, B. (2014). Methods of conflict resolution in African traditional society. *African Research Review: An International Multidisciplinary Journal*, 8(2).

Afon, A. O., & Badiora, A. I. (2016). Accounting for variation in perception of police: A study of residents in a Nigerian city. *The Police Journal*, 89(3), 241–256. doi:10.1177/0032258X16658926

Agbakoba, J., & Nwauche, E. (2006). African conceptions of justice, responsibility and punishment. *Cambrian Law Review*, 37, 73.

Aihiokhai, S. A. (2012). *Ancestorhood in Yoruba Religion and Sainthood in Christianity: Envisioning an Ecological Awareness and Responsibility*. www.saintleo.edu/media/

Ajayi, A. T., & Buhari, L. O. (2014). Methods of conflict resolution in African traditional society. *African Research Review*, 8(2), 138–157. doi:10.4314/afrrev.v8i2.9

Ajetunmobi, R. O. (2012). Theories and Concepts in Migration and Settlement Studies: The Case of the Coastal Yoruba. *Social Sciences*, 7(2), 289–296. doi:10.3923science.2012.289.296

Ake, C. (1986). Editorial: Reason D'Etre. *African Journal of Political Economy*, 1.

Akinnawo, E. O., & Akpunne, B. C. (2016). The Influence of gender on the level of drug consumption and psychological health of inmates of Lagos Medium Security Prisons. *International Journal of Gender and Development Issues*, 1(4), 196–207.

Albert, I. O., Hérault, G., Awe, T., & Omitoogun, W. (2013). *Informal channels for conflict resolution in Ibadan, Nigeria*. Ibadan, Nigeria: Institut français de recherche en Afrique.

Allen, T., & Macdonald, A. (2013). Post-conflict traditional justice: A critical overview (JSRP Paper 3). London: LSE.

Ani, C. C. (2012). Crime and Punishment in African Indigenous Law. In Legal Pluralism in Africa: A Compendium of African Customary Laws. NIALS.

Anon. (1991). *A Dictionary of the Yoruba Language*. University Press.

Assaye, A. G., Anteneh, K. S., Dinberu, A. D., & Ali, M. S. (2021). The Nexus between Shimglina as ADR and the Formal Criminal Justice System: The Case of the Amhara Regional State, Ethiopia. *AJCR, 1*. Retrieved on January 3, 2022, from https://www.accord.org.za/ajcr-issues/the-nexus-between-shimglina-as-adr-and-the-formal-criminal-justice-system-the-case-of-the-amhara-regional-state-ethiopia

Atanda, J. A. (1967). *The New Oyo "Empire": A Study of British Indirect Rule in Oyo Province, 1894-1934* [Unpublished Ph.D. Thesis]. University of Ibadan.

Ayandele, E. A. (1992). *The Ijebu of Yorubaland 1850 – 1950: Politics, Economy And Society*. Heinmann Educational Books.

Ayandele, E. A. (1967). The Mode of British Expansion in Yorubaland in the Second Half of the Nineteenth Century: The Oyo Episode. *Odu, 3*, 2.

Ayodele, J. O. (2017). Restorative Justice and Women's Experiences of Violence in Nigeria. Handbook of Research on Global Perspectives on Therapeutic Jurisprudence and Overcoming Violence against Women, 44-62.

Badamasiuy, J., & Bello, M. (2013). An appraisal of administrative justice and good governance in Nigeria. *Journal of Politics and Law*, 6(2), 216–230. doi:10.5539/jpl.v6n2p216

Bellessa, S. B. (2012). *Study guide criminal justice essentials*. John Wiley & Sons, Inc.

Berkowitz, K. (2016). *San Francisco Unified School District Restorative Practices Whole School Implementation Guide*. San Francisco Unified School District. https://cupdf.com/document/restorative-practices-whole-school-implementation-guide.htm

Biobaku, S. O. (1957). *The Egba and Their Neighbours*. Oxford University Press.

Bowd, R. (2009). Status Quo or Traditional Resurgence: What is Best for African Criminal Justice Systems. In The Theory and Practice of Criminal Justice in Africa (p. 9). Academic Press.

Bunikowski, D., & Dillon, P. (2017). Arguments from Cultural Ecology and Legal Pluralism for Recognising Indigenous Customary Law in the Arctic. In Experiencing and Protecting Sacred Natural Sites of Sámi and other Indigenous Peoples. The Sacred Arctic. doi:10.1007/978-3-319-48069-5_4

Cassell, P. G. (1994). Balancing the Scales of Justice: The Case For and the Effects of Utah's Victim's Rights Amendment. *Utah L. Rev.*, *1373*, 1402–1404.

Coleman, J. (1963). Nigeria – Background to Nationalism. Academic Press.

Cooper-Knock, S. J., & Owen, O. (2015). Between vigilantism and bureaucracy: Improving our understanding of police work in Nigeria and South Africa. *Theoretical Criminology*, *19*(3), 355–375. doi:10.1177/1362480614557306

Crowder, M. (1978). The Story of Nigeria. Academic Press.

Danish Institute for Human Rights (2012). *Informal Justice Systems: Charting a Course for Human Rights Based Engagement.* United Nations Development Program, United Nations Children's Fund, United Nations Women.

Dierk, L. (2011). Yoruba Origins and the Lost Tribes of Israel. *Anthropos*, *106*(2), 579–595. doi:10.5771/0257-9774-2011-2-579

Doolin, K. (2007). But what does it mean? Seeking definitional clarity in Restorative justice. *Journal of Criminal Law*, *71*(5), 427–440. doi:10.1350/jcla.2007.71.5.427

Durkheim, E. (2001). Introduction (C. Cosman, Trans.). In The Elementary forms of Religious Life. Oxford University Press.

Edo, V. (2010). The Practice of Democracy in Nigeria: The Pre-Colonial Antecedent. *LUMINA*, *21*(2), 1–7.

Ekhator, E. (2019). *Traditional oath-taking as an anti-corruption strategy in Nigeria.* In A. Agada (Ed.), *Combating the Challenges of Corruption in Nigeria: A Multidisciplinary Conversation* (pp. 323–324). Black Towers Publishers.

Elliot, E. M. (2011). *Security with Care (Restorative justice and Healthy societies).* Fernwood Publishing.

Fadipe, N. A. (1970). *The Sociology of the Yoruba.* Ibadan University Press.

FBI Factbook. (2012). *The world Factbook, Africa, Nigeria.* Retrieved from https://www.cia.gov/library/publications/the-world-factbook/geos/ni.html

Gabagambi, J. J. (2020). *UPDATE: A Comparative Analysis of Restorative Justice Practices in Africa*. Retrieve on January 13, 2022, from https://www.nyulawglobal. org/globalex/Restor ative_Justice_Africa1.html

Gross, S. R., O'Brien, B., Hu, C., & Kennedy, E. H. (2014). Rate of false conviction of criminal defendants who are sentenced to death. *Proceedings of the National Academy of Sciences, 111*(20), 7230–7235. doi:10.1073/pnas

Hunter, E. (2011, November). Access to justice: To dream the impossible dream? *The Comparative and International Law Journal of Southern Africa, 44*(3), 408–427.

Ibhawoh, B. (2013). Imperial Justice: Africans in Empire's Court. Oxford University Press.

Idowu, E. B. (1963). Olodumare: God In Yoruba Belief, New York. *Fredrick Praeger, 1963*, 56.

Ifemeje, S. C. & Ozuru, G. (2021). Restorative Justice as a Useful Tool for Victims' Justice in Nigeria: An Appraisal. *AFJCLJ, 6*.

Igbafen, M. (2014). The Concept of Person in African and Chinese Philosophies: A Comparative Inquiry. *International Journal of Philosophy and Theology, 2*(3).

Ikponmwosa, F., & Evbayiro, A. (2017). The Native Courts System in Benin Division 1900-1945. *University of Benin Journal of Humanities, 5*(1), 154.

Imam, I. (2016). Exploring shariah measures for curbing judicial corruption in northern Nigeria. *Jurnal Syariah, 24*(3), 465–494. doi:10.22452/js.vol24no3.6

International Center for Prison Studies. (n.d.). Available at: https://www.prisonstudies. org/country/nigeria

Isaac, Y. O. (2018). Role of Traditional Institution in Nigeria Democratic Space: Contending Perspectives, Issues, and Potentials. *Journal of Public Value and Administrative Insight, 2*(3).

Jemiriye, T. F., & Awosusi, A. (2007). Irunmole (Spiritual Entities) of Yoruba Traditional Religion. *Pakistan Journal of Social Sciences, 4*(4), 548–552.

John, A., & Musa, A. (2014). Delay in the administration of criminal Justice in Nigeria: Issues from a Nigerian viewpoint. *J Law Pol Glob, 26*, 130–138.

Johnson, S. (1921). *History of the Yorubas: From the Earlies Times to the Beginning of the British Protectorate by Samuel Johnson (1846 - 1901)*. Routledge.

Joireman, S. F. (2001). *Inherited Legal Systems and Effective Rule of Law: Africa and the Colonial Legacy*. Political Science Faculty Publications. 113. http://scholarship. richmond. edu/polisci-faculty-publications/113

Kalu, K., & Falola, T. (Eds.). (2019). Introduction: Exploitation and Misrule in Colonial and Postcolonial Africa, African Histories and Modernities. doi:10.1007/978-3-319-96496-6_1

Kamara, H. (2019). *Breaking the school to prison-deportation pipeline through restorative justice*. Retrieved from https://www.thepraxisproject.org/blog/2019/8/21/breaking-the-school-to-prison-deportation-pipeline-through-restorative-justice

Kaplan, F. (1997). Runaway Wives: Native Law and Custom in Benin, and Early Colonial Courts, Nigeria. *Annals of the New York Academy of Sciences*, *810*(1), 245–313. doi:10.1111/j.1749-6632.1997.tb48132.x

Kariuki, L., Lambert, C., Purwestri, R. & Biesalsk, H. K. (2016). *Trends and consequences of consumption of food and non-food items (pica) by pregnant women in Western Kenya*. Elsevier GmbH on behalf of Society of Nutrition and Food Science e.V. doi:10.1016/j.nfs.2016.09.001

Kariuki, F. (2014). Applicability of Traditional Dispute Resolution Mechanisms in Criminal Cases in Kenya: Case Study of Republic v Mohamed Abdow Mohamed [2013] eKLR. *Alternative Dispute Resolution, 2*(1), 202-228.

Ladan, M. (2013). Towards Complementarity in African Conflict Management Mechanisms. In *UPDATE: A Comparative Analysis of Restorative Justice Practices in Africa*. Retrieve on January 13, 2022, from https://www.nyulawglobal.org/globalex/Restorative_Justice_Africa1.html

Laleye, S. A. (2014, December). Punishment and Forgiveness in the Administration of Justice in Traditional African Thought: The Yoruba Example. *International Journal of Philosophy and Theology*, 2(4), 165–176. doi:10.15640/ijpt.v2n4a10

Lewis, P., Robinson, P., & Barnett, R. (1998). Stabilizing Nigeria: Sanctions, Incentives, and Support for Civil Society. In *Preventive Action Reports*. The Century Foundation Press.

Leyh, B. (2011). *Procedural Justice? Victim Participation in International Criminal Proceedings*. Utrechti: Intrsentia.

Lloyd, P. C. (1962). *Yoruba land Law*. Oxford University Press.

Llwelyn, J. J., & Howse, R. (2002). *Restorative Justice: A Conceptual Framework*. Law Commission.

Louw, D., & Wyk, D. (2016). The Perspectives of South African Legal Professionals on Restorative Justice: An Explorative Qualitative Study. *Social Work, 52*(4).

MacFarlane, J. (2006). *Restorative justice in Ethiopia: a pilot project.* University of Windsor.

Mangena, F. (2011). Restorative Justice's Deep Roots in Africa. *South African Journal of Philosophy.*

Michael, C. O. (2016). Communication of an interpreter and fair trial under Nigerian criminal justice system. *International Journal of Legal Discourse, 1*(1), 213–233. doi:10.1515/ijld-2016-0006

Morillo, S., & Pavkovic, M. (2017). *What is Military History?* Polity Press.

Mutua, M. (2016). Africa and the Rule of Law. *SUR, 13*(23), 159 – 173.

Nnam, M. U. (2016). Responding to the problem of prison overcrowding in Nigeria through restorative justice: A challenge to the traditional criminal justice system. *International Journal of Criminal Justice Sciences, 11*(2), 177.

Nweke, K. (2012). The Role of Traditional Institutions of Governance in Managing Social Conflicts in Nigeria's Oil -Rich Niger Delta Communities: Imperatives of Peace-Building Process in the Post-Amnesty Era EEE. *British Journal of Arts and Social Sciences, 5*(2), 202–219.

Nwolise, O. B. C. (2004). Traditional approaches to conflict resolution among the Igbo People of Nigeria: Reinforcing the need for Africa to rediscover its roots. *AMANI Journal of African Peace, 1*(1), 59–80.

Nwosu, K. (2011). *Nigerian Criminal Law and Procedure in Prospective.* National Strategic Training/Workshop on Fast Track Trials, Case Diversion Measures; Non –Custodial Options; Plea Bargaining; Use of ADR for Crimes and Restorative Justice, Abuja, Nigeria.

Oamen, P., & Aigbokhan, P. (2018). Customary Law Arbitration in Nigeria: An Appraisal of Contending Legal Issues. *Benin Bar Journal, 1*(1), 214–247.

Ocran, M. (2006). The Clash of Legal Cultures: The Treatment of Indigenous Law in Colonial and Post-Colonial Africa. *Akron Law Review, 39*(2), 465–481.

Odoh, B. (2015). *Creative Approaches to Crime: The Case for Alternative Dispute Resolution (ADR) in the Magistracy in Nigeria Journal of Law* (Vol. 36). Policy and Globalization.

Office of the Comptroller of Kirikiri Medium Security Prison. (2015). *Data on prison population as sourced by Ani Comfort Chinyere restorative justice: victim offender mediation during a visit on 23/9/2015*. Office of the Comptroller of Kirikiri Medium Security Prison.

Ojo, M. O. D. (2014). Incorporation of Ayelala traditional religion into Nigerian criminal justice system: An opinion survey of Igbesa community people in Ogun State, Nigeria. *Issues in Ethnology and Anthropology, 9*(4).

Okunoye, A. (2022). *Owo Attack: Ondo women perform ritual to help arrest assailants*. Retrieved on June 11, 2022, https://www.premiumtimesng.com/regional/ssouth-west/535490-owo-attack-ondo-women-perform-ritual-to-help-arrest-assailants.html

Olaoba, O. B. (2002). *Yoruba Legal Culture Ibadan*. FOP Press.

Olusola, A. G. (2005). *Animals in the Traditional Worldview of the Yorùbá*. .Retrieved on May 30, 2022, from https://www.folklore.ee/folklore/vol30/olusala. pdf doi:10.7592/FEJF2005.30.olusala

Oluwole, S. B. (2014). *Socrates and Orunmila: Two Patrons Saints of Classical Philosophy*. Arik Publishers.

Omale, J. (2006). Justice in History: An Examination of African Restorative Traditions and the Emerging Restorative Justice Paradigm. *African Journal of Criminology and Justice Studies, 2*(2).

Omotoye, R. W. (2011). The study of African Traditional Religion and Its Challenges in Contemporary Times. *Ilorin Journal of Religious Studies, 1*(2), 21–40.

Osemwonwa, U. I. (2000). *The Customary Laws of The Binis*. Myke Commercial Press.

Osifo, V. (2017). *7 Roles of Traditional Rulers in Achieving Stable Democracy in Nigeria*. Information Guide in Nigeria. Retrieved on December 26, 2021, from https:// infoguidenigeria.com/roles-of-traditional-rulers-in-achieving-stable-democracy-in-nigeria

Phillips, K. (1969). *The Emerging Republican Majority*. Arlington House.

Pimentel, D. (2010, Summer). Can Indigenous Justice Survive? Legal Pluralism and the Rule of Law. *Harvard International Review, 32*(2), 32–36.

Rawls, J. (1999). *A Theory of Justice* (Revised ed.). Oxford University Press. doi:10.4159/9780674042582

Salawu, A. (2016). Media Narrative Construction of human rights abuses in Nigeria. *Loyola Journal of Social Sciences*, *30*(1), 107–124.

Salihu, H. A., & Gholami, H. (2018). Mob justice, corrupt and unproductive justice system in Nigeria: An empirical analysis. *International Journal of Law, Crime and Justice*, *55*, 40–51. doi:10.1016/j.ijlcj.2018.09.003

Sangroula, Y., & Sangroula, Y. (2016). Use of informal justice mechanisms in criminal justice system: Critical observation of principles, theories and prospects. *Journal of Civil and Legal Sciences*, *5*(3), 1–13. doi:10.4172/2169-0170.1000193

Shajobi-Ibikunle, G. D. (2014). Challenges of imprisonment in the Nigerian penal system: The way forward. *American Journal of Humanities and Social Sciences*, *2*(2), 94–104. doi:10.11634/232907811402535

Shapland, J., Robinson, G., & Sorsby, A. (2011). *Restorative Justice in Practice: Evaluating what works for victims and offenders*. Routledge. doi:10.4324/9780203806104

Sherman, L., Strange, H., Mayo-Wilson, E., Woods, D., & Ariel, B. (2015). Are Restorative Justice Conferences Effective in Reducing Repeat Offending? *Journal of Quantitative Criminology*, *31*(1), 1–24. doi:10.100710940-014-9222-9

Skelton, A. (2013). The South African Constitutional Court's restorative justice jurisprudence. *Restorative Justice*, *1*(1), 123–127. doi:10.5235/20504721.1.1.122

Stewart, J. (2010). Arenas of anguish – tracking multiple perpetuation trauma in HIV/ AIDS and gender- based violence intersections. In Gender Based Violence in Africa: Perspectives from the Continent. Pretoria: University of Pretoria.

Strang, H., Sherman, L. W., Mayo-Wilson, E., Woods, D., & Ariel, B. (2013). *Restorative Justice Conferencing (RJC) Using Face-to-Face Meetings of Offenders and Victims: Effects on Offender Recidivism and Victim Satisfaction. A systematic review*. The Campbell Collaboration.

Tamuno, T. N. (1962). *The Development of British Administrative Control of Southern Nigeria, 1900-1912* [Unpublished Ph.D. Thesis]. London University.

The Advancement Project. (2014). *Restorative practices: Fostering healthy relationships and promoting positive discipline in schools: A guide for educators*. Cambridge, MA: Schott Foundation. http://schottfoundation.org/sites/default/files/restorative-practices-guide. pdf

The Network of University Legal Aid Institutions. (2018). *More than half of Nigeria's awaiting-trial-prisoners under age 30 — Group*. Retrieved on June 11, 2022, from https://www.premiumtimesng.com/news/more-news/284830-more-than-half-of-nigerias-awaiting-trial-prisoners-under-age-30-group.html

Tobi, N. (1996). Sources of Nigerian Law. Lagos: M.J. Professional Publishers Ltd.

Umbreit, M. S., & Armour, M. P. (2010). *Restorative justice dialogue: An essential guide for research and practice*. Springer. doi:10.1891/9780826122599

Umbreit, M. S., Coates, R. B., & Vos, B. (2008). Victim-Offender Mediation: An evolving evidence-based practice. In D. Sullivan & L. Taft (Eds.), *Handbook of Restorative Justice* (pp. 52–62). Routledge.

United Nations. (2016). *Human Rights and Traditional Justice Systems in Africa. United Nations Human Rights*. Office of the High Commissioner.

Van Ness, D., & Strong, K. H. (2015). *Restoring justice. An introduction to restorative justice*. Routledge.

Werner, K. (2010). Rediscovering indigenous peacebuilding techniques: the way to lasting peace? *Africa Peace and Conflict Journal, 3*(2), 60.

WHO, LSHTM, & SAMRC. (2013). Global and regional estimates of violence against women: Prevalence and health impacts of intimate partner violence and non-partner sexual violence. WHO.

Wojkowska, E. (2006). Doing Justice: How Informal Justice Systems Can Contribute. United Nations Development Programme, Oslo Governance Centre.

Wojkwoska, E., & Cunningham, J. (2010). *Justice reform frontier*. International Development Law Organisation.

UN Women, UNICEF, & UNDP. (2013). *Informal Justice Systems: Charting a Course for Human Rights based Engagement*. Author.

Wourji, T. W. (2012). Coexistence between the Formal and Informal Justice Systems in Ethiopia: Challenges and Prospects. *African Journal of Legal Studies*, *5*(3), 269–293. doi:10.1163/17087384-12342012

Chapter 3

The Traditional Restorative Justice Practices That Have Influenced Southern Africa

Angelo Kevin Brown
Arkansas State University, USA

ABSTRACT

The indigenous peoples of Southern Africa have a tradition of using restorative justice practices. The region has used restorative justice practices primarily until European colonization had enforced a Western criminal justice and legal system. During and after colonization, Southern Africa has continued to use traditional methods for public safety and resolving conflicts in communities. This led to governments having a dual system in which nonserious violations are usually handled in the traditional courts, and the more serious crimes are handled in the formal criminal courts.

INTRODUCTION

Throughout the known history of Southern African justice systems, there have been restorative justice practices and traditions used by the indigenous people of the land (Anderson, 2003). The traditional method of justice in this region has shared many similarities with modern restorative justice practices including the goal of restoring peace, reconciliation, and promotion of community norms, with the perspective that crime harms the victim and the community. They also share the emphasis on informality, community participation, and restitution (Mangena, 2015; Murhula

DOI: 10.4018/978-1-6684-4112-1.ch003

& Tolla, 2021). In Southern Africa, nations like Botswana, Eswatini (Swaziland), Lesotho, South Africa, and Namibia have used traditional and restorative justice practices that they have combined with Western legal systems under their governmental systems (Gavrielides & Artinopoulou, 2016).

The traditional justice practices have focused on restorative practices in contrast to the Western justice practices of punishment, imprisonment, and vengeance. The traditional justice practices in the region rely heavily on restorative justice to promote the healing of the victims, perpetrators, and the community. These nations in Southern Africa share many similarities in their legal systems, as they have been greatly influenced by Roman-Dutch law through colonization (Wessels, 2013). These nations also share similar history and culture as they are all made up of primarily Bantu people and are the five nations that make up the Southern African Customs Union (SACU).

The traditional justice practices throughout pre-colonial Southern Africa had been used for minor crimes and violent and serious crimes including rape and murder. The Bantu of Southern Africa have terms that define restorative justice in their tradition. These terms include *Ubuntu*. The Ubuntu philosophy is based on the concept of a community to achieve just there must be a restoration of the accused perpetrator so they will no longer cause harm to others (Elechi et al., 2010). This perspective of justice was founded on the understanding that when wrongdoing is done, it is in the community's best interest to help reintegrate the wrongdoer back after being rehabilitated. When a crime happens, the entire community is harmed, and the community is responsible for its members, so they must work together and not marginalize the perpetrator (Rautenbach, 2015).

The focus of the chapter will be on restorative justice practices regarding traditional justice. Restorative justice in Southern Africa attempts to engage everyone that was affected by the crime in an attempt to create a process where each person can heal from the harm that was caused and move on from the incident (Skelton & Batley, 2021). The process allows the victim and perpetrator to better understand the situation and attempt to create improved relationships. The chapter will review the indigenous justice practices, the history of traditional justice practices in Southern Africa, and how colonization has impacted the traditional justice systems.

SOUTH AFRICA

South Africa is the largest nation in Southern Africa, with over 60 million people. The majority of South Africa is made up of indigenous Black South Africans, with minority groups of White South Africans (8%), Multiracial 9% (Coloured South Africans), and Asian mostly Indian South Africans but more recently Chinese

South Africans. The nation is predominantly Christian (78%), and around 4.5% have traditional religious faiths.

South Africa's Truth and Reconciliation Commission (TRC) institutionalized traditional restorative justice practices under the presidency of Nelson Mandela to help create a peaceful transition from the instability that was present after apartheid (Llewellyn & Howse, 1999). TRC brought traditional practices that were used by the indigenous people of the region and instilled them into the legal system. TRC combined indigenous and Christian values.

Restorative justice in the South African approach is a justice approach whose purpose is to address the harms that were caused by another person or a group of people. Restorative justice is meant to promote "Healing rather than hurting, moral learning" (Braithwaite, 1999). This approach has differences from the adversarial criminal justice system that was implemented by the colonial settlers of South Africa. The adversarial system of justice often focuses on retribution, while TRC brought transitional justice that was more concerned with healing the broken relationships that were created. TRC in South Africa used Christian theology and language to promote forgiveness and reconciliation.

Apartheid had created decades of racial oppression that created resentment, anger, and hate that remained after apartheid. This process was established to provide peace in the post-apartheid era and to promote humanness or in the Zulu language *Ubuntu*, to help create a peaceful and stable nation (Llewellyn & Howse, 1999). The process even provided amnesty to the perpetrators of apartheid if they confessed to their crimes (Gade, 2013).

Precolonial

Throughout pre-colonial South African history, there has been both restorative and retributive justice. Traditional leadership has always been a foundation of justice throughout the region. The elders and traditional leaders historically acted as the governors of the community and controlled various aspects of everyday life, especially judicial matters. These leaders often did not rely on democratic forms of government, as they had been granted the power to decide for the community on justice-related issues.

Throughout the region, there were various types of traditional justice practices as several indigenous groups such as the Bantu agricultural community had migrated to South Africa a couple of hundreds of years before the European settlers. Other indigenous groups in South Africa were hunter and gathering groups such as the San, which had different forms of justice as they lived differently from the agricultural Bantu groups. Other ethnic groups like the Khoikhoi were herding groups that migrated down to South Africa and implemented herding in the region, which brought distributive justice practices and customs.

The ancient wisdom of traditional justice practices in South Africa reemerged in the late 20th and early 21st centuries as traditional practices like restorative justice were becoming accepted by the government (Gade, 2013). The modern criminal justice system that relies on courts and prisons was brought to the region through colonization by the British and Dutch. The restorative justice practices were often regarded as soft on crime and impractical by government officials. Despite the narratives that surrounded restorative practices in South Africa, the value and utility of the practices have been becoming more respected and accepted.

Colonial and Apartheid

The indigenous South African communities often distrusted the settler's justice that was enforced on them. As Europeans began to settle in the region, the traditional leadership and restorative justice practices were not valued by them. The indigenous people remained using such practices for their communities, but the White settlers were not interested in accepting this type of justice. There was often an attempt to avoid bringing law enforcement into the villages as the people did not want to deal with the often-corrupt criminal justice officials to handle their disputes and issues. This allowed for the traditional justice systems of South Africa to be carried over through the colonial period to modern-day.

The Dutch were the first Europeans to colonize the land and first arrived in the Western Cape in the 17th century. The Dutch and the indigenous groups had fought over the land and the Dutch had forced out the Khoi and other groups and forced them to work on their farms. The Khoi members who avoided working on the Dutch farms often transited to becoming hunter-gatherers like the San people, which created competition between the tribes.

In the 18th century, the Dutch settlers implemented policies to force the indigenous people to have papers to be able to move around the region. During these times, the tribal conflict created clans to separate from their original tribal groups and become rivals, as the Nguni tribe did, which led to violent disputes over resources and land. The Dutch often used these tribal disputes to their advantage.

The British gained control of much of Southern Africa starting in the 19th century. The British and Dutch settlers worked together to exploit the Black populations. These settlers had worked together to attack the tribes and steal their resources, especially their cattle, as it was an important source of food for the settlers and a source of survival for the indigenous populations (Worden, 1994).

With the British influence, the region moved away from slavery-based labor systems and started to invest in wool production. The new economic developments created poverty for many of the immigrants of South Africa and they started to leave the colonized areas of South Africa for the untapped land of the interior. This migration led to violent battles between the indigenous tribes and settlers. The settlers discovered the diamonds in the South African interior in the mid-19th century, which led to the British Empire expanding its rule to control the areas where diamonds were found.

With the British needing to exploit the minerals for economic incentives, they had to expand their territory. This led to the creation of railways on indigenous land, which displaced more tribes and continued to create hardships for the indigenous people. The British government created new taxes on the tribes and used the indigenous people for labor in the diamond and mineral mines for extremely low pay. The settlers also created a justice system that reinforced an unequal society, that harshly punished those who were unwilling to follow the new laws of the land.

The expansion and focus on diamond mines created many hardships for the African farmers. In the late 19th century, there was an infestation of rinderpest insects that destroyed farms in the region and ruined many farmers' ability to survive. With the farms becoming less reliable, the British exploitation, and violent disputes between the indigenous tribes and settlers created an environment in which most of the indigenous tribes could not survive independently.

The difficult economic situation led to a major war between the British and Boer. After various conflicts, the Union of South Africa (South Africa) was established on May 31st, 1910, which unified the Cape, Natal, Transvaal, and the Orange River colonies. The Boers of about 65,000 had battled against about 500,000 soldiers of the British Empire and the indigenous South Africans had been divided and fought for both the Boers and British. The British had implemented concentration camps that killed thousands of African and Boer people, especially innocent women, and children.

Throughout the 20th century, the White settlers in South Africa had perceived the other racial groups, especially the Black South Africans, as inferior. This treatment led the White lawmakers to create laws that limited other racial groups to succeed in education, society, career, and other aspects of life. The government would punish those who did not conform to the racialized order of society as they saw these people as a threat. This led to political groups that were trying to create equality among racial groups illegal and these groups went underground and often became radicalized and violent in response to this treatment.

The practice of White supremacy was implemented into the constitution of the Republic of the Union of South Africa. The South African government gave power to people through property ownership, which was held by the White population.

The Black population was also excluded from being members of the parliament and the official measures of segregation of Black and Whites were soon initiated. The 1913 Land Act provided most of the region (90%) to be reserved only for Whites who were the minority of the population (around 21%).

In 1927, the Black Administration Act 38 established the civil and criminal courts of South Africa. The law was based on common law to establish a European-style legal system in South Africa in an attempt to move away from African customary law that was based on indigenous laws and customs. South Africa had used these two parallel legal systems, but the common law often superseded the customary law when the rules were contrary to the common law.

The African National Congress (ANC) had been forming groups of resistance to the land grab of the Whites and the racist policies that were created. The ANC became enemies of the state and there was violent oppression against the ANC and its members. The laws continued to enforce White supremacy over the land as the Black population had no political power, and this led to the official creation of the apartheid state. The apartheid state created countless racial injustices and human rights violations that divided racial groups that still affect society to this day.

The TRC Final Report listed the racial laws as injustices that needed to be reconciled. Some of the laws and policies including the Immorality Act of 1927, made any extra-marital affairs between a Black person and a White person illegal, which later included, Coloured people and Asian people. Next was the Prohibition of Mixed Marriage of 1949, which criminalized any White person who marries a person from another racial group. These laws created various hardships for the children who were created by mixed-race parents because their existence was a sign of a crime, and the child often faced many barriers in life.

Other laws that created social injustices included the Internal Security Act of 1950, also known as the Suppression of Communism Act of 1950, which made certain political organizations illegal, especially those that had any perceived connection to communism. The Group Areas Act of 1950 enacted a requirement that geographical areas be designated for certain racial groups. This made each racial group become segregated from one another throughout South Africa. The Population Registration Act of 1950 created laws that each person be registered at birth under a certain racial group either Black, Coloured, White, or Other.

The Blacks Act of 1952 (Pass Law) was implemented next. This law made each Black person be required to always carry identification. The documentation needed by Black people included their place of origin, employment records, tax payment history, criminal records, police contacts, and a photograph. Later in 1954, the Blacks Resettlement Act was implemented and removed Black people from the townships.

In 1960, the Unlawful Organizations Act of 1960 was enacted into law. This law made any organization that the government saw as a threat to public order or public safety prohibited. This made the ANC and other political groups unlawful. These were just some of the laws that facilitated the human rights violations against non-White South Africans.

As about a third of South Africa still live in rural areas, the need for informal justice practices is essential, especially where tribal ties are still strong. This is because many of the community members in these areas do not have the legal knowledge, or resources to pay for legal representation and fees that are required from the formal legal system. There is also a lack of trust in the formal legal system by many in these rural communities. The largest tribe in South Africa is Zulu and followed by Xhosa and Sotho. The cultural influence of these tribal groups helped ensure traditional restorative practices continue in South African communities, even with the Western legal system in place.

The traditional justice system in South Africa has the goal of settling disputes and restoring the social harmony of the community. The written legislation of customary law goes back to 1878 with the implementation of the Natal Code of Zulu Law, which eliminated the uncertainties of customary law. Since colonization, the South African justice system had become a hybrid system where the Western system was mixed with the traditional practices. Traditionally, most of South Africa was community-based and collective groups it was important to reconcile the disputing parties for the good of the community. The outcomes of the settlement often are based on a resolution to bring back the status quo before the harm was done.

When it came to homicide and other serious crimes, the solution would differ for different tribes and communities. The Xhosa practice of restorative justice often used the community leader (king or chief) to decide on how perpetrators of homicide should be dealt with, as he would be the main victim, as the actual victim is no longer alive. This is similar to how the United States of America handles crimes, as it is a crime against the state when people are taken to trial. The king or chief is given the information of the incident, and the decision is made with intake from the community, but the chief or king makes the ultimate decision and becomes the final court decision or *Inkundla*. The typical decision in a homicide case is that the perpetrator must pay for the harm done by giving cattle to the family and the chief or king.

The use of imprisonment had not been a common punishment in traditional South African practices, there were no jails or prisons to place the offenders in and there is a lack of purpose in this type of punishment for traditional justice goals. In certain circumstances, they did use banishment and even death in some cases, especially for witchcraft and murder. The Western-style justice is not a good fit with many of the traditional South African justice practices because the Western justice system is impersonal while the South African traditional system was very personal.

As modern justice practices rely on factual evidence, the traditional justice system did not rely on the same type of evidence. The lack of factual evidence in the modern system will often lead to the acquittal of a guilty person while the traditional system relies more on community knowledge of the victims and perpetrators. The focus of factual evidence in the modern system can leave victims losing trust and hope in the criminal justice system when they are not able to prove that the crime was committed, while without these requirements of proof there could be more room for those falsely accused to be treated as guilty perpetrators.

The lack of trust in the modern justice system has become an important part of many of the rural communities, which led to vigilante justice in extreme circumstances in South Africa. During Apartheid many of the townships and villages would use traditional means of justice instead of the formal justice system because of the mistrust of the official governmental rule of law. The African National Congress had even created alternative structures of governance in opposition to the apartheid government to impose their version of justice (Leebaw, 2003).

Post-Apartheid

As the National Party lost power in the latter part of the 20th century, Apartheid was coming to an end. The Black population especially continued to resist apartheid and the physical resistance became more and more common. The government would utilize the military to use force against any resistance but eventually, the government fell. This led to South Africa becoming a democratic nation.

As the new government was created, an interim constitution was implemented in 1993. The new government had created the Promotion of National Unity and Reconciliation Act (PNURA), which first established an official Truth and Reconciliation Commission (TRC). This came about right before the first democratically elected president was selected, Nelson Mandela. President Mandela was part of the previously banned ANC.

The end of apartheid brought about a new South African Constitution, which helped give customary law equal respect to common law. In the case of Alexkor Ltd v Richtersveld Community, it was acknowledged that "While in the past indigenous law was seen through the common-law lens, it must now be seen as an integral part of our law... Its validity must now be determined by reference not too common law, but to the Constitution." This created an equal but parallel legal system that is under one government. The Western-based legal system includes incarceration, retribution, revenge, as well as procedural justice, and the traditional court system is based on a different set of values and is meant to compensate the victims, rehabilitate the preparators, seek the truth, and create reconciliation.

There are a variety of judicial courts in South Africa, including the Constitutional Court, the Supreme Court of Appeal, the High Courts, the Magistrates Courts, as well of other courts that are established in s.166 of the South African Constitution and the informal courts that use the traditional methods. This is how legal pluralism is built as the customary courts provide an alternative to the common law courts. The traditional courts are more flexible than the formal courts and allow for the law to be applied to the context of the area.

The traditional court proceedings would often take place in an informal and open court, and without any legal representation allowed for either of the parties. The purpose of having these proceedings in this structure is to try and facilitate reconciliation between the two parties in conflict. In these communities, the conflicts often have impacted the community as a whole, so the community members are expected to participate in the process under the leadership of a traditional community leader. Also, female community members were generally excluded from these court hearings, but a male member of their family can be there for them (Rautenbach, 2018). International human rights advocates have been critical of the lack of gender inequality in these courts, as they have led to problematic procedures and results.

The South African government had imposed various legal frameworks and policies to establish a traditional practice in the government. One such framework was the Traditional Leadership and Governance Framework Act, 2003, which included a code of conduct for the traditional leaders. Under this framework, the traditional leader must follow and perform their duties in "good faith diligently honestly and in a transparent manner."

The TRC was a government-funded commission to help the human rights violation that was common throughout apartheid against the Black population. TRC was greatly influenced by restorative justice theory (Llewellyn, 2013). The TRC commissions used both formal as well as informal practices to ensure that the benefits of both were utilized. These commissions also used domestic techniques with international norms. A former chair of TRC Archbishop Desmond Tutu explained the purpose of restorative justice with the statement "restorative justice is being served when efforts are being made to work for healing, for forgiveness, and for reconciliation."

The purpose of the TRC was to not forget what happened but to understand what had happened to ensure that it does happen in the future. Those who created the framework for TRC had considered other atrocities that have happened in the world. The Holocaust that killed millions throughout Europe and the victims of the Nazis had helped create the International Military Tribunals that brought the perpetrators of human rights abuses to trial and justice was an important process that was considered in the formation of TRC. TRC used more of an indigenous approach than the International Military Tribunals as many of the victims in South Africa had a more indigenous culture and values. The Military Tribunals also differed as they were based on retributive justice, while the South African method was more of a restorative justice approach.

There were many critics of TRC who were critical that the government was not using criminal trials against the perpetrators in South Africa. Some of the criticisms included that TRC did not require the perpetrators to show any kind of remorse for their actions as long as they fully disclosed their wrongdoings. The critics of TRC claimed that this process would legitimate the apartheid law because the process limited it to the crimes that were defined under the previous apartheid-based laws. This created an environment in which apartheid a violation of human rights was not a focus of the process. The abuses that Black people and other discriminated groups under apartheid faced due to the apartheid state were not eligible to be considered, which made only the extreme acts that were even wrong under apartheid be considered.

Another important criticism of the TRC process was that it included the violence that was used against the apartheid state and equated it with the violence that was used against people by those in support of the apartheid state. This process failed to have any leaders of the apartheid state take any responsibility for the systematic discrimination and state-sponsored violence. The victims of the apartheid state would be put under unnecessary pressure in TRC because they would be asked if they had forgiven their abusers. The victims were not given any reparations in the beginning, even though the human rights abuses were immediately granted amnesty.

Eventually, after the approved recommendations for reparations were made so victims could be compensated. The process of reparations was facilitated by the Reparations Committee, which created recommendations for reparations to be paid by the perpetrators of the wrongs and the beneficiaries of the wrongful acts. The payments were also planned to be gathered by an "apartheid tax," donations, levies, wealth taxes, and surcharges on corporations. The South African government had rejected these recommendations for reparations to victims. The victims were defined as people who had "physical or mental injury, emotional suffering, pecuniary loss or a substantial impairment of human rights." The Act had defined the term "gross violations of human rights as:

violation of human rights through – (a) the killing, abduction, torture or severe ill-treatment of any person; or (b) any attempt, conspiracy, incitement, instigation, command or procurement to commit an act referred to in paragraph (a), which emanated from conflicts of the past and which was committed during the period I March 1960 to 10 May 1994 within or outside the Republic, and the commission of which was advised, planned, directed, commanded or ordered, by any person acting with a political motive

During apartheid as many people join political originations that often resorted to violence to make their demands known, which led to many people being hurt in these political acts. The victims of the political violence included the political activists who were hurt targeted and the innocent bystanders who were hurt by the collateral damage. The victims of the violence included innocent children and the elderly, as well as many government officials. The TRC tried to help restore the harm these victims faced and gave them an active part in the seeking of justice post-apartheid in order for the nation to face its past and create a better future.

TRC invited the victims to the hearings. The estimated victims were in the millions and many of them were dead, while others were not interested in the process. As the actual victims were so large, the TRC was not able to include the majority of the victims. This created a clear but restricted mandate, which was limited to the acts that were committed between March 1960 to May 10[th.] 1994. With the restrictions, there were still over 50,000 reports made of human rights violations. There were over 21,000 South Africans that volunteered to share their experiences under apartheid

Some of the perpetrators of human rights violations were asked to come forward and speak during the Amnesty hearings of TRC. The hearings were meant for the perpetrators to tell the whole truth of their wrongdoings, which the Amnesty Committee would assess and evaluate if they met the threshold to be given amnesty for their actions. There were about 20,000 amnesty applications from the perpetrators of the human rights violations.

The hearings were often very emotional as victims shared their stories of suffering. Many victims and perpetrators spoke different languages, which made it even more difficult for the victims to be fully understood by the perpetrators and the community. TRC had to use many translators to assist in the process as well as using counselors to help with the emotional event. The translators that were used had spoken one of the 11 different official languages of South Africa. The victims were supported in speaking the native language that they were most comfortable using during the TRC.

After the TRC hearings, South Africa continued to use restorative practices. The traditional restorative practices or tribal councils are now known as traditional councils. The traditional councils help cover the traditional communities throughout the region and deal with justice issues and civil issues like land development. The rural areas often prefer and rely on this method but as with other forms of governance, this can be corrupted. The risk for the traditional councils to be biased and give favor to certain people is a problem that can happen. To counteract this, the councils are made up of a diverse set of community members.

The South African Department of Justice has continued to support restorative justice approaches as it has been an effective way to prevent re-offending and bring more satisfaction to both victims and communities. A current example of how restorative justice is practiced is with the convicted South African Paralympic athlete Oscar Pistorius, who killed his girlfriend Reeva Steenkamp in 2013. Steenkamp's father had chosen to meet with his daughter's killer in June 2022 before his expected 2023 release from prison. The victim-offender dialogues are supervised by government officials throughout the process and in this case, is a step before Pistorius is eligible to be paroled.

BOTSWANA

The Republic of Botswana is a landlocked nation in Southern Africa. After British colonization, the nation gained independence in 1966. As the British had implemented a Western justice system in Botswana, the use of restorative justice and other customary practices had been neglected by the colonial government. The nation is one of the most sparsely populated in the world, with about 70% of the land covered by the Kalahari Desert, which creates many rural communities that have little interaction with government institutions. The rural communities of Botswana rely greatly on their local leaders to help resolve conflicts between their people. Like the other nations in the region, Botswana is predominantly Christian, and this plays a significant role in the way that its justice system is implemented. The legal systems of Botswana share many similarities with the customary and common law framework of South Africa (Rautenbach, 2016).

Customary law generally handles the standard of community violations and is used to resolve disputes among community members. Restorative practices throughout Africa are used within the Customary law framework (Elmangoush, 2015). The government of Botswana often relies on customary law to handle low-level law violations, conflicts, and civil disputes (Fombad, 2004). Like the other nations in Southern Africa, Botswana's traditional system relies on tribal leaders to help promote peace in a traditional restorative process. In Botswana, the Kgotla is a meeting place for traditional conflict resolution (Moumakwa, 2011). The Kgotla is used for both civil and minor criminal issues. The Kgotla uses the restorative justice process to help resolve conflicts and prevent future disputes between their citizens.

One common crime that is taken seriously in Botswana is theft. Throughout Southern Africa, theft between community members has historically been handled issues like this through restorative practices. Cattle are an exceptionally valuable stock in the nation and are often the target of thieves. The criminal penalties that are given through the customary courts can be prison time for those who are found guilty.

As restorative justice is implemented through the customary courts it has had various criticism about the inequality that can occur. The courts have a lack of oversight, which has led to discriminatory practices that greatly impact women and their ability to have equal rights within marriage, protection against domestic violence, inheritance, and child custody. Restorative justice has shown promise in the country's juvenile system but is still rarely used (Cole, 2010). The Juvenile Justice system in the country is provided independently from the Adult System through the Children's Act, which identifies juveniles as those of the age of 14-17, and children as under 14. The customary juvenile justice system continues to also be punished through corporal punishment for juvenile males instead of imprisonment (Mutsvara, 2020).

A serious criticism of the customary court system is the lack of safeguards and the lack of civil rights given to suspects in this process, which can lead to innocent people being put into unsafe prisons. The customary courts' lack of safeguards leads to convictions of people when they would have been likely acquitted in a trial court if they opted for the Magistrates court. The trial courts are much better equipped to investigate the facts of the case and give more rights to the defendants (Makhari, 2021). As people in Botswana often lack the resources to hire attorneys to go to trial, the customary court is often the only choice people feel they have. There are options to appeal cases in Botswana, but few people ever do because of the lack of knowledge about the law and lack of resources to pay for fees and representation, as most people are in poverty and uneducated in the law.

LESOTHO

The Kingdom of Lesotho is another small nation in Southern Africa of about 2 million people. The vast majority of the nation is made up of a Christian Bantu-speaking ethnic group, the Basotho people (99% of the population). The Basotho had split into different and conflicting groups because of colonization and regional conflicts. Lesotho is a landlocked nation that is encircled by South Africa. Lesotho gained independence in 1966 after almost a century of British colonization. The legal system is a dual system that uses customary law and a mixed general system of Roman-Dutch civil law and the English Common Law system.

Similar to South Africa, Lesotho has customary law based on indigenous values and history (Skelton & Batley, 2021) and Western-based law that was established through European colonization (Modo, 2002). Lesotho integrates traditional indigenous values of restorative justice along with Christian values of forgiveness into its justice system, especially when children are the perpetrators. Children are believed to be less legally culpable when they break the law, while adults are perceived as being legally culpable for their actions (Skelton & Batley, 2021). The traditional communities are often based on the belief that "It takes a village to raise a child."

The traditional justice system was greatly impacted in 1938 when the traditional courts were replaced through colonization by the Local and Central Courts.

The traditional practices of the nation go back to Moshoeshoe the Great who is known as the founder of the Basotho Kingdom (Modern-day Lesotho). The kingdom has been based on a communal effort that if one person offends the community it is the right and responsibility of the community as a whole to re-integrate that person. To reintegrate the person back into society the Basotho tradition expects that the perpetrator accepts responsibility for their wrongdoing, compensation to the victim to help with the reconciliation process between victim and offender, agreement of peaceful settlement, and a symbolic show of remorse known as *itiha* (Foley, 2014).

The implementation of restorative justice in the official justice system started with juvenile justice. Due to an ineffective juvenile justice system, the nation revised the system through the 1980 Children Protection Act, which helped reintegrate Basotho values into the justice system to help with juvenile delinquency. The Children Protection and Welfare Act of 2011 put into law the restorative justice practices to be used when children are involved in the justice system (Foley, 2014). The law allows for traditional justice values to be combined with international legal norms to protect the rights of children. The act is based on the standards defined in the 1989 United Nations Convention on the Rights of the Child as well as the 1999 African Charter on the Rights and Welfare of the Child (Foley, 2014).

The act has brought restorative justice practices from the village level to the official child justice system. The act created the Village Child Justice Committee (VCJC). The VCJC is composed of the village chief and six members that are chosen by the village. In Lesotho, restorative justice is also used for adult offenders but normally for only minor offenses such as theft, conflicts with neighbors, and domestic issues. A criticism of the traditional courts has been the lack of seriousness that they take domestic violence issues when females are the victims. The courts have generally been controlled by men and the cultural norms provide a gender imbalance where men are prioritized over women, leaving women less satisfied with the outcomes and their protection within the home.

ESWATINI

Eswatini is also known as Swaziland (Name changed in 2018) in Southern Africa. Eswatini is one of the smallest nations in Africa and has just over a million people. The majority of the nation is made up of ethnic Swazis that are primarily Christians. The Christian values that are present in the nation help reinforce the restorative practices used in the nation. Eswatini is an incredibly poor nation that struggles with various health issues, including tuberculosis, and about a fourth of the adult population has human immunodeficiency virus (HIV).

Eswatini uses a dual legal system that implements both the traditional law and customs as well as the Roman-Dutch influenced common law system similar to other nations in the region, including Lesotho, Namibia, and South Africa. The Western system includes the Court of Appeals and High court, and the magistrates' courts, while the traditional courts primarily deal with minor violations. The sentences that are given by traditional courts are reviewed by the Court of Appeals and High court and can be appealed by these courts as well (Makhari, 2021).

The communities are often governed by traditional chiefs who volunteer and have the power to arrest suspected perpetrators of minor violations. The trial is then led by a council within the chiefdom, while more serious crimes are handed to the Royal Eswatini Police Services. Most people that deal with the legal system in the nation do so through one of the 13 traditional courts. The judicial officers in these courts are appointed by the King. The court is determined by the director of public prosecution. The police often do not give the case to the director in the traditional courts as the evidence standard is not as high as compared to the civil judicial system. When a suspect is convicted in the traditional courts, they have the right to appeal the conviction to the High Court (Skelton & Batley, 2021).

The traditional courts are usually presided over by the local chiefs who act as court presidents. These courts deal with both civil and criminal matters but have various limitations. The traditional courts can only impose a fine of about 17$ (240 emalangeni), and a maximum sentence of 12 months in jail or prison. The traditional restorative practices are especially important and commonly used in the juvenile justice system in the nation. The government and many people in this nation believe that children should be treated separately from adults in the justice system. Restorative justice is the primary method used for children who get into legal trouble because of the belief children are better able to be rehabilitated through restorative means.

Traditional courts do not allow defendants to have legal counsel and can be assisted by informal advisors. The courts are often problematic especially for rural women, who are often perceived as 'disobedient' and the courts were unsympathetic to domestic abuse that they are victims of (Mavundla et al., 2022). Women are still accused of witchcraft in these traditional practices, which can lead to them being physically harmed. This disparate treatment based on gender within the legal system has been a serious issue that is in part a reason why the nation is ranked low on the Gender Inequality Index.

NAMIBIA

Namibia is a nation in Southern Africa with about 2.5 million people. Namibia had been part of South Africa until 1990 and shares a similar history and cultural background. The nation is made up of mostly Ovambo ethnic groups that are primarily Lutheran Christians. The Namibian justice system uses religious values similar to the other nations in the region in support of implementing restorative practices. Namibia, like other nations in the region, uses both traditional courts that practice customary law and a separate system of courts that are implemented through the Ministry of Justice based on the Roman-Dutch system inherited from South Africa that is parallel to the traditional system.

Traditional authorities are officially recognized in Namibia, by the Constitution of Namibia, which also recognizes customary law in the legal system. This is an important recognition as many of the traditional communities throughout the nation still live-in close-knit communities especially the indigenous peoples the Himba and San. These indigenous people have continued using the traditional justice system to resolve most of the issues in their communities, especially with juveniles and instances of theft (Horn & Bösl, 2008).

Namibia has 49 officially recognized traditional authorities. The traditional justice systems are detailed in the law under the Traditional Authorities Act (No. 25 of 2000) and the Community Courts Act (No. 10 of 2003). Numerous unrecognized traditional authorities enforce customary laws in the nation (Hinz, 2008). The Traditional Authorities Act gives the traditional authorities the function to promote peace and welfare of the communities. These traditional authorities can adjudicate the cases and create customary law. The traditional authorities also have executive functions, as there is no separation of powers like some other governmental systems have. As Namibia has a vertical structure where the traditional justice systems are the lowest level of the courts in the legal system.

The traditional courts are usually led by community elders and the courts have a chief who is the community's head. The chief's role is to help restore the harm that has been caused by breaking the community norms and rules. The communities are also divided into separate districts, which have senior headmen who take lead over the district's traditional courts. Each district is under separate villages and the village is under the leadership of a headman.

Most cases in Namibia are seen at the village level before moving up to the district level. For some issues especially, low-level problems like petty theft that only impact the village the headman can deal with them but can also refer the case to the district level or even higher. For the more serious crimes such as murder, it is customary that it goes directly to the chief. As these are based on traditional values, there is often a serious gender inequality that takes power away from women, which is in opposition to the international legal norms for equality of genders within a legal system. More recently women have been given more active rules including as traditional leaders and senior councilors (Ubink, 2011).

The Namibian government has currently tried to pursue restorative justice and reparations for the genocide of Namibians in the early 20th century by German Troops. This was partly inspired by the TRC policies of South Africa. The German government did give an official apology to the Hereros of Namibia for the genocidal murder that occurred. Some of the decedents of the genocide had brought the case to US federal court one member Ngondi Kamatuka stated "All we are asking for is restorative justice for genocide. "The plaintiffs are arguing for reparations similar to the holocaust survivors who were awarded after World War II."

CONCLUSION

The chapter explored how traditional justice practices have continued to play an active role in many communities of Southern Africa, especially in rural villages. Most of the research on traditional and restorative justice practices in the region has focused on South Africa, which made it the focus of the chapter. The traditional restorative values that have been used throughout the region for many generations have started to be respected and implemented throughout the world, especially in North America and Western Europe.

South Africa has been an exceptional case that has inspired many other governments to implement similar practices. The other nations in the region have shown that restorative and traditional practices could be used within their specific context to help support peace and justice within their communities and formally implement traditional practices into the legal system. There have been various studies on the impact of using these practices in South Africa that show a variety of positive benefits and limitations, but the research has been lacking in the surrounding nations.

It is important to learn from the ancient wisdom of our ancestors and to understand how the indigenous philosophies of justice can help improve the effectiveness of justice systems. As colonization started to take away these traditional ways of life, they were too important for the people of the land to give up and the restorative justice practice lived on because of how necessary the practices are for communities to live in peace. The Western use of punitive treatment towards the people was used more often in the urban areas which led to more animosity between the government and certain segments of the population. The restorative practices are continued to be used especially in the rural areas of these countries as they have more of a community-based culture and natural understanding of the importance of restorative justice for the cohesion of their society to be maintained. These governments have shown that the traditional and modern practices can be combined and create a functional mixed legal system.

REFERENCES

Anderson, A. M. (2003). Restorative justice, the African philosophy of Ubuntu and the diversion of criminal prosecution. In *17th International Conference of the International Society for the Reform of Criminal Law* (pp. 24-28). Academic Press.

Cole, R. (2010). Juvenile offenders and the criminal justice system in Botswana: Exploring the restorative approach. *Reflections on Children in Botswana, 2010,* 54.

Elechi, O., Morris, S. V., & Schauer, E. J. (2010). Restoring justice (ubuntu): An African perspective. *International Criminal Justice Review, 20*(1), 73–85. doi:10.1177/1057567710361719

Elmangoush, N. (2015). *Customary Practice and Restorative Justice in Libya.* United States Institute of Peace.

Foley, E. A. (2014). It still 'takes a village to raise a child'-an overview of the restorative justice mechanism under the Children's Protection and Welfare Act, 2011 of Lesotho. *Article 40, 16*(1), 15-19.

Fombad, C. M. (2004). Customary courts and traditional justice in Botswana: Present challenges and future perspectives. *Stellenbosch Law Review, 15*(1), 166–192.

Gade, C. B. (2013). Restorative justice and the South African truth and reconciliation process. *South African Journal of Philosophy= Suid-Afrikaanse Tydskrif vir Wysbegeerte, 32*(1), 10-35.

Gavrielides, T., & Artinopoulou, V. (2016). *Reconstructing restorative justice philosophy.* Routledge. doi:10.4324/9781315604053

Hinz, M. O. (2008). *Traditional courts in Namibia–part of the judiciary? Jurisprudential challenges of traditional justice.* Academic Press.

Horn, N., & Bösl, A. (2008). *The independence of the judiciary in Namibia.* Macmillan Education.

Leebaw, P. (2003). Legitimation or Judgment? South Africa's Restorative Approach to Transitional Justice. *Polity, 36*(1), 23–51. doi:10.1086/POLv36n1ms3235422

Llewellyn, J. (2013). Truth commissions and restorative justice. In *Handbook of restorative justice* (pp. 373–393). Willan. doi:10.4324/9781843926191.ch19

Llewellyn, J. J., & Howse, R. (1999). Institutions for restorative justice: The South African truth and reconciliation commission. *University of Toronto Law Journal, 49*(3), 355–388. doi:10.2307/826003

Makhari, M. R. (2021). *Legal history of the reform of traditional courts in South Africa: insights from Botswana and the Kingdom of eSwatini* (Doctoral dissertation). North-West University.

Mangena, F. (2015). Restorative justice's deep roots in Africa. *South African Journal of Philosophy=Suid-Afrikaanse Tydskrif vir Wysbegeerte, 34*(1), 1-12.

Mavundla, S. D., Strode, A., & Essack, Z. (2022). Access to Justice for Women in Eswatini: HIV- Positive Women as a Vulnerable Population. In Violence Against Women and Criminal Justice in Africa: Volume II (pp. 339-370). Palgrave Macmillan.

Modo, I. V. O. (2002). Dual legal system, Basotho culture and marital stability. *Journal of Comparative Family Studies, 33*(3), 377–386. doi:10.3138/jcfs.33.3.377

Moumakwa, P. C. (2011). *The Botswana Kgotla system: a mechanism for traditional conflict resolution in modern Botswana: case study of the Kanye Kgotla* (Master's thesis). Universitetet i Tromsø.

Mutsvara, S. (2020). *Inhuman sentencing of children: A foucus on Zimbabwe and Botswana* (Doctoral dissertation). University of the Western Cape.

Rautenbach, C. (2015). Legal Reform of Traditional Courts in South Africa: Exploring the Links Between Ubuntu, Restorative Justice and Therapeutic Jurisprudence. *Journal of International and Comparative Law*, 275.

Rautenbach, C. (2016). A family home, five sisters and the rule of ultimogeniture: Comparing notes on judicial approaches to customary law in South Africa and Botswana. *African Human Rights Law Journal, 16*(1), 145–174. doi:10.17159/1996-2096/2016/v16n1a7

Rautenbach, C. (Ed.). (2018). *Introduction to legal pluralism in South Africa.* LexisNexis.

Skelton, A., & Batley, M. (2021). A Comparative Review of the Incorporation of African traditional justice processes in Restorative Child Justice Systems in Uganda, Lesotho and Eswatini. *Comparative Restorative Justice*, 245-264.

Ubink, J. M. (2011). Gender Equality on the Horizon: The Case of Uukwambi Traditional Authority, Northern Namibia. *Northern Namibia*, (3), 51–71.

Wessels, J. W. (2013). *History of the Roman-Dutch law*. Read Books Ltd.

Worden, N. (2011). *The making of modern South Africa: Conquest, apartheid, democracy*. John Wiley & Sons.

ADDITIONAL READING

Dambe, B. J., & Fombad, C. M. (2020). The stock theft act and customary courts in Botswana: Justice sacrificed on the altar of expediency? *Journal of Legal Pluralism and Unofficial Law*, *52*(1), 65–81. doi:10.1080/07329113.2020.1734381

Section 2
Indigenous Wisdom: Middle East

Chapter 4

Capacities of Restorative Practices Within Domestic Customs and Traditions:
The Societal-Cultural and Legal Experiences of Iran

Mehrdad Rayejian Asli
The Institution for Research and Development in Humanities (SAMT), Iran

ABSTRACT

Despite the recognition of the concept of 'restorative justice' in the Persian literature of criminal sciences during recent decades, Iran has a long history of traditional customs and heritages with restorative function that their origins could be found in both pre-Islamic and post-Islamic historical eras. However, the restorative practices have entailed contradictory outcomes of reception and censure. The sympathizers believe that they are a specific means for interaction and relations between tribes, clans, and ethnic groups, or mechanisms of social control. But the opponents criticize such practices due to their potential detrimental consequences particularly in some cases of forced marriage. Notwithstanding these considerations and concerns, one approach to this issue alongside the subject of the present book is to inquire the capacities of restorative practices within domestic customs and traditions of Iranian society. In addition, the legislative manifestations of restorative practices within the Iranian legal system and challenges of the related legislation deserve to be discussed.

DOI: 10.4018/978-1-6684-4112-1.ch004

INTRODUCTION

There are at least two traditional rituals that have still been applied between ethnic groups in some areas of Iran (Khanmohammadi and Ehsani, 2019, p. 140; Nozarpoor, 1991, p. 44).[1] These traditional rituals that could be described as restorative practices are 'cease-blood' or 'peace-blood' ('blood stop' and 'blood peace' in other references, e.g., Osanloo, 2020, p. 11; *khoon-bass* or *khoon-solh* in Persian) and 'resolution' (*fasl* in Persian). Both traditional rituals have compensatory and remedial functions based on their cultural and religious bases, and thus, are recognized as restorative justice practices. Some authors argue that reconciliation rituals and practices frame some of particular characteristics of Islamic teachings like compassion and grace in suffering, and also demonstrate the specific features of ancient Persian culture including chivalry and conciliation or peacemaking. However, religious law in the form of *Shari'a* (Islamic law) or *fiqh* (Islamic jurisprudence) has played more significant role in development of these reconciliation and restorative rituals and practices particularly after Islamic government since the 1979 Revolution in Iran (Osanloo, 2020, pp. 11-12). Accordingly, when a crime is likely to cause a bloody or serious conflict or dispute between two tribes or ethnic groups, the elders or fathers of the tribe or group seek to find a way to resolve the conflict and to avert the danger of bloodshed (Yarahmadi, 2010, pp. 57-8).

In relation to criminal justice policies, the Iranian legal system seems to be influenced by these traditional rituals and customs at two levels:

At the first level, we witness a superficial coexistence or concurrence of the traditional rituals and criminal justice system according to which criminal justice agencies tolerate the existence and occurrence of such rituals and customs. In other words, they are allowed to remain in subsistence and continuation under the authority of legal-judicial system. Such a coexistence or concurrence can be understood in the light of a semi-participatory criminal policy as well as Islamic thoughts. According to a participatory criminal policy, formal and informal criminal justice agencies and organizations cooperate or participate together in response to crime in a definite society. But based upon the Islamic doctrine, which has specifically been promoted in the post-revolutionary Iran, practices such as forbearance, forgiveness and reconciliation are as values and virtues that demonstrate the religious beliefs of Iranian people as the 'Islamic unified nation' (*umma vaahedah*).

At the second level, we see a development in the domestic criminal justice policy based upon the restorative justice doctrine. This process is sometimes referred to as 'translational criminology' through which prevention, reduction and management of crime require that the scientific discoveries are translated into policy and practice by creating a dynamic interface between study/research and policy/practice (Laub and Frisch, 2016, p. 11). The notion of restorative justice arose and grew in the Persian literature of criminal sciences through many scholars' activities and contributions including academic teachings and publications during the late 90s and the beginning of 2000s. For example, in a preface for a book in Persian entitled "New Horizon of Criminal Justice: Penal Mediation." (2003), there is a reference denoting a few miscellaneous references in literature in Persian about penal mediation and restorative justice till the beginning of 2000s (Nadjafi Abrand Abadi, 2003, p. 19). By introducing, study and research on some of the domestic reconciliation and restorative rituals and practices, i.e., cease-blood and resolution, these efforts have gradually influenced the Iranian criminal justice policies, particularly at legislative level, and several legislations have been laid down by translating the academic literature into criminal justice policy that are explored in this chapter.

QUESTIONS AND PROBLEMATIC POINT

The present chapter seeks to answer two key questions. First, what capacities of restorative practices are there due to the traditional rituals and customs in Iran? Second, what challenges the Iranian legal system does face in recognition of restorative justice at legislative and implementation levels?

The problematic point of the chapter is formed through finding an answer to these questions on the presumption that in despite of the current domestic reconciliation rituals and customs, Iranian criminal justice system, in particular, and Iranian society, as a whole, face challenges to achieve the goals of restorative justice. At the same time, this tipping point seems in accordance with the subject and aim of the present book in 'minding the gap between restorative justice, therapeutic jurisprudence, and global indigenous wisdom', because it addresses the reconciliation and resolution rituals and customs as a domestic model of restorative justice as well as their function in social reintegration, and their characteristic as the therapeutic justice that are utilized by certain ethnic groups or tribal communities as the indigenous people of Iranian society.

THE ORGANIZATION OF CHAPTER AND OBJECTIVES

To answer the questions and their correspondence hypothesis, the contents consist of three main parts:

Part one introduces and examines two prominent examples of domestic reconciliation rituals including cease-blood (*khoon-bass*) and resolution (*fasl*) which are applied between tribes and ethnic groups in some areas of Iran. These traditional rituals are as restorative justice practices within the domestic customs and heritages of Iranian society, particularly based on its post and pre-Islamic dimensions and capacities.

Part two focuses on adopted legislations that are based on restorative justice doctrine or practices. Restorative justice doctrine or practices denote two series of academic literature and traditional experiences that the chapter assumes their influence on the contemporary criminal justice policy in Iran.

For all the influence, part three of the present chapter analyzes the challenges of restorative justice practices and criminal justice policies at the practical (social and cultural contexts) and strategic (public and legal policy) levels.

For the purpose of this chapter, these three parts are spelled out as experiences of [contemporary] Iranian society at traditional and policy levels.

Domestic Reconciliation Rituals

In addition to long time history of reconciliation rituals, some of them have been developed in the modern era. Notwithstanding some challenges relating to trends of globalization (Laing and Frost, 2017), these rituals seek to remain as regards their restorative function, to the extent that they have formed a part of elements of the restorative justice definition. For the reason, some of the pioneers of restorative justice idea, like Braithwaite, regards it as "the dominant model of criminal justice throughout most of human history for all the world's peoples" (Braithwaite, 2002, p. 323). Such a function indicates a point of view that makes it possible to see ritual as a way of defining or describing humans, because it is a specific, observable mode of behavior which is exhibited by all known societies, and the nature of ritual is to be defined in terms of its function in a society (Penner, 2016).

From the perspective of informal or non-state justice, reconciliation and restorative rituals and practices may be a part of global span of indigenous traditional dispute resolution systems or customary justice systems (CJS). The main distinction between these two forms of systems relates to their applicability. Unlike indigenous traditional dispute resolution systems, CJS provide access to justice for marginalized or impoverished communities that may otherwise have no other options for redress (World Justice Project, 2013).

Regarding the causes of conflicts or hostilities in traditional communities from a sociological viewpoint, the Durkheimian theory about mechanical solidarity seems a proper explanation, because such communities demonstrate the social cohesiveness of small, undifferentiated societies which is called 'mechanical' by Durkheim. According to him, mechanical solidarity is found in societies with the social integration of members of a society who have common values and beliefs (Britannica, 2020). In these societies, common values and beliefs constitute a collective conscience that connects individual members to each other and cause them to cooperate and coordinate (Evans, 1977, p. 39).

In relation to Iranian society,[2] there are two major examples of reconciliation rituals having restorative function. Before exploring these typical specimens, some points about the Iranian society from the above-mentioned perspectives seem necessary. In terms of informal justice model, these domestic examples appear to be a global span of indigenous systems for conflict resolution rather than CJS because the communities that utilize or perform these rituals or practices are not marginalized or impoverished as to access to justice. In other words, they always have an option to refer their case to the official justice system. As regards the sociological typology of societies, focusing upon Durkheimian theory, the existence or prevalence of these domestic rituals and restorative practices may be defined as a mechanical solidarity in communities with social integration between the members with common values and beliefs.

Cease-blood and resolution are two typical examples of such indigenous traditional settlements in Iran.

Cease-Blood (Khoon-bass)

According to a definition contained in Center for the Great Islamic Encyclopedia (Ebrahimi, 2020), cease-blood, also called 'peace-blood',[3] is one of the oldest customs of some ethnic groups in Iran for resolution of conflicts and cessation of hostilities in disputes or bloodsheds resulted in death upon which a blood money as the satisfaction is paid by the murderer family or group to the murdered counterparts. In other words, when a murder occurs in a tribe or ethnic group, members of the tribe or group seek to end the resultant conflict or fighting through reconciliation or mediation instead of resorting to blood disputes. Despite linked to certain detrimental consequences, e.g., in forced marriage, as a main criticism and serious challenge, (see, no. 3-a), this custom is traditionally regarded as a peaceful resolution for the indigenous people upon which a girl of the murderer family or group, sometimes without her consent, marries a man of the murder victim's family or group.[4]

Other examples of cease-blood have been reported between tribal communities of Iraq, Jordan, Syria, and Morocco, and it shows that this has been common in the Middle East (Arjmandi and Noroozi, 2010, p. 16), and from this chapter's outlook, it could be defined as part of a global span of indigenous systems for conflict resolution.

In addition to cases which may be overlapped with forced marriage, this type of traditional ritual with a compensatory function is applied in some areas including southwest of Iran. For example, in Izeh, a city in Khuzestan Province, cease-blood which is called '*khoon-bori*' (i.e., cutting bloodshed), is used as a traditional method of resolution of ethnic conflicts resulted from homicide. It is applied in other areas including between Arabs of Khuzestan, and the Baloch people in southeast of Iran (Sistan and Baluchestan Province). The manner or style of this traditional ritual differs in terms of its formalities or the kind or amount of compensation. The difference is attributed to social, cultural, or economic development. Moreover, religious beliefs may play an important role, specifically when compensation is determined on the Islamic orders relating to blood money/wergild (*diyaa*). Despite some differences between *Shi'a* and *Sunni*'s attitudes to Islamic orders, provisions of *diyaa* are similar in both branches. In Islamic criminal law, *diyaa* is applied in cases of homicide including as an alternative to *qisas* (retaliation in kind) in murder cases (For further study about the function of *diyaa* as a compensatory sanction and forbearance/forgiveness mechanism, including within indigenous communities, see: Osanloo, 2012, pp. 308-326).

In reference to accessibility of justice system, a case study showed that many families of tribal communities in Izeh prefer to refer their case to cease-blood in spite of availability of legal justice system (Arjmandi and Noroozi, 2010, p. 1). Even if a case referred to the system, the conflict might not be resolved, and thus, cease-blood is to be preferred. According to this research, in respect of the formalities and methods of cease-blood, a number of cases are still done in the form of marriage of a girl (often without her consent) from the murderer family with a man of the murder victim's family (Arjmandi and Noroozi, 2010, p. 14).

Finally, as regards the conflicts and hostilities between tribal communities or ethnic groups, they are mainly rooted in economic, cultural, and psychological contexts and conditions,[5] and this could be justifiable by the Durkheimian theory of mechanical solidarity that requires, inter alia, domestic reconciliation rituals and customs as a main form of social response mechanisms to resolution of conflicts.

Resolution (Fasl)

Another traditional ritual that has particularly been common between Iranian Arabs (as an important ethnic group in south of Iran) is resolution (*fasl*). In Persian literature, the word '*fasl*' has several meanings that seem related to intended concept of this traditional ritual. These are (1) separating (i.e., cause to move or be apart), (2) settle or find a solution, (3) barrier (i.e. a circumstance or obstacle that keeps dispute parties apart in order to preventing the continuation of a hostility or bloodshed), and (4) attaching or joining two or more parties in order to repair or restore a damage, loss or an injury (Mo'in, 2002, p. 2550). As a traditional ritual, it is usually applied in crimes including murder, rape, adultery, battery, abducting a woman, insult especially insulting a married woman, and theft (Nozarpoor, 1991, p. 47). Resolution is defined as a traditional practice for resolving interpersonal disputes and tribal conflicts resulted from the mentioned-above crimes.

Regarding the history of this traditional ritual, Iranian Arabs of Khuzestan argue that its origin is traced back into Pre-Islamic Arabia (Arjmandi and Noroozi, 2010, p. 17). Due to its long-time history, Islam acknowledges the existence of this tradition afterwards. Compared with cease-blood (*khoon-bass*), marriage has a key role in this traditional ritual between Iranian Arabs, to the extent that in recent decades, two women with their dowry in murder cases, and one woman with her dowry in manslaughter cases have been determined as the amount of resolution. Also, under the Islamic orders, *diyaa* has been recognized as an alternative to compensation marriage (Nozarpoor, 1991, p. 47). Compensation marriage is one of the prevailing practices in some Islamic countries according to which the elders of a tribe gather to resolve the dispute in murder by forcing a girl from their community to marry a member of the victim's family (See, Rayejian Asli and Amrollahi Byouki, 2016, p. 735).

In addition to Arab region of Iran, resolution has been applied in some parts of Borujerd of Lorestan Province in western Iran. In its rural areas, this traditional ritual is sometimes called '*khoon-bass*' or '*khoon-solh*' like the Arab region (Yarahmadi, 2010, p. 57). Yet, Arabs of Khuzestan often use terms including 'resolution' (*fasl*), 'aid' (*owneh*), or 'settlement' (*jars/fasl*) (Rayejian Asli & Daneshnejad, 2015, p. 92). All these terms indicate various forms of participation and cooperation with characteristics of restorative and community justice. Meanwhile, resolution, as a form of mechanical solidarity, is a continuous social action within a traditional community that is applied between stakeholders of a conflict in order to reach a settlement or conciliation. Through this social process, mediation is used as an endeavor to achieve a peaceful goal. From the perspective of ritual functions, it requires the respect for traditions and customs emphasizing upon social conventions (Rayejian Asli & Daneshnejad, 2015, p. 93), and even may create emotional states and responses similar to interaction ritual chains in Randall Collins' theory (Collins, 2004). By distinguishing various rituals, Collins argues that successful rituals create symbols of group membership and increase individuals with emotional energy contrary to unsuccessful rituals that deprive individuals of emotional energy. "Each person flows from situation to situation, drawn to those interactions where their cultural capital gives them the best emotional energy payoff" (Collins, 2004, p. 102). Accordingly, restorative justice practices could demonstrate a model for recognizing an interaction ritual chains through which success of traditional ritual like resolution may generate emotional energy between members of social groups and reinforce the social solidarity.

LEGISLATIVE MANIFESTATIONS

The traditional rituals and customs discussed in the previous section seem to have an influence on domestic criminal justice system in the light of legal policies adopted since 2000s. Indeed, this could be described as a domestic criminal policy which has also been influenced by academic teaching of restorative justice doctrine in faculties of law as well as their departments of criminal law and criminology in the universities around Iran. It should be noted that criminal law and criminology programs are offered at master and postgraduate (doctoral) levels in the universities of Iran. Restorative justice doctrine and teachings could be discussed in courses such as criminology, criminal sociology, the history of criminal law development, theoretical criminology, criminal policy, and sociology of punishment at both master and postgraduate levels. One of the notable references in this area is a series of lectures entitled "Issues of Criminal Sciences" that includes, inter alia, the specific themes on restorative justice with an attitude to Iranian legal and justice system (Ebrahimi, 2011, 2026 pages). Two chapters of this series contain the topic of 'restorative justice' which were respectively taught in master and doctoral levels (Ebrahimi, 2011, pp. 1507-1658, 1659-1716). Meanwhile, many references about restorative justice in the Persian literature of criminal sciences have mentioned or alluded to examples (particularly cease-blood/*khoon bass* and resolution/*fasl*) of the domestic practices with restorative function. For instance, in one of the chapters of a series of lectures entitled "Issues of Criminal Sciences" (Ebrahimi, 2011, p. 1661), 'resolution' as a traditional ritual between the Arab tribes of Khuzestan is defined as an example of restorative justice in Iranian history. In addition to these academic literature and teachings, there have been some Islamic dimensions such as 'reconciliation between two parties' (*islah-e-zaatolbein*) which is based upon the *qoran* (the Holly Book of Muslims) and other primary sources of Islamic law,[6] and has an influence on Iranian law, specifically in the field of criminal procedure.[7] In a sense, it could be said that in the course of incorporating the restorative practices into legal system, formal criminal justice policy has been inspired by Islamic capacities, and at the same time, has been made its acquaintance with the traditional customs and rituals esp. cease-blood and resolution through the academic teachings.

Such an influence may be regarded constructive as a positive step to develop the legal system and its criminal justice part. In other word, domestic customs, and traditions such as cease-blood and resolution prima facie have restorative function, and in this regard, are considered as capacities that could bring about development in domestic legal system, in particular, and in Iranian society, as a whole, notwithstanding challenges they may entail. This part of the present chapter, therefore, discusses about significant manifestations of Iranian model of restorative justice at the level of legislative criminal policy.

The Emergence of Dispute Resolution Councils (DRC) in the Light of Restorative Justice

Traditional societies have preserved their customs and heritage for centuries that form a body entitled cultural values. Resolving disputes amicably is one of these traditional mechanisms which finds itself woven in its social fabric. Its aim is to facilitate the ordinary people in getting their problems or issues (esp. trivial matters) to be resolved in a friendly and peaceable manner through the restorative justice model involving members of civil society. DRCs are indeed the institutional form of a strong tradition of dispute resolution through reconciliation and mediation based on restorative justice. The purpose of DRCs is to develop the peoples' cooperation in solving disputes of informal and formal nature, as well as settlement of matters of judicial nature with less complexity, whether in criminal or non-criminal cases.

Recognizing DRC in the Iranian legal system is traced back into the establishment of Houses of Equity (Justice) in pre-revolutionary period of Iran's history (Bigdelou, 2020, p. 101). Its function was investigating and handling rural disputes amicably through reconciliation and mediation. Judicial functions in the field of private law in the pre-revolutionary Iran were categorized into five organizations: The civil courts, military courts, locally elected lay-courts, Houses of Equity, and Councils of Arbitration. Two recent organizations were respectively exercised in rural areas and cities (Baldwin, 1973, p. 497). The aims of house of equity were to prevent the spread of petty disputes into complex ones, and that villagers no longer needed to travel to the towns and cities to access to justice. Moreover, the participation of peoples in electing their judge gave them a significant role in administration of justice as well as induced them to resolve their own disputes.

The establishment of Houses of Equity has been attributed to the historical characteristics of procedural tradition in Iran, including non-formality, self-governance, and relative independence of judicial institutions. In the contemporary history of Iran, modernization of institutions and procedural practices is defined as reformation process during the *Qajar* and *Pahlavi* era, and Houses of Equity were recognized as a modern judiciary institution based on the domestic traditional capacities in the form of the White Revolution during the 1960s. Some scholars have analyzed the establishment of the Houses of Equity in the context of the goals of the White Revolution as such in order to promote state bureaucracy in procedural areas and develop the law enforcement in the context of non-formal justice (Bigdelo, 2020, p. 101).

In the post-revolutionary Iran, we witness two sub-periods in respect of the domestic legal system. The first sub-period coincided with the beginning decades of Islamic revolution between 1979 and the late 90s through which criminal laws and provisions were mainly changed according to Islamic law, and some of the pre-revolutionary criminal laws, esp. the General Penal Code 1973, were repealed due to their secular characteristics. The criminal legislations of this sub-period consisted of *hudud*, *qisas*, *diyaa*, and *ta'zir* that were later codified in the Islamic Penal Code 1991. In Islamic law, *hudud* are acts prohibited by God and punished by defined mandatory penalties. *Qisas* is a specified punishment in the Quran and Sunna, with the decision to inflict it resting with the victim's closest kin as the avenger of the physical harm done to the victim. *Diyaa* is applied in cases of homicide including as an alternative to *qisas* in murder cases or as a separate criminal sanction in some of the non-intentional offences. *Ta'zir* is a punishment that the judge is given discretion in sentencing and applied to crimes for which there are no specified penalties in the Quran or Sunna (Arafa, 2018, p. 8).

Restorative justice, as a concept, was not realized by the Iranian jurists and legal scholars, and thus, was not recognized by the Iranian policy makers in this sub-period. However, implications of restorative justice could be found in some of these Islamic provisions. For example, recognizing *diyaa* as an alternative to *qisas* or granting pardon to the perpetrator instead can reflect a restorative capacity that requires the victim and the offender to enjoy reconciliation or mediation.

The second sub-period includes two recent decades through which a development has been occurred in the form of a gradual shift in the domestic criminal justice policy by realization of restorative justice in Persian literature of law and criminal sciences, as well as by its recognition at policy-making level. Therefore, such a shift could be justified by the academic considerations and other circumstances that required the government to adopt new measures and policies based on the contemporary developments in the modern world. It could also be understood as a retreat or drawing back from absolute commitment to Islamic law based on a feverish haste in the beginning years of the Revolution. Notwithstanding this retreat, the government retains the Islamic bases of its domestic legal system. The official underpinning of this system is recognized in Art. 4 of the Islamic Republic of Iran's Constitution which stipulates: "All civil, penal financial, economic, administrative, cultural, military, political, and other laws and regulations must be based on Islamic criteria. This principle applies absolutely and generally to all articles of the Constitution as well as to all other laws and regulations, and the wise persons (*fuqaha'*) of the Constitutional Council (also known as the 'Guardian Council') are judges in this matter." Accordingly, some of the Iranian authors who have discussed about the DRC, regard the primary sources of Islamic Law (see footnote 15), and *figh* concepts e.g., 'reconciliation between two parties' (*islah-e-zaatolbein* – see: no. 2 and footnote 16) as foundations and backgrounds of this domestic institution (Fathi, 2005, p. 85).

Thus, following the translation of 'restorative justice' in the Persian literature of criminal sciences, this sub-period has witnessed new legislations reflecting the contemporary developments in the fields of criminology, penology, victimology and criminal policy that formed in the context of development policies, esp. judicial development in the beginning of 2000s. Accordingly, DRC became the starting point of these policies based on the domestic model of restorative justice.

Emergence of DRC in the Context of Development Programs

The pre-revolutionary legislations relating to the development policies narrowed to economic dimension (focusing on civil engineering). The first program of development in the pre-revolutionary Iran was a temporary 7-year program (1948-1954). The last program (The Fifth Program of Development Act) was enacted in 1973 (https:// olgou.ir/downloads/asnad/ghableenghelab/ghanoonOmrani1.pdf; https://qavanin.ir/ Law/PrintText/86928). In addition to economic matters, some other dimensions of development, including public and social affairs were also seen in this act. These policies expanded into other aspects of development in the post-revolutionary Iran, particularly after the end of the Iran-Iraq War in the late 80s. The first post-revolutionary legislation relating to development policies was enacted in 1990 with the new title of 'the Program of Economic, Social and Cultural Development of the Islamic Republic of Iran' (https://rc.majlis.ir/fa/law/show/91755). The origins of criminal sciences' doctrine that led to next progress in the second sub-period of the post-revolutionary Iran could be found in this act, such that no. 9 of the General Objectives regarded criminological studies and research as an effort to establish the judicial security and administer the justice. One of the significant parts of this objective in the context of restorative justice accomplished in the Third Program of Economic, Social and Cultural Development Act 2000.

Art. 189 of Act 2000 is indeed the first notable provision at level of the post-revolutionary criminal justice policy in Iran that reflects the restorative justice doctrine. The article provided a way by establishing DRC under the authority of the judiciary in order to reduce the number of people referring to the courts, in accordance with the development of public participation, and in order to resolve some of conflicts such as local disputes that its judicial nature is less complex (Islamic Parliament Research Center of the Islamic Republic of Iran, 2000). The Administrative Regulation of Article 189 (2002) recognizes the competence of DRCs in those criminal matters called 'non-indictable offences' in which complaint of a victim is needed (Islamic Parliament Research Center of the Islamic Republic of Iran, 2002). In these cases, the DRC is competent to hear the criminal case in order to reconcile the dispute through negotiation.

The Establishment of DRC in Their Special Act by the Parliament

The Dispute Resolution Councils Act (DRC Act) is the most important source of the legislative criminal justice policy in Iran based on restorative justice. This act has been changed several times in recent decade. The latest change resulted in the Act 2015 (The Government Gazette, no. 20652, 2016). The Act 2015 recognizes the competence of DRCs to hear all non-indictable offences and the private aspect of indictable offences in order to reconcile the dispute provided to consent of the parties. According to Iranian criminal law, the consent of the victim (as victim forgiveness of an offender) in indictable offences is a mitigating factor to reduce the punishment of the offender or to change it to a lesser degree (Art. 13-b of Iranian Criminal Procedure Code 2014).[8]

Incorporating Restorative Justice into Criminal Laws and Provisions

In addition to provisions of the Program of Economic, Social and Cultural Development Act, and the Special Act of DRC, setting down special provision with respect to criminal matters seemed to be necessary. Accordingly, the Criminal Procedure Code 2014 and the Regulation of Mediation in Criminal Matters 2016 were enacted in order to recognition of criminal/penal mediation as a significant method of restorative justice model.

The Victim-Offender Mediation: The Criminal Procedure Code 2014 (CPC 2014)

In 2003, a quarrel broke out between two cousins in one of the rural areas in west of Iran that bears malice and vengeance resulting in death of one of them by shooting of another man. The defendant argued that he made a mistake in identity of the victim. But the victim's kin demanded *qisas* based of an argument that a murder occurred. However, the elders of village sought to resolve the dispute through irenic and peaceful manners. By continuation of the dispute, the case was referred to the court and it was held that the defendant could be found guilty of manslaughter by paying *diyaa* to the victim's kin. Yet, because of his inability to pay compensation, the case was then referred to mediation with the assistance of a headman of the village (Beytoote, n.d.). Considering the silence of internal law in recognizing criminal mediation, CPC 2014 (The Government Gazette, no. 20135, 2014) stipulates the victim-offender mediation as a way in achievement of restorative justice goals. According to Art. 82 of CPC 2014, in some minor offences including those of which they are suspendable, judicial authorities may, at the request of the accused provided to the consent of the victim or a private plaintiff, determine a maximum period of three months to the accused in order to ask the forgiveness of victim or offer the restitution for him/her. However, the judicial authority may also refer the matter to the DRC or to a person or institution for mediation, if the parties reach an agreement, in order to reconcile the dispute.

The mechanisms contained in this article are the victim forgiveness of the offender, restitution by the offender, and the victim-offender mediation. While the latter is provided by a person or institution for mediation, but the offender and his/her victim would also be able to resolve their dispute by their own mediation. From a victimological viewpoint, the victim-offender mediation is considered as programs of the restorative justice model. Its effectiveness and benefits are in favors of the needs and rights of victims and serve the advantage and expediency of offenders and the society (Moran, 2017, p. 1). Also, it is sometimes referred to as 'victim-offender reconciliation' and defined as an important part of restorative justice (Britannica, 2013). As this mechanism is often applied with the aid of a specially trained mediator (Britannica, 2013), it could be said, the term 'victim-offender mediation' denotes cases involving such a mediator, but the term 'victim-offender reconciliation' refers to cases in which the victim and offender decide to resolve their dispute without intervention of an official mediator. Thus, Art. 82 of CPC 2014 indeed endorses both forms of the victim-offender reconciliation and mediation.

Mediation in Criminal Matters: The Regulation 2016

For the purposes of Article 82, the Regulation of Mediation in Criminal Matters 2016 has been adopted by the Cabinet following the offer of Department of Justice and agreement of the head of Judiciary (Cabinet Decision, no. 52773/95749, 2016). Article 1-a of the Regulation 2016 defines criminal mediation as a process through which the victim and offender converse together about causes, effects, and consequences of crime, and the ways of remedy and reparation for that crime under the supervision of a mediator in an appropriate circumstance, intending to reach a conciliation. Regarding the victim-offender mediation/reconciliation contained in Art. 82, Arts 1-b and 1-d of the Regulation 2016 recognize natural and legal persons as the mediator. Accordingly, a mediator may be a person or an institute/organization (e.g., DRC) who manages or facilitates the process of dialogue and reconciliation between parties. Nevertheless, the formal characteristic of criminal mediation in the Regulation 2016 appears more significant than its informal feature, because the Judiciary is recognized as the authority having administrative power and control over the process of criminal mediation. For this reason, Art. 1-e of the Regulation 2016 stipulates submitting the meeting minutes of mediation to the competence judicial authority.

All these provisions demonstrate the governmental feature of restorative justice model in Iran. In this regard, DRC was renamed the Development Center for Dispute Resolution after it merged with Arbitration Center by the Judiciary in 2016. At the time of writing the present chapter, the Office General of Development of Mediation and Arbitration of the Judiciary Development Center for Dispute Resolution has announced an invitation to register for receiving the mediation license in November 2021 (https://shoradad.eadl.ir/).

CHALLENGES OF RESTORATIVE JUSTICE PRACTICES AND CRIMINAL JUSTICE POLICIES

Notwithstanding the traditional capacities and legal developments, restorative justice practices and policies in Iran face challenges at both practical and legislative levels. These challenges could be classified as three series of considerations and concerns including those relating to human rights and justice system, to social and cultural contexts, and to implementation of policymaking and legislation.

Human Rights Considerations and Justice System's Concerns

Although the rituals including cease-blood (*khoon-bass*) and resolution (*fasl*) could be seen as restorative capacities within the domestic customs and traditions of Iranian society, but they sometimes face serious challenges in terms of disagreement with some aspects of human rights, and probable contradictions with criminal justice system (For the attitude of Iran to the international instruments, particularly in the human rights areas, see, e.g.: Rayejian Asli, 2021, pp. 69-82).

Human Rights Considerations

In respect of human rights considerations, there is a serious concern when these rituals overlap with or result in forced marriage. Ali, one of the relatives of a girl who was married as a result of cease-blood (*khoon bass*), narrates the story of this ritual as follows:

There were two men named Ata'ullah Khan and Rasool Khan who owned many lands, including seventy yards real estates in villages. They encountered serious conflicts. Rasool Khan won the competition and became the chieftain of the lands. However, he showed strange behaviors so that he married many girls and women by abusing his position. Thus, Ata'ullah Khan and his sons decided to kill Rasool Khan and carried out their plan. Due to the difficulties of establishing the murder, Ata'ullah

Khan and his relatives decided to use cease-blood (khoon bass) as their traditional ritual. Therefore, one of their girls named Azimeh was married to one of the Rasool Khan's sons without her consent and notwithstanding her romantic relationship with her boyfriend. Azimeh experienced serious challenges in her marriage to the extent that she was repeatedly battered and tortured by her husband. Azimeh's family ignored her grievances and complaints. After a long time, enduring suffering, and pains, she is now in treatment with psychiatrists (http://www.ensafnews.com/257781/).

In addition to this true story, some research, and studies (Bakhtiarnejad, 2009, p. 24) show that marriages occurred following cease-blood cause specific forms of victimization. One major type of such victimization is honor killing (Rayejian Asli and Amrollahi Byouki, 2016, p. 746). This type of murder has still been found in some of countries like Iran due to the provisions of Islamic Penal Code 1996 (IPC 1996). According to Art. 630 of IPC 1996, a husband is allowed to kill his wife and her lover when the husband sees they are committing adultery ('*zina*'). This provision has been recognized in Art. 302 of new IPC 2014 that exempts the husband from retaliation ('*qisas*') as a result of killing his wife and the man committing adultery with her. According to a study (Bakhtiarnejad, 2009, p. 24), forced marriage is a ground that may cause honor killing. Other factors and grounds are ethnicity, prejudice, suspicion or cautious distrust, and intensive social strain and control. This study shows that provinces in northwest, west and southwest are the so-called 'hotspots' of honor killing in Iran (Bakhtiarnejad, 2009, pp. 37-42). In terms of relation between occurrence of honor killing and traditional customs and rituals, this finding may be confirmed at least in the west and southwest of Iran.

From a human rights-oriented point of view based upon international standards and norms as well as a criminological-victimological standpoint, honor killing is an example of violence against women as well as domestic violence (Rayejian Asli, 2021, p. 78). But at the same time, honor killing as a result of forced marriage is committed because of a traditional ritual like cease-blood (*khoon-bass*) or resolution (*fasl*). Cases of honor killing arise in a variety of situations. For example, women who are forced into marriage through such traditional customs or rituals later feel saddened, disappointed, or inconvenienced of their married life, and thus, decide to have an affair with another man in order to make up for their emotional and sexual frustrations (Rayejian Asli and Amrollahi Byouki, 2016, p. 746). Even if such a marriage does not result in an unfaithful or disloyal situation, the mere status of forced marriage could be regarded as inequitable and unfair.

Criminal Justice System's Concerns

In relation to criminal justice system, traditional rituals and restorative practices may also be described as private justice mechanisms in contradiction with the philosophy of criminal justice based on the notion of public order. According to penal philosophy and justice theories, punishments and criminal sanctions have evolved throughout the history in a two-stage process from private justice into public justice. Consequently, imposing punishment on offenders and providing criminal sanctions for offences are under the state's monopoly in terms of necessities or requirements of public order. However, in this modern thinking, we witness a coexistence between the state justice and the private justice. In this context, states respect some traditions and customs in the course of the goals of their societies.

A major example in Islamic law that has been recognized in post-revolutionary Iran's legal system is certain provisions of retaliation (*qisas*) and wergild (*diyaa*). In *qisas* crimes which are defined as offenses against the physical integrity of the person, including intentional injury and homicide, *qisas* is considered a matter to be settled between the offender and the victim (Warren, 2019). Decision of doing or not *qisas* is at the hands of the victim or his/her heirs against the convicted perpetrator of murder or intentional bodily injury. If *qisas* is required due to a murder, the victim's heirs have the right to take the life of murderer provided that the court approves it. Also, all persons who are entitled to decide about *qisas* have a choice to receive *diya* or forgive (pardon) the murderer instead (Esposito, 1931). The state's possession or control over these punishments or criminal sanctions are provided in IPC 2014 that stipulates executing *qisas* by authorization of the supreme leader or his representative/the Judiciary (Art. 417). While Art. 421 specifies the absolute right of the victim or his/her heirs to *qisas*, but it is overshadowed by the political power or governmental authority.

Another example relates to cases in which we could see a state tolerance to some forms of a private justice. As might be expected, there is a similar mechanism in Iran's constitution that allows the recognized religious minorities to exercise their religious ceremonies and rituals within the limits of the law so that they are free to exercise matters of personal status and religious education and to follow their own rituals (Art. 13 of the Constitution). But with respect to other ethnic groups and communities, there is a *de facto* situation in which some forms of a private justice model are permitted. Yet, as regards the state's monopoly of criminal justice policies, some social-cultural conflicts and challenges seem inevitable.

One area of such conflicts and challenges concerns the relationship between criminal justice system and traditional customs and rituals. From a historical background, as documented in certain of sources (Yarahmadi, 2010, p. 57), in the past, indigenous peoples seldom raised a legal action and were reluctant to refer their disputes to judicial authorities because they believed that legal proceedings make a bad situation or negative experiences with the criminal justice system, and such a decision is deemed a stain or disgrace to their family or tribe. Today, however, in some areas (e.g., Ilam and Lorestan in west of Iran), to be resolved a dispute, legal services or the judicial system are often demanded (Yarahmadi, 2010, p. 60). Nevertheless, whenever the indigenous peoples act on their traditional rituals, the criminal justice system does not intervene insofar as the dispute or its resolution process disturbances or threatens or endangers public order or national security. Such an issue is narrated by Jalal Al-e-Ahmad, Iranian novelist, in his book Triennial Memoir (*Kār-nāma-ye se sāla*) (Al-e-Ahmad, 1968, p. 37) when he made a telling observation about his last journey to Khuzestan (in southwest of Iran). Al-e-Ahmad describes the day of his arrival in Ahvaz (capital of Khuzestan province) where they came to a bizarre roadblock at the front of the hall of justice, because a vast concourse of Arab peoples appeared forcing an entry to the hall and police officers were struggling to impede them. He was informed that a homicide was occurred and then the case was referred to the justice system by taking the defendant into custody. The objectors claimed that they would resolve the dispute by the resolution ritual (*fasl*), and thus, they demanded the immediate release of the defendant (Nozarpoor, 1991, p. 46).

While the narrator wondered about this event, the fact is that such a conflict or challenge between criminal justice system and traditional rituals or customs (notwithstanding the coexistence between these two social institutions) is inevitable.

Considerations Relating to Social and Cultural Context and Social Solidarity as a Challenge

In the light of translational criminology-victimology, restorative justice whether as traditional restorative practices or academic teachings has been reflected into Iranian criminal justice policy in recent several decades. This development has had a more significant mirroring at the legislative level. At the relevant level of criminal policy, a major deficiency is that these legislations have been adopted irrespective of social and cultural context and setting within which the restorative justice would be applied. In other words, the ways of policymaking, on the one hand, and sociocultural contexts and conditions, on the other hand, do not seem to be consistent or coextensive. This argument implies the fact that traditional restorative practices represent a small portion of the Iranian current society as a whole. In other words, ethnic groups or communities who are bounded to their traditions or rituals are indeed a smaller part of a group opposed to the majority of Iranian people who do not know or realize these rituals.

This relevant argument proclaims a different kind of social attitude that explains at least two forms of behavior or practice. These two forms seem appropriate with the Durkheimian idea of mechanical and organic societies which was denoted before (See no. 1). Accordingly, the majority of Iranians appears to tend a way of life and living in a modernization context that is defined as organic society while the minority ones may occasionally behave in a particular way or customarily have a certain characteristic opposed to majority of the society. In addition to observations of the author, there are several research and studies that show an evolution based on modernization in the contemporary society of Iran. One of the latest sociological works about Iran is a book entitled "Social Solidarity and Its Enemies" (2021) in which the author argues that in Iranian society, as a social and class structure resulting from rentier capitalism, the question is how to lead people to the rearrangement of the social structure and convince the governmental bourgeoisie to revive institutions such as syndicate, councils and unions in order to achieve the justice as well as to achieve an ideal solidarity? (Zakeri, 2021, p. 522). Other studies have analyzed modernization as an acquisitive identification in Iranian society which was began from the capital 'Tehran' in the nineteenth century (Towhidian et al., 2018, p. 167).

This perception of the before-mentioned argument does not necessarily contravene restorative justice in a modern society or developed country. However, social solidarity as a main variable, whether in traditional or modern social-cultural context, plays a role in people's tendency toward traditional or modern identification insofar as higher level of social solidarity brings about a higher tendency to national or local identification, and conversely, a lower tendency to modern identification. As this hypothesis is documented in some studies in Persian literature (Maghsoodi, 2018, pp. 44-45), thus, restorative justice practices seem underwhelmed by Iranian society due to decline of social solidarity and traditional identification.

In addition to solidarity challenge, there seems to be some forms of a social disorganization, an anomic situation, or a structural strain in some parts of the Iranian society, as such in its modernization process, which take people away from dispute resolution methods based on restorative justice. In line with this consideration, different views arise about the temperaments and social values of Iranians. Some have merely praised Iranian culture and the prevalence of positive values, and some others have solely referred to common negative values, or seen both types side by side.

One of the studies (Hamshahri-Online, 2012) shows that many of Iranians do not tend to recognize the prevalence of positive values in their society, and in contrast, acknowledge the prevalence of negative values within their own country. The findings indicate to some extent a pessimistic attitude toward the social system and the positive values belonging to the system, and respondents generally consider negative perceptions of Iranian personality more than positive values. Accordingly, Iranians appraised the prevalence of benevolence as moderate, fidelity as low, forgiveness as high, adherence to promises as low, honesty and truth as low, and fairness as low. On the contrary, from the perspective of respondents, negative values were, inter alia, fraud and deception more prevalent (Hamshahri-Online, 2012).

Earlier, in another study entitled "Investigating Social Attitude and behaviors of Residents of the Country's Urban Areas" (1996), the researchers found similar results (Tavassoli, 1996, p. 452). More recently reports show that social problems may result in an insecurity in the society (ISNA, 2017). Moreover, one of the latest studies (Dargahi and Beiranvand, 2021, p. 260) suggests that the active population of Iran is exposed to the effects of the devastation caused by the instability of the family foundation, the spread of drug abuse and addiction, and crime. Efficient use of this active population in the path of growth and development must be the most important concern of the government and policy makers, insofar as they are convinced to meet the economic and political requirements of growth and development. The continuation of a weak and sluggish economy and the increase of social harms and problems would, in the medium term, confront the country with poverty and a young population active in disarray of social anomalies, and in the long run, with a crisis of an aging population in need of public resources (Dargahi and Beiranvand, 2021, p. 260).

All these facts and circumstances can undoubtedly weaken restorative capacities of the society, and consequently, any policy making, including any legislation adopted or enacted to develop or promote the restorative justice may fail because of the contradictory characteristics of social and cultural contexts. Several studies affirm that the spread and increase of social harms and problems, particularly crime and deviance have a direct correlation with undermining and weakening human dignity as well as self-transcending values like virtuousness and piety (See, e.g., Tanha, 2021, p. 40). These positive values have a determining role in the process of restorative justice programs and practices.

Considerations Relating to Implementation of Policymaking and Legislation

Another challenge of domestic restorative justice practices and policies that may be described as a deficiency in achievement of the restorative justice goals is that the relevant legislations reflect the restorative justice doctrine on paper rather than in reality or in practice. In terms of legislative criminal justice policy, the provisions of dispute resolution, reconciliation and mediation in the domestic legal system have sought to reflect the restorative justice doctrine. However, they encounter shortcomings in fulfilment of goals of restorative justice model. This weakness is caused by the attitude or frame of mind of the policymakers in implementing the legislations in question. In general, Iranian law system have experienced a series of legislations and regulations among which many of them have been necessary. Yet, they have mainly faced the challenge of implementation. In respect of restorative justice, the relevant provisions, particularly those incorporated this model into criminal legislation (see, section b in this chapter) do not appear implemented appropriately. For this reason, notwithstanding the provisions of victim-offender mediation in CPC 2014, and mediation in criminal matters in the Regulation 2016, establishment of mediation institutes have not been realized yet because, as mentioned before (see 2-b-ii), the Office General of Development of Mediation and Arbitration of the Judiciary Development Center for Dispute Resolution as the governmental organ of DRC has recently announced an invitation to register for receiving the mediation license in order to establishing the mediation institution. In regard to the DRC, as another institution which could have a restorative function, it still appears deviated from its standard and intended course because of employing and working the non-professionals and non-experts as mediators and conciliators.

CONCLUSION

Taking into account the discussions and considerations in this chapter, the conclusion remarks could be summarized as follows:

1. In the context of domestic customs in Iran, some examples of dispute resolution patterns, particularly in the form of traditional rituals are still found that could be described as restorative justice practices.
2. Despite the restorative capacities of these practices, they have not been developed nationwide, and some governmental attempts, e.g., suggestion of national register of cease-blood/*khoon-bass* as a cultural heritage (Hamshahrionline, 2020) have faced notable debates and serious criticism in the light of human rights considerations, specifically in terms of forced marriage.
3. No doubt the existence of such traditional rituals and practices can be acceptable insofar as they meet certain important considerations esp. in respect of with public order and social security.
4. In the context of criminal justice policy, Iran's legal system have demonstrated some trends to recognize restorative justice that seem to deserve the potential credit. However, the system in fact operates in a conventional stream based on penal philosophy that is rooted in Islamic law (*fiqh*).
5. Accordingly, the provisions of restorative justice model, including those relating to DRC, and incorporating restorative justice into criminal legislations (e.g., the victim-offender mediation/penal mediation) are mainly overshadowed by the large-scale criminal laws and provisions contained in IPC 2014, CPC 2014,

and other similar legislations which are based upon the criminalization and penalization mechanisms. Moreover, these provisions are subordinated to the constitutional principle of superiority of *Shari'a* that reflects in *qisas, diyaa,* and *islah-e-zaatolbein.*

6. In the post-revolutionary, a domestic criminal justice policy based upon restorative justice has gradually become integrated into Iran's legal system. This policy has been influenced by academic doctrines and teachings in the last two decades that enjoy the traditional customs and rituals as examples of a domestic restorative justice. Therefore, these doctrines offered a pattern for policymaking from the perspective of a translational criminology-victimology according to which restorative justice got a chance to incorporate into criminal justice policy.

7. Finally, from a macro-level perspective, and considering sociocultural conditions and circumstances that are to some extent documented by certain research and studies, Iranian society, except for in certain domestic traditional parts, faces obstacles and challenges to achieve an ideal model of restorative justice and its desired goals.

REFERENCES

Al-e-Ahmad, J. (1968). Triennial Memoir [Kār-nāma-ye se sāla]. Tehran.

ArafaM. A. (2018). Islamic Criminal Law: The Divine Criminal Justice System between Lacuna and Possible Routes. *Journal of Forensic and Crime Studies, 102.* https://ssrn.com/abstract=3189521

Arjmandi, G., & Noroozi, A. (2010). Conflict Resolution among the Bakhtiaris of Izeh: 'Khoon-bori' or 'Khoon-bas' as a Custom. *Iranian Journal of Social Problems in Iran, 1*(1), 1–44. https://journals.ut.ac.ir/article_20744.html

Bakhtiarnejad, P. (2009). *Faaje'eye Khamush: ghatlhaye namusi* [The Silent Tragedy: Honor Killing]. https://engare.net/honor-killing/

Baldwin, G. B. (1973). The Legal System of Iran. *International Lawyer, 7*(2), 492-504. https://scholar.smu.edu/til/vol7/iss2/19

Bigdelou. (2020). Houses of Equity; judicial modernization or a return to procedural traditions. *Journal of Iran History, 13*(1), 101–120. doi:10.52547/irhj.13.1.101

Britannica. The Editors of Encyclopaedia. (2010). Mechanical and Organic Solidarity. *Encyclopedia Britannica*. https://www.britannica.com/topic/mechanical-and-organic-solidarity

Britannica. The Editors of Encyclopaedia. (2013). Victim-offender reconciliation. In *Encyclopedia Britannica*. https://www.britannica.com/topic/workhouse

Britannica. The Editors of Encyclopaedia. (n.d.). People of Iran. *Encyclopedia Britannica*. (https://www.britannica.com/place/Iran/The-Abbasid-caliphate-750-821

Burton, J. (1990). *Conflict: Resolution and Prevention* (1st ed.). St. Martin's Press.

Cabinet Decision. (2016). *The Regulation of Mediation in Criminal Matters 2016*, no. 52773/95749. https://rrk.ir/Laws/ShowLaw.aspx?Code=12750

Collins, R. (2004). Interaction Ritual Chains. Princeton University Press.

Dargahi, H. & Beiranvand, A. (2021). *Macroeconomics and Social Harms/Problems: Investigating the Interaction between Divorce, Crime and Drug Addiction with Economic Growth in Iran*. Donya-ye-Eqtesad Publications.

Dignan, J. (2005). Understanding Victims and Restorative Justice. In Crime and Justice. Open University Press.

Ebrahimi, M. (2020). *Khoon-bas* [Cease-Blood]. Center for the Great Islamic Encyclopedia. https://www.cgie.org.ir/fa/article/246533/%D8%AE%D9%88%D9%86-%D8%A8%D8%B3

Ebrahimi, S. (Ed.). (2011). *Issues of Criminal Sciences: A Series of Lectures of Professor Ali-Hossein Nadjafi Abranabadi*. http://adminshop.mizanlaw.ir/Content/upload/Tblbooklet/be55ab6b2fb54c62a1999d5aa383b85d.pdf

Esposito, J. L. (Ed.). (1931). Qisas. In *The Oxford Dictionary of Islam*. Oxford Islamic Studies Online. https://www.oxfordislamicstudies.com/article/opr/t125/e1931) (https://www.oxfordislamicstudies.com/article/opr/t125/e1931

Evans, A., & Evans, A. (1977). An Examination of the Concept 'Social Solidarity.'. *Mid-American Review of Sociology*, 2(1), 29–46. https://www.jstor.org/stable/23254926

Fathi, H. (2005). Dispute Resolution Councils: A Critic and Evaluation. *Islamic Law (Figh and Law)*, 1(4), 85-108. http://hoquq.iict.ac.ir/article_22698.html?lang=fa

Hamshahri. (n.d.). Combatting with Street Crime. *Weekly Annex of Hamshahri Newspaper*, 175.

Hamshahri-Online. (n.d.). A *Narration of the National Register of a Traditional Ritual: Khuzestan laid claim to Cease-Blood (Khoon-bass).* https://www.hamshahrionline.ir/news/541113/

Islamic Parliament Research Center of the Islamic Republic of Iran. (2000). *The Third Program of Economic, Social and Cultural Development Act.* https://rc.majlis.ir/fa/law/show/93301

Islamic Parliament Research Center of the Islamic Republic of Iran. (2002). *The Administrative Regulation of Article 189 of The Third Program of Economic, Social and Cultural Development Act.* https://rc.majlis.ir/fa/law/show/121958

ISNA. (2017). *Social Problems and the Danger of Insecurity in Society.* https://www.irna.ir/news/83054077/

Khanmohammadi, K., & Ehsani, H. (2019). Anthropological Study of the Phenomenon of "Khunbas" in the Seydun Region of Khuzestan. *Islam and Social Studies, 1*(21), 140–169. doi:10.22081/JISS.2018.66171

Laing, J. & Frost, W. (Eds.). (2017). Rituals and Traditional Events in the Modern World. Routledge.

Laub, J. H., & Frisch, N. E. (2016). Translational criminology: A new path forward. In *Advancing Criminology and Criminal Justice Policy* (1st ed.). Routledge. doi:10.4324/9781315737874

Maghsoodi, M. (2018). Assessment of Iranian Collective Identity, Emphasizing Social Solidarity. *National Studies Quarterly., 19*(75), 23–46. 20.1001.1.1735059.1397.19.75.2.5

Mo'in, M. (2002). *Mo'in Persian Encyclopedic Dictionary* (19th ed.). Amirkabir Publisher.

Moran, F. (2017). Restorative Justice: A Look at Victim Offender Mediation Programs. *21st Century Social Justice, 4*(1), 1–5. https://fordham.bepress.com/swjournal/vol4/iss1/4

Nadjafi Abrand Abadi, A. H. (2003). "Penal Mediation: A Manifestation of Restorative Justice" (Preface). In *Abbasi, M. New Horizon of Criminal Justice: Penal Mediation* (1st ed.). Daneshvar Publications.

Nozarpoor, A. (1991). The Mechanism of Social Control (Resolution as a Ritual) in Tribal Community of Arabs of Khuzestan. *Development of Education of Social Sciences, 8*, 44-51. http://ensani.ir/fa/article/213346/

O'Brien, M., & Yar, M. (2008). *Criminology: The Key Concepts*. Routledge.

Osanloo, A. (2012). When Blood Has Spilled: Gender, Honor, and Compensation in Iranian Criminal Sanctioning. *Political and Legal Anthropology Review*, *35*(2), 308–326. doi:10.1111/j.1555-2934.2012.01205.x

Osanloo, A. (2020). Forgiveness Work: Mercy, Law, and Victims' Rights in Iran. Princeton University Press.

Penner, H. H. (2016). Ritual. In *Encyclopedia Britannica*. https://www.britannica.com/topic/ritual

Rayejian Asli, M. (2021). Incorporating the United Nations Norms into Iranian Post-Revolution Criminal Policy: A Criminological-Victimological Approach. In H. Kury & S. Redo (Eds.), *Crime Prevention and Justice in 2030* (pp. 69–82). Springer Nature Switzerland. doi:10.1007/978-3-030-56227-4

Rayejian Asli, M., & Amrollahi Byouki, M. (2016). Forced Marriage in Islamic Countries: The Role of Violence in Family Relationships. In *Women and Children as Victims and Offenders: Background, Prevention, Reintegration* (pp. 729–753). Springer International Publishing Switzerland. doi:10.1007/978-3-319-08398-8_26

Rayejian Asli, M., & Daneshnejad, A. (2015). Informal Settlement of Criminal Conflicts without Police Intervention. *Journal of Research Police Sciences*, *17*(2), 83–100.

Rigoni, C. (2016). Restorative justice and mediation in penal matters. A stock-taking of legal issues, implementation strategies and outcomes in 36 European countries. *Restorative Justice*, *4*(2), 276–279. doi:10.1080/20504721.2016.1197539

Rush, G. E. (2003). *The Dictionary of Criminal Justice* (6th ed.). Dushkin/Mc-Graw-Hill.

Shoradad. (n.d.). https://shoradad.eadl.ir/

Tanha, A. (2021). The Economy of Crime. *Tejarat-e-Farda Magazine.*, *435*, 40–41.

Tavassoli, G. A. (1996). Urban Sociology. Payam-e-Noor University Press.

The Government Gazette. (2014, Apr. 23). *Criminal Procedure Code 2014*, no. 20135. https://dotic.ir/news/5584/

The Government Gazette. (2016, Jan. 27). *Dispute Resolution Councils Act 2015*, no. 20652. https://rrk.ir/Laws/ShowLaw.aspx?Code=9094

Towhidian, Y. (2018). Exploring Threatening Factors of Social Solidarity within Neighborhoods. *Urban Sociological Studies (Journal of Islamic Azad University, Dehaghan Branch), 8*(28), 165-188.

Warren, C. S. (2019). Islamic Criminal Law. *Oxford Bibliographies.* (https://www.oxfordbibliographies.com/view/document/obo-9780195390155/obo-9780195390155-0035.xml)

World Justice Project. (2013). *Customary Justice: Challenges, Innovations and the Role of the UN*. International Development Law Organization (IDLO). https://worldjusticeproject.org/news/customary-justice-challenges-innovations-and-role-un

YarAhmadi, Q. (2010). The Ritual of Resolution (*Fasl*) in Besri Village of Borujerd City. *Najvaa-ye Farhang, 14*, 57-60. https://www.magiran.com/paper/742430

Zakeri. (2021). Social Solidarity and Its Enemies. Nashr-e-Nay.

KEY TERMS AND DEFINITIONS

Criminal Justice System: It is a body of governmental agencies, organizations, and institutions (emphasizing upon police, prosecution services, courts, and corrections) that their aims are to respond past crimes and criminals by a series of criminal sanctions, including deterrent, incapacitative, rehabilitative, and restorative ones, as well as to prevent future crimes and criminals by a series of measures and mechanisms, and finally, to protect and support for victims of crime (Rush, 2003).

Dispute Resolution Council: It is a societal institution which acts through processes to help people for resolving their disputes without a legal action whether as a criminal or civil case. In some countries like Iran, Dispute Resolution Council (DRC) is a governmental organization under the authority of the Judiciary (Burton, 1990).

Domestic Customs and Traditions: These are certain ways of behaving or a series of actions that some ethnic groups or tribal communities regularly carry out or perform in a particular situation or context based on their own custom and or beliefs. Two major examples of such domestic customs and traditions that still exist in the Iranian society are cease-blood (*khoon-bass*) and resolution (*fasl*) (Laing and Frost, 2017).

Penal Mediation: It is a form of alternative dispute resolution outside the court that is in general applied in the settlement of civil disputes, but also in practice often applied in criminal cases by discretion of a judicial authority and referring to a mediator or conciliator (Rigoni, 2016).

Restorative Justice: It is an approach to and a model of justice that seeks to repair or restore harm or injury by seizing an opportunity for those who are suffered harmed or injured and those who take responsibility for the harm or injury, and by communicating about and address the needs, interests and rights of all actors of criminal occurrence, i.e., the victim, offender, and society (Dignan, 2005).

ENDNOTES

[1]   As seen later, these ethnic groups belong to a part of communities or populations with common cultural background or descent who usually live in some rural and urban areas of west and south of Iran and consist of the Kurds, the Lurs, and the Arabs.

[2]   The definition of Iran, Iranian people and culture particularly requires the understanding of its sociological features and variables including ethnic groups, languages, religion, settlement patterns and demographic trends (Britannica, n.d.). In terms of ethnicity, Iran is a culturally diverse society with the predominant ethnic and cultural group generally called as Persian. But, at the same time, Iran also consists of further ethnic groups such as Kurds, Baloch, Bakhtyārī, Lurs, and other smaller minorities e.g., Armenians and Assyrians. Due to the ethnic and cultural diversity, Iranian people speak a number of languages and dialects notwithstanding the recognition of Persian (*Farsi*) as the predominant and official language of this country. The vast majority of Iranians belongs to *Shi'a* branch of Islam as the official state religion. But other ethnic groups are the followers of *Sunni* Muslims, and a small part of the population consists of religious minorities of Christians, Jews, and Zoroastrians who are as the recognized religious minorities by the Constitution of Islamic Republic of Iran. In terms of settlement patterns, over three quarters of Iran's population is urban. But even so the rest population of rural, as discussed later, plays a key role in domestic reconciliation rituals.

[3]   In Persian literature, the word '*khoon*' means blood, and '*bass*' refers to cessation of bloodshed, and thus, to reach a peace deal.

[4]   It is obvious that if the offender's family does not have a female relative to offer, an alternate way such as compensation may be replaced.

[5]   Economic conditions as an operative cause of this type of reconciliation ritual may contribute to shift its manner. For example, exponential growth and rising prices (including in the rate of wergild/*diyaa* officially announced by the Judiciary every year) that Iran's economy has experienced specifically in recent years, may impact on such a shift to use alternatives (e.g., transfer of property or livestock) to this monetary sanction.

6   Besides *qoran*, the other primary sources of Islamic law include the *sunnah* (the traditions or known practices of the Prophet Muhammad), *ijma'* (consensus), and *qiyas* (analogy).

7   Such an influence could be found in both pre-revolutionary and post-revolutionary periods of Iranian law. According to Art. 262 of old Criminal Procedure Code (1912), "in matters that may lead to peace, the court shall make every effort to reconciliation between two parties (*islah-e-zaatolbein*) before the issuance of the verdict, and, if it does not succeed, the court shall rule". A similar provision was contained in Art. 195 of the Criminal Procedure Code 1999 that has been replaced by the provisions of the new Criminal Procedure Code 2014, as will be discussed later.

8   This provision is restricted to *ta'zir* crimes in which judges have a power in sentencing. Therefore, *hudud* and *qisas* crimes are not included in Art. 13-b of Iranian Criminal Procedure Code 2014.

Section 3

Indigenous Wisdom: India

Chapter 5
Restorative Justice and Therapeutic Jurisprudence:
Two Sides of the Same Coin

Beulah Shekhar
National Forensic Sciences University (NFSU), India

Ranjani Castro
iD https://orcid.org/0000-0002-7927-6354
Karunya Institute of Technology and Sciences, India

Hitesh Goyal
National Forensic Sciences University (NFSU), India

ABSTRACT

The research will conceive restorative justice and therapeutic jurisprudence as two sides of the same coin, and one is the result of the other as a major development in criminological thinking. Notwithstanding, roots in a variety of indigenous cultures, including spirituality and holistic healing traditions and strives to re-connect offenders with their surroundings and communities. The objective of this research is to explore the experiences of victims and offenders involved in restorative justice practices, concerning increase in their general well-being, self-esteem, and satisfaction of the process and decrease in their feeling of shame, guilt, stress, regret, and anger. Restorative justice mechanisms enhance therapeutic jurisprudence through restoration, resilience, reconciliation, reintegration, rehabilitation, reformation, and resocialization among victims and offenders. Another objective is to understand from practitioners whether restorative practices facilitate conflict resolution and discuss the alternate conflict resolution model for restorative justice and therapeutic jurisprudence.

DOI: 10.4018/978-1-6684-4112-1.ch005

INTRODUCTION

The authors conceive therapeutic jurisprudence emerging from the restorative justice practices, as a major development in criminological thinking, having roots in a variety of indigenous cultures, including spirituality and holistic healing traditions, that aims to re-connect offenders with their surroundings and communities. Restorative justice and therapeutic jurisprudence have been proposed as solutions to many of the issues confronting modern criminal justice. Despite citing indigenous legal systems as a source for current concepts of restorative justice and therapeutic jurisprudence, both the theory and practice of it have been developed substantially around the world in recent years. Therapeutic jurisprudence and restorative justice can be intimately tied to the formation of a disagreement or harmful behaviour, and competent emotion management is vital in the conflict resolution processes. Therapeutic jurisprudence investigates the impact of the law on the well-being including the emotional well-being of its people. It suggests legal reform based on behavioural science to reduce negative consequences and boost positive effects on wellbeing. Meanwhile, restorative justice addresses disrupting behaviour, whether related to legal action or not, which can cause not just physical but also emotional or psychological suffering that must be healed if the problem is to be fully remedied. The fundamental healing technique is a mediated contact between victim and offender in which each emotion can be addressed and comforted by addressing the events, their consequences, and what the offender can do to take responsibility for their wrongdoings or make apologies to the victims for their harms (King, 2008).

The development of restorative justice concept can be traced in the article written by Albert Eglash 'Beyond Restitution: Creative Restitution.' The idea of justice which he referred to is not new but was not practiced widely. Such provisions of justice have been noted in human history also. John Braithwaite has observed and mentioned in his studies that restorative justice has been the dominant model of criminal justice in most of the human histories across the world.

Restorative justice theory addressed the failures in the justice system and suggested adequate therapeutic jurisprudence in many cases. As mentioned by Bajpai (2002) in his article 'towards restorative justice' the theory of restorative justice is developing new ways of 'doing justice.'

Van Ness and strong (1997) have identified a few movements for developing restorative justice. These movements are the following:

1. There is a movement on informal justice also called as the informal justice movement majorly addresses that there should be informal procedures with a view to increasing access to and participation in the legal process. The intention of this movement is de-legalization concerning with minimizing

the stigmatization and coercion which are in existing practices in the criminal justice system. This will help in removal the stigma to the victims in criminal justice system.

2. A concept of restitution which was discovered in 1960s to response to a crime rediscovered. This movement also more focused on the victims. It addressed that there is need of maintaining the meeting of victim and offender which will sever the best interest of society. It has also addressed that offender shall bear the losses occurred to the victim due to his wrong-doing or act.

3. Another a big movement that may also classified as victim's right movement. This has addressed the right of the victim to participate in the legal process.

4. Later a movement developed to address the reconciliation/conferencing between the victim and offender. It has majorly addressed in two ways:

   I. Victim/offender Mediation: It has originated from the efforts of the Mennonite Central Committee; this process helps to address the problem by having a mediator along with the victim and offender. So that an alternate way can be developed to resolve the conflict.

   II. Family group conferencing movement in New Zealand: This was inspired from the Maori traditions in New Zealand.

The development of restorative justice in history is available in several different dimensions but the philosophy will be same to address the conflict in a peaceful manner. Keeping this in mind this chapter attempts to explore the ground report where victims and offenders are involved in restorative justice practices. And how restorative justice facilitates conflict resolution in India. The chapter also assesses the 7 R's model which is responsible for an effective restorative justice mechanism that helps in enhancing the therapeutic jurisprudence in India. The 7 R's model tends to key elements of restorative justice mechanisms such as restoration, resilience, rehabilitation, reintegration, reformation, reconciliation, and resocialization among victims and offenders. Based on the primary data collected from the experiences of victims and offenders involved in restorative justice practices, this chapter is also addressing the practitioner's point of view that how it helps in conflict resolution in India.

Zehr, 1997 mentioned the concept of restorative justice is healing the victims and suggests the right correction for the one who is wrong. Restorative justice is a form of the justice system based on the concept of reparation, which means an action that addresses repairing the damage caused by the crime. Marshall (1995) has defined restorative justice as a process of dealing with the victims and offenders. In this process majorly we need to focus on the settlement of the conflict that occurred by the crime and resolving the causes of the problem.

In other words, we can say restorative justice redefines the crime which considers the crime is not only the breaking laws perhaps crime is an injury or a wrong done to an innocent person or group of persons. This finds a different way to deal with the offenders through a mediation process which helps in resolving the conflict through dialogue and negotiations.-

RESTORATIVE JUSTICE AND THERAPEUTIC JURISPRUDENCE IN INDIA

Restorative Justice

The essential fundamental elements of restorative justice are forgiveness, acceptance of guilt, and confession of a mistake. Also, it has been added in terms of principles in the legal instruments of reformation of juvenile delinquencies in India such as the Juvenile Justice (Care & Protection) act. The essence of restorative justice also can be noticed in the process of delivering justice. In India's Criminal Justice System, which is a legacy of colonial times, there is almost no type of restorative justice. It has been observed that courts in the majority of countries support alternate methods of settling issues to avoid lengthy trials and to avoid the clutter of litigation.

Articles 41 and 51A of the Indian Constitution promote the use of restorative justice in terms of providing victim compensation. Clause 8 of the UN declaration of basic principles of justice for the victim of crime and abuse of power deals with the restitution of the victims of crime which directly reveals the essence of restorative justice. Based on the declaration provision of victim compensation and restitution lies an offender to bound a responsibility to recurred the losses of victim.

The essence of the essence of restorative practices in the criminal justice system of India is shown in Figure 1. Such procedures have been utilized since ancient times and are known as Panchayats which is recognized as a constitutional body and legally is known as arbitration. These derive from traditional indigenous village councils, literally assembly (yat) of five respected village elders (pancha). Similarly, Lok Adalat, meaning people's (lok) court (Adalat) was established can be considered as people's court where the disposal of matter pending in Panchayat occurs speedily and decisively in a binding decision. Also, the people get the chance to negotiate with their opponent party and justice comes through a peaceful settlement and mediation. The petitioners emerge to the Court in sorrow and anguish for justice and have faith in the Court because they believe that they will receive justice. However, in reality, the courts take a long time to decide cases, causing physical and psychological injury to both the parties, prompting them to seek alternative conflict resolution for a faster, less expensive, and less stressful resolution of disputes. Justice delayed is justice denied, and the cases should not be dismissed but rather decided.

The restorative justice and traditional way of delivering the justice in panchayats can expedite relief to the victim and stabilize all parties.

Figure 1. The Essence of Restorative Justice Practices in India's Criminal Justice System
Source: The Authors

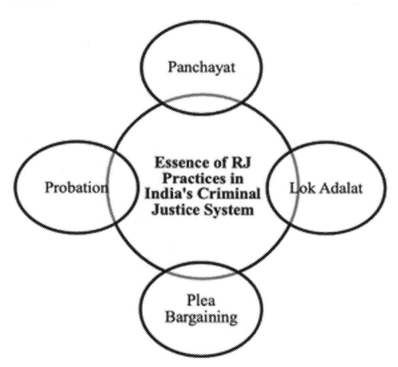

Alternate Conflict/Dispute Resolution (ADR) can aid victims in receiving prompt relief. The parties are more involved in the outcome and have more control over it, which leads to a sense of satisfaction among the parties. The approach used here is flexible and not as formal as the strict procedure used in ordinary cases. The goal of ADR is to create a solution that is agreeable to both parties, reconciliation between the victim and offender is also preserved through this approach. ADR entails negotiation, mediation, conciliation, Lok Adalat, and counseling.

Further, the concept of plea bargaining allows cases to be resolved without going to trial. The stakeholders resolve the matter and reach an agreement, and the judge approves the solution. It is a process of active bargaining. The development of restorative justice methods has the potential to remedy many problems in the current criminal justice system, such as long trials, dissatisfied victims, and communities, and so on. As the custodian of basic rights, the state is obligated to ensure prompt justice and avoid any delay that leads to a miscarriage of justice. Sticking to a lengthy criminal procedure and a protracted court process will never make the system faster. To address this, an alternative must be found. There is also a lack of victim-centered justice, and the alternative is to lessen victimization, and justice should be given at the time to the victim.

Therapeutic Jurisprudence

In India, therapeutic jurisprudence is used mostly in matrimonial courts and the field of family law, it is focused primarily on restorative justice theory. In a country with a population of around 1.3 billion people and widening inequality, the existing justice system, like its colonial underpinnings, is so apathetic to societal realities. Although mainstreaming therapeutic jurisprudence is not the most practical option, it must be implemented in domestic abuse and sexual harassment cases. With the upsurge of the #MeToo movement, redressal has become a pressing concern. With an unempathetic justice system, appropriate redress for survivors of sexual harassment and domestic violence appears unlikely. This prompts concern about the efficacy of Indian legal education and how restorative justice can be incorporated into the current system to promote empathy among law school students and the legal community in general (Charles, 2020). Therapeutic justice is widely used in many countries, including Australia, as well as in Drug Courts in the United States. According to various studies, mainstreaming therapeutic justice is an extremely costly endeavor that necessitates a massive number of resources and manpower. It addresses societal issues such as providing adequate redressal, reducing the burden on the courts, and providing healing to victims while rehabilitating those who have caused suffering.

The research study by the authors focused on the concept of restorative justice and therapeutic jurisprudence in India. This chapter has extensively reviewed the literature available on restorative justice which also is a form of therapeutic jurisprudence in India. The study promotes the instances of therapeutic jurisprudence use in several categories of cases such as correction of juvenile delinquency, victim compensation/restitution, and settings for restorative justice. The literature has found the indigenous justice system is active through panchayats and people's courts to deliver justice within the deadline. To address the RJ and TJ in the object of two sides of a coin primary data was collected from the six case studies, six in-depth interviews, and 12 questionnaires. The cases were actual and interviewed through in-depth interviews. Based on empirical data, the results have shown that restorative justice is a form of therapeutic justice. It can help in providing a therapeutic way to treat the suffering of one who suffered. This is the best way to deliver justice in a legal setting without any due delay and other mistakes.

THEORETICAL BACKGROUND AND PRACTICES

There is an ample amount of literature available on restorative justice practices in India and Abroad. But as it is advancing day by day based on victim and offender experiences. The experiences are a subjective reality, and it is a matter of individual experiences. This can be explained as follows:

Restorative Justice

The roots of restorative justice can be traced in a variety of distinct approaches in criminology and law that emerged during the 1960s and 1970s, and they provide a backdrop for the current growth of restorative justice as a social movement. Among these beginnings is the emergence of 'informal justice,' such as victim-offender mediation. Besides that, several intellectual traditions supported the development of restorative justice, including European critical abolitionism, religious traditions emphasizing reconciliation and healing, and those in North America, Australia, and New Zealand highlighting Indigenous cultural values and conflict resolution processes in post societies (Daly & Immarigeon, 1998). The theories of punishment are therapeutic, preventive, and corrective serve as the foundation for the concept of restorative justice.

Restorative justice is a notion that seeks to modify how crime is perceived and, as a result, how justice is administered. Most criminal justice systems regard crime as an offense against the state that must be punished by the state, with victims playing a little, if any, involvement in the process. Restorative justice is frequently presented as an alternative to retributive justice since it places the victim at the center of any process, rather than as a witness or spectator, as in a strictly punitive approach. Restorative justice views misbehavior in terms of relationship harms and seeks to rebuild relationships between people and communities: achieving justice entails healing and solving the wrongs (Zehr, 1997). The most apparent relationship harmed by an offense is that between victim and offender, but a restorative justice process seeks to repair all relationships harmed by wrongdoing. As a result, restorative procedures emphasize the role of communities as both victims and responders to crime (Robins, 2009).

A restorative practice is a method of dealing with conflict that fosters positive connections and generates or restores a feeling of community (Wachtel & McCold, 2004). Offenders are tasked with reflecting on the impact of their acts and behaviors in restorative interventions, and they must accept responsibility for such actions and behaviors. Restorative practices are not limited to the traditional criminal justice system. It is used in any case where an offensive activity has occurred (Wachtel & McCold, 2004). It aids in the development of individuals' problem-solving abilities, as well as the maintenance and restoration of relationships, without minimizing blame or dispensing punishment. Restorative approaches are founded on important questions such as, what happened? who has been harmed? how does one involve everyone who has been impacted in coming up with a solution?

Restorative justice has varied substantially in practice, both in terms of method and the amount to which key ideals and aims are satisfied. Restorative justice encompasses a variety of methods that may occur at various stages of the criminal justice process, such as pre-court diversion, collaborative processes with the court, including at the time of sentencing, and post-sentencing with prisoners (Shekhar B., 2021). Restorative justice can be seen in victim-offender mediation, family group and youth justice conferencing, restorative circle, family support programs, diversionary programs, victim impact panels, transitional programs, and community conferencing. Restorative justice claims can also be found in post-conflict and transitional justice situations like Truth and Reconciliation Commission for South Africa, Sierra Leone, and Sri Lanka (Ranjani, 2021). Furthermore, restorative justice approaches have been employed in a variety of settings other than criminal law, such as workplaces, schools, and child protection cases.

Restorative Practice Models

Victim-Offender Mediation (VOM)- It allows victims and offenders to meet with the assistance of a qualified mediator to discuss the crime and agree on the next measures toward justice (Van Ness & Strong, 2006). Family Group Conferencing (FGC)- It differs from VOMs in that they are facilitated rather than mediated, and attendees include victim and offender family members, as well as the investigating officer, psychologist, social worker, and other criminal justice officials (Batley & Dodd, 2005). Restorative Circle- It encourages discussion in a successive circular sitting configuration, this model emphasizes the worth and integrity of each member. Circles are a community-based decision-making process that is increasingly being employed in restorative programs (Van Ness & Strong, 2006). Alternative or Diversionary Programs- It seeks to redirect cases away from or give an alternative to some aspect of the criminal justice system. It obligates the offender to perform community service to make amends for the harm he or she has inflicted. Diversion is the process of diverting young offenders away from the legal systems and into formal reintegrative programs in which the young person accepts responsibility for the transgression. It provides young people with the opportunity to avoid a criminal record, as well as the stigma and brutalizing impacts of the criminal justice system (Bezuidenhout & Joubert, 2003). Victim-Impact Panels or In-Prison Seminars- Seminars are gatherings in which the victim and family members express the impact of the offense or crime on them (Van Ness & Strong, 2006). Transitional Programs- It offers aftercare programs aimed to reintegrate a young person into the community post imprisonment (Zehr, 2002). Family-Support Programs- It is specifically designed to assist offenders' families by enhancing their ability to keep young people in their homes (Fulcher, 2001). Elements of Encounter- It engages meeting between victims and offenders with the components of narrative (each presenting their account of the actual offense), expression of emotion, attaining understanding, and agreement- through negotiation and co-operation (Van Ness & Strong, 2006). Restorative or Community Conferencing- It is a structured conference with the offender, victim, and significant persons in both the offender's and victim's lives, which goes beyond victim-offender mediation. Offenders are told in person how their actions have affected people other than the victim.

Therapeutic Practice

Therapeutic jurisprudence is a legal approach that examines and evaluates legal rules, procedures, and processes through the lens of wellbeing. It contends that any legal change can have either therapeutic or anti-therapeutic effects. In other words, it can have a beneficial or bad impact on people's emotional and psychological well-being (Wexler, 2000). The supporters of therapeutic jurisprudence strive to make the law a beneficial social force that promotes well-being.

The approach originated in the United States. The term was coined in 1987. It originated as a novel perspective on mental health legislation, but support for therapeutic jurisprudence has increased dramatically since then, and it is currently being utilized in a wide range of legal sectors. The blog 'Therapeutic jurisprudence in the mainstream' provides a variety of foreign examples, ranging from non-adversarial resolution of civil issues to novel judicial procedures in criminal and family courtrooms. The Glasgow Drug Court in the United Kingdom is an excellent example of a therapeutic jurisprudence approach in action. It offers offenders an 18-month therapy and testing regimen to battle drug dependency, with a focus on long-term rehabilitation.

Therapeutic jurisprudence is particularly significant in legal practice in two aspects- the first method is concerned with how the legal profession employs and implements the law in their practice. The technique can be implemented in the practice of individual legal practitioners as well as across entire firms or organizations. For example, by seeking less combative methods of dealing with opponents, using empathy in client discussions, and collaborating with psychologists or other specialists to provide a holistic solution to client difficulties; the second way of therapeutic jurisprudence applies to legal practice is that it acknowledges that the law can have both therapeutic and anti-therapeutic impacts on legal actors, including legal practitioners. Thus, it throws a crucial spotlight on the well-being of those in the profession and fosters discussion and debate on this hitherto overlooked topic.

Therapeutic jurisprudence has a lot to offer individuals who want a legal system that recognizes and incorporates insights into wellbeing. There are also plans in the UK to establish a Centre for Therapeutic Jurisprudence to bring together academics, legal professionals, and others to investigate how to harness and develop this further. Apparently, in this era of political, legal, and regulatory transformation, there is a potential to confront legal culture's traditional conventions and recast the law as a therapeutic tool.

LITERATURE REVIEW

Swagata Raha in her research chapter *'Pathways and Possibilities for Restorative Justice in India's Juvenile Justice System'* explored the restorative justice concept in the correction of the juvenile justice system in India. Also, she has cited the practical approach through a case law *Tamil Nādu v. Union of India, AIR 2017 SC 2546*. It has emphasized the exploitation of children in orphanages in Tamil Nadu state. As she explained in her article the criminal justice system denotes 'crime is a violation of the law and the state whereas restorative justice considers crime is a violation of people and obligation. The Supreme court of India has given several therapeutic judgments in the cases of juveniles in conflict with the law. Also, the Honourable court has advised the lawyers to practice therapeutic and preventive lawyering (Supreme Court Committee on Juvenile Justice (2016)).

Jessica Traguetto & Tomas de Aquino Guimaraes (2019) in their research, *"Therapeutic Jurisprudence and Restorative Justice in the United States: The Process of Institutionalization and the Roles of Judges"* discussed that many countries' legal systems and judiciaries have been shifted and transformed to provide justice more efficiently and decisively. Some initiatives, such as Therapeutic Jurisprudence (TJ) and Restorative Justice, have attempted a less adversarial approach to resolving legal disputes (RJ). The focus of this research is to describe how institutionalized these movements are in the United States, as well as the roles that judges play in the development. Document analysis, court-hearing observation, and interviews with 13 judges from various judicial areas involved in TJ and RJ judicial proceedings in the

United States were used to collect data. The findings show that these movements are in the stages of enacting divergent change; judges who engage with these approaches act as organizational actors; and the judges consulted can be divided into four complementary roles in the promotion of TJ or RJ- promoter, author, convener, and maintainer (Traguetto & Guimaraes, 2019).

Michael S King (2008) in his article, *"Non-adversarial Justice and the Coroner's Court: A Proposed Therapeutic, Restorative, Problem-solving Model"* proposes a model for using therapeutic jurisprudence, restorative justice, mediation, and problem-solving in coroner's court to minimize the negative effects of coroner's court processes on the families of the victims and to promote a more holistic resolution of issues at hand, including the perseverance of the cause of death and the coroner's role in promoting health and safety of the victims (King, 2008).

Daniela Bolivar (2010) in her paper, *"Conceptualizing Victims 'Restoration' in Restorative Justice"* presents that how restorative justice literature has been defined and how restoration is measured trying to discover the hidden approaches adopted in both theory and research and analyze their repercussions and constraints for the development of restorative justice theory and practice (Bolivar, 2010). The analysis reveals that approaches widely in terms of how harm is defined and how the victim's role is conceived, as well as in terms of the aspects deemed most useful for restorative justice practices.

Dena M. Gromet (2012) in her article, *"Restoring the Victim: Emotional Reactions, Justice Beliefs, and Support for Reparation and Punishment"* argued that psychological effects to criminal misconduct have primarily concentrated on the perpetrator, specifically how and why offender punishment meets people's need for justice. However, restoring the victim provides another avenue for addressing the 'psychological itch' caused by injustice. The author discussed two theories of how crime victims can be restored- the belief that victim harm should be directly restored i.e., a restorative justice approach, or the belief that victim harm should be addressed through the punishment of the perpetrator i.e., a retributive justice approach (Gromet, 2012). These two lay theories are discussed in terms of their emotional and ideological underpinnings, as well as positional and severe factors that can influence whether people are willing to accept a restorative or punitive "justice mindset" when dealing with victim and crime oriented.

Dijk et al., (2020) in their paper, *"Victim-Offender Mediation and Reduced Reoffending: Gauging Self-Selection Bias"* compared reoffending rates among three categories of offenders: those who agreed to participate in mediation, those who are already willing to participate but whose counterparts' declined mediation, and those who were reluctant to participate. The data was collected from 1,275 samples. The findings confirmed that participation in mediation anticipates lower reoffending rates and implying that this effect also reduces the shame and guilt after the mediation among the participants than non-participants (Dijk, Zebel, Classen, & Nelen, 2020).

Tanya Rugge & Terri-Lynne Scott (2009) researched, *"Restorative Justice's Impact on Participants' Psychological and Physical Health"* claims that restorative justice processes satisfy both victims and offenders (Rugge & Scott, 2009). This study explores positive effects on participants' well-being and specifically examined the impact of restorative justice processes on victims' and offenders' psychological and physical well-being using specific health indicators. They used a quasi-experimental design to study changes in sense of wellbeing with 50 victims and 42 offenders who participated in a restorative justice process. The findings show that the majority of victims and offenders experienced increased levels of well-being, decreased levels of stress and regret from before to after intervention.

Josep Tamarit & Eulalia Luque (2016) in their research, *"Can Restorative Justice Satisfy Victims' Needs? Evaluation of the Catalan Victim-Offender Mediation Programme"* evaluates the program's ability to achieve restorative justice objectives from the perspective of victims' needs. The study confirmed the findings from other countries, emphasizing how the mediation process aids in the emotional recovery and self-esteem of the victims and offenders. The effect of low self-esteem for the offenders who served sentencing in prison and the victims who suffered from the crime have regained self-esteem after the intervention (Tamarit & Luque, 2016). The findings also illustrate the potential of restorative processes to provide victims with a better sense of fairness than the criminal justice proceedings in both the contexts of due process and therapeutic dimensions after analyzing the various factors involved.

Heather Kristian Strang (2002) in her book, *"Repair or Revenge: Victims and Restorative Justice"* used a quasi-experimental design to compare victims and offenders who received restorative justice to those who received contemporary justice. She discovered that those who engaged in conferencing were satisfied more than those who went through the contemporary justice process (Strang, 2002). This study also looked at emotional restoration and discovered that participants who went through the restorative approach were less angry and fearful post-process than they were before.

Tali Gal & Vered Shidlo-Hezroni (2011) in their article, *"Restorative Justice as Therapeutic Jurisprudence: The Case of Child Victims"* explores the concept of restorative justice as it relates to a therapeutic jurisprudence framework and concentrates on child victims in the criminal justice system (Gal & Shidlo-Hezroni, 2011). The vulnerability of young victims in the present criminal justice system and the concept of restorative justice, together with its core aspects, philosophy, and accommodating progressions, this article suggest various ways in which justice authorities could provide better therapeutic outcomes to child victims. The paper also highlights the significance of child participation in the judicial proceedings as an ideal therapeutic outcome that will enable children, family members, and societies.

George Mousourakis (2021) in his study, *"Restorative justice, criminal justice, and the community: fostering a collaborative approach to addressing conflict and crime"* supported that restorative justice is indeed a mode of understanding crime and steps for dealing with the issues that crime causes in modern societies. The basic principle of restorative justice is not the implementation of one process over another; it is the parenthood of any process that embodies restorative principles and seeks to achieve the restorative desired outcomes (Mousourakis, 2021). This paper describes the broad ideology of restorative justice, discusses the distinctions among restorative justice and other prevalent conceptualizations of justice, and helps to identify the constitutive elements required for restorative justice practices. The paper also observes restorative justice practices, providing information on key principles, practices, and objectives, as well as identifying some issues that must be addressed in the development and implementation of such approaches.

Patrick Bashizi Bashige Murhula & Aden Dejene Tolla (2021) in their research, *"The Effectiveness of Restorative Justice Practices on Victims of Crime: Evidence from South Africa"* states that restorative justice is a comprehensive philosophy that has gained attraction in criminal justice debates and criminological research. However, there is some discourse about whether its programs satisfactorily address the needs of victims. This paper examines the impact of restorative justice practices on crime victims. The results of this study, which are based on interviews with victims of crime and legal professionals in South Africa, assist the efficacy of a restorative justice approach that addresses victim satisfaction. Restorative justice allows victims' requirements to be more taken into an account during the criminal proceedings. This is in stark contrast to modern criminal justice, which has frequently effectively precluded victims from every aspect of its litigation despite significant reforms to encourage and safeguard victims' rights (Murhula & Tolla, 2021).

CONCEPTUAL INVESTIGATION

Restorative justice can be considered as a victim-centered approach that conceptualizes criminal behavior in a fundamentally different way than conventional theories of criminal justice. It has come to exhibit an increasingly strong influence over juvenile justice systems in recent years, as policymakers have become increasingly concerned about the traditional criminal justice system's ability to deliver participatory processes and fair outcomes that benefit victims, offenders, and society at large (O'Mahony & Doak, 2009). Although the victim-offender relationship is the most obvious relationship destroyed by an offense, a restorative justice process attempts to mend all relationships harmed by wrongdoing.

As a result, restorative procedures highlight the relevance of communities as both victims and responses to crime (Robins, 2009). The panchayat system participating in delivery of justice to petty cases to provide the immediate solution to such offences is an example given its village origins now in urban settings. The Restorative justice is a practice in which all parties involved in an injustice could debate the repercussions for individuals and decide what should be done to try to repair the injustices. It is based on three key concepts: harms and needs, obligations, and engagement (Zehr, 2002). Restorative justice is a response to crime that focuses on recovering victims' losses, holding criminals accountable for the harm they have caused, and fostering community harmony. To meet the requirements of these three groups, the criminal justice system must prioritize restoration, healing, responsibility, and prevention (Shekhar B., 2002). Restorative processes such as mediation models, child welfare conferencing models, community justice conferencing models, and circle models, have emerged in recent years, mostly in the context of criminal offenses, but their value in civil law conflicts should not be underestimated (McCold, 1999). Children's restorative circles concentrate upon concepts such as socio-emotional learning, anger management, accountability, self-awareness, and connections (Manoharan, 2021). The four Rs of restorative justice are reformation, resocialization, rehabilitation, and reconciliation (Shekhar B., 2020). Restorative justice is not something that can be bottled. It is a collection of ideas and practices that work together to create a plan for obtaining justice that includes all parties involved, including the perpetrator, victim, and community (Ranjani, 2021). Restorative justice practices in India, such as those of the Enfold Proactive Health Trust, aim to reduce gender-based violence and sexual abuse among children through education, awareness, rehabilitative assistance for child sexual abuse survivors, and restorative procedures with children in schools and the Juvenile Justice system. The organization works to build safe environments in which people of all genders are appreciated and treated equally, where every child is safe, and where people of all genders feel empowered and accountable (Manoharan, 2021).

Therapeutic jurisprudence refers to the court's approach of effecting and fostering healing for crime victims and offenders. It demonstrates how the legal system can have a large impact on people's psychological and physical well-being. Therapeutic jurisprudence was primarily concerned with the therapeutic or anti-therapeutic effects of the legal system on criminals, though it also acknowledged the possibility of having an effect on crime victims and the general public (Erez & Hartley, 2003). The purpose of therapeutic jurisprudence is to reduce the psychological trauma that crime victims experience as a result of the crime, as well as secondary victimization by the criminal justice system. Furthermore, therapeutic jurisprudence recognizes, emphasizes, and studies the possibility of both positive and negative repercussions for crime victims (Wexler, 2014). The three key procedures of therapeutic jurisprudence are apology, forgiveness, and reconciliation (Daicoff, 2013). These can be used to help crime victims or anyone else hurt by criminal behavior heal, as well as to heal the damage of crime on individuals, communities, or conflicting systems. While these may not always and successfully resolve the disagreement, they can help or promote conflict resolution.

The holistic worldview is a circle of justice that brings everyone together concerned in a problem or conflict on a continuum, with all eyes on the same point. Restorative and reparative procedures are used to resolve the problem. They place a higher value on healing frayed personal and societal relationships. The victim is the center of attention, and the goal is to restore and renew the victim's physical, emotional, mental, and spiritual health (Lord et al, 2015). It also includes the offender's conscious activities to regain dignity and trust, as well as restoration to a proper physiological, psychological, and spiritual status and even the restoration of personal and social harmony as prescribed by the therapeutic jurisprudence principle. Rather than punishing activities that result in a win-win situation, settlement is founded on truth-based concessions based on truth, justice, and fairness with societal peace as the most essential goal to achieve. Indigenous conflict resolution provides local solutions to local challenges, putting today's popular conflict resolution methodologies and conceptual frameworks to the trial. As a result, in today's conflict-ridden culture, it is more vital than ever to research indigenous conflict resolution practices and their positive effects on communal harmony (Tamang, 2015). Indigenous conflict resolution processes are always founded on the principle of restorative justice. Restorative justice's expanding role in dealing with transitional justice, international criminality, and egregious violation of human rights (Ranjani, 2021). Traditional dispute resolution, peace-making, talking circles, family or community meetings, and traditional mediation are all indigenous conflict resolution techniques that are defined only in the tribal community's language (Shekhar B., 2002).

Restorative Justice and Therapeutic Jurisprudence as two sides of the same coin. Justice and therapeutic jurisprudence both arose from an examination of modern criminal justice as an inhumane, ineffective process in which professionals impose their preferred outcomes on citizens rather than reaching more authority, sensitive, healing, and constructive conclusions through respectful, inclusive deliberation (Daicoff, 2000). Several characteristics are shared by restorative justice and therapeutic jurisprudence. They are both highly contentious concepts, and both combine socially constructed frameworks and methodologies that are constantly refined and rearticulated (Wexler, 2000). We know that the two sides of a coin are different, and yet they share a value. We can say logically that all restorative justice is consistent with therapeutic jurisprudence, and yet not all therapeutic jurisprudence is restorative justice because the therapeutic reformation of law and legal process includes other practices. Both disciplines have matured in recent years, with successive generations of thinkers identifying and addressing theoretical limitations and contradictions while attempting to build on early practices, overcome implementation barriers, and establish and evaluate new approaches (Jones & Kawalek, 2019).

Undoubtedly, both fields' practices are rapidly evolving. Restorative justice has evolved from small-scale victim-offender reconciliation programs in the United States and Canada, penal mediation in Europe, family group conferencing in New Zealand, specialized restorative services with a diverse range of practice options. The institutionalization of restorative and therapeutic practices has resulted in their dilution that both fields have faced significant challenges as advancements under their purview deviate significantly from their core principles and research evidence on best practices (Cooper, 2019). Their facilitators must consider not only how to persuade the criminal justice system to adopt these ideas, but also how to achieve a greater degree of participatory justice without losing essential preventative devices within existing processes (Christie, 2007). Restorative justice facilitators are increasingly adopting the language of restorative practices as a comprehensive philosophy and method for relational engagement with colleagues and citizens, both proactively and, as restorative justice theorists originally envisioned, in response to crime, injury, and dispute (O'Connell, 2019).

Therapeutic jurisprudence practitioners are also interested in expanding its array of uses. They use its basic theoretical foundation as combining the legal rules and procedures as well as the roles and behavior of legal actors to emphasize the connection between the therapeutic design of the law and the critical, yet more difficult to sustain component- the therapeutic judicial process. In other utterances, both disciplines are looking far beyond the institutionalization of their highly specialized and peripheral applications to the mass acceptance of their principles and processes in the criminal justice system (Wexler, 2015). Furthermore, it has focused on family courts and child welfare, schools, and institutional cultures in the case of restorative justice (Kierstead, 2012).

OBJECTIVES OF THE RESEARCH

- To explore the experiences of victim offenders involved in restorative justice practices to increase well-being, self-esteem, and satisfaction of the process; and decrease shame, guilt, stress, regret, and anger.
- To study if restorative justice mechanisms enhance therapeutic jurisprudence through 7R's i.e., restoration, resilience, rehabilitation, reintegration, reformation, reconciliation, and resocialization among victims and offenders.

- To understand from practitioners whether/how the restorative justice practices facilitate conflict resolution in India.

Research Design

A mixed-method research design considers the collection of both qualitative and quantitative methods in a single study in which the data is collected concurrently or progressively and incorporates the data integration at one or more stages within the research method (Creswell et al., 2003). Moreover, while mixed-method research considers borrowing components from both qualitative and quantitative research, the application of this strategy is frequently driven by the research question that must be answered. In other words, the goal of mixed methods research is to answer research questions using a combination of qualitative and quantitative procedures.

Research Methodology

The study is based on a mixed-method research design which included both qualitative and quantitative methods for data collection and analysis. The research combined three parts of collecting data by using a self-administered questionnaire, in-depth interviews, and case study methods. Further, the study utilized convenience sampling (opportunity sampling) for collecting qualitative data by using in-depth interviews and case studies. The snow-ball sampling (chain sampling) method is a non-probability sampling to collect quantitative data by using a self-administered questionnaire to measure the variables of victim offenders' well-being, self-esteem, satisfaction of the process, shame, guilt, stress, regret, and anger. These variables were used before and after the victim-offender mediation to measure the outcomes of restorative justice and therapeutic jurisprudence practices. The qualitative analysis of comprehensive case studies was experimented with, to study and understand therapeutic jurisprudence when enhanced through the use of restorative justice among victims and offenders. Moreover, the researchers conducted in-depth interviews with the restorative justice and therapeutic jurisprudence practitioners to understand whether or how the restorative justice practices facilitate conflict resolution in India.

Table 1. Methods adopted for Data Collection

S. No.	Method/Techniques adopted for Data Collection	Number of Samples	Research Design
1.	Case Studies	06	Qualitative
2.	In-depth Interview	06	Qualitative
3.	Questionnaire	24	Quantitative

A total Six cases studies and six in-depth interviews were conducted for collection of qualitative data for this study through convenience sampling technique. Followed by a total 24 samples given the data through the questionnaire technique.

Research Tool and Construction

The research utilized both quantitative and qualitative instruments for data collection. The self-administered questionnaire with subtle variables for quantitative data collection was taken before and after the victim-offender mediation followed by a discussion on the qualitative interviewing and case study.

TESTING THE QUESTIONNAIRE

The concept of reliability and validity can be used to assess the precision of measurements and the findings of a study. A researcher must determine the questionnaire's reliability and validity. The questionnaire is valid if it measures what it is supposed to measure, and it is reliable if the instrument is consistent and steady (Sekaran, 2003). Thus, having a reliable and valid questionnaire is essential for excellent research.

Content Validity

To ensure content validity, the questionnaire was distributed to restorative and therapeutic practitioners, criminologists, psychologists, victimologists, and research specialists. The primary reason was to determine whether the objectives were adequately covered and to focus on various perspectives. Appropriate changes were made based on the expert group's suggestions to create an ideal questionnaire. To achieve face and content validity, some questions have been added and a few have been omitted by the instructions provided.

Content Reliability

The Test-Retest method was used to determine the tool's reliability. The self-administered questionnaire was distributed before and after the mediation to the participants through convenient sampling. The responses gathered are assessed by using the test-retest method. It is the most common measure of reliability and the significance level of 0.05 is considered acceptable, indicating that the values are internally consistent and reliable.

Analysis of Data

IBM SPSS 28 software was used to analyze the obtained data. The variables are categorical, so the test-retest reliability method was used to determine the reliability, and Pearson's chi-square was used to analyze the relationship between variables. The last three objectives were qualitatively interpreted and produced as descriptive and case studies.

Limitations

There are always certain limitations available in every research. This also has some major limitations such as:

1. The researchers were time-bound so, the study was conducted in a short time. This research project was self-funded. So, the few samples only covered to address the issues and situation of restorative justice in India.
2. Due to a lack of time and budget the data a larger sample could not be obtained.
3. Access to data for the study was not easy due to confidentiality in the collection of data.

RESULTS AND DISCUSSION

Quantitative Analysis - Test-Retest reliability assesses the consistency of the results when the same test has been conducted with the same sample before and after the mediation process. Pearson Chi-square was used to test the hypothesis to know the relationship between variables.

Well-Being and Before and After Mediation

H0 – There is no significant relationship between well-being and before & after mediation.

Table 2.

Test-Retest	Pearson Correlation	Significance 2-tailed
Well-Being and Before & After Mediation	0.867	0.001

Table 3.

Pearson Chi-Square	Asymptotic Significance
Well-Being and Before & After Mediation	0.007

The Pearson Correlation analysis in table 2 shows that the p-value of 0.001 is less than 0.05 and the Pearson correlation value of 0.867 is greater than 0.07 is significant and reliable. The Pearson Chi-Square analysis in table 3 shows that the asymptotic significance of 0.007 is less than 0.05 is also significant. Thus, the null hypothesis is rejected which indicates that there is a significant relationship between well-being and before & after mediation.

The findings show that the victims and offenders are more concerned about their well-being after the mediation process. The process makes them aware of their physical, psychological, and emotional well-being. Similarly, Tanya Rugge & Terri-Lynne Scott (2009) in their study also support those victims' and offenders' well-being has increased after the mediation. The findings illustrate that there were positive changes in victims' and offenders' physical, psychological, and emotional well-being.

Self-Esteem and Before and After Mediation

H0 – There is no significant relationship between self-esteem and before & after mediation.

Table 4.

Test-Retest	Pearson Correlation	Significance 2-tailed
Self-esteem and Before & After Mediation	0.717	0.020

Table 5.

Pearson Chi-Square	Asymptotic Significance
Self-esteem and Before & After Mediation	0.045

The Pearson Correlation analysis in table 4 shows that the p-value of 0.020 is less than 0.05 and the Pearson correlation value of 0.717 is greater than 0.07 is significant and reliable. The Pearson Chi-Square analysis in table 5 shows that the asymptotic significance of 0.045 is less than 0.05 is also significant. Thus, the null hypothesis is rejected which indicates that there is a significant relationship between self-esteem and before & after mediation.

The findings show that participants have low self-esteem before mediation has been associated with feelings of shame. But after the mediation, the victims and offenders aid in emotional recovery, self-worth, and an increase in self-esteem. Similarly, Josep Tamarit & Eulalia Luque (2016) in their research illustrates the effect of low self-esteem for the offenders who served sentencing in prison and the victims who suffered from the crime have regained self-esteem after the intervention (Tamarit & Luque, 2016).

Stress and Before and After Mediation

H0 – There is no significant relationship between stress and before & after mediation

Table 6.

Test-Retest	Pearson Correlation	Significance 2-tailed
Stress and Before & After Mediation	0.816	0.026

Table 7.

Pearson Chi-Square	Asymptotic Significance
Stress and Before & After Mediation	0.197

The Pearson Correlation analysis in table 6 shows that the p-value of 0.026 is less than 0.05 and the Pearson correlation value of 0.816 is greater than 0.07 is significant and reliable. The Pearson Chi-Square analysis in table 6 shows that the asymptotic significance of 0.197 is less than 0.05 is not significant. Thus, the null hypothesis is accepted which indicates that there is no significant relationship between self-esteem and before & after mediation.

The findings show that victims and offenders have moderate positive changes after the mediation compared to before. Crime has created a great impact on both victims' and offenders' mental health because they are routinely marginalized and, victimized by the criminal justice process. However, Tanya Rugge & Terri-Lynne Scott (2009) studied that victims' and offenders' stress has been reduced after the mediation. Thus, the results in tables 6 and 7 don't support the study because stress, fear, helplessness, shame, trauma, guilt, and anger have been observed as early emotional reactions to violent crime which may be associated with a sense of vulnerability, disrupted safety, loss of trust, and lowered self-esteem.

Shame and Guilt and Before and After Mediation

H0 – There is no significant relationship between shame and guilt and before & after mediation.

Table 8.

Test-Retest	Pearson Correlation	Significance 2-tailed
Shame and Guilt and Before & After Mediation	0.732	0.016

Table 9.

Pearson Chi-Square	Asymptotic Significance
Shame and Guilt and Before & After Mediation	0.036

The Pearson Correlation analysis in table 8 shows that the p-value of 0.016 is less than 0.05 and the Pearson correlation value of 0.732 is greater than 0.07 is significant and reliable. The Pearson Chi-Square analysis in table 9 shows that the asymptotic significance of 0.036 is less than 0.05 is also significant. Thus, the null hypothesis is rejected which indicates that there is a significant relationship between shame and guilt and before & after mediation.

The results show that shame is felt when a people's bad behavior is contributed to an intrinsic and unalterable feature. Shameful people believe that there is no point in attending a mediation program to correct their actions, but the mediation has reduced the victims' and offenders' feelings of guilt and shame. As a result, they are open to mediation and optimistic about its potential impact. Similarly, Dijk et al., (2020) research findings confirmed that participation in mediation anticipates lower reoffending rates and implying that this effect also reduces the shame and guilt after the mediation among the participants than non-participants (Dijk, Zebel, Classen, & Nelen, 2020).

Regret and Before and After Mediation

H0 – There is no significant relationship between regret and before & after mediation.

Table 10.

Test-Retest	Pearson Correlation	Significance 2-tailed
Regret and Before & After Mediation	0.947	0.001

Table 11.

Pearson Chi-Square	Asymptotic Significance
Regret and Before & After Mediation	0.007

The Pearson Correlation analysis in table 10 shows that the p-value of 0.001 is less than 0.05 and the Pearson correlation value of 0.947 is greater than 0.07 is significant and reliable. The Pearson Chi-Square analysis in table 11 shows that the asymptotic significance of 0.007 is less than 0.05 is also significant. Thus, the null hypothesis is rejected which indicates that there is a significant relationship between regret and before & after mediation.

The findings show that an apology for regret from the offender associated with effective action can have a long-term positive impact on the victim. While an apology cannot because it is not the primary outcome of a crime, it is one of the factors that, as much as anything, provides some sense of peace to the victim. Tanya Rugge & Terri-Lynne Scott (2009) research findings show that the majority of victims and offenders experienced decreased levels of regret from before to after intervention.

Anger and Before and After Mediation

H0 – There is no significant relationship between anger and before & after mediation.

Table 12.

Test-Retest	Pearson Correlation	Significance 2-tailed
Anger and Before & After Mediation	0.802	0.005

Table 13.

Pearson Chi-Square	Asymptotic Significance
Anger and Before & After Mediation	0.011

The Pearson Correlation analysis in table 12 shows that the p-value of 0.005 is less than 0.05 and the Pearson correlation value of 0.802 is greater than 0.07 is significant and reliable. The Pearson Chi-Square analysis in table 13 shows that the asymptotic significance of 0.011 is less than 0.05 is also significant. Thus, the null hypothesis is rejected which indicates that there is a significant relationship between anger and before & after mediation.

The results show that massive positive effect on victims and offenders reported less anger and fear and more show empathy in victim-offender mediation. Heather Kristian Strang (2002) discovered that participants who went through the restorative approach were less angry and fearful postprocess than they were before.

Satisfaction of the Mediation Process Among Victims and Offenders

It is inferred from the above table 14 that satisfaction of the mediation process among victims and offenders are 2.80 and 2.40; the standard deviation of victims and offenders are 0.447 and 0.548. Thus, the satisfaction of the process is high among both victims and offenders. Victim-offender mediation profoundly recognizes the victims need to be engaged at all stages of the mediation. It is only equitable that the individual whose been treated unfairly receives an effective response for his or her needs. When the case is handled in the way that the victim prefers, the consequence of the dialogue is likely to be satisfactory to them as well. Heather Kristian Strang (2002) discovered that those who engaged in conferencing were satisfied more than those who went through the contemporary justice process.

Table 14.

Satisfaction of the Mediation Process	N	Mean	Standard Deviation
Victims	5	2.80	0.447
Offenders	5	2.40	0.548

Qualitative Analysis - The data collected by interviews and the case studies are illustrated below to understand the restorative justice mechanisms that enhance therapeutic jurisprudence and facilitate conflict resolution. Based on the interviews with the practitioners have claimed that restorative justice and therapeutic jurisprudence as two sides of the same coin, therefore, restorative practices enhance therapeutic jurisprudence through seven R's- restoration, resilience, rehabilitation, reintegration, reformation, reconciliation, and resocialization among victims and offenders.

Restorative Justice and Therapeutic Jurisprudence as Counterparts

Restoration - Restoration highlights the notion that crime causes damage associated with the experience of unfair treatment, disgrace, or embarrassment. The victim's humanity has been harmed, and his or her society has been transformed. Victims may have lost faith in society. Thus, restorative, and therapeutic techniques comprehend damage not only on a micro scale but also on a social level and restore aspects such as equality, due process, peace, and social integration. Shock, fear, anger, helplessness, disbelief, and guilt are common early reactions to overcome crime. Victims will need information, assistance, and aid in dealing with the consequences of crime; psychological help, practical support, and a support group for rehabilitation; the victim should feel relieved, aided, and able to return to normal life. The state must therefore take responsibility for providing protection, rights, and restoration to the victim if those rights are violated.

Resilience - Resiliency is a term that describes a person's tendency to remain balanced in the face of adversity. Victims of crime are likely to exhibit a variety of emotions, positive and negative coping, and strengths to keep moving forward. These victims may still require some assistance, but it should be focused on the criminal proceedings. Each victim has specific positive qualities that increase their resiliency. People deal with the issue of criminal victimization by implementing a variety of coping strategies, both positively and negatively. These strategies can either help or hinder them in their progress. It can be necessary to remind all who deal with victims that positive coping and resiliency are significant considerations in a victim's ability to be aware of what took place and keep moving forward. Even the most disturbed victim of crime can identify the potential core of strength. Victims can make sense of events that happened to them more quickly if that strength is nurtured and positive coping skills are developed.

Rehabilitation - Rehabilitation of criminals is the central process of assisting offenders in developing, transforming, and enabling them to move from the circumstances that led to their criminal behavior. The notion is to address each one of the main factors that contribute in addition to helping an offender live a crime-free existence after they have been freed from jail. One of the most difficult problems for offenders is being institutionalized or having spent so much time in incarceration that they are no longer understand how to survive outside. This forces some of them to re-offend in returning to jail. The following techniques to rehabilitate offenders are, hearing of victims' opinions in parole examinations to hear crime victims' views about offenders' parole; communication of victims' sentiments to probationers to communicate crime victims' sentiments to offenders on probation; victim notification system to notify crime victims about the treatment status of the offenders; and provide counseling to crime victims with advice and support (The Ministry of Justice, 2021).

Reintegration – Crime can also lead to stigmatization for both the victim and the offender. Thus, restorative justice encourages the reintegration of both the victim and the offender. The ultimate goal is for them to become intact, contributing community members. Victims are frequently stigmatized by their family, friends, and the community. It can often be due to the hopelessness felt during and after a crime. However, it might be since victims serve as unsettling prompts to everyone around them that crime can happen to anyone. People who would normally help victims seek to describe what occurred by blaming victims or wanting he/she will indeed 'let it go' out of fear. Reintegration is the phenomenon of a person returning to society after serving time behind bars. Imprisoned people can benefit from reintegration programs that help them receive employment training and seek jobs. When a victim or criminals can become active and productive members of their communities, they are said to be reintegrated. To provide it, victims and offenders must seek out communities that share the three components- respect and understanding of people in the community; equal responsibility to those in the community; and intolerance for deviant behavior by the community members.

Reformation – Diversionary strategies are used to help the offender to reform through personalized therapy. The reformation of the offender emphasizes the humanitarian principle to strengthen the offender's personality by counseling him in the proper direction. It holds that a serious penalty without addressing the offender's intuitions is harmful to the offender, the victim, and society as well. The ultimate goal and rationale of a detention order or other unlawful imprisonment are to safeguard the public against crime. This ideal can only be realized if the time spent in prison is used to ensure that the criminal is not only committed but also capable of leading a law-abiding and conscience life when he returns to society (Rule 58, United Nations Standard Minimum Rules for the Treatment of Prisoners). It is anticipated that labeling them as criminals will enhance their resentment and turn them into unrecoverable criminals as a treatment for the sickness of criminality. They can take the form of institutionalized and non-institutionalized measures like parole, probation, community work, house arrest, revocation, an apology to the victim, and court orders. It also proposes a total overhaul of the prison system, including the establishment of open prisons, recreation, education, and work opportunities.

Reconciliation – Victim-offender reconciliation engages the victim and the offender to talk about the crime and the consequences. The victim and the perpetrator commonly act on a plan with the help of a professionally trained mediator. The concept of making reconciliation is - the action of enabling two persons or groups to become cordial again after the reconciliation program; the process of determining how to make two opposing concepts, truths, or assertions exist or be simultaneously true; a situation in which two persons or groups of individuals rekindle their friendship; the process of bringing two opposed opinions, concepts, or situations together; and the re-establishment of cordial ties, reconciliation, or reunion is the process of bringing individuals together being friendly again, and reaching an agreement.

Resocialization – Resocialization is the method through which a person or a group is exposed to a different culture, requiring them to abandon their old culture and accept a new one. They must acquire the customs, beliefs, and ways of living in new surroundings that they are introduced to encounter during this process. The individual must abandon or unlearn their past values and, perhaps their personality to accept those particular to their surroundings. This is an intentional and rigorous process. The contrast between resocialization and the formative, lifelong process of socialization though is that it leads to a person's development, whilst the latter redirects it. People who have never been socialized from the beginning, such as seriously abused children, require resocialization. It's especially important for those who haven't had to behave socially for a long time, such as incarcerated inmates.

CASE STUDY

The case studies for this research discussion are a composite of typical factual situations for the purpose of addressing the forms of therapeutic jurisprudence in the cases of juvenile and mediation.

Victim-Offender Mediation - Creative Restitution, Restoration, and Rehabilitation

Kathir stole a piece of gold jewellery from a house in a small village in Kanyakumari, and it was discovered that the gold jewellery belonging to one of the houses had been stolen. Immediately, the leader of the hamlet asked all the village members to gather in a panchayat and insisted that whoever taken the gold had to return, therefore, the hamlet had given a chance to everyone that the people had to put a piece of a cow pat in the bucket so that the thief was also allowed to restore the crime by putting the ornament back. So, the offender hasn't been punished but had a chance of creative restitution. Through creative repatriation, rehabilitation, resocialization, and repentance, the relationship of trust is fostered between the victim and the village, resulting in the offender's willingness to return the ornament and realize his mistakes.

Alternative or Diversionary Programs - Reparation, Reformation, and Therapeutic

Ravi, a 15-year-old boy, caused a teenager's accident and a complaint was brought against him. According to the Indian Motor Vehicles Act, 1988, driving a vehicle and obtaining a license is not authorized until the age of eighteen. Ravi's rash driving and his unresponsive parents, who bought him a bike at this age, are to blame for the accident. Unfortunately, the adolescent was saved from danger but suffered serious injuries. Ravi's parents were teachers, then the board asked them to teach the juveniles at the Observational home. The Juvenile Justice Commission took up the matter and directed Ravi to visit the government hospital to witness the unexpected cases and their suffering. Ravi and his parents were instructed to look after the injured victim and compensate for his treatment costs. This approach made them understand their mistakes and allowed them to atone for their wrongdoings and heal their connection with the victim. Ravi and the victim became friends, and his parents began making pamphlets and raising awareness to prevent accidents.

Circle Sentencing - Restoration, Reintegration, and Resocialization

A 16-year-old boy named Jeevan was brought to a circle sentencing for a sexual offense. A 13year-old girl, Ganga was the victim. Social media platforms brought Jeevan and Ganga together. They arranged to meet in Ganga's area after several interactions on social media. Jeevan was charged with possessing carnal knowledge of a minor under the age of 16 and was sent to a restorative circle by the investigating officer. After the assault, Ganga requested expert help because she had endured a lot, including the loss of a best friend she had known for a long time. This acquaintance was also the closest friend of Jeevan. Through her counselor, Ganga indicated that she mourned the loss of this companionship every day. Following a meeting with both the parties, their families, and therapeutic experts, a circle conference date was set to mitigate the harm caused by social media commentary. This had become excruciatingly unpleasant, hateful, and harmful to both individuals and their families over the course of six months. During the preconference discussion, Jeevan and his father expressed their apprehension about meeting Ganga's father, saying, 'If that was my daughter, I'd be so angry and broken.' Jeevan and his parents, Ganga and her parents, counselors for each of the parties, a community spokesperson from a sexual offense support service, the investigating officer, and two facilitators were all present at the conference. During the circle, all participants were allowed to discuss their experiences with the offense, both directly and indirectly. A Victim Impact Statement was used by Ganga to explain her feelings to her counselor. Counselors and investigating officers examined the ramifications for the community as a whole. When Ganga's father spoke about how he had been affected, he became emotional and sobbed multiple times. Ganga's father further said,

'Our women and children need to be protected by men. The #MeToo movement is very common now, and we, as men, must lead the fight to safeguard our women.'

By being honest and frank about what he had committed, Jeevan accepted responsibility for his conduct. He said, *'Everything was my fault,'* in an attempt to alleviate Ganga's guilt and shame, which she had expressed in her testimony. *'There was nothing wrong with you.'* After that, he apologized to the victim. Ganga was the driving force behind the establishment of the agreement, stating that she needed to feel safe in her area. Jeevan agreed to remain out of her neighborhood, realizing that it was her home and that she had the right to feel comfortable there. He also promised to continue receiving rehabilitative counseling. There was a prolonged conversation among families about what the community as a whole could do to cope with the loss of Ganga's best friend. Then, Jeevan agreed to speak with their mutual friend and reaffirm that Ganga had done nothing wrong, as well as help their friendship to be restored. This would be extremely significant to Ganga and indicated,

'That communicating with the offender put her at peace.'

Family Group Conferencing - **Healing, Reconciliation**, and **Resocialization**

A 10-year-old boy named Ram from a remote town flung an object at the victim's head and threatened to have someone sexually abuse his sister. Ram was charged with common assault and issuing threats. These crimes were committed in a classroom setting, both the boys and their families knew each other. Before this occurrence, the two boys regarded their connection as best friends. Both boys' parents were interviewed extensively before the conference. The lack of friendship between families and boys was a major issue for parents. All participants wanted their relationships to be the same as they were before the offense. Ram originally understated his conduct, claiming that the threats were 'just a jest.' Both boys, their parents, as well as the school counselor and a Police Officer attended the conference.

During the conference, Ram's father gave a heart-touching talk on the traditional role of men, and the significance of respecting women, which brought some attendees to tears. Ram gained a greater understanding of the consequences of his actions as a result of the conference. He expressed regret to the victim and his parents. Both boys exchanged handshakes and pledged to be better friends. Ram hugged his mother and praised her for her support. The conference aided in the restoration of the damage caused by Ram's actions, as well as the promotion of healing and reconciliation. Both boys have become best friends and the two families' bond has been restored.

CONCLUSION AND RECOMMENDATIONS

The findings of the research addressed the gap in existing literature found. Most of the studies in Indian context related to restorative justice also have been appreciated by the judiciary of India. This approach can be taken as an initiative to provide therapeutic justice. For example, the contemporary adaptation of the village panchayat and lok adalat people's court are part of restorative justice system process. The data shows that people are benefiting from the indigenous understanding of community about the speedy justice delivery. Mediation has also been followed to address the restorative justice delivery system as a form of therapeutic justice. The findings also discussed about the treatment to the offenders in terms of providing restitution to the victim in several cases which makes the offender accountable for the victim's loss. It makes restorative justice and therapeutic justice the sides of the same coin.

The research shows that the victims and offenders increase their general well-being, self-esteem, and satisfaction with the process; and decrease their feeling of shame, guilt, stress, regret, and anger after the victim-offender mediation. A community orientation is required to address the importance of restorative justice system. Through the panchayat justice system it can be achieved. Its capacity to interact with victims and offenders in a potential yield, offers them some sort of reparation, healing, restoration, reconciliation, reintegration, resocialization, reformation, rehabilitation, and assist them in recovering from the consequences of crime is indeed very essential. According to various international studies and the same, this research shows that these techniques can provide victims and offenders with high levels of satisfaction about the process they go through and how they are treated as humans. The victims and offenders are also satisfied with the results of the programs, which normally seek to proactively address their needs, according to the study. Regarding offenders, these measures provide a process for holding them accountable. It requires offenders to accept responsibility for their actions and recognize the influence of their acts on others. It also provides an opportunity for offenders to atone and put things better. Restorative justice and therapeutic jurisprudence empower individuals who have already been adversely harmed by crime in numerous ways in conversely to more traditional criminal justice models that have been condemned for stigmatizing victims and even criminals.

Law enforcement, legislatures, and the public at large have all taken notice of the recent decision to disband the police departments and demands for criminal justice reform toward a more therapeutic approach. Stakeholders would have a constant involvement in the procedures, perhaps enhancing satisfaction and lowering recidivism. The research without a doubt supports that restorative justice and therapeutic jurisprudence as two sides of the same coin to address criminal justice reform and restore community cohesion, the criminal justice system must seek a suitable journey ahead that is fair to victims, offenders, and all the stakeholders. These practices contribute as an alternative to retributive justice to close those gaps between restorative justice, therapeutic jurisprudence, and indigenous wisdom.

Scope for Further Research

This study has opened the various scopes for further research in the domain of restorative justice. As the findings of the research are very interesting it can be conducted on a broader level to generalize the situation and develop a theory. Restorative Justice has not much developed in India due to its not continuous practice. Further research can address its challenges. Proper plans and funds can advance the situation of restorative justice in India based on community models such as the panchayat and lok adalat. The study also directs the young researchers to think about the more practicing therapeutic jurisprudence in India and there is a need of aware the officials of the criminal justice system of therapeutic jurisprudence and restorative justice.

REFERENCES

Bajpai, G. S. (2002). Towards Restorative Justice. Development Without Disorders.

Batley, M., & Dodd, J. (2005). International Experiences and Trends. In Beyond Retribution: Prospects for Restorative Justice in South Africa. Pretoria: Monograph Series No 111.

Bezuidenhout, C., & Joubert, S. (2003). *Child and Youth Misbehavior in South Africa: A Holistic View*. Van Schaik.

Bolivar, D. (2010). Conceptualizing Victims 'Restoration' in Restorative Justice. *International Review of Victimology*, *17*(3), 237–265. doi:10.1177/0269758010017300301

Charles, C. (2020). Therapeutic jurisprudence in India and its scope in cases of domestic violence and sexual harassment. In *International Academic Conference on Access to Justice to End Violence*. UNODC & TISS.

Christie, N. (2007). *Limits to Pain: The Role of Punishment in Penal Policy*. Wipf and Stock Publication.

Cooper, C. (2019). Evaluating the Application of TJ Principles: Lessons from the Drug Court Experience. In *The Methodology and Practice of Therapeutic Jurisprudence*. Carolina Academic Press.

Creswell, J. W., Plano Clark, V. L., Gutman, L. M., & Hanson, E. W. (2003). Advanced Mixed Methods Research. In *Handbook of Mixed Methods in Social & Behavioral Research*. Sage Publications.

Daicoff, S. (2000). The Role of Therapeutic Jurisprudence within the Comprehensive Law Movement. In *Practicing Therapeutic Jurisprudence: Law as a Helping Profession*. Carolina Academic Press.

Daicoff, S. (2013). Apology, Forgiveness, Reconciliation & Therapeutic Jurisprudence. *Pepperdine Dispute Resolution Law Journal*, *13*(1), 131–180.

Daly, K., & Immarigeon, R. (1998). The Past, Present, and Future of Restorative Justice: Some Critical Reflections. *Contemporary Justice Review*, *1*(1).

Dijk, J. J., Zebel, S., Classen, J., & Nelen, H. (2020). Victim-Offender Mediation and Reduced Reoffending: Gauging Self-Selection Bias. *Crime and Delinquency*, *66*(6-7), 949–972. doi:10.1177/0011128719854348

Eglash, A. (1959). Creative restitution: Its roots in psychiatry, religion and law. *Brit. J. Delinq.*, *10*, 114.

Erez, E., & Hartley, C. C. (2003). Battered Immigrant Women and the Legal System: A Therapeutic Jurisprudence Perspective. *Western Criminology Review*, 155–169.

Fulcher, L. (2001). Cultural Wisdom: Lessons from Maori Wisdom. *Reclaiming Children and Youth*, *10*(3), 153–157.

Gal, T., & Shidlo-Hezroni, V. (2011). Restorative Justice as Therapeutic Jurisprudence: The Case of Child Victims. In *Therapeutic Jurisprudence and Victim Participation in Justice: International Perspectives*. Carolina Academic Press.

Gromet, D. M. (2012). Restoring the Victim: Emotional Reactions, Justice Beliefs, and Support for Reparation and Punishment. *Critical Criminology, 20*(1), 9–23. doi:10.100710612-011-9146-8

Jones, E., & Kawalek, A. (2019). Dissolving the Stiff Upper Lip: Opportunities and Challenges for the Mainstreaming of Therapeutic Jurisprudence in the United Kingdom. *International Journal of Law and Psychiatry, 63*, 76–84. doi:10.1016/j. ijlp.2018.06.007 PMID:29996972

Kierstead, S. (2012). Therapeutic Jurisprudence and Child Protection. *Comparative Research in Law & Political Economy*, 31-44.

King, M. S. (2008). Non-adversarial Justice and the Coroner's Court: A Proposed Therapeutic, Restorative, Problem-solving Model. *Journal of Law and Medicine, 16*(3), 442–457. PMID:19205307

King, M. S. (2008). Restorative Justice, Therapeutic Jurisprudence and the Rise of Emotionally Intelligent Justice. *Melbourne University Law Review, 32*(3).

Lord, V., Shekhar, B., & Stokes, T. (2015, March 4). *Juvenile Victim-Offender Restorative Justice Program: Process Evaluation.* Academy of Criminal Justice Sciences, American Society of Criminology.

Manoharan, A. (2021). *Handbook for Facilitation of Restorative Practices in Child Care Institutions.* Enfold Proactive Health Trust.

Marshall, T. F. (1999). *Restorative justice: An overview.* Home Office.

McCold, P. (1999). Restorative Justice: The state of the field 1999. *Building Strong Partnerships for Restorative Practices Conference.*

Mousourakis, G. (2021). Restorative justice, criminal justice, and the community: fostering a collaborative approach to addressing conflict and crime. *Acontinental de R Atura Jurídica, 2*(2), 88.

Murhula, P. B., & Tolla, A. D. (2021). The Effectiveness of Restorative Justice Practices on Victims of Crime: Evidence from South Africa. *International Journal for Crime, Justice and Social Democracy, 10*(1), 98–110.

O'Connell, T. (2019). The Best Is Yet to Come: Unlocking the True Potential of Restorative Practice. In Routledge International Handbook of Restorative Justice. Theo Gavrielides.

O'Mahony, D., & Doak, J. (2009). Restorative Justice and Youth Justice: Bringing Theory and Practice Closer Together in Europe. In *JReforming Juvenile Justice*. Springer. doi:10.1007/978-0-387-89295-5_10

Raha, S. (2019). Treatment of Children as Adults under India's Juvenile Justice (Care and Protection of Children) Act, 2015: A Retreat from International Human Rights Law. *International Journal of Children's Rights*, 27(4), 757–795. doi:10.1163/15718182-02704004

Ranjani, R. (2021). Victims in Post-Conflict Sri Lanka seeking Transitional Justice on the Road to Peace and Reconciliation. In B. Shekhar & S. P. Sahni (Eds.), *Victims of Crime and Victim Assistance - A Global Perspective*. Bloomsbury.

Robins, S. (2009). Restorative approaches to criminal justice in Africa - The case of Uganda. In *The theory and practice of criminal justice in Africa*. African Human Security Initiative.

Rugge, T., & Scott, T.-L. (2009). *Restorative Justice's Impact on Participants' Psychological and Physical Health*. Public Safety Canada.

Sekaran, U. (2003). *Research Methods for Business: A Skill Building Approach*. John Wiley & Sons.

Shekhar, B. (2002). Restorative Justice System - An Alternative to the Existing Retributive Justice System. *Social Defence*, 53(152), 56–74.

Shekhar, B. (2020). From the Frying Pan into the Fire? Victim Turned Offender. In B. Shekhar & S. P. Sahni (Eds.), *A Global Perspective of Victimology & Criminology – Yesterday, Today and Tomorrow*. Bloomsbury.

Shekhar, B. (2021, September 2). *Restorative Justice – A New Lens for Holistic Justice*. Dr. Harisingh Gour Central University.

Strang, H. K. (2002). *Repair or Revenge: Victims and Restorative Justice*. Clarendon Press.

Tamang, G. M. (2015). *Indigenous Methods of Conflict Resolution in Sikkim: A Study of Dzumsa*. Sikkim University.

Tamarit, J., & Luque, E. (2016). Can Restorative Justice Satisfy Victims' Needs? Evaluation of the Catalan Victim-Offender Mediation Programme. *Restorative Justice*, 4(1), 68–85. doi:10.1080/20504721.2015.1110887

The Ministry of Justice. (2021). Retrieved from https://www.moj.go.jp/ENGLISH/m_hisho06_00046.html

Traguetto, J., & Guimaraes, T. (2019). Therapeutic Jurisprudence and Restorative Justice in the United States: The Process of Institutionalization and the Roles of Judges. *International Journal of Offender Therapy and Comparative Criminology*, *63*(11), 1971–1989. doi:10.1177/0306624X19833528 PMID:30829089

Van Ness, D., & Strong, K. (2006). Restoring Justice (3rd ed.). Lexis Nexis Publishing.

Van Ness, D., & Strong, K. H. (2014). *Restoring justice: An introduction to restorative justice*. Routledge. doi:10.4324/9781315721330

Wachtel, T., & McCold, P. (2004). Building a Global Alliance for Restorative Practices and Family Empowerment. In *The IIRP's Fifth International Conference on Conferencing, Circles, and Other Restorative Practices*. International Institute for Restorative Practices.

Wexler, D. B. (2000). Therapeutic Jurisprudence: An Overview. *Thomas M. Cooley Law Review*, *17*, 125–134.

Wexler, D. B. (2012). New Wine in New Bottles: The Need to Sketch a Therapeutic Jurisprudence 'Code' of Proposed Criminal Processes and Practices. SSRN *Electronic Journal, 14*(7). doi:10.2139/ssrn.2065454

Wexler, D. B. (2014). Two Decades of Therapeutic Jurisprudence. *Touro Law Review*, 1–14.

Wexler, D. B. (2015). Moving Forward on Mainstreaming Therapeutic Jurisprudence: An Ongoing Process to Facilitate the Therapeutic Design and Application of the Law. In Therapeutic Jurisprudence: New Zealand Perspectives. Warren Brookbanks.

Zehr, H. (1997). *Restorative Justice: When Justice and Healing Go Together*. Track Two.

Zehr, H. (2002). *The little book of restorative justice*. Good Books.

Zehr, H. (2015). *The little book of restorative justice: Revised and updated*. Simon and Schuster.

Chapter 6

Looking at Community–Based ADRS in India Through a Restorative Justice Perspective

Swikar Lama

Sardar Patel University of Police, Security, and Criminal Justice, Jodhpur, India

ABSTRACT

Restorative justice is a type of alternative dispute resolution, but not all ADR (Alternative Dispute Resolution) procedures constitute restorative justice. This chapter examines community-based alternative dispute resolution systems, attempting to distinguish the similarities and differences between ADRS (Alternative Dispute Resolution Systems) and restorative justice procedures. It examines whether these community-based ADRs adhere to restorative justice principles such as victim empowerment, deliberate effort by those involved in decision-making to reduce stigmatization and punishment of the offender, emphasis on strengthening or repairing interpersonal relationships, and so on. It also looks into whether formal restorative justice processes could imbibe some of the good features of these community-based ADRs.

INTRODUCTION

There are a number of variations or types of justice like retributive justice, restorative justice, natural justice, distributive justice, etc. In criminal justice the two types of justice are retributive justice and restorative justice. After the offender's guilt has been confirmed, retributive justice is concerned with a reasonable response to the offence by imposing a just and proportionate penalty on the culprit. The criminal

DOI: 10.4018/978-1-6684-4112-1.ch006

is thought to have fully merited the sentence. The doctrine of retributive justice, or lex talionis (eye for an eye, tooth for a tooth), holds that the penalty should be commensurate to the crime; "life for life, wound for wound, stripe for stripe" (Tripp, 2001; p 197). Only fair and just punishment is the focus of retributive justice. The severity of the crime and the offender's purpose are used to determine the fairness of the sentence, but other variables such as caste, race, and age are not considered. Unjust punishments include chopping off an offender's hand for stealing a rupee or condemning someone to death for an accident or irresponsible behavior.

Restorative justice, on the other hand, is not focused on the philosophy of vengeance and punishment, but rather on healing the victim's harm and reintegrating the perpetrator into society. Restorative justice frequently brings the offender and victim together in order for them to gain a better understanding of how crime affects the victims.

In Part 3, this chapter offers the indigenous practices of Nyaya Panchayats (Justice Assembly) and the more recent Mahila Panchayats (Women's Assembly), as well as the Nari Samaj (Women's Society) as practices that provide an understanding of community necessary for reintegration of the offender into society, while at the same time revealing the distinction between those traditional practices and the imposed idea of restorative justice.

RESTORATIVE JUSTICE

Instead of focusing on the state, Restorative Justice views crime as an act against the individual or community. Restorative justice systems allow the offender to accept responsibility and accountability for their acts, and the victim has the chance to play an important role in the process. In the majority of cases, the wrongdoer/offender apologizes or compensates the victim.

Restorative justice is a broad word that refers to a growing social movement that seeks to codify peaceful measures to repair harm, resolve conflicts, and protect the rule of law and human rights (Cremini, 2007). In contrast to the Criminal Justice System, a restorative justice approach eliminates or reduces the involvement of the law, experts, and the government. In order to repair the harm and restore relationships, restorative justice actively involves victims, wrongdoers, and their communities. Restorative justice aims to create collaborative enterprises in order to restore reciprocal accountability for good responses to wrongdoing in our society. Restorative justice seeks to balance the needs of the victim, the perpetrator, and the community through processes that preserve each stakeholder's well-being and self-respect (Bazemore and Walgrave, 1999; Umbreit, 1995). Restorative justice also includes compensatory justice. Compensatory justice is a type of justice in which victims are fairly compensated for the harm they have suffered as a result of their wrongdoers' actions. A person's compensation should be proportional to the harm he or she has suffered.

The restorative justice movement has just lately gained traction.The founders of the Contemporary Justice Review wrote:

There still remain a considerable number of people involved in the administration of criminal justice, and many who teach about justice issues at the university level, for whom issues of restorative justice, and even the term itself, remain quite foreign. ~(Sullivan et al., 1998, p.8)

Today, most administrators and scholars in the field of criminal justice, at least in industrialized nations, are familiar with the word. Restorative justice is increasingly being used in a variety of situations, including schools, workplaces, corporations, and politics.

Many people are unfamiliar with the term "restorative justice," despite the fact that it has grown popular. The term 'restorative justice' does not appear to have a single, well-defined meaning, as it is employed in a variety of contexts. Restorative justice is a hotly debated topic. Restorative justice does not apply to all alternatives to traditional criminal justice. According to Johnstone and Van Ness(2007), a restorative justice process must include one or more of the following elements:

1.   There will be an independent or court-annexed in which victims, offenders, and anyone involved in the crime will discuss how the crime occurred, the harm it caused, and what should be done to repair the crime or resolve future disputes.
2.   The empowerment of crime victims will be emphasized.
3.   The parties participating in the decision-making process will make a concerted effort to reduce the stigmatization and punishment of the offender. They should concentrate their efforts on helping the offender acknowledge and rectify the harm they have caused, and eventually reintegrate them into society.
4.   Certain ideals, such as respect for others, the avoidance of aggression, and compulsion during interaction, will drive the process and its outcome.
5.   The victims' injuries and needs will be prioritized by the decision-makers or facilitators.
6.   There will be a focus on healing or improving interpersonal relationships.

Most restorative justice advocates and professionals agree that one or more of these elements should be included in the process. The participants and decision makers must decide which of these ingredients is the most important.

Traditional Criminal Justice System vs. Restorative Justice

Restorative justice is also concerned with the administration of justice. Restorative justice is based on a different basis than retributive justice in that it focuses on restoring peace and repairing harm, yet it is ultimately a form of justice. Although restorative justice is not a substitute for the criminal justice system, and is rarely adopted as a unified model, its idea and principles may be adopted by it in a hybrid form (Walgrave, 2013). Restorative justice, on the other hand, should be recognized as a theory and practice of justice in and of itself, with equal relevance but a different philosophy and scope than the Criminal Justice System. Victims who want to ask questions of criminals can do so through restorative justice, which allows them to acquire an answer through a meaningful discourse (Umbreit, Vos., & Coates,2006). Many people believe that restorative justice can help people heal by correcting the harm and engaging in meaningful discussion (Conners, 2003).

Restorative justice is a program that aims to bring victims, criminals, and the criminal justice system together in the most positive way possible. Restorative justice advocates claim that RJ is based on the following beliefs: victims should play a central role rather than being sidelined during the process, victims and offenders do not need to feel animosity toward one another, victims' primary need may not be revenge, and incarceration may not be the best way to reform a criminal. These concepts go counter to the assumptions that underpin the traditional justice system (Zehr,1995). Proponents of restorative justice argue that incorrect assumptions have led to growing public dissatisfaction with criminal justice systems around the world. One assumption is that offenders and victims are completely opposite to one another. Such an assumption is incorrect, and it could have a severe impact on the Criminal Justice System's operation. It may urge the system to seek punishment against perpetrators while victims may merely want an apology and an expression of regret for the crime. The reality that most perpetrators have been victims themselves, some as children, is generally forgotten. Many commonalities exist between the criminals and victims, which may aid in bringing them together. Because lawyers perform the role of opponents in the courts, traditional justice expects that their clients (victims and offenders) should have adversarial relationships as well. This attitude undervalues and dismisses the victims' and offenders' roles and demands. Restorative justice, on the other hand, focuses on finding ways for victims and offenders to work together in order to repair harm and avoid future crimes. The largest blunder of retributive justice is treating offenders as if they will never return to society, while in reality, the vast majority of them do (Dressler,1990). The hope is that they do not repeat their conduct and cause harm to society at that time. As a result, the system should also prioritize the offender's rehabilitation and reintegration. The high recidivism rates indicate that the necessary efforts are not being made.

When an offender is pressured or threatened with legal action, the criminal justice system often works. Restorative justice, on the other hand, only works when it is completely voluntary, as it is built on the principles of cooperation and empowerment (Latimer, Dowden & Muise, 2005). Another viewpoint is that restorative justice is not diametrically opposed to traditional justice, and that compensation and reintegrative shame should be considered forms of punishment as well (Daly, 2000).

Ideally, restorative justice should be voluntary for both the victim and the perpetrator as well as any community participant. When a transgression occurs, the victim may not be the only one who is terrified; the perpetrator may lack the courage to confront the victim, even if they accept responsibility for their acts. Despite the fact that people may be persuaded to participate in a restorative justice process, proponents of restorative justice believe that participation is always voluntary (Umbreit, Vos, & Coates, 2006; Daly,2002; Volpe & Strobl, 2005). While restorative justice theorists and practitioners may value restorative justice for its ability to promote forgiveness, victims are neither pressed nor asked by the state to forgive their offenders. The state requests, but does not compel, the parties to resolve their differences.

Importance of Restorative Justice

The restorative justice movement is a multifaceted global social movement whose major goal is to alter how modern societies understand and respond to crime and other types of anti-social behavior. Restorative justice can be utilized as an alternative or complement to the present criminal justice system, which is more punitive in nature. For example, hybrid models may begin with restorative justice processes and continue with it as long as the participants are benefiting from it or introduce it later at the stage where the practices are deciding on consequences. It is stated that by using community-based reparative justice, crime can be managed in a better manner, but it can also help both victims and offenders(Johnstone & Van Ness,2013). In order to reintegrate the offender, restore victims, and repair relationships, restorative justice enlists the help of family, friends, and practitioners. Victims of crime are given a larger involvement in the judicial process and have the opportunity to recuperate from the trauma they have experienced. Offenders, on the other hand, are more likely to recognize the seriousness of their crime and reintegrate into society. Economic capital spent on experts such as lawyers could be put to better use, such as preventing crime. Restorative justice has been shown in studies to promote victim satisfaction, social control, proper resource utilization, and establish new avenues for crime prevention (Koss, 2000).

Restorative Justice differs from other processes in that victims, offenders, and others affected by the incident meet face to face in a safe and supportive environment and participate actively in discussion and decision-making rather than remaining passive while criminal justice agencies make their decisions. Rehabilitation (changing the offender's attitude), deterrence (it is difficult for offenders to meet with their victims as well as their own friends and families), restitution for victims, reducing the victims' fear, and helping them understand the offender's side of the story are some of the benefits of restorative justice (Bazemore,1998).

Community and Restorative Justice

Most proponents of restorative justice believe that the community has a role to play in the process. The community is also important in restorative justice since the offender must eventually be accepted as a part of the community. However, there are differences in opinion about what constitutes a community and how to effectively engage and empower it. In restorative justice, for example, McCold (2004) warns about the consequences of an ill-defined community. He argues that a community justice model could define community as local hierarchical formations built along lines of power, domination, and authority.

Restorative justice processes can be community-based, which means they take place in the neighborhood where both the victims live or work. The fact that community-based restorative justice initiatives involve the entire community is the most significant element. It is inclusive in nature, treating both victims and perpetrators as members of the community. Anything that occurs within the community concerns the entire community. In contrast to retributive justice, which places the state at the center of the courtroom, restorative justice gives the community control over the process (Daly 2002).

Despite the fact that Bazemore (2005) suggests that restorative justice might be utilized to strengthen communities, there has been very little research on the relationship between community involvement and restorative justice processes. Problems may occur in inter-communal societies where meaningful interaction is impossible owing to differences in viewpoints. Restorative justice in the community may only be effective in a homogeneous community (Braithwaite, 2007). Restorative justice practices, including their implementation, must be evaluated to ensure that they do not instill a hierarchical structure and adhere to ideals that are shared by the entire community. It is critical to notice substantial sociocultural context discrepancies and disparities that may result in an oppressive atmosphere (Conners, 2003).

Restorative justice, in a larger sense, empowers the community by incorporating it in the decision-making process following a crime. When an occurrence has ramifications beyond the victim-offender conflict, community participation increases the likelihood that the remedy will benefit and repair the community as a whole. At the village level, and in urban adaptations, the Nyaya Panchayat, Mahila Panchayat and the Samaj in Darjeeling are examples of organic indigenous practices that resonate with restorative justice ideas and provide a clear understanding of constitutes community.

In practice there are also issues about community involvement, such as the possibility of community excesses such as vigilantism. Others have expressed concern about engaging and empowering the community in an unhealthy state. Involving a hierarchical, patriarchal culture may only reinforce or deepen patterns of abuse, according to First Nation women (a volunteer group) in Canada (Cayley, 1998). Others, however, have argued that if the community is properly engaged and empowered, restorative processes can lead to community and individual healing (Pranis 2001; Ross 1996). Carsten Erbe (2004) even goes so far as to say that restorative justice should remain a community-based movement, as opposed to institutions where decisions are made by professionals. He claims that having such a procedure handled by professionals would be contrary to the notion of restorative justice. The tension between a preference for a community facilitator known to the community or a professionally trained neutral one is often one that depends on whether the process is indigenous and organic, or mainstream and imposed.

The idea that the hurt inflicted by crime is the concern of the victim, offender, and their local community is one of the core principles of Restorative Justice. "The underlying concepts of restorative justice necessitate a fundamental shift in power in society in terms of who controls and owns crime – a move from the state to individual citizens and local communities" (Umbreit, 1994, p. 162). The settlement and prevention of crime necessitates a positive effort on the side of society as well as community responsibility. At the moment, such responsibility is evaded on two fronts: by the public in placing criminal problems solely in the hands of statutory agencies, and by the latter in believing that once a perpetrator has been found guilty and sentenced, that is the end of their responsibility (Marshall, 1992).

Ideally, this responsibility begins before a crime is committed. It is necessary to "communize" crime control policy. The majority of crimes are disputes inside a community between a perpetrator and a victim. The majority of violent crimes are committed by people who live in the same neighborhood. As a result, it is a problem that must be addressed by all members of the community, including members who are specialists rather than by specialists who are outsiders to the community as understood by the participants. (Bianchi, 1978, cited in Mackey, 1981, p. 52)

Another crucial part of restorative justice is the local community. The more crime and crime interventions are envisaged in terms of social conflict, the more interpersonal interactions will be prioritized in procedures. Reparation proceedings should increasingly incorporate the local community as part of socially integrative dispute resolution strategies. Existing social networks should be activated, and new ways to cope with deviant conduct should be encouraged. Decriminalization could be aided by active community participation: aberrant behavior becomes a social issue, and the causal and relational elements of delinquency are more clearly disclosed. (Messmer & Otto, p. 2-3, 1992)

Strong Restorative Justice programs are defined by a local community-controlled environment. Victim-offender reconciliation programs that have been most successful have responded to community needs and local culture; planning and implementation have remained local initiatives; and services have made use of or worked closely with local resources. (Mika, p. 564, 1992) It is possible that a lack of a sense of "community" is contributing to the difficulty of addressing crime on a local level. Criminal conflict is both a cause and a result of the deplorable conditions in our inner cities (Stark, 1987). If our experience with "community corrections" and "community policing" has taught us anything, it is evident that we must define more precisely what we mean by "community" or "communities," and how and why it or they would be involved. (Harris, 1989, p. 35)

The community in the holistic Restorative Justice paradigm cannot be defined *a priori* because it is determined by the nature of the conflict to which it is applied. According to Restorative Justice: "Concepts are directly applicable to injuries suffered in the course of ordinary life and routine dispute, and where the event is not characterized as a crime," (Peachey, 1992, p. 552). The community with standing in any given disagreement will be determined by a number of factors, including the severity of the harm, the relationship between the disputants, and the size of the aggregate. There are several levels of community, just as there are various levels of conflict. Each perpetrator and victim belong to a variety of communities and informal organizations, including family, friends, neighborhood and school groups, churches, and community organizations. We are all members of our "communities" at the local, municipal, metropolitan, state, federal, and societal levels. We are all, in the end, members of the human community.

Consider the following scenario: two young siblings are fighting. Given the likely extent of injury incurred, the community whose interests are at issue is restricted to the family. If there is a quarrel between married partners and the injury involves physical harm, the community with an interest is bound to expand to include, at the very least, other non-primary family members and associates. Similarly, more violent crimes should include a larger circle of family and the community members.

ALTERNATIVE DISPUTE RESOLUTION SYSTEMS (ADRS)

As discussed above, Alternative Dispute Resolution System (ADR) is an attempt to create a mechanism that can serve as a substitute for traditional forms of justice. In addition to criminal and civil courts, India has a number of alternative conflict resolution mechanisms. These alternative conflict resolution mechanisms assist the traditional criminal and civil courts to manage their caseloads, which are currently tens of thousands of cases. Rather than retributive justice, these processes encourage compromise, making amends through restitution, and other ideals that are consistent with restorative justice even when not fully involving the community and society.

Alternative dispute resolution (ADR) refers to a variety of methods for resolving disputes without resorting to formal litigation. The current ADR movement began in the 1970s in the United States, propelled by a desire to avoid the cost, delay, and adversarial character of litigation. Court reformers are attempting to promote its use in underdeveloped countries for these and other reasons. Some countries' interest in ADR derives from a desire to resurrect and reform traditional mediation methods. Today, ADR is divided into two primary types: court-administered choices and community-based conflict resolution mechanisms. Mediation/conciliation—the traditional method in which a neutral third party supports disputants in achieving a mutually acceptable solution—as well as early neutral evaluation, a summary jury trial, a mini-trial, and other procedures are all included in court-annexed ADR. Supporters believe that these strategies reduce litigation costs and time, boosting access to justice and lowering court backlog while also retaining vital social bonds between disputants. ADR in the community is frequently designed to be independent of a formal court system, which can be prejudiced, expensive, distant, or otherwise unavailable to a people. Traditional concepts of popular justice, which relied on elders, religious leaders, and other community figures to assist resolve conflict, are sometimes incorporated into new efforts. In the 1980s, India adopted lok adalat village-level people's courts, where professional mediators attempted to resolve common disputes that had previously been addressed by the panchayat, a council of village or caste elders.

Restorative Justice and Alternative Dispute Resolution Systems

While both restorative justice and alternative dispute resolution share the ideals of re-integrative shaming, reparation, and restitution, there are some distinctions. Restorative justice is a type of alternative dispute resolution, but not all ADR procedures constitute restorative justice (Omale, 2011). Alternative Dispute Resolution (ADR) and some indigenous or customary law may share some key restorative ideas with restorative justice, but not all ADR procedures do. According to Barton (2003), there are fundamental philosophical and ideological differences that are easily discernible in both practices because, within restorative justice programs, practitioners must choose between 'the surface approach' and 'the deep approach' to how restorative justice processes and meetings should be conducted. The 'surface approach' is defined by a focus on establishing concrete agreements and certain fairly specified material results, such as restitution and compensation to victims, keeping the matter out of court, and avoiding a criminal conviction and prison sentence for the offender. These are principles shared by both restorative justice and ADR mechanisms. However, while the aforementioned outcomes and purposes are significant, they do not exhaust, let alone do justice, to the concept of restorative justice, reconciliation, and mending the wounds of crime (Barton, 2003). As a result, competent restorative justice practice goes beyond the 'surface approach,' beyond the types of material externalities outlined before. In its best practice, it should use the "deep approach" when available. For example, this might include the use of symbolic ceremonies. Because the major goal and objective of restorative justice is to bring closure and healing to the impacts of crime, particularly the emotional harm, disconnectedness, and social isolation suffered by those who have been most severely impacted by the wrongdoing.

South Asia is no stranger to practices based on restorative justice concepts and principles. Panchayat in India, Salish in Bangladesh, and melmilap in Nepal are examples of community based ADRS that date back to the pre-colonial era (Asadullah et al., 2021). In India, customary law plays an essential part in dispute settlement and, and its procedural structure adheres to the notion of community-centric justice. The Indian Constitution, in Article 13(3), recognizes customs as a source of law. The tribes of the Garo Hills, for example, hold the entire community responsible for an offence rather than stigmatizing and blaming a single person.

ADRS process is essential for introducing the reparation process of a restorative justice system into the mainstream court system, but the extent to which such bodies or agencies would achieve the anticipated purpose in enacting the restorative justice system is also subject to periodic inquiries and reviews. The underlying possessive character of such operating agents in capturing such power-steering in the guise of rendering restorative process within such local community would be to take control of it, which could negatively affect the noble pursuits of justice and harmonious order in such restorative process once again (Ghosh, 2014).

Examining Various Forms of ADRS in India Through the Lens of Restorative Justice

Nyaya Panchayats

The Constitutional support for local justice administration led to efforts by the Law Commission in 1986 to begin efforts to organize village Nyaya Panchayat in such a way these could be annexed to mainstream court logistical, and justice needs (Thilagaraj, 2017).

In India, Nyaya Panchayats have existed since ancient times and played very important role in dispute resolution in villages. The Nyaya Panchayat, that means justice (nyaya) assembly (yat) of five respected village elders (pancha) is a traditional community judicial body in India, mediates disagreements and prevents them from growing into major issues. The principle underlying Panchayat is "Panch Parmeshwar" which means God speaking through five. In India, Nyaya Panchayat is a type of ADRS that takes place at the village level (Meschievit & Galanter, 1982). The members of the Nyaya Panchayat are elected by the residents of the community or village. Nyaya Panchayats operate under the principles of natural justice and have relatively simple procedures. Civil and minor criminal cases are handled by them. For example, prison sentences are not permitted. The amount of fines are limited, and certain crimes and civil actions are not in its jurisdiction. There are also provisions for transferring cases to and from the Nyaya Panchayat and the courts, and also to the court from the Nyaya Panchayat. If the Nyaya Panchayat has no jurisdiction due to amount exceeding its limit or any reason, the case should be tried by the court (Chakroborty, 2021).

Family problems are frequently handled to a local panchayat in rural areas. Panchayat is a village court made up of well-respected members of the community. The panchayat is a kind of community-based Alternative Dispute Resolution (ADR). According to Natarajan (2005, p. 91), "[s]uch informal justice is tailored to match the requirements of villagers and is regarded inexpensive, immediate, accessible, and reliable."

Although the community accepts the decisions, either willingly or out of fear, members frequently advise women to modify to avoid ostracism from others(Moore,1993). In a conservative society like India, where women often experience discrimination due to role expectations, they face social and cultural obstacles, making it more difficult for them to find justice through men-controlled processes (formal or informal).

Panchayats used extrajudicial power in the past. Post -colonial reforms in law and policy were intended to restore some of the benefits of these process. This platform, however, is under decline, with major ramifications for Indian communities. India's democratization, economic development, and urbanization have all had an impact on panchayats. The panchayat, which has been the traditional institution of community justice and has served to perpetuate the caste system, is losing its ability to settle conflicts as a result of the inter-caste and interpersonal confrontations that democratic forces have unleashed. However, caste prejudices and biases can be seen in the official justice system as well.

There is a great deal of ambiguity about the manner of dispute resolution, the process of dispute resolution, and the dispute resolution bench. For example, Clause 3 (4) of the Nyaya Panchayat Bill, 2006 states, "The Nyaya Panchayat Pramukh shall appoint two Panches by rotation from the Nyaya Panchayat to sit with him to determine all aspects of the disputes or the controversy," and Clause 3(5) states, "The Nyaya Panchayat shall have the powers to co-opt two persons from the names suggested by the parties to the dispute or controversy and they

Some states created NPs to combine the benefits of formal legal institutions such as due process, standard law, and procedures with the benefits of informal traditional institutions such as easy access, flexibility, low cost, and a friendly atmosphere. Nyaya Panchayats (T) have three different roles and goals: to function as a branch of the state judiciary, a community program, and finally, an adapted form of the village panchayat. The village leaders' talent and knowledge were to be channeled through new elective bodies. Furthermore, NP was to function as a familiar, easy-to-access body both figuratively and literally and would adopt most of the features of village panchayats to bolster this role.

In reality, victims do not always receive the justice they deserve after approaching the panchayat. Dominant castes govern the majority of these panchayats. For example, women aren't even invited to the hearing/meeting, so they can't expect to get justice. A simple thumbprint or signature suffices as confirmation of her presence (Moore, 1993). Panchayats encourage members to settle domestic violence matters at the family level, seeing it as a private problem. Members discourage Domestic Violence victims from filing formal complaints with the Panchayats. Compromises reached through an informal or non-formal process are the most common way for cases to be resolved. Domestic violence cases are never reported to the Panchayats unless they are referred to the police or the courts. Domestic violence agreements are often broken, and the Nyaya Panchayats are powerless to enforce them.

Nyaya Panchayats are consistent with restorative justice's qualities and methods to some extent. There is an informal or semi-formal procedure that involves victims, offenders, and others involved in the crime in a discussion about how the crime occurred, the harm it caused, and what should be done to repair the crime or mediate future conflict. Victims are empowered to a degree, although this is largely dependent on caste and group dynamics. People participating in decision-making make no attempt to reduce the stigmatization of the offender. They should concentrate their efforts on helping the offender acknowledge and rectify the harm they have caused, and eventually reintegrate them into society. Although some emphasis may be placed on improving or restoring interpersonal ties, the complainant will frequently be forced to compromise with the transgressor. One remedy is that according to Chapter VI, the order of a Nyaya Panchayat may be "revised" in the absence of jurisdiction or in the case of material irregularity, with a remand from the Judicial Magistrate with instructions to the Nyaya Panchayat or even to be tried by the Magistrate. However, the remedy might not be practical since parties are not permitted legal counsel in the nyaya panchayat, and often are of limited means.

Mahila Panchayats

Mahila Panchayats are a type of women courts. Most women courts are run by NGOs, often with financial support from foreign donor agencies or, in some cases, from governmental or semi-governmental agencies such as State Women's Commissions or Legal Aid Societies. Their decisions are not recognized by the judicial system of the state (Vatuk, 2013).

Mahila means "woman", so these are women's assembly. Mahila Panchayats provide crisis intervention and legal assistance on a local level, and deal with community-level legal problems, as well as assisting in the prevention of violence against women and family conciliation. It is an initiative taken up for legal empowerment of women and for distress redressal at the community level. Groups of community women, identified by NGOs, form a panchayat in their area, take up local disputes, counsel the two parties and assist them in reducing violence in their locality. There are two para-legal workers in a panchayat. These women are selected from the community, are trained in the different laws pertaining to women and guided in the process of handling a case and counselling women in distress.

Looking at Delhi as an example, various Non-Governmental Organizations in the National Capital Region presented their approaches and ideas for assisting women in asserting their legal rights. The Committee overwhelmingly agreed and adopted the model given by Action India, a Non-Governmental Organization. The Delhi Commission for Women backed the creation of Mahila Panchayats. Mahila Panchayats are a new cooperative approach to community conflict resolution that is gaining traction. Leaders are chosen after consultations with the community's women, and these women are then invited to volunteer as Mahila Panchayat members. The Mahila Panchayat members are trained in laws relating to crimes against women, conflict resolution mechanisms, and current legal status in regard to custody, property, maintenance, marriage, and other issues, as well as counselling, First Information Report writing, police station procedures, and legal procedures. Following their training and orientation, Mahila Panchayat members are capable of dealing with any sensitive family or women's issue. They make an effort to approach problems on a local level with the help of community workers. Lawyers are also affiliated with Mahila Panchayats, and issues that cannot be addressed at the Mahila Panchayat are either handled by lawyers or other options are selected after consultation with leading Non-Governmental Organizations, legal experts, and the Delhi Commission for Women which includes sending the matter to formal courts.

All of the Non-Governmental Organizations that have created Mahila Panchayats have taken on the responsibility of educating the surrounding community about the law. The Mahila Panchayats select community members to participate in these legal awareness programs. The majority of conflicts and lawsuits involving bigamy, maintenance, domestic violence, alcoholism, and other issues are resolved at the community level by Mahila Panchayats. However, in certain circumstances, they needed the assistance of law enforcement to pressure men who were bothering or causing difficulties for women.

Mahila Panchayats are held at a communal location so that women who have been victims of violence have a regular forum to express their grievances. Both victims and perpetrators attend the meetings and air their grievances in a calm setting. Paralegals engage the community and discover people who can become active members in order to develop a mahila panchayat. When a party brings a subject to the panchayat's attention, the opposing party is notified to appear. The panchayat fosters and facilitates open communication between the two sides in order to reach a mutual accord. The compromise or settlement is written on letterhead paper and signed in the presence of witnesses.

Every resolved case is followed up on by the paralegals, as this step is critical to ensuring the protection of the victims and the family's serenity. The Mahila Panchayat members ensure that the compromise/settlement is upheld by visiting the family as often as necessary. The Mahila Panchayat is unique in that it harnesses the community's combined strength to empower women by encouraging them to make decisions. This institution's strength is social control. Both parties accept and follow the Mahila Panchayat's decisions because failing to do so would result in social marginalization and disgrace. Members of the Mahila Panchayat are usually vociferous and go to great lengths to prevent domestic abuse, including publicly shaming the perpetrator.

According to Lemons (2010), despite creating more democratic, woman-centered adjudication settings, panchayats reinscribe gendered norms that they openly seek to challenge through their politics of livability or compromise, which involves teaching women to live with and through patriarchal norms. She mentions that many victims of domestic violence are persuaded to return to their husbands/in-laws and advised to behave appropriately and maintain peace in the household. Mahila panchayat, on the other hand, gives the space and time that women require to discuss and work through their problems. In her dissertation on love and marriage in a Delhi basti, Shalini Grover uses Kandiyoti's term "bargaining with patriarchy" to describe the mahila panchayat's enforcement of domestic gender roles, including the subordination of women to their husbands, as women are asked to compromise and follow the sterotypical roles prescribed by a patriarchal society(Grover, 2009).

Despite their flaws, the Mahila Panchayats or women courts are entirely composed of women mediators who come from the same cultural and social background as the complainants/ victims. Hence, they share and understand the traditions within which solutions have to be designed. They aim to provide 'social justice' rather than 'legal justice'(Vatuk,2013).

Samaj

Samaj are "societies" found in the Darjeeling area in West Bengal.

Apart from the review-based literature on various community based ADRS mentioned above, the researcher has also conducted empirical study on Samaj which are community based ADRS in Darjeeling in West Bengal.

This study has been done using exploratory case studies. Case studies have been done through a Multi model approach of data collection by using semi-structured interviews and participant observation.

Convenient sampling was used in this study. Ten samajs from towns/villages of Kurseong, Darjeeling, Mirik and Kalimpong from West Bengal were selected. Victims of domestic violence have been taken for the study. Convenient sampling method was also used to select 20 samples (2 women complainants from each Samaj) who had approached the Samaj. Apart from victims, 10 transgressors/defendants (1 from each Samaj) and 10 Samaj members (1 from each Samaj) were also taken as samples for this study. The researcher also made observations of the sessions which took place in the Samaj.

Indian Nepalis corroborate to the idea of a speech community that is composed of both caste Hindus and Indo-Mongoloid groups. Caste system has been the historical basis of Nepali social structure. Since Nepali caste system in Darjeeling hills has been lax in nature compared to its Nepal counterpart (Munshi & Lama, 1978). It successfully accommodated the Indo-Mongoloid groups into its fold. Sanskritization had been at work in the hills ever since the mid-19th century. The Nepali community of the Darjeeling Hills is not as patriarchal as in the rest of India and Nepal (Bhadra & Shah, 2007). It is noticeable through clothing styles and gender relationships for instance. In Darjeeling town, young men and women spend time together (Allendorf, 2012). Darjeeling contains a mix of various castes and ethnic groups. The Tibeto-Burman groups (which forms a majority of the population), which are indigenous to the hills, customarily have more egalitarian gender relations (Morgan & Niraula 1995).

Darjeeling is generally characterized by greater gender equality than plains in India (Allendorf, 2009). Son preference is non-existent or rare in Darjeeling and according to the Census of 2011; the child sex ratio is 993 females per thousand males in Darjeeling District (excluding the plains which have different demographics and culture) which is much higher than the national average. The tradition of dowry has never existed in Darjeeling. Women share equal responsibilities in the Nepali society. Apart from earning or working women often take care of running the household and education of children. They are consulted on important matters like finance, education and marriage of children. Separation and remarriage are not uncommon in the society (Thapa, 1983). Women have a lot of liberty in the society as women's mobility and visit to natal homes are not restricted by their spouses or in-laws.

Equality of men and women, which is a yet a dream for the rest of India, is a striking reality in Darjeeling. (Mishra, 2000, p. 18)

The West Bengal government abolished the three-tier Panchayat system in Darjeeling after the Gorkhaland agitation in 1986 and the founding of the Darjeeling Gorkhaland Hill Council(Subba,1989). Samajs were founded in Darjeeling's numerous villages and towns, similar to Nyay Panchayats. The Samaj Members were elected or chosen members from the town's villages and neighborhoods. Separate Nari Samajs, made up of elected or chosen women from the hamlet, were formed in various villages and cities. In their particular villages or localities, the Samaj or Nari Samaj looks into issues of development and justice/dispute resolution.

When someone in the village wants to settle a disagreement, the Samaj members convene a meeting in which other villagers or community members are invited to attend or participate. Because Samaj members are nominated or elected by the entire village or locality, the Samaj has a lot of power in society. Local police outposts and stations frequently support the Samaj because they believe that domestic problems should be settled by Samaj itself, unless they have escalated to a serious problem. The fact that the Samaj represents the entire community or neighborhood gives it power. The number of Samaj members varies, but they often do not exceed five. Members of the Samaj tended to be the most educated and well-respected residents in the area. After a few years, the Samaj's membership frequently changes. When a person works as a Samaj member, it is viewed as a socially responsible deed. The Samaj members meet once a month to discuss developmental topics, but when disputes or problems arise, the Samaj members gather to settle the matter.

Looking at Samaj From the Perspective of Restorative Justice

After attending the sessions/sittings of the Samaj and interviewing the complainants, transgressors and Samaj members(mediators), analysis and evaluations on various aspects of restorative justice, such as empowerment, emotional rehabilitation, and interviews of the victims, the transgressors and the mediators, the following observations were made:

Empowerment of the Women Complainants

The Samaj lacked a well-defined and well-organized procedure. In the majority of cases, the women were requested to tell their stories in front of the transgressor and other members of the community. It did, in some situations, prevent some of the female complainants from fully opening up.

Though the Samaj members were generally supportive of the women complainants and allowed them to air their grievances, they were also domineering and proactive at times. The mediators often forced the complainants to accept the transgressor's apology and reconcile in order to keep the family together, especially in cases when the domestic abuse was not physical in nature. Family was given a lot of value by the family members, even though the complainant was unable to reconcile.

In certain situations, the complainants were also subjected to a great deal of negotiating, which is a patriarchal product. She was asked to adjust her behavior if her husband and in-laws complained that she was not doing her domestic duties properly or was disrespectful to her husband and in-laws.

The views of primary stakeholders, including other family members, were always at risk of being drowned out by the voices of other secondary stakeholders. Women who complain often reflect the views of their maternal family members. The complainant's parents were hostile and shouted at the transgressor in one of the situations. After repeated requests, the Samaj members had no choice but to ask them to leave the room for a while. It was frequently seen that the complainants' and transgressors' families and relatives interjected frequently, posing a barrier to the complainant's empowerment.

The majority of the complainants interviewed said they had the opportunity to interact with the Samaj members and the transgressor. During the mediation process, the majority of the complainants felt that the Samaj members were supportive and made them feel at ease. Because the complainants were familiar with the Samaj members in most cases, they did not feel threatened by them; however, because only a few of the Samaj's held separate sessions with the complainants, some of the complainants found it difficult to express themselves freely.

Emotional Repair

Because both the complainants and the Samaj members were familiar with each other and shared the same cultural and economic background, the Samaj members were able to understand the complainants' sentiments. The majority of the time, especially in the case of Nari Samaj members, the Samaj members grasped the context and position of the complainants. They were compassionate and offered the complainants comfort and emotional assistance. Even the complainants expressed their feelings without being formal or hesitant.

Even while the Samaj inquired about personal problems and listened to grievances in greater depth than the mediators at the mediation center, this did not guarantee that the Samaj would be able to adequately repair the emotional harm caused to the complainants. Despite the fact that the outpouring of emotions may have aided the complainants to some extent, no psychological counselling was provided to them.

The majority of the complainants believed that the members of the Samaj were sympathetic to their plight. Women Samaj members, in particular, were regarded to be particularly compassionate and empathetic by complainants. Only a few complainants felt emotionally better after the whole procedure since the Samaj members empathize with them and listened to their concerns and stories about their past violence.

The Samaj members were criticized by several of the complainants. They believed that the Samaj members were solely interested in settling the issue and that they did not care to learn about the complainants' injuries or make any effort to repair them.

The majority of Samaj members had no idea what constituted "domestic violence." Almost everyone in the Samaj had no idea that emotional abuse, verbal abuse, and other forms of abuse were considered domestic violence. The majority of Samaj members did not consider yelling or verbal abuse to be serious offences. They saw arguing as a regular part of married life.

They agreed that women require a great deal of emotional support since they recognize that most women do not complain unduly about their spouses. The majority of women in the Samaj believed they could relate to the complainants.

"Only if the situation is truly severe," one Samaj member added, "would a lady complain about her husband in public. When a lady marries, she comes to her new house with complete faith in her husband. When the husband betrays that trust by inflicting pain on the woman, it has a significant impact on her."

Re-Integrative Shaming

The need of making an apology was emphasized. The Samaj made certain that the injured party received an apology. The Samaj frequently overstepped its bounds, and in certain cases, members of the Samaj not only made the transgressor feel terrible, but even scolded the transgressor/husband. The transgressors had to face the brunt more when the Samaj members were women or when the session was led by the Nari Samaj. A Nari Samaj member said the transgressor was a "devil" at one of the meetings. Members of the Nari Samaj would sometimes chastise transgressors angrily.

Furthermore, because the procedure was not performed in a private way, the entire process was watched by neighbors and other members of the community. Though shaming the transgressor might aid in social control, the transgressor is sometimes verbally attacked by the complainant's family and relatives. This then went against the restorative justice principle, which emphasizes that both parties should treat each other with respect.

When a Samaj meeting was held in the village of the woman complaint, the people present were frequently angry and disapproving of the transgressor. They even threw insults at the transgressor in several cases. This went completely against the re-integrative shaming principle, which calls on the transgressor to recognize their error and repent of their actions. Some of the transgressors were subjected to public humiliation.

Because the Samaj members were well-known to the transgressor, re-integrative shaming appeared to be effective in the case of Samaj. On the other hand, because the sessions were held in front of other village members, including family and neighbors, when the Samaj members were harsh this had a humiliating effect in some situations. Sometimes the opposite could also be seen. Since, the transgressors knew the Samaj members in most situations, the Samaj members were not as harsh as the transgressors in some cases and even seemed to blame the complainant to produce a balanced effect and satisfy the transgressor.

On one occasion, when a woman was sexually mistreated by her husband, because he forced her to perform unnatural sex, the Samaj members were furious and severely reprimanded him. Furthermore, the women present began verbally attacking him and calling him a pervert. The husband appeared to be completely humiliated. This was the worst kind of stigmatization, not reintegrative shaming.

When asked if the Samaj had shamed the transgressors, the majority of the complainants agreed that the Samaj had done a good job of doing so. The complainants claimed that the mediators were harsh in their criticism of domestic violence, particularly in cases of physical abuse. The complainants believed that disclosing the transgressor's history of violence in front of the community would in some way shame the transgressor.

"The Samaj members chastised my husband and in-laws," Neeru stated. I'm relieved that they didn't pay attention to any of their excuses. When the Samaj members figured out who was telling the truth, they were quite embarrassed."

The complainants believed that when Samaj members knew the transgressors well or lived in the same neighborhood as them, they were less critical of them.

"Three members of the Samaj live in close proximity to my husband," Radha explained. "Their families have been friends for centuries. Why would they be so harsh with my husband and ruin their relationship? They were giving us advice as if it were my fault. I'm not pleased with the way they're handling my issue."

When the transgressors were asked if the mediation center had made them aware of their wrongdoings, the majority of them said yes. The transgressors were split on whether they thought the mediators were considerate or whether they felt humiliated or ashamed during the procedure. Some of the transgressors believed the Samaj members were harsh and humiliating them.

"The Samaj members were too critical of me," Raju said. "They don't get it. I had no choice but to resort to violence because I didn't have any other options. They were belittling me as if I had committed a heinous crime. Furthermore, it was carried out in the presence of the general public. It was a total embarrassment."

"The Samaj members were really judgmental," Kamal claimed. How can they just take my wife's word for it? In addition, my in-laws and their family were constantly abusing me. It was quite offensive, and the entire experience was unpleasant."

Problem-Solving and Inclusiveness

In many circumstances, sharing feelings and discussing conflict/violence and the harm caused by it turned out to be different. Both sides were respectful to each other in most circumstances, but Samaj members had to intervene in other cases to stop the blame game between the two parties. Because the members of the Samaj were not specifically trained in domestic violence issues, the meetings frequently turned heated because, rather than expressing sentiments of pain, hurt, and betrayal, the complainants became hostile and began accusing the transgressor. This outburst of rage and aggression elicited a retaliatory outburst of rage and counter-blaming from the transgressors.

In one case, the complainant's father became so enraged by the fact that his daughter had been tortured that he threatened to send his son-in-law and his family to prison. The majority of Samaj members were found to be lacking in their ability to direct emotions so that they might be channeled properly and produce more good outcomes. This could be due to their lack of understanding of the feelings that a victim of domestic violence goes through.

The members of the Samaj placed a high value on accountability. They made the transgressors aware of their errors and requested that they apologize but the Samaj Members did not make much effort in analyzing the sincerity of the apology.

The majority of complainants were pleased with the discussions that were held in order to find a solution to the situation. They believed that each party had been given ample opportunity to tell their stories and engage in meaningful dialogue with one another. Concerns about the Samaj's environment were divided among the complainants. Some found the process to be relaxing and conducive to problem solving, while others did not find it to be relaxing and found it to be stressful.

"There was so much noise during the process," Rita added. "The people out there were constantly having a conversation. Both parties were making quite a racket. People were yelling and squabbling with one another. Members of the Samaj had to step in and help. They had to scream at the top of their lungs just to be heard."

Accountability

The complainants were pleased with the Samaj members' efforts to persuade the transgressors to admit their conduct and apologize. When they were asked to apologize for being disrespectful to their in-laws or initiating the violence, some of the complainants were upset. Some of the complainants believed that the Samaj members' request for the transgressors to apologize to the complainants was merely a formality. Some of the victims were still unsure whether the transgressor's apologies were sincere and that he would not repeat the violence. "I am happy that the Samaj forced my husband to apologize to me," Neetu remarked. It means a lot to me that the community recognizes that he has offended me and that he is aware of it as well."

The majority of transgressors were also pleased with the problem discussions and efforts to find a solution. They also thought that they had been given ample opportunity to convey their narrative, and that the meetings had been held in a calm and pleasant environment. Many others believed that the Samaj had failed to preserve order and decorum throughout the procedure. The men/transgressors had a different perspective than the complainants. The majority of them objected to the Samaj's inclusion of all members of society, believing that it encompassed even those who were uninterested in the issue.

"People are shouting here like this is a fish market," Raju remarked. "Everyone is behaving as if they are attorneys. Members of the Samaj should be stricter and only allow people to speak in turn."

"The Samaj should only accept persons who are related to or know both parties," Kamal remarked. "There is a large crowd, and the most of them have come to see the drama. It is unnecessary for so many people to gather here to observe the procedures."

The perpetrators failed to see that domestic violence has an impact on the community, as does the disruption of family peace. Their discontent could be related to their embarrassment at having to confront a larger group of people.

Reparation of Relationships

The majority of complainants believed that the mediators placed a high value on the rehabilitation of relationships. They believed that the mediators had provided both the complainants and the transgressors counselling to help them realize the value of a family. They also believed that the mediators had given them sound advice on whether or not to give their spouses and in-laws another chance.

The members of the Samaj believed that family was extremely important. The majority of the mediators believed that every effort should be made to keep the family together. They believed that only cases of serious physical abuse, dowry, and extreme substance abuse, in which the women's safety would be jeopardized, should be resolved outside of criminal courts. "Fights between husband and wife are like a side dish in marriage," one Samaj member said. "It happens to every couple at some point. The only stipulation is that no physical violence be used. Finally, people must put their egos aside and reconcile for the sake of the family."

The Samaj members believed that in times of minor violence or verbal spats, both parties needed to recognize that relationships require more understanding between persons. The Samaj members did everything they could to help the husband and wife reconcile. Even if divorce was unavoidable, the Samaj members attempted to persuade the couples to agree on a financial settlement or alimony for the complainants.

"We try to settle the situation here," one Samaj member remarked. We strive to reconcile both parties if they cannot, but if they cannot, we try to settle the divorce peacefully by agreeing on monetary compensation or monthly alimony. By doing so, we hope to avoid having to deal with alimony issues in the civil courts for both parties."

Other Issues

The majority of Samaj members believed that they did not need to be psychologists to handle problems, but they did feel that additional training would be beneficial. They believed that psychological counselling and legal expertise would enable them to be more effective mediators. They also agreed that they needed to strike a fine balance between dealing with the complainants' concerns and not being too harsh on the transgressors.

CONCLUSION

After studying the various community-based ADRS(both through secondary and primary data) and examining them from a restorative justice perspective, it is clear that, while these community-based ADRS adhere to some restorative justice principles, they still need to implement various restorative justice mechanisms in order to instill its principles. Though there still might be some loopholes, a sincere attempt was made by these community based ADRS to empower the women, solve problems with inclusiveness, repair the emotional harm, repair relationships and hold the transgressors accountable. Since, there is a thin line between re-integrative shaming and humiliation, there were instances in which the community ADRS were successfully implementing while in few cases they overstepped that thin line.

What is Needed for Community Based ADRS to be Reflect all Principles of Restorative Justice?

Restorative justice procedures must be taught to the mediators of these community based ADRS through intensive training in order to put this into reality. The members of Mahila Panchayats were trained to a certain extent in legal related to crimes against women, conflict resolution mechanisms, and current legal status in regard to custody, property, maintenance, marriage, and other issues, as well as counselling, but further training in restorative justice procedures would be more beneficial.

Too much emphasis must not be given on reconciliation. Mediators of community based ADRS must be trained in victimology and victim psychology to make them understand that sometimes reconciliation may not be the best solution for a victim. This will also help the mediators to become more effective in their attempt to repair the emotional harm of the victims.

Mutual respect must be strictly maintained and there should be no stigmatization of the transgressor. This must be strictly implemented by not allowing the participants to speak out of turn, use rude or provocative words and loud tone.

What the Community Based ADRS Contribute to an Organic Restorative Justice Process

Restorative justice procedures, on the other hand, might learn a lot from community based ADRS, such as follow-up processes and active stakeholder participation.

Even though, the decision of these community based ADRS are not enforceable in the courts or not even supported by the judicial systems of the State, their decisions are often accepted and followed by the participants due to 'social control'. The advantage of these community based ADRS lies in the fact that mediators come from the same cultural and social background of the participants (complainants and transgressors) and share the same cultural beliefs and traditions which help them come up with mutually acceptable solutions and decisions. Since, the mediators come from the same locality and community, it is also easier for them to follow-up on the process or decisions given by them vis-a-vis the court annexed ADRS or restorative justice practices. This goes to show that restorative justice practices embedded in community based ADRS specially located in collectivist societies or rural/semi-rural settings would go a long way in promoting restorative justice in the society.

REFERENCES

Allendorf, K. (2012). Like daughter, like son? Fertility decline and the transformation of gender systems in the family. *Demographic Research*, *27*(16), 429–454. doi:10.4054/DemRes.2012.27.16 PMID:27147902

Allendorf, K. E. E. (2009). *The quality of family relationships, women's agency, and maternal and child health in India* [Doctoral dissertation]. University of Wisconsin-Madison.

Asadullah, M., Kashyap, R., Tiwari, R., & Sakafi, N. (2021). Community and Restorative Justice Practices in India, Nepal, and Bangladesh: A Comparative Overview. In T. Gavrielides (Ed.), *Comparative Restorative Justice*. Springer. doi:10.1007/978-3-030-74874-6_11

Barton, C. K. (2003). *Restorative justice: The empowerment model*. Hawkins Press.

Bazemore, G. (1998). Restorative justice and earned redemption communities, victims, and offender reintegration. *The American Behavioral Scientist*, *41*(6), 768–813. doi:10.1177/0002764298041006003

Bazemore, G. (2005). Whom and How Do We Reintegrate? Finding Community in Restorative Justice. *Criminology & Public Policy*, *4*(1), 131–148. doi:10.1111/j.1745-9133.2005.00011.x

Bazemore, S. G., & Walgrave, L. (1999). *Restorative juvenile justice: Repairing the harm of youth crime*. Criminal Justice Press.

Bhadra, C., & Shah, M. T. (2007). *Nepal: Country gender profile*. Report prepared for JICA.

Braithwaite, J. (2007). Encourage restorative justice. *Criminology & Public Policy*, *6*(4), 689–696. doi:10.1111/j.1745-9133.2007.00459.x

Cayley, D. (1998). *The expanding prison: The crisis in crime and punishment and the search for alternatives*. Toronto: House of Anansi.

Chakraborty, N. (2021). The Role of Nyaya Panchayat in Delivery of Rural Justice in India: A Critical Analysis. *VIPS Student Law Review*, *3*(1), 83–93.

Conners, R. (2003). Oppression Theory Critique. *Racial issues in criminal justice: The case of African Americans*, 255.

Cremini, H. (2007). *Peer Mediation: Citizenship And Social Inclusion Revisited: Citizenship and Social Inclusion in Action*. McGraw-Hill International.

Daly, K. (2000). Revisiting the relationship between retributive and restorative justice. *Restorative justice: Philosophy to practice*, 33-54.

Daly, K. (2002). Restorative justice: The real story. *Punishment & Society*, *4*(1), 55–79. doi:10.1177/14624740222228464

Dressler, J., Murphy, J. G., & Hampton, J. (1990). Hating Criminals: How Can Something That Feels So Good Be Wrong? *Michigan Law Review*, *88*(6), 1448–1473. doi:10.2307/1289323

Erbe, C. (2004). What is the Role of Professionals in Restorative Justice? In H. Zehr & B. Toews (Eds.), Critical Issues in Restorative Justice (pp. 289–297). Academic Press.

GhoshP. (2014). Restorative Justice: The New Paradigm in the Province of Justice in India? doi:10.2139/ssrn.2467373

Grover, S. (2009). Lived experiences Marriage, notions of love, and kinship support amongst poor women in Delhi. *Contributions to Indian Sociology*, *43*(1), 1–33. doi:10.1177/006996670904300101

Harris, M. K. (1996). Key differences among community corrections acts in the United States: An overview. *The Prison Journal*, *76*(2), 192–238. doi:10.1177/0032855596076002006

Johnstone, G., & Van Ness, D. W. (2007). The idea of restorative justice. Handbook of restorative justice, 1-23.

Johnstone, G., & Van Ness, D. W. (2013). The meaning of restorative justice. In *Handbook of restorative justice* (pp. 27–45). Willan. doi:10.4324/9781843926191-8

Koss, M. P. (2000). Blame, shame, and community: Justice responses to violence against women. *The American Psychologist*, *55*(11), 1332–1343. doi:10.1037/0003-066X.55.11.1332 PMID:11280942

Latimer, J., Dowden, C., & Muise, D. (2005). The effectiveness of restorative justice practices: A meta-analysis. *The Prison Journal*, *85*(2), 127–144. doi:10.1177/0032885505276969

Lemons, K. (2010). *At the margins of law: Adjudicating Muslim families in contemporary Delhi*. UC Berkeley: Anthropology. Retrieved from https://escholarship.org/uc/item/6f66n4dn

Mackey, V. (1981). *Punishment: In the scripture and tradition of Judaism, Christianity and Islam.* Paper presented to the National Religious Leaders Consultation of Criminal Justice, Claremont, CA.

Marshall, T. F. (1992). Restorative Justice on Trial in Britain. In H. Messmer & H.-U. Otto (Eds.), *Restorative Justice on Trial* (pp. 15–28). Kluwer Academic Publishers. doi:10.1007/978-94-015-8064-9_2

McCold, P. (2004). Paradigm muddle: The threat to restorative justice posed by its merger with community justice. *Contemporary Justice Review, 7*(1), 13–35. doi:10.1080/1028258042000211987

Meschievitz, C. S., & Galanter, M. (1982). In search of Nyaya Panchayats: The politics of a moribund institution. In *Comparative Studies* (pp. 47–77). Academic Press. doi:10.1016/B978-0-12-041502-1.50007-3

Mika, H. (1992). Mediation interventions and restorative justice: responding to the astructural bias. In *Restorative Justice on Trial* (pp. 559–567). Springer. doi:10.1007/978-94-015-8064-9_40

Moore, E. P. (1993). Gender, power, and legal pluralism: Rajasthan, India. *American Ethnologist, 20*(3), 522–542. doi:10.1525/ae.1993.20.3.02a00040

Morgan, S. P., & Niraula, B. B. (1995). Gender inequality and fertility in two Nepali villages. *Population and Development Review, 21*(3), 541–561. doi:10.2307/2137749

Munshi, S., & Lama, U. (1978). The Tamangs of Darjeeling: Organized Expression of the Ethnic Identity-Part II. *Journal of the Indian Anthropological Society, 13*(3), 265–286.

Natarajan, M. (2005). Women police stations as a dispute processing system. *Women & Criminal Justice, 16*(1-2), 87–106. doi:10.1300/J012v16n01_04

Omale, J. O. (2011). Restorative justice and alternative dispute resolution: An analytical discourse for African professionals. *Int'l J. Advanced Legal Stud. & Governance: An International Journal of Policy, Administration and Institutions, 2,* 102.

Peachey, D. E. (1992). Restitution, reconciliation, retribution: Identifying the forms of justice people desire. In *Restorative justice on trial* (pp. 551–557). Springer. doi:10.1007/978-94-015-8064-9_39

Pranis, K. (2001). Restorative justice, social justice, and the empowerment of marginalized populations. In G. Bazemore & M. Schiff (Eds.), *Restorative community justice: Repairing harm and transforming communities* (p. 287). Anderson Press.

Ross, R. (1996). Leaving our White eyes behind: The sentencing of Native accused. In M. O. Nielsen & R. A. Silverman (Eds.), *Native Americans, crime, and justice.* Westview.

Stark, R. (1996). Deviant places: A theory of the ecology of crime. *Criminology, 25*(4), 893–910. doi:10.1111/j.1745-9125.1987.tb00824.x

Subba, T. K. (1989). *Dynamics of a Hill Society. Mittal Publications.*

Sullivan, D., & Tifft, L. (2007). *Handbook of restorative justice: A global perspective.* Routledge. doi:10.4324/9780203346822

Thapa, S. (1989). The ethnic factor in the timing of family formation in Nepal. *Asia-Pacific Population Journal, 4*(1), 3–34. doi:10.18356/a0ff19ee-en PMID:12315769

Thilagaraj, R. (2017). Nyaya Panchayat. In *Restorative Justice in India* (pp. 3–12). Springer. doi:10.1007/978-3-319-47659-9_1

Tripp, T. M. (2001). The Rationality and Morality of Revenge. *Justice in the workplace: From theory to practice, 2,* 197.

Umbreit, M. S. (1995). Holding juvenile offenders accountable: A restorative justice perspective. *Juvenile & Family Court Journal, 46*(2), 31–42. doi:10.1111/j.1755-6988.1995.tb00815.x

Umbreit, M. S., Vos, B., & Coates, R. B. (2006). *Restorative Justice Dialogue: Evidence-based practice.* Center for Restorative justice Peacemaking, University of Minnesota.

Vatuk, S. (2013). The "women's court" in India: An alternative dispute resolution body for women in distress. *Journal of Legal Pluralism and Unofficial Law, 45*(1), 76–103. doi:10.1080/07329113.2013.774836

Volpe, M. R., & Strobl, S. (2005). *Restorative justice responses to post–September 11 hate.* Academic Press.

Walgrave, L. (2013). Integrating criminal justice and restorative justice. In *Handbook of restorative justice* (pp. 581–601). Willan. doi:10.4324/9781843926191.ch26

Zehr, H. (1995). Justice paradigm shift? Values and visions in the reform process. *Mediation Quarterly, 12*(3), 207–216. doi:10.1002/crq.3900120303

ADDITIONAL READING

Basu, S. (2006). Playing off courts: The negotiation of divorce and violence in plural legal settings in Kolkata. *Journal of Legal Pluralism and Unofficial Law*, *38*(52), 41–75. doi:10.1080/07329113.2006.10756591

Baxi, U. (1976). Access, Development and Distributive Justice: Access Problems of the" Rural" Population. *Journal of the Indian Law Institute*, *18*(3), 375–430.

Kiss, E. (2000). Moral ambition within and beyond political constraints: reflections on restorative justice. In R. Rotberg & D. Thompson (Eds.), *Truth v. justice: The morality of truth commissions* (pp. 68–98). Princeton University Press. doi:10.1515/9781400832033-005

Mika, H. (1992). The Practice and Prospect of Victim-Offender Programs. *SMU Law Review*, *46*, 2191.

Sarkin, J. (1997). The truth and reconciliation commission in South Africa. *Commonwealth Law Bulletin*, *23*(1-2), 528–542. doi:10.1080/03050718.1997.99 86472

Saxena, R. C. (1972). *Commentaries on the U.P. Panchayati Raj Act 1947*. Eastern Book Co.

Sophia, A. (2021). Women's Empowerment in Manipur. *Journal of Social and Political Sciences*, *4*(1). Advance online publication. doi:10.31014/aior.1991.04.01.247

Tinker, H. (1967). *Foundation of Local Self-Government of India*. Lalvani Publishing House.

Chapter 7

Extra Marital Affairs, Breach of Trust in Marriage, and Therapeutic Jurisprudence:
A Critical Analysis From the Perspectives of Ancient Hindu Codes, Customs, and Contemporary Laws

Debarati Halder
Parul Institute of Law, Parul University, India

ABSTRACT

Therapeutic jurisprudence (TJ) emphasizes the law's healing touch to cure the socio-legal evils that may hamper the wellbeing of people at large. The chapter deals with extramarital affairs, breach of trust in marriages, and the role of TJ in restitution of justice for spouses, especially female spouses who may be pushed to trauma, extreme depression, frustration, and anger due to extramarital affairs by unfaithful husbands with special reference to India. In ancient Hindu Codes and customary laws, extramarital affairs by husbands did not find specific mention as offensive behavior in marriage. This has led the contemporary laws to not acknowledge extramarital affairs as offences in marriage. But in the ancient times, women in India had rights to seek restitution of justice from family elders and community elders. This alternative dispute resolution mechanism provided much needed healing touch. The chapter researches on the hidden role of TJ in the ancient and contemporary laws in India dealing with victimization of women by way of extramarital affairs by husbands.

DOI: 10.4018/978-1-6684-4112-1.ch007

INTRODUCTION

In 1980's Bruce Winnick and David Wexler evolved the concept of Therapeutic jurisprudence (TJ) specially to signify the therapeutic aspects of law for restitution of justice (Wexler D, 2000). Research of Winnick and Wexler showed that law and its applicability to specific cases have deep impacts on the litigants, victims, and common individuals as a whole. At the beginning, TJ played a significant role in promoting the therapeutic aspects of mental health laws. But slowly TJ researchers started looking into other areas of law including criminal laws, family laws, laws related to cyber space, workplaces related laws etc. This research could bring significant impacts on contemporary legal proceedings and judicial cognitive mindsets that would help litigants and especially victims of crimes. (Perlin, 2016). In India, the concept of TJ had its long history through the ancient scripts and customary laws. This may best be understood from the ancient understanding of victim's rights and duties of the king for restoration of justice, acknowledgement of rights of the accused, compensatory jurisprudence etc., where the focus of the ancient legal texts known as Manusmriti, Artha Shashtra, Danda Neeti etc, was on wellbeing of the people and justified satisfaction of the litigants, victims etc. (Umashankar.P, 2022).

Some of these are reflected in the modern Indian judicial understandings like the landmark decision of Justice Krishna Iyer in the 1977 case of Mohammed Ghiyasuddin vs State of Andhra Pradesh (Halder,2015), where Justice Iyer emphasised on rights of the accused and convicted prisoners to undergo a therapeutic correctional administration system. In the contemporary world, TJ is being applied to resolve matrimonial disputes in many jurisdictions (Freeman, 2008). The principle is also being applied for resolving child custody issues. TJ in my understanding has worked wonderfully worldwide to provide a therapeutic touch to many litigants in family dispute matters.

Marriage has been considered as the strongest unit in a society from primitive period. Traditionally it has been understood that mutual trust plays a significant role in strengthening the bond between two heterosexual individuals who will eventually go ahead for procreation.

Marriage in India, especially in Hinduism is considered to be a sacred institution where not only the bride and bridegroom unite for conjugal life on the basis of mutual trust and devotion to each other, but the respective families of the parties to the marriage also get connected as relatives. (Mitra, S.K. and Fischer, A., 2002).

Customary laws flowing from ancient scripts like the Vedas. Artha Shashtra, Smritis including Manu Smriti etc, governing marriages, succession, adoption etc, have indicated that in a marriage *"dampati"* or legally wedded heterogeneous couple have several duties towards each other, towards the children, their families and to the society as a whole. (Kalita.S, 2022). It is necessary to mention here that ancient Hindu texts did not however put a complete restriction on bigamy for specific categories of people including some sects of Kshatriyas (the warrior community) like the kings, kulin Brahmana (high class Brahmana) etc. But this has been construed differently than unfaithfulness of spouses in marriages. The former had been sanctioned by customary laws majorly for social needs. For example, a Hindu king could marry multiple women from imperial families of other states mainly to establish family relationships that would prevent war like situations between two countries.[1] The later had been considered as a moral sin.

But not many examples in literature show rights of women against unfaithful and promiscuous husbands. Some ancient texts including Manusmriti however strongly recommends punishments for unfaithful wives (Krishnamurthy.V(2017). But this does not mean that women in ancient Hindu scripts did not have any legal recourse against unfaithful husbands. A married woman had right to seek the guidance of family elders and community elders against family disputes, breaches in marriage vows by unfaithful husband. Several researchers have also indicated that such disputes were mostly resolved by family elders and community elders (Vatuk.S, 2013) including the Nyaya Panchayats who would follow traditional customary practices (Thilagraj.R, 2017) for dispute resolution.

The limited research that is available in this regard presents a gap in the understanding of how cheating in Hindu marriages by husbands had been treated in the ancient Hindu texts, whether the said issue was addressed by any customary laws, and whether the colonial rule could address this issue for the purpose of restitution of justice for wives who had been victims of in marriage due to unfaithfulness of the husbands. This book chapter aims to address this lacuna from TJ perspectives.

It may be noticed that such women who witness extramarital affairs of unfaithful husbands may undergo prolonged trauma, depression, anger, and frustration. As the ancient texts suggest, family elders and community leaders may provide a therapeutic support by hearing the pain of such women and suggesting for her rights to lead dignified life by making the matrimonial family allow her to stay in the matrimonial home respectfully (Vatuk.S, 2013). But it may also be seen that ancient texts could influence the social norms to blame such women especially when they could not produce any children out of the marriage including male heirs (Vatuk.S, 2013). In such cases matrimonial families could justify the unfaithfulness of the husbands. This system continued for thousands of years. Much later this system of blame game would shift to apply within the meaning of torture and domestic violence to the wife in modern independent Indian understanding. Such inclusion has a good significance from TJ perspective as this acknowledged the idea of mental wellbeing of women who may have gone through the pain of witnessing extramarital affairs of their husbands.

Even though customary laws flowing from ancient Hindu scripts including Vedas and Smritis had been regulating marriage related laws, grounds for divorce etc, the colonial British laws had their significant influence on developing Hindu laws regulating marriages, grounds and procedures for divorces, adoption, inheritance, succession of the properties etc. Such influences may be seen through several provisions in the Indian Penal Code including Ss.493(cohabitation caused by a man deceitfully inducing a belief of lawful marriage), 494(marrying again during the lifetime of the spouse), 495 (marrying again during the life time of husband or wife concealing the first wife/husband to the person to whom the offender is getting married), 496 (marriage ceremony fraudulently gone through without lawful marriage, 497 (adultery), 498 (enticing, illegally taking away or detaining with criminal intent a married woman) etc, which was later adopted by the lawmakers of independent India. Such provisions also played its role in determining marriage related offences (Mitra, S.K. and Fischer, A., 2002).

This chapter examines the issue of breach of trust in marriage to demonstrate the hidden or lost therapeutic jurisprudence in the Hindu texts, specifically by way of extramarital affairs and its impact on female spouses in India. The concept of *breach of trust in marriage* can be expanded to include romantic affair with another man/ woman by the spouse which may involve physical and virtual sexual connection etc, without the knowledge and consent of the other spouse. Such romantic involvement may include extramarital affair, which may include adultery, or romantic sexual relationship with another unmarried, divorced, or widowed man or woman.

In 2018, the Supreme Court of India had decriminalised adultery. S.497 of the Indian Penal Code addresses adultery as a criminal offence and says as follows:

Whoever has sexual intercourse with a person who is and whom he knows or has reason to believe to be the wife of another man, without the consent or connivance of that man, such sexual intercourse not amounting to the offence of rape, is guilty of the offence of adultery, and shall be punished with imprisonment of either description for a term which may extend to five years, or with fine, or with both. In such a case, the wife shall not be punishable as an abettor.

The court observed that the term adultery as per S.497 indicates position of wife (with whom an adulterous relationship has been established) as mere property of the husband. But this author would not concentrate solely on why adultery has been decriminalised. This chapter emphasises on the fact that while the court had decriminalised adultery, establishing extramarital romantic affair by one spouse (including sexual relationship) with third party while the marriage is still existing, has not been considered as a criminal offence under the Indian Penal Code. A romantic attachment may include persuading, exchanging romantic messages, physical touching with sexual intention, hugging, kissing and also having penetrative sexual connection with the romantic partner (Perlin, M.L. and Lynch, A.J., 2015). Unfortunately Indian Penal Code does not recognise extramarital affair by husband which may necessarily include breaching the trust within marriage. However, the Protection of women from Domestic Violence Act, 2005 recognises psychological torture as an offence within marriage. This statute very narrowly addresses 'emotional abuse,' which is not explained broadly.[2]

This author argues that extramarital affairs in Hindu marriages were not considered as offence against women in marriage since the ancient times. But this was neither ignored as an acceptable behaviour by male spouse in the marriage. This behaviour was acknowledged as moral sin and the extremely narrow restorative justice mechanism for supporting the aggrieved spouse did have some essence of TJ. This was however not prominently evident until the 21st century

Indian criminal as well as family laws have failed to define the concept of extramarital affair and breach of trust in the marriage. Extramarital affair is a broader understanding which may or may not include adultery. This author suggests that an extramarital affair by husband which necessarily amounts to breach of trust in marriage need to be recognised as a civil offence within the meaning of cruelty to wife and the restitution of justice mechanism must adopt TJ approach. An extramarital affair may lead to negligence to wife and deserting her. It may also lead to negligence in maintaining wife and children born out of the marriage. While S.125 of the Indian Criminal Procedure Code penalises negligence in maintaining wife and children, this chapter further argues that the wife may suffer tremendous physical, financial, and psychological victimisation while the court procedure may go ahead in this regard. The problem must therefore be addressed at the initial stage. If the conduct of extramarital affair (as explained in the above paragraph) is considered as offence, the victim, i.e., the wife can get legal recourse.

This chapter is divided into three main parts including the first part, introduction. The second part discusses about the concept of marriage as a whole including the offences in a marriage under the ancient Hindu texts as well as under the contemporary laws. The third part offers suggestions and conclusion.

MARRIAGE UNDER THE ANCIENT HINDU CODE AND THE CONTEMPORARY LAWS

Meaning of marriage: Traditionally marriages in Hinduism are considered as sacred union of two heterosexual human beings for the continuation of family and lineage. The sources of Hindu rituals and practices for marriage and succession of property by heirs are necessarily found in ancient texts including Shruti which can date back to Vedic era, Smritis, which include several codified versions of Hindu practices and rituals, Shashtras and Upanishads (Ray, S. N. (1908). Among the Smritis, Manu Smriti is considered as most prominent source of Hindu rituals and practices (Asati, G. (2019). Later Artha Shashtra strengthened the verses of Manusmriti by laying down the rules for good governance, protection of the rights of people and emphasising on the basic duties of man as well as that of the king to protect the rights of people (Asati, G. (2019). All of these texts have contributed significantly towards building up a codified version of Hindu rituals and practices which provided it recognition as customary laws which survived for thousands of years until now. These customary laws remained almost untouched by different rulers who had invaded India during different ages in Indian history. Europeans including the Dutch, French and English rulers being the last 'foreign rulers' of India, also did not disturb the customary laws. However, it cannot be ignored that the uniform penal laws created by the British rulers did leave a benevolent impact on the Hindu customary laws, especially related to child marriages, Sati practices and widow remarriages. Over the ages, Hindu rituals and practices have accommodated several progressive practices like banning *Satidaha* (burning of the young widow in pyre of the husband), banning child marriages etc., which have been supported by modern contemporary laws (shredding several age-old customs and practices which infringed the basic rights of women and children. In this context, it is necessary to understand the meaning of marriage and the essential elements of the same as per the modern Hindu laws.

The ancient texts mention about several forms of marriages which had gained strong recognition under customary laws over the years. These include Brahma (most practiced forms of marriage which includes Kanyadaan or gifting the daughter by father to the bridegroom), Prajapatyay (where father of the bride along with other elders in the family may instruct the bride and the bridegroom to follow the Dharma etc,), and Gandharva (a marriage where bride and bridegroom may have the liberty to choose their respective partners and which is also recognised as love marriage which may or may not have the approval of the family elders) etc(Gupta, H., & Singh, Y.(2019). As such, any of the forms of marriages followed by Hindus may be considered valid when two main conditions are satisfied. These include eligibility of the parties to enter into a marriage and the mandatory performance of *shashtric* rituals that may find its roots in ancient texts like the Manu Smriti, etc. The first condition amongst the above two conditions has however gone through several changes due to the development of human rights including the women and child rights. This set of conditions which frame up the eligibility for any individual to enter into a Hindu marriage includes religious affiliation to Hinduism, age of marriage, consent to marriage and the pre-marriage relationship between the families of the bride and the groom. The second set of conditions include performance of certain ancient *shashtric* rituals which may make the marriage sacred and which if not followed, may annul the marriage. These customary rituals are still practiced in Hinduism and in the modern contemporary world they have been recognised as essential elements of marriage (Kumar, V, 2017). These include pre marriage, marriage and post marriage rituals like engagement ceremony or roka or tilak ceremony, Haldi ceremony or sacred bathing of the bride and the groom in their respective family homes with turmeric paste that should be touched by both the bride and the groom at auspicious times, Yagna and Homa for worshipping and getting the blessing of the ancestors etc, before the beginning of the marriage ceremony, yagna or homa,, var mala, kanyadaan, sindoor daan, tying of mangal sutra, saptapadi and vidai during the marriage and grihapravesh of the married couple in the matrimonial home after the marriage. Noticeably, the above-mentioned rituals which form the second set of conditions for making a marriage valid from the customary law perspectives have also undergone several changes especially due to different customs in different regions in India. The modern Hindu law however has recognised the basic conditions of a valid Hindu marriage on the basis of the most practised customs and rituals. These can be found in Ss 5 and 7 of the Hindu Marriage Act, 1955. The former lays down the eligibility of the parties to enter into a valid marriage by stating the followings:

"Marriage may be solemnized between any two Hindus, if the following conditions are fulfilled, namely:

(i)   *neither party has a spouse living at the time of the marriage;*

(ii)   *at the time of the marriage, neither party (a) is incapable of giving a valid consent to it in consequence of unsoundness of mind; or (b) though capable of giving a valid consent, has been suffering from mental disorder of such a kind or to such an extent as to be unfit for marriage and the procreation of children; or (c) has been subject to recurrent attacks of insanity*

(iii) *the bridegroom has completed the age of twenty-one years and the bride, the age of eighteen years] at the time of the marriage;*

(iv)   *the parties are not within the degrees of prohibited relationship unless the custom or usage governing each of them permits of a marriage between the two;*

(v)   *the parties are not sapindas of each other, unless the custom or usage governing each of them permits of a marriage between the two."*[3]

Here before we take the discussions ahead to understand about the rituals which may make the Hindu Marriages valid as per the existing personal laws, we need to understand about the concepts of eligibility of entering into a Hindu marriage. The first condition for a valid Hindu marriage is the religious affinity of both the parties to Hinduism. The other conditions for a valid Hindu marriage can be divided into two categories: one flowing from the ancient Hindu texts which has now become customary law and has been supported by the modern Hindu Marriage Act, 1955. The second is a group of criteria that have been developed by the modern parliamentarians in accordance with the evolution of the human rights and child rights. In the latter falls the issues of age and consenting power. Hindu Marriage Act prohibits any Hindu man under twenty-one years of age and any Hindu marriage woman under eighteen years of age to enter into marriage.[4] The Hindu Marriage Act also makes mental maturity and sound mental health mandatory for the bride and bridegroom to enter into marriage so that both can consent for the marriage independently and without any coerce. These conditions are influenced by the universal human rights which prohibits child marriages and prevents exploitation of men and women including sexual exploitation in the name of marriage. The first criteria of the other essential conditions of Hindu marriage as has been mentioned in the above, falls in the usages and customs flowing from the ancient texts: these include prohibition of marriage in the sapinda relationships or within the closest blood lines. But here the Hindu marriage Act has further considered regional customary practices amongst the Hindus from different geographic regions in India which may permit marriage between close family members like cousins, maternal uncle and niece etc.

Apart from these conditions, there lies another essential condition of monogamy for a Hindu marriage to be a valid marriage: as such, the parties to the marriage must not have a prior marriage existing while conducting a second marriage. This very condition distinguishes Hindu marriage as a sacred marriage built on sacred vows of commitment and trust to spouses taken in the presence of sacred fire of the Yagna, priests and family and community elders. Courts in India on numbers of occasions have held that a Hindu man can marry a Hindu woman following the shashtrik rituals to validly solemnise the marriage under the Hindu Marriage Act, 1955. However, it must also be noted that in the ancient and medieval period, Hindu marriage related rules and customs did permit polygamy. This is evident from Ramayana and Mahabharata, the two great epics of India. Polyandry was however permitted for separate reasons: for example, Kshatriya kings could practice polygamy with daughters of other kings to avoid war and to create family relationships with other kingdoms. Kulin (Brahmana from decent and aristocratic families) Brahmans were also permitted to practice polyandry. But the modern Hindu Marriage Act turned Hindu marriages to monogamy marriages since 1955 and it was largely due to the influence of Hindu social reformers who could influence the colonial lawmakers as well as post-independence Indian lawmakers (Karlekar, M. (1995).

Further, neither the existing modern law, nor the customary laws and practices as has been flowing from the ancient scripts permit any Hindu individual to marry any non-Hindu heterogeneous individual to claim the validity of Hindu marriage under the Hindu Marriage Act. The customary practices and the modern Hindu law relating to marriage neither permits any of the spouses to convert to another religion other than Hinduism to perform a second marriage in the presence of the first wife who was legally married to the former as per the Hindu marriage rituals as has been mandated by Hindu Marriage Act, 1955. This is evident in the case of Sarla Mudgal vs Union of India, 1995 and Lily Thomas vs Union of India, 2000. In both these cases the Supreme Court of India while dealing with the validity of the second marriages by Hindu men who converted to Islam observed that Hindu marriages unlike the Muslim marriages, do not permit polygamy as per the modern Hindu Marriage Act even if the first wife consents for the second marriage. The monogamous nature of marriage also prohibits and punishes bigamy which is reflected in S.494 of the Indian Penal Code which says as follows:

Whoever is having a husband or wife living, marries and such a marriage is void by reason of its taking place during the life of such husband or wife, shall be punished with imprisonment of either description for a term which may extend to seven years and shall also be liable to fine.

S.494 of the Indian Penal Code further provides exception to the offence of remarriage during the lifetime of a validly married spouse by stating that *"This Section does not extend to any person whose marriage with such husband or wife has been declare void by a court of competent jurisdiction, nor to any person who contracts a marriage during the life of a former husband or wife, if such husband or wife, at the time of the subsequent marriage, shall have been continually absent from such person for the space of seven years, and shall not have been heard of by such person as being alive within that time provided the person contracting such subsequent marriage shall, before such marriage takes place, inform the person with whom such marriage is contracted of the real state of facts so far as the same are within his or her knowledge"*.[5]

It is interesting to note that while in the ancient Hindu texts bigamy was not prohibited as a whole, the issue of extramarital affairs breaching the marriage vows for trust between the spouses was considered as a moral wrong with heavy punishment especially for adultery. Male and female partners in marriage were expected to respect the marriage as an institution. The same concept is reflected in S.494 Indian Penal Code. Adultery on the other hand was considered as a punishable offence, but presently the Supreme Court of India has decriminalised the same. This will further be discussed in the following paragraphs.

SUGGESTIONS AND CONCLUSION

Patterns of Extramarital Affairs its Impact on Marriages and Legal Significance as an Offence

The laws of marriage in ancient Hinduism have indicated that love and trust in each other are the two prime elements in marriage which if broken may deeply affect the family as a significant unit of the society. Extramarital affairs or emotional, physical, and sexual relationships with persons other than legally married spouses are considered as sin because such behaviour in spouses indicate breaking the trust in the other spouse and cheating on the other spouse. We must understand that extramarital affairs can be of different types: this can include emotional and physical connection with another married woman by a married man (known as adultery), emotional and physical connection with another unmarried individual, emotional and sexual relationship with one's student or teacher or people who may be associated with the offending individual within the meaning of guardian and minor, teacher and student, temporary guardian for adult/child female/male whose parents/ husbands/ guardians have entrusted the responsibility of protecting the said person/ child/disabled person etc. The above understanding about the types of extramarital affairs can be explained through the following flow chart:

Figure 1. Types of Extra-Marital Affairs

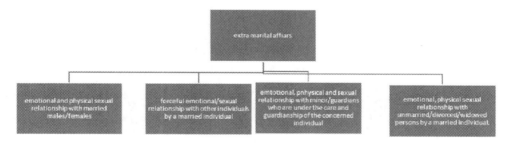

The above chart may clearly indicate four distinct types of relationships that may be *exploited* by the married spouse for personal satisfaction breaching the marriage vows and trust of the other spouse. The categories of the extramarital relationships are further discussed below:

(a) Adultery

The first category of the relationship falls within the meaning of adultery and the same has been considered as sin by ancient texts and customary laws not only of India, but in many other religions including Christianity. Loving and having sexual relationship with a legally wedded wife or husband of another individual by a married individual was considered as violation of the settled norms of the society as this behaviour not only violates the normative rules of law, but sociological understanding about the meaning and significance of family units in the society as a whole. The Vedic scripts, Smritis and Shrutis have prescribed strict punishment for such relationships to save the purity and sacred nature of marriage which includes capital punishment, pecuniary fines etc., for the male adulterers (Sinaha. K, 2014). Female adulterers on the other hand were also prescribed punishments including restricting their worldly pleasures of clothes and food to bare minimum, abandoning them from the family set up etc. Nonetheless adultery has the essential element of breaching the trust in the marriage. But we must also not ignore the fact that the concept of punishment for adultery as may be seen in the ancient texts which framed the customary laws for marriage in the mediaeval period and later in the European influenced Indian criminal laws in S.497 of the Indian Penal Code essentially shows women as 'properties of their husbands' and therefore adultery with married women was considered as a crime against the property of the husband of the married woman. This concept of considering wife as the property of the husband had unfortunately remained unchanged in the colonial laws as well. S.497 of the Indian Penal code reflects this when it says

Whoever has sexual intercourse with a person who is and whom he knows or has reason to believe to be the wife of another man, without the consent or connivance of that man, such sexual intercourse not amounting to the offence of rape, is guilty of the offence of adultery, and shall be punished with imprisonment of either description for a term which may extend to five years, or with fine, or with both. In such case the wife shall not be punishable as an abettor.

The Indian Supreme Court very recently had examined this law largely in the light of women's right to prosecute adulterous husbands in the case of Joseph Shine vs Union of India, 2018. The court observed that S.497 of the Indian Penal Code does not permit wives of men who commit adultery to make it as a ground for divorce: wives were not recognised as victims of breach of trust in marriage when the husbands commit adultery. The problem that the court identified was an inherent patriarchal problem where women are considered as mere properties for sexual and reproductive purposes. While the court has declared S.497 of the Indian

Penal Code as unconstitutional as the very provision did not adhere to the equal right provision of the Constitution of India, it cannot be said that adultery has been decriminalised in its literal sense. A clear reading of the observation of the judges in the above-mentioned case may indicate that if the action of extramarital affair is done by the married man with a married woman where both had consented, the other spouse of the respective adulterers may consider this as grounds for divorce for breaching the trust in the marriage. in such case the existing modern law does not necessarily prescribe punishment to the adulterous party, but rather gives the spouse of the adulterous party right to have divorce and claim matrimonial alimony and the said right may not be denied by any courts where such divorce case may be filed.

(b) Non-Consensual Emotional/Sexual Intimacy With Other Individuals by a Married Individual

In case of adultery, we can see that if the married man and married woman consensually involve in sexual relationship, the same may now be considered as offence against marriage for respective persons and the spouses of the respective adulterers may take this as grounds for divorce. But when the concerned spouse indulges in sexual relationship with another man or woman without the consent of the latter it may not provide a cloak of immunity from criminal responsibility to the former against latter. Indian governmental reports have suggested that every year several sexual abuse cases targeting women and girls are reported to the police and there are rare cases where adult men are victimised sexually by adult women. In majority of such cases, it may be seen that married men may be committing the offence (Pandey, M. (2018). Consider the 2012 infamous case of Nirbhaya or Delhi gang rape case, where one of the perpetrator's wives wanted to file divorce suit before the execution of the said perpetrator because she did not want to live with the shame of being the wife of a convicted rapist (Dey, A., & Orton, B. (2016). In such sorts of offences, we may see that such affair may necessarily be extramarital. Here we need to understand about the factor of lack of consent and nature of the association and behaviour of the man and his target victim who is not his legally wedded wife. At the very first step we may see that the perpetrator may develop a psychological bonding with the victim which may or may not be a one-sided affair. The perpetrator may not disclose his marital status to the victim. The perpetrator may further try to dominate and coerce the victim to accept his love and behave with him as intimately as possible. This very nature of the behaviour of the perpetrator may change the entire nature of the relationship to offensive relationship of stalker and his victim (Halder, Debarati,2015). While initially the victim in such cases may consider showing a sympathetic attitude towards the perpetrator as the latter may try to attract the attention of the former by sharing about his frustrations with his job, his family or with his wife (in case the former knows about the latter's marital status), later the victim may try to withdraw from such relationships igniting more aggressiveness in the perpetrator to coerce her for staying in the extramarital relationship. There may be possibilities that the victim may try to contact the wife and/or the police as resorts to free herself from such abusive relationships. Such actions from the victim may further create shock to the spouse of the perpetrator and the said spouse may go for a denial mode. This indeed may cause domestic violence as the male spouse may never want the female spouse to raise questions about his infidelity. In majority of cases in India where the female spouse may be socio-economically dependent on the husbands, they may not have any other option but to accept the extramarital affair and stay in the relationship allowing the husband to go ahead for more such extramarital affairs. Here the wives may also have to suffer doubly as the victim 'girlfriend' of the husband may bring criminal complaints against the wife in case the latter continues to support the husband and denies any claim of stalking and extramarital affair.

Ironically, such extramarital affairs by husband had not been considered as 'sinful' or grave moral wrongs as we get to see in cases of adultery in the ancient Hindu texts that governed laws related to marriage. Further, married men were also allowed to keep concubines and visit brothels and this system is still existing in a more refined manner especially since prostitution is not legally banned in India (Goyal, S. (2020). The modern criminal laws however have considered such behaviours as wrong behaviours that may cause cruelty to spouses.

(c) Extramarital Emotional and Sexual Intimacy With Persons Within the Fiduciary Relationship

There are several cases where adult married male or female individuals may get involved in emotional and sexual intimacy outside the marriage with adults as well as minors falling within the fiduciary relationships. Such relationships may happen between children and their adult caregivers, disabled people and their caregivers, students, and teachers etc. often it is seen that adolescent children may have infatuation towards their teachers and caregivers . This may not be considered legally wrong because the children may not be matured enough to understand the nature of the relationship and the consequences of the same. But when there is a vice versa reciprocation from the adult teachers or caregivers and later both the children and the teacher/caregiver get indulged in emotional and sexual intimacy, it then turns into a legally prohibited and punishable relationship especially for the adult teacher /caregiver. Laws in different jurisdiction including India have prescribed strict punishment for such exploitation of fiduciary relationships.[6] Unlike the second category of the extramarital affair discussed above, the present category of offences attracted penal punishments since the ancient times and the Smritis, Shrutis and Vedas had indicated that teachers and guardians play the role of parents in the absence of biological parents. Such sexual intimacy with people in the fiduciary relationship may also indicate unfaithfulness of the husband.

Extramarital Affair as Normal Behaviour Versus Morally Wrong Behaviour and Restitution of Justice: Possible Therapeutic Jurisprudential Solution

While the above paragraphs discussed about extramarital affairs by both genders and its legal implications on marriage, looking at the socio-legal understandings regarding position of women especially in Indian social system it becomes necessary to analyse the situation and rights of female spouses who may be victimised due to extramarital affairs of their husbands. The above discussion may show that extramarital affairs by husband may not be considered as offensive in the marriage unless the same is reported by the wife as mental torture, part of domestic violence or the same has instigated the wife for committing self-harm including suicide. Traditionally Indian women are discouraged to discuss about the infidelity of their husbands: reasons for such oppressive tradition varies from socio-economic condition of the women, fear of social taboo, fear of blaming the incapacity of the wives to sexual and material gratification of the husbands etc (Khan.A & Majumdar, 2021). Resultant, majority of women may be forced to stay in abusive and toxic relationships for ever. But this does not mean that women may not have any rights against such behaviour of their husbands. Indian criminal laws which are largely based on colonial European moral laws, have provided significant consideration to the orthodox socio-economic cultures which may prevent women to visit government offices including police offices dominated by male police officers: for example, women police stations have been established to enable women to approach the women police and to register cases of violence including domestic violence (Jassal, N. (2020). But in reality such initiatives may not gain full satisfactions because traditionally extramarital affairs may not attract penal actions unless the wives consider it as offensive behaviour as discussed above.

Suggestions

Does it then mean that women who are silenced by their orthodox societies may not have any right against such violation of marriage rights? The answer lies in the possible application of Therapeutic jurisprudential approach of laws for marital disputes. Criminal justice machinery would not infringe the privacy of marriage unless it is invited to. Women who suffer victimisation due to extramarital affairs need to be empowered to understand about their rights against such extramarital affairs. In a recent case the Allahad High Court had emphasised on the right of the wife to complaint against polygamous nature of Hindu husband: the case dealt with court's decision to uphold the order the of the lower court dismissing the appeal for discharging the accused husband who was charged with abetting the suicide of his second wife. He apparently got married suppressing the facts of his first marriage. When the second wife got to know that the man was preparing to get married for the third time she lodged a criminal complaint against the husband and then committed suicide. Even though the case highlighted domestic violence due to the polygamous nature of the husband, a deep reading into the facts of the case would also reveal that criminality of extramarital affairs have been broadly addressed here from the perspective of wife's right to have complete commitment from the husband. But we also need to understand that marriage necessarily includes psychological bonding between the spouses. In the Indian orthodox patriarchal social set up where wives are expected to satisfy the husbands materially and sexually, a spouse with infidelity may not be expected to become faithful to the other spouse (especially female spouse) after the latter complaints to the criminal justice machinery about the extramarital affair of the former especially when the complaint may be made not as a preparatory step for separation and divorce, but as a step for re-establishing conjugal rights of the spouses . Good marriage counselling may make the faulting spouse to understand the mistakes that are created by extramarital affairs. But there may be chances that the said spouse may take this opportunity to inflict more harm on the other spouse (especially for wives) and in such cases complaint to the criminal justice machinery by the wife may become extremely anti therapeutic as this may make the husband more aggressive and revengeful. In the absence of any customary laws and practices criminalising extramarital affair as an offence in Hindu marriage, it has become necessary to treat the same as an offence especially when it has created domestic violence against the other spouse.

Given this situation which calls for addressing legal vacuum, this author argues that extramarital affair must be considered as within the meaning of cruelty to the wife within the meaning of S.498A of the Indian Penal Code and domestic violence within the meaning of S.3 of the Protection of Women from Domestic Violence Act, 2005. The former states as follows:

S.498A: Husband or relative of husband of a woman subjecting her to cruelty. — Whoever, being the husband or the relative of the husband of a woman, subjects such woman to cruelty shall be punished with imprisonment for a term which may extend to three years and shall also be liable to fine. Explanation. —For the purpose of this section, "cruelty" means—

a. *any wilful conduct which is of such a nature as is likely to drive the woman to commit suicide or to cause grave injury or danger to life, limb, or health (whether mental or physical) of the woman; or*

b. *harassment of the woman where such harassment is with a view to coercing her or any person related to her to meet any unlawful demand for any property or valuable security or is on account of failure by her or any person related to her to meet such demand.*[7]

S.3 of the Protection of Women from Domestic Violence Act, 2005 states as follows:

For the purposes of this Act, any act, omission or commission or conduct of the respondent shall constitute domestic violence in case it— (a) harms or injures or endangers the health, safety, life, limb or well-being, whether mental or physical, of the aggrieved person or tends to do so and includes causing physical abuse, sexual abuse, verbal and emotional abuse and economic abuse; or (b) harasses, harms, injures or endangers the aggrieved person with a view to coerce her or any other person related to her to meet any unlawful demand for any dowry or other property or valuable security; or (c) has the effect of threatening the aggrieved person or any person related to her by any conduct mentioned in clause (a) or clause (b); or (d) otherwise injures or causes harm, whether physical or mental, to the aggrieved person. Explanation I.—For the purposes of this section,— (i) "physical abuse" means any act or conduct which is of such a nature as to cause bodily pain, harm, or danger to life, limb, or health or impair the health or development of the aggrieved person and includes assault, criminal intimidation and criminal force; (ii) "sexual abuse" includes any conduct of a sexual nature that abuses, humiliates, degrades or otherwise violates the dignity of woman; (iii) "verbal and emotional abuse" includes— (a) insults, ridicule, humiliation, name calling and insults or ridicule specially with regard to not having a child or a male child; and (b) repeated threats to cause physical pain to any person in whom the aggrieved person is interested; (iv) "economic abuse" includes— (a) deprivation of all or any economic or financial resources to which the aggrieved person is entitled under any law or custom whether payable under an order of a court or otherwise or which the aggrieved person requires out of necessity including, but not limited 5 to, house hold necessities for the aggrieved person and her children, if any, stridhan, property, jointly or separately owned by the aggrieved person, payment of rental related to the shared house hold and maintenance; (b) disposal of household effects, any alienation of assets whether movable or immovable, valuables, shares, securities, bonds and the like or other property in which the aggrieved person has an interest or is entitled to use by virtue of the domestic relationship or which may be reasonably required by the aggrieved person or her children or her stridhan or any other property jointly or separately held by the aggrieved person; and (c) prohibition or restriction to continued access to resources or facilities which the aggrieved person is entitled to use or enjoy by virtue of the domestic relationship including access to the shared household. Explanation II.—For the purpose of determining whether any act, omission, commission or conduct of the respondent constitutes "domestic violence" under this section, the overall facts and circumstances of the case shall be taken into consideration.[8]

A close read into both these provisions would show that none of the provisions have included extramarital affair or any pattern of extramarital affair as cruelty. This author argues that both the provisions may include extramarital affair as cruelty so that the victim wife may claim right for restitution of justice especially regarding offences in marriage. This may not only help the female spouse to seek compensation and matrimonial alimony in case she wishes to make this as a ground for divorce, but it may also establish extramarital affair not only as a moral wrong, but also as a penal offence in marriage. Such inclusion of the behaviour of extramarital affair as cruelty to wife may also go a long way to achieve the aims of Therapeutic Jurisprudence as the wife may get support from restorative justice practitioners, lawyers, counsellors, and the judiciary which may not be possible from the society or her matrimonial family if the latter does not treat extramarital affair as a moral wrong and punishable behaviour. This may also help to heal the mental health condition of the aggrieved wife as such behaviour of extramarital affair may instigate the wife to commit self-harm, harm the children in anger and frustration and also take certain irrational coping mechanisms like attacking the 'girlfriend' of the husband or the husband himself for taking revenge etc, which in turn may attract criminal liability for her.

CONCLUSION

Extramarital affairs in Hindu marriages by unfaithful husbands have been considered as trivial behavioural wrong for long. As we understand from the above paragraphs, the ancient Hindu code did not consider it as an offence in marriage, but the norms and customary practices did to a certain extent sympathize with aggrieved women. This shows hidden existence of TJ norms in the ancient Indian understandings which encouraged restitution of justice for women through family counselling and counselling by village and community elders. But this was not of much help. Women who had been cheated in marriage due to extramarital affairs of unfaithful husbands could not get proper legal attention till the contemporary period in modern India when the judges started considering the mental wellbeing of the victims of marriage related wrongs. With the expansion of scope of application of TJ principles in matrimonial issues, courts are encouraging litigants and victims to seek alternative dispute resolution mechanisms. In case of family matters India is witnesses more involvement of ADR mechanisms which include family elders to reach an amicable solution for the issue. The positive point is, women who had been victimised by extramarital affairs, can speak to the counsellors and family elders and members to express their concerns, their anger and frustration. Most of these discussions may follow TJ approaches and may provide a healing touch to the victims especially because such discussions are dismissing social blame game on the aggrieved wives. Even though many women may opt for divorce due to extramarital affairs of their husbands, traditional approaches based on ancient understandings offer a range of options. The present TJ connected trends are also empowering women to understand their rights in this regard. It is expected that Indian family laws may explore and apply TJ principles more to address the issue of unfaithfulness of husbands and extramarital affairs as punishable behavioural wrongs and such behaviours may be construed as causing mental cruelty which may further help aggrieved women to be saved from social blame game and be empowered against oppression.

REFERENCES

Ahmad, J., Khan, N., & Mozumdar, A. (2021). Spousal violence against women in India: A social–ecological analysis using data from the National Family Health Survey 2015 to 2016. *Journal of Interpersonal Violence*, *36*(21-22), 10147–10181. doi:10.1177/0886260519881530 PMID:31642354

Asati, G. (2019). The Correlative Notion of Dharma as Duties in Hindu Law. *Supremo Amicus*, *10*, 106.

DebaratiH. (2015). Cyber Stalking Victimisation of Women: Evaluating the Effectiveness of Current Laws in India from Restorative Justice and Therapeutic, in Jurisprudential Perspectives. *TEMIDA*, 103-130. doi:10.2298/TEM1504103H

Dey, A., & Orton, B. (2016). Gender and caste intersectionality in India: An analysis of the Nirbhaya case, 16 December 2012. In *Gender and race matter: Global perspectives on being a woman*. Emerald Group Publishing Limited. doi:10.1108/S1529-212620160000021006

Freeman, M. B. (2008). Love Means Always Having to Say You're Sorry: Applying the Realities of Therapeutic Jurisprudence to Family Law. *UCLA Women's Law Journal*, *17*(2), 215. doi:10.5070/L3172017812

Goyal, S. (2020). Prostitution: Legalising the White Slavery Abode. *Supremo Amicus*, *22*, 64.

Gupta, H., & Singh, Y. (2019). *Emerging trends of Hindu marriage and their impact*. Retrieved from https://www.researchgate.net/profile/Yogendra-Singh-57/publication/359002312_EMERGING_TRENDS_OF_HINDU_MARRIAGE_AND_THEIR_IMPACT/links/6221ba5a97401151d2fab5ef/EMERGING-TRENDS-OF-HINDU-MARRIAGE-AND-THEIR-IMPACT.pdf

Halder, D. (2015). *Cyber Stalking Victimisation of Women: Evaluating the Effectiveness of Current Laws in India from Restorative Justice and Therapeutic Jurisprudential Perspectives*. Academic Press.

Jassal, N. (2020). Gender, law enforcement, and access to justice: Evidence from all-women police stations in India. *The American Political Science Review*, *114*(4), 1035–1054. doi:10.1017/S0003055420000684

Kalita, S (2022). Introducing goddesses as role models: a selective examination of some sahadharmini ideals in goddesses. *Women and Nation Building*, 23.

Karlekar, M. (1995). Reflections on Kulin Polygamy—Nistarini Debi's Sekeley Katha. *Contributions to Indian Sociology, 29*(1-2), 135-155. Retrieved from https://www.cwds.ac.in/wp-content/uploads/2016/09/ReflectionsonKulinPolygamy.pdf

Krishnamurthy, V. (2017). The concept of dharma in Indian jurisprudence. *VIDHIGYA: The Journal of Legal Awareness*, *12*(2), 31–37. doi:10.5958/0974-4533.2017.00011.2

Kumar & Associates. vs State of UP & Another CRIMINAL REVISION No. - 1092 of 2022. https://www.livelaw.in/pdf_upload/sushil-kumar-and-6-others-v-state-of-up-and-another-criminal-revision-no-1092-of-2022-allahabad-hc-416420.pdf

Kumar, V. (2017). Bigamy and Hindu marriage. *Journal of the Indian Law Institute*, *59*(4), 356–382.

Mitra, S. K., & Fischer, A. (2002). Sacred laws and the secular state: An analytical narrative of the controversy over personal laws in India. *India Review*, *1*(3), 99–130. doi:10.1080/14736480208404635

Pandey, M. (2018). *"My mother is a goddess","I am an inmate here": Male prisoners' attitudes towards women and their perceptions of culpability from Delhi Prison* [Doctoral dissertation]. Anglia Ruskin University.

Perlin, M. L., & Lynch, A. J. (2015). Love is just a four-letter word: Sexuality, international human rights, and therapeutic jurisprudence. *Canadian Journal of Comparative and Contemporary Law*, *1*, 9.

Perlin, M. L., & Lynch, A. J. (2016). Therapeutic Jurisprudence. In Sexuality, Disability, and the Law (pp. 145-157). Palgrave Macmillan. doi:10.1057/9781137481085_6

Pothen, S. (1989). Divorce in Hindu society. *Journal of Comparative Family Studies*, *20*(3), 377–392. doi:10.3138/jcfs.20.3.377

Ray, S. N. (1908). Sources of Hindu Law. *Allahabad LJ*, *5*, 249.

Sinha, K. (2014). Be It Manu, Be It Macaulay: Indian Law and the Problem of the Female Body. *J. Indian L. & Soc'y*, *5*, 61.

Thilagaraj, R. (2017). Nyaya Panchayat. In *Restorative Justice in India* (pp. 3–12). Springer. doi:10.1007/978-3-319-47659-9_1

Umashankar, P. (2022). Study of the Judiciary and Administration in Ancient India with Special Reference to Manusmriti and Arthashastra and Its Relevance in Present Indian System. *Issue 2 Int'l JL Mgmt. &. Human.*, *5*, 534.

Vatuk, S. (2013). The "women's court" in India: An alternative dispute resolution body for women in distress. *Journal of Legal Pluralism and Unofficial Law*, *45*(1), 76–103. doi:10.1080/07329113.2013.774836

Wexler, D. (2000). Therapeutic jurisprudence: An overview. *TM Cooley L. Rev.*, *17*, 125.

ENDNOTES

[1] For example, consider the second marriage of Kind Pandu with Madri, the princess of Madra Desha which was done for strengthening political ties between the two kingdoms.

[2] See S.3(a) of the Protection of women from domestic violence Act, 2005, which says as follows: For the purposes of this Act, any act, omission or commission or conduct of the respondent shall constitute domestic violence in case it(a) harms or injures or endangers the health, safety, life, limb or well-being, whether mental or physical, of the aggrieved person or tends to do so and includes causing physical abuse, sexual abuse, verbal and emotional abuse and economic abuse; This has been further discussed later.

[3]   See in S. 5 of the Hindu Marriage Act, 1955, Act no.25 of 1955. Available @ https://highcourtchd.gov.in/hclscc/subpages/pdf_files/4.pdf

[4]   While this book chapter was being written, the Indian parliamentarians were also considering making a uniform age of twenty-one years as the legal age for entering into marriage for Hindus.

[5]   See in S.494 Indian Penal Code, 1860, Act no 45 of 1860.

[6]   This can be seen in Protection of Children from Sexual Offences Act, 2012, The Sexual Harassment of Women at Workplace (Prevention, Prohibition and Redressal) Act 2013.

[7]   See S.498A of the Indian Penal Code, Act no. 45 of 1860.

[8]   See S.3 of the Protection Of Women From Domestic Violence Act, 2005, ACT NO. 43 OF 2005.

APPENDIX: CASES

Joseph Shine v. Union of India, 2018 SCC On Line SC 1676.
Lily Thomas vs Union of India, AIR 2000 SC 1650
Sarala Mudgal vs Union of India, AIR 1995 SC 1531.

Section 4

Indigenous Wisdom: Native American and First Nation

Chapter 8
The Drum Speaks

Rosemary White Shield
Council of State Governments Justice Center, USA

Rod Robinson
Center for Strength Based Practices, USA

ABSTRACT

Many aspects of global Indigenous wisdom teach us that true justice is a spiritual force that allows for the ebb and flow of balance to enter and sustain human reality. Within this form of justice is the organic movement of healing and restoration for the continuation of life. Indigenous perspectives on the concept and practice of restorative justice are often expressed as a process that acts to open a pathway for justice intended to restore balance and to engage the healing process for individuals, families, communities, and creation. The chapter presents the kinship system model as a non-linear structure within an indigenous paradigm to reference principles of restorative justice, therapeutic jurisprudence, and Indigenous wisdom through a non-colonial process of discernment, understanding, and ways of knowing.

INTRODUCTION

In Native American and First Nation justice philosophy and practice, healing, along with reintegrating individuals into their community, is more important than punishment. The Native peacemaking process involves bringing together victims, offenders, and their supporters to get to the bottom of a problem. While contrary to traditional Eurocentric justice, this parallels the philosophy and processes of

DOI: 10.4018/978-1-6684-4112-1.ch008

the modern restorative justice movement. In the Native worldview there is a deep connection between justice and spirituality: in both, it is essential to maintain or restore harmony and balance (Mirsky, 2004).

As illustrated above, the process of Indigenous restorative justice and therapeutic jurisprudence from many perspectives rests on the understanding that all of Creation is interconnected and individual actions create "ripple" effects that affect the whole of Life. As Unci Edna Little Elk stated, "A child is taught that an ant, a butterfly, a plant, a tree, the fish, the sky is just as important as they are…when a person or being dies, the universe shifts to accommodate that loss" (White Hat, L. 2003). Indigenous restorative practices often point to the healing principles of Traditional Law, and that Elders are the embodiment of Indigenous Law (Johnson, 2014). Established through the course of thousands of years of lived experience, the Law provides foundational security, safety and wellness but also moves to accommodate the individual and the experience of societies. When offered to victims of crime and those who perpetrate the crime, global Indigenous wisdom contained in traditional oral libraries and the keepers of those libraries, our Elders, has and continues to provide direction to attain effective results in bringing forth the power of justice, safety, and healing.

Need for an Indigenous Paradigm

This effort seeks to examine and present the conceptual understanding and thematic principles from several diverse tribal perspectives of restorative justice and therapeutic jurisprudence which has been present for millennia and retains its resiliency in face of colonization. In order to form context for a conceptual understanding of this reality and to clearly optimize it, an Indigenous frame of reference needs to be brought into the discussion. A number of Native peoples are calling for the employment of worldviews, paradigms, theories of knowledge, and methods Indigenous to Native cultures in intellectual endeavors (Simpson, 2001). Kuokkanen (2000) discusses the need and significance of an "Indigenous paradigm" as a way of decolonizing Indigenous minds by "re-centering" Indigenous values and cultural practices. Kuokkanen (2000) cites the move toward an Indigenous paradigm as an essential piece of Indigenous peoples' struggle for self-determination and psychological decolonization which moves away from prevailing Western models and Euro-centered thinking.

Another significant reason for the use of an Indigenous paradigm is connected to the on-going concerns and questions regarding who decides what knowledge is relevant, and how it is relevant, to Indigenous people. In addition, concerns about the decision making process in knowledge construction related to Indigenous peoples also center on the identification and interpretation of ways of knowing and theorizing.

Indigenous acquisition of knowledge is reflected in an Indigenous cultural context, which is infused and founded upon a spiritual reality and experience of that spiritual reality (Kuokkanen, 2000).

This knowledge might come to us from relationships, experiences, storytelling, dreams, participation in ceremonies, from the Elders, the oral tradition, experimentation or observation; from children or from teachers in the plant and animal worlds. (Peat, 1994, cited in Simpson, 2001).

It is essential in the examination of the restorative justice and therapeutic jurisprudence that the employment of an Indigenous paradigm is used in understanding the deep contexts and principles that bring the healing of the Law into being.

METHODOLOGY

The methodology that was used for the study was a qualitative culturally responsive research method based on relational axiology perspectives which include non-Western values based co-construction of knowledge and ways of knowing where the research process underscores collective connectedness and non-hierarchical relationships between the researcher and participants. Data was collected primarily through a philosophic sagacity interview method which allowed the researchers to find wisdom held within cultural communities that often may not be in written literature.

Approach

Based on this qualitative, culturally responsive research, the authors understood the following. Native societies are relationship based. Traditional relationships and roles were refined over thousands of years of lived experience and have been effective cultural strengths and sources of resilience for Indigenous Nations. These relationships and roles have sustained and promoted the continuing life of Indigenous peoples in all its facets: spiritual, mental, emotional, physical, and social. They have enabled Native peoples to fully embrace life-giving experiences, protect them from destruction during colonization and continue the foundation for restorative justice and therapeutic jurisprudence.

However, the effects of colonization, historical trauma and its systemic encroachment have oftentimes disrupted these relationships and roles. Social competencies within a traditional context have often been distorted or removed. Expectations and education about how to treat oneself and others have become unclear and confusing in some situations. Relying on Indigenous systems and principles of restoration and justice revitalizes our tribal consciousness and rebuilds our sense of belonging to heal from the effects of colonization, trauma, victimization and committed crimes against people.

The authors introduce a **Kinship System Model** of restorative justice and therapeutic jurisprudence that embraces the revitalization of a traditional kinship network, a Circle of greater understanding that surrounds each individual with support and guidance to promote healing and peacemaking. It is based on the traditional spiritual view of family-relatives supporting, providing care through honesty, responsibility, accountability, and the expectation of courage when helping one another to fully be the people the Creator created intended them to be, which in turns infuses healing into the Community, all of our Relatives and Creation itself.

By uniting around individuals, the Circle brings forth organic and natural systems inherent for thousands of years in the traditions and values, which powerfully provide effective healing and recovery approaches for those that are suffering. With intensely centering these culturally intrinsic systems into a structure that specifically focuses on life affirming solutions versus attempting to "fix" a problem or worse yet, punishing the individual for wrong choices, it is believed that it is more important to seek spiritual healing and fair and accountable justice for persons and community in order to arrive at a place of safety and restoration. Successful results are anticipated to be substantially increased, and further effects from the victimization and perpetration experiences can be reduced in families and Communities.

Drawing on the vast expanse of the global Indigenous wisdom found in the oral libraries, lived experience, and the embodiment of the Law, our Elders, the Kinship System Model embodies several aspects. The four aspects of the Kinship System Model are:

Knowledge
Synergistic Participation
Interpretation
Expression

The authors recognize that our Ancestors teach us that within these aspects are certain principles that rest on the power of the sacred four directions, ancient traditions, and the sacred winds which bring them into being in our human endeavors. The principles can act as guiding methods of inquiry into the inherent Indigenous wisdom which is tribe and community specific and can support the bringing of justice and therapeutic jurisprudence to the forefront of healing. The principles can function as a lens for possible consideration in the reflection of actualizing justice, restoration, and healing for all concerned **as tribally determined**. The principles are:

1. The deeper purpose of justice is to bring the restoration of balance to the Community
2. Inherent in the restoration process is healing for all concerned
3. Therapeutic jurisprudence is understood within the context of the worldview that all is interdependent and connected; therefore, it cannot be understood as transactional, individual or as a compartmentalized process-it must be relational in all its processes in order for the Circle to be complete.

Author Dr. White Shield reflects: "In moving through the process of receiving the wisdom of those who know so much more than I, I was guided to a sense of choice about what I would listen to, what I would see, what I would take into myself, what I would offer to others, and what I would pass by because of the effects of colonization on my thinking and feeling. I was encouraged to not struggle to remove the effects but focus on all the words uttered by Creation I could listen to, all that I could see, all that I was given to me to carry forth to offer to others for their consideration. I was invited to move from my head to deeper in my heart.

The choice of carrying that from others who knew so much more than I was an honor and affected me profoundly. I humbly stood in front of the wisdom, seeing that it was not only words that were spoken and written, but every moment of the Elders' lives that brought them to this space and time on their life journey where the wisdom was held. It shimmered and flowed, alive and vibrant with the breath of those who generously gave it as messages to the world, as Medicine to ease suffering and bring healing that comes from true justice.

I was assured that this choice and action of what to see, what to listen to, and understand was a healing for the effects of colonization on myself, and that process, if undertaken not only by myself, but also by others in their own ways, would contribute to the healing and restoration of balance, which is true justice, from several Indigenous perspectives. I was shown that the Kinship System was not compartmentalized, not linear, but a description of a structure that allowed the braiding of the three principles between the Model's areas of focus and the application of those principles. I was shown that knowledge could not live in isolation as a single entity without connection to expression, that interpretation of knowledge could move to deeper levels if there was a synergistic participation **together** of all concerned in the restorative justice and therapeutic jurisprudence experience in Community. I learned that the four aspects of the Kinship System Model could not be prescriptive but were intertwined with the principles. Understanding the Model in this way illuminated that true justice was not only limited to offense and accountability but could help revitalization of all areas of Indigenous life and move us away from the effects of colonization." As a Potawatomi Elder shared, "Traditional Justice would benefit individuals, families, clan groups and Tribal Nations significantly. Reinstating traditional belief systems and practices would go hand in hand with Native endeavors to bring back languages, customs, and community development" (Cross Bear, 2022).

A Ponca Elder explained that true justice requires an end to injustice by the person who commits the injustice and "ending bad behavior which the community has witnessed, offering to do good things and ending the Black Road that one walked and going over to the Red Road." (Stubben, 2022). The author Dr. White Shield comments "I was reminded that there are many languages in Creation that generously offer guidance and help for these things to happen. I understood that a powerful voice in Creation, the Drum, gathers us once again. All we have to do is Listen."

LISTEN TO THE DRUM

The author R. Robinson comments "Before I offered these words on paper, I traveled to my ancestral homeland to speak with a Northern Cheyenne Elder and Holy Man, Two Moons, who gave me permission to speak as I have. I prepared my words in prayer offering our sacred herbs, cedar, sage and sweetgrass, asking that Creator guide my words so that they may reach those that are suffering, as well as those that are searching for meaning, in hopes that they will serve as a light on their path to the Creator. Aho, White Eagle."

Both authors offer the following understanding from the wisdom offered to them. It is impossible to list all those who have contributed to our understanding over our lifetimes. Each of us will at several point(s) in our lives be faced with needing to listen to the wisdom offered by those who have walked before us, our Elders, the drum keepers, the pipe carriers, the wisdom keepers, the Medicine people, the holy women, and men. At these times, we will have little choice but to consider and listen, as the course our life has taken us naturally or painfully to a place where certain questions must be answered. What is happening in my life, where is my life going, what is my purpose, where do I belong, who do I belong to, where is my home and when it finally comes to my time to cross over, alas what have I given to life that will last or have I simply taken from others?

We are all given choices from early on to listen to the teachings given by our parents, grandparents, and relatives, not just through hearing, more so through our senses. If we are fortunate, we will have teachers that have encouraged us to, "listen to the wind, it talks - listen to the silence, it speaks - listen to your heart, it knows" (Native American Proverb).

This is where, whether we realize it or not, we are called to gather our many life lessons in a manner that will serve as us *well of wisdom*. For years or decades to come, we will fill it with many items, as we journey forward. It will not be until we stop looking forward ever striving to get, to experience, to achieve, to own, that there will come a time when we need to slow in our taking and accelerate our need to give, to share, to serve. We will look back at so many memories, many that are joy filled – holding in our arms new life as it comes into this world, as well as sorrow filled days – holding in our arms fathers as they pass from this world. We have gathered smells, tastes, touches, stories, experiences, thousands of images, all have stayed with us indelibly and have formed the very ground that we stand on.

Realization will begin to sink in that we now must begin teaching those that are coming behind us. We will now honor the teachings we have been given, even though we seemed to have ignored or seemingly forgotten them as we passed from youth into our Elder years. We will no longer regret our past, rather we will use it as wisdom to be passed on. We will gain a profound realization that we now must begin giving away every morsel of what our life has taught us, we will cease to take and will begin to serve.

This now becomes our life framework, this is what will shape us, the experience, strength, and hope that will guide us and give us the emotional, psychological, and spiritual balance we seek, we realized that without it we had been left vulnerable to the influence of the behaviors of negative forces and others that may not have had our best interests at heart and the result became painful, if not catastrophic, not only for ourselves but those that love us.

This speaks directly to the reality of addiction and the destructive path it has carved throughout Indigenous lives, homes, communities, and land. It has become the "root cause" of the violence that we see committed on ourselves and others. The cause of losing hope to the point of self-harm, the reason the jails are full of Native despair, and why all that are experiencing this darkness will find themselves standing at a turning point and need to be given the opportunity to turn from these ways. This can also be referred to in the Western world as including therapeutic jurisprudence, that social force that will bring with it either positive or negative consequences and a reaction to our choice of action. It is important, however, that the Western system of crime and punishment recognize that there are other powerful healing ways that will encourage our sisters and brothers to listen, to learn, and to act on what must be changed in their lives, they recognize that if allowed a path, their time is now.

There are sayings, often given by grandparents, to Native children that act as the influence of Indigenous social force-they are intended to help the child see and strike a balance for understanding life; "if you are not looking for trouble, you do not have to worry about finding it, because trouble is not looking for you, however if you are looking for trouble, trouble will always find you". Another saying is, "whatever you put out into the world in words or actions, will come back to visit you. If it is kindness, then kindness will be returned to you, if it is malice, then malice will be returned to you."

The importance of listening to these teachings will cause one to decide, is this a task that must be done against my youthful will or rather an encouragement to choose the right path for our journey to a new adventure. We will face these kinds of choices many times and must learn to braid them in a way that builds a strength of character needed to give rather than take? In many of the Indigenous cultures and customs, these teachings are the most important lessons the Elders are going to teach, because if you have strength of character, you have respect of and for others and stand to achieve the balance that we seek and what is wanted for us by those that love us.

This is meant to say that all balance comes from a system of justice, which is what all of society is built on, both natural law and man-made laws. We all must recognize and adhere to these laws if we are to live together in a good way, a natural way. This chapter is offering an examination and question of culturally based perspectives on justice. How does a mainstream culture pursue justice against how an Indigenous population believes justice needs to be seen?

These perspectives will determine the path that either tries to "fix the problem and have the person pay the price of consequence for a wrong choice or to teach each person that has wronged another, how to choose a path that has more balance and leads to a healthier solution for living. Tradition teaches that justice in its true and intended form, must be respected, and honored as the Creator has given freedom of choice to all and tools to be used either as a swift sword, in the Western way, or as principles for living in the Indigenous world, which are intended to guide a person to a balanced way of living versus being punished in equal measure for the crime. Neither is all right and certainly not wrong, however it becomes critical that consideration be given to the difference in culture(s) that each live in and abide by.

These guiding principles are at the heart of every culture, ever reminding us to put principles before personalities… which asks of us to use the right lens to allow one to see and the quietness to hear what answer the drum, the wisdom keepers are telling and leading us to do. That time is now!

The Elders will rarely give us a direct answer to a direct question, rather the answer is buried inside of a story, such as, "whenever you are faced with a difficult question or challenge, it is important for you to think like water. Water always knows where home is and how to get there by many paths and nothing will keep it from getting there" (Northern Cheyenne Elder).

Translated, if we are painstaking in our efforts to change we need to remain patient and learn the lesson that if we are able to wait, listen to counsel and not act on the immediate emotion, we will save ourselves and others from the "ripple effect of dropping a stone (emotion/word/action) into a still body of water," which causes rings of reaction to our actions, be it positive or negative. All must stand accountable for our words and actions, that is what natural law calls for.

Restoration and healing are the primary base of solution that is the most sought after in our Indigenous ways, rather than making sure that the punishment fits the crime. However, the Western way of justice is encouraged to consider the Indigenous ways of applied solutions as they are not always as black and white as one would want and certainly not simple. In fact, often they can be quite severe if the actions the person committed on another are called for, however they are always intended to teach rather than simply punish and often times will require that the person committing the action restore as much as possible in kind, what has been taken from the victim as a result of their violation.

To bring these teachings into a contemporary context and better fit with therapeutic jurisprudence and a restorative model of justice the following model and method for change that is parallel to Indigenous ways is offered by the *Heart and Soul of Change* (Hubbel, Duncan and Miller, 1999). Housed within the four aspects of the Kinship System Model, it can provide reference points for actionable application of the Kinship System Model. These concepts are translated as follows:

Extra-Therapeutic Factors

Creating a non-judgmental teaching versus treatment environment designed to help the person to recognize that they carry an inherent ability to change attitude and actions within themselves regardless of an outside intent to help and that this natural healing ability can be actualized regardless of their circumstances or environment. To treat a person's clinical condition is a Western approach to change, the Indigenous approach is to teach a person how to harness their own power to create and live in a recovery environment.

Therapeutic Alliances

Recognizing each person as an individual deserving of respect and reserving any judgement of the person's circumstances for how they arrived at this point in time, allows for a welcoming opportunity to be attracted to change rather than having it promoted as a "change or else approach." If a helper is sincere in this approach, it will create a strong rapport between each person and their helper or mentor.

Notice that we refer to a helper or mentor rather than therapist as this reference fits more with the Indigenous practice of teaching a person to create and maintain a skillset of solutions that they can own for life, rather than coming to the therapist for the answers as if the person lacks the ability to change unless if comes from an outside source.

Method and Technique

The Western approach to change often wants to create or employ a "best practice" approach to solving problems that can simply be adjusted or adapted to multiple persons and ethnic populations, when in fact the Indigenous approach says there is no right way. "It matters not how you come to this time in your life requiring change, it matters most that you simply come with an honest desire to change and a willingness to be taught new ways and solutions for living. The intent here is to guide a person toward what motivates them for change versus telling them through a particular philosophic approach what they need to do to "fix their problem."

Hope and Expectancy

This is what is at the heart of the Indigenous practice of healing versus treating a disease or diagnosed clinical disorder. If we are painstaking and present in our approach to the above three principles for activating long-term change, then hope will naturally begin to flare for every individual. They will be less resistant to change and more willing to commit to it, if they have a sense of hope that this can work for them as well. Hope is not just for the lucky few, they too are able to hope for a better life.

When one studies the origins of the justice system, it is believed that the intent of incarceration is to rehabilitate a person back to where they were a contributing member of society. The Indigenous approach meets the person where they are at and teaches that this opportunity, no matter how challenging, is a gift from Creator that you that encourages you to reach out for the hope and the desire to take your life back, to recognize who you are, where you come from, where your home is and like water, change becomes the most natural course. To realize that there actually is an easier softer way to walk than what we have been doing and there are many people in our lives who will teach us how to walk more softly through our life.

Aho!

CONCLUSION

In the approach the authors took in bringing forth Indigenous wisdom within the realm of true justice and therapeutic jurisprudence, spiritual practices were emphasized which allowed the teachings of the Elders and Holy Ones to be made more visible. According to Ms. Fania Davis, a leader in this field, "unlike our prevailing justice system that sees religion or spirituality as something that must be kept out of and divorced from the process, restorative justice (RJ), rooted in indigenous worldviews, embraces a life-affirming, non-sectarian spirituality. Restorative justice sees justice as healing, relational, community-based, inclusivist, participatory, needs and accountability-based, and forward-looking. RJ is not merely a conflict resolution tool; it is a set of principles and a way of life" (Davis, 2017).

In coming full circle, the authors traveled to the North, South, East and West to gather the gifts of Indigenous wisdom from different Indigenous perspectives and ways of knowing to outline these principles and a way of life. We traveled to ancestral homelands and understood the gifts were not limited to space and time but had lived continuously in the lives of ancestors and relatives who ensured they would be kept for many others who would come after them. We bring them to a sacred common ground and offer them for your consideration in the journey we all are invited to take for true justice and healing in the global Indigenous community. We look forward to sharing the stories, experiences, and all the gifts the wisdom offered here might bring to an understanding of restorative justice practiced with the visibility of spiritual practices and acknowledgement of Kinship

REFERENCES

Davis, F. (2017). *Restorative Justice: Spiritual Resources for Sustainable Peace in Communities*. Harvard Divinity School News Archive. https://news-archive.hds.harvard.edu/news/2017/10/03/restorative-justice-spiritual-resources-sustainable-peace-communities

Hubble, M. A., Duncan, B. L., & Miller, S. D. (Eds.). (1999). *The heart and soul of change: What works in therapy*. American Psychological Association. doi:10.1037/11132-000

Johnson, S. (2014). Developing First Nations courts in Canada: Elders as foundational to Indigenous therapeutic jurisprudence +. *Journal of Indigenous Social Development, 3*(2). http://hdl.handle.net/10125/34473

Kuokkanen, R. (2000). Towards an "Indigenous paradigm" from a Sami perspective. *The Canadian Journal of Native Studies, 20*(2), 411–436.

Mirsky, L. (2004, April 27). *Restorative justice practices of Native American, First Nation and other Indigenous People of North America*. International Institute of Restorative Practices. https://www.iirp.edu/news/restorative-justice-practices-of-native-american-first-nation-and-other-indigenous-people-of-north-america-part-one

Simpson, L. (2001). Aboriginal peoples and knowledge: Decolonizing our processes. *The Canadian Journal of Native Studies*, *21*(1), 137–147.

White Hat, L. (2003, November 26). Seeking Our Wellness workshop offers positive resources to public. *Tribune/News*.

ADDITIONAL READING

Duncan, B. L., Miller, S. D., & Sparks, J. A. (2004). *The heroic client* (Revised ed.). Jossey-Bass.

Hand, C., Hankes, J., & House, T. (2012). Restorative justice: The indigenous justice system. *Contemporary Justice Review*, *15*(4), 449–467. Advance online publication. doi:10.1080/10282580.2012.734576

Hewitt, J. (2016). Indigenous restorative justice: Approaches, meaning & possibility. *UNBLJ*, *67*, 313.

Leeds, S. (2008, December 11). *The role of Tribal courts in promoting safety, justice, and healing: A Tribal justice perspective* [Keynote address]. 11th National Indian Nations Conference, reservation of the Agua Caliente Band of Cahuilla Indians, CA.

Zion, J. (2015). Navajo therapeutic jurisprudence. *Touro Law Review*, *18*(3). https://digitalcommons.tourolaw.edu/lawreview/vol18/iss3/9

Conclusion

Authors were invited to add closing comments, in any style, if inspired. These comments represent the metaphysical, epistemological, and ontological distinctiveness of their writing through stories, narratives, poetry, and teachings of their choice. These are their words.

THE COCKROACH WILL FIND NO JUSTICE IN THE COURT OF THE CHICKENS (Ghanaian Proverb, Translated From Twi)

COCKROACH HAVE NO BUSINESS IN FOWL HOUSE (Caribbean Proverb)

Seth Tweneboah & Anthony Richards

This proverb is used to comment on the inherent biases of insiders against the outsiders in any society. The use of an allegorical court to deliver this message is telling. Enslaved people were not allowed testify in court until after Emancipation. Despite national independence and other reforms of the late 20th century the processes of the courts in Commonwealth countries remain firmly enshrined in British tradition, to the exclusion of those of afro-descended peoples and their diverse world views.

A singular intersection with cultural diversity occurs at the swearing of a sacred oath on a holy book such as the Bible, Q'ran or Bagavahad Gita. This option is not typically extended to african-derived religions. For one, they often lack a canonical holy book as their beliefs have been transmitted orally. More importantly, these religions have been suppressed for centuries and, in places, devotees have been forced to gather in the dead of night in order to avoid invasions by police. However, adherents in the Americas are increasingly assertive. A case in point is the orisa religion derived from the Yoruba people of south-eastern Nigeria which flourishes as the spectacular Candomble of Brasil, and Santeria of Cuba. During the 59th Grammy Awards, the popular African-American singer Beyonce performed *Lemonade's*

"Love Drought" draped in brilliant golden maternity robes, representing the river orisa Osun, deity of love, sweetness, wealth and fertility.

The stern orisa Ogun, deity of mettalurgy and war is also the harbinger of divine justice. In Yorubaland of Nigeria, people traditionally swore oaths by Ogun. During the 1990s adherents in Trinidad & Tobago petitioned to be allowed to swear by the Iron of Ogun in courts. Although the approximately 200 orisha shrines represent only 1% of the population, they were supported by other civil society groups, and eventually won this right.

Trinidadian elder, Iya Eintou Springer wrote to us as follows: "The pieces of metal were fashioned by Babalorisa Sam Phills with the approval of the Council of Orisa Elders headed by Iya Gbogbo Melvina Rodney. There were seven pieces of metal that being the number sacred to Ogun, the father of truth and justice. Iya Rodney's shrine, Egbe Orisa Ile Wa was central to this initiative. On Iya's spiritual transition, her children myself, Rawle Gibbons and Funso Aiyejina as well as Iyalorisa Shangowumi and Baba Sam himself were central to the negotiations with the Attorney General's office. I believe it was in 2000"

****

OUR CONCLUSION

Beulah Shekhar, Ranjani Castro, and Hitesh Goyal, India

In conclusion, it's time to revisit our justice system that existed in the country, prior to the arrival of the British having the basic principles of restorative justice intertwined in their quaint way, when the offender, the victim, their families and the the community sat together under the village banyan tree and dispensed justice with a focus of the victims' needs'. With the advent of time our ancient justice system was replaced by the common law system and the focus shifted to the accused and I guess we 'threw the baby out with the bath water.'

Though not well documented, India can also, like the Maoris and the Aboriginal people and the Red Indians, pride itself on the indigenous wisdom in the justice delivery mechanism for holistic justice and healing. The time is finally ripe to reintroduce the healing components of therapeutic jurisprudence on the one side and the basic tenets of restorative justice on the other and see them as two sides of the same coin. In the words of a Tamil poet in chapter 55 of the Thirukural, his collection of couplets says that, "investigating intensely, leading fairly without unduly favouring anyone, analysing and acting, constitute justice".

****

204

IN CONCLUSION

Swikar Lama, India

The two objectives of the study are- (1) To evaluate the pros and cons of some community based ADR systems in India and to understand necessary conditions under which principles of restorative justice may be implemented. (2) To find out the needs and changes which the participants desire in the existing alternative dispute resolution systems.

The community based ADRS chosen for this study were viewed through the restorative justice perspective. Even though the ADRS were not formal forms of restorative justice, the agenda and aim of both ADRS and Restorative Justice were similar to each other. Hence the study tried to explore whether these ADRs followed the principles of Restorative Justice. Apart from looking at these institutions through the restorative justice perspective, the study also examined whether these ADRS are also affected by the patriarchal ideology which affects society even today.

Women victims often desire matters of domestic violence to remain private so that the honour of family remains intact. In these community based ADRS, the arena is public as well as private. It is public because it takes place in the presence of family, neighbors, and the community but at the same time it does not bring the matter outside the closed community of known people which happens in criminal and civil courts. Hence the 'public-private' distinction gets blurred but remains distinct when seen through different perspectives. At the same time some involvement of the community is often desired by the victims because they want the wrongdoing done to them to be validated by the society. They also want their transgressors to be shamed or vindicated by the community so that the abuse does not get repeated. The community provides social control so that the Samaj members and members of the community keep an eye on the transgressor.

Looking at the findings of the study from a holistic perspective we can point out a few things. These community based Alternative Dispute Resolution Systems prove to be a blessing for many women victims of domestic violence who are not willing to approach the criminal justice system or civil system due to social or economic reasons. However, it is still a sad situation that women have no other choice but to fall back on these ADRS because of the patriarchal society. In most cases these ADRS act as a platform for the women to negotiate with their spouses and in-laws to ensure their safety.

Finally, the last suggestion is that although marriage and family are institutions which are important and need to be preserved as much as possible through reconciliation or mediation but not at the cost of the safety or happiness of an individual. Hence it is a very important responsibility which has been bestowed upon the mediators and Samaj members to decide what is best for the participants as well as the accused and advise them accordingly. The success of an institution lies in whether they make correct judgements and make this society a safer and happier society to live in.

Eventually, institutions and ADRS can only help to a certain extent but unless until the people and community do not address the issues of patriarchy, gender inequality and sexism and in doing so, change women's and men's socialization (perceptions of masculine and feminine behaviour) domestic violence will continue to happen and institutions including both Criminal Justice system and ADRS will struggle to deal with it.

****

The Shuddering

By Rosemary White Shield

Did the sun rise that morning?
I couldn't know when I was carrying my son's casket to the grave
A beloved life on Earth taken by the hands of another.
Each step requiring a commitment to Love no matter what.
Questioning in those steps, where was justice?
As my feet and spirit felt the weight of all in my hands
I saw through my ways
Creation shuddering with me
There was comfort in that
A holy silence born by my ancestors with me
A time out of time
Like when one is in love
Or bearing the impossible
the unspeakable
the ultimate wrong
And where does the heart go then?
To the only place that really matters
Love in its fullest form
With all the gifts in her hands

Beckoning to understand
What true justice is
The balancing
The restoration
Not of so much of what has been lost
But what is found on the Trail
Of Life, of continuing to Love
For those that will accept it
The Drum from my ancestors beckons, invites, speaks
To embrace Love from the sunrise within ourselves
To encourage the sun rising in others who are not blinded by the light,
To hear the deep shuddering of Creation
As the beginning sounds of healing
Where we can carry our ancestors' words
Spoken through others in present day
And give them to the world,
To have them burn for all others who come after us.

****

The Eagle and the Condor: A Prophecy

By Marta Vides Saade

Wait five hundred years.
Now. Eagle and Condor fly.
Together. Unite.

These lines represent a prophecy related by a Quechuan Elder during the First Encuentro of Indigeneous Peoples in Quito, Ecuador in 1990 at a gathering of over 200 representatives from the north, central and south parts of the hemisphere (Appla-Yala). It tells of an encounter between the Condor of Urin (the south) and the Eagle of Hanan (the north) The Condor and the Eagle join their tears from Jahanpacha (the sky) to Ucupacha (the underground) to cauterize the wounds of Out of this union sprang present-day Central America. In this piece of earth was concentrated the wisdom of Hana (the North) and Urin (South). Nature and the Universe will rejuvenate the old and nourish the reunited people with pure energy.

This was related orally by a well-regarded Elder. This resonated with those present as consistent with some of their own prophecies about the return of ceremony, tradition, and healing. Those present went on their way after being told to maintain their traditions and that the time for hiding traditions in order to preserve them was passing. That the time for healing was now. From this moment arose many actions. One of them is a ceremonial run known as the Peace and Dignity Journeys that run from Alaska in the north and from Tierra del Fuego in the south, to unite in a middle place. https://realpeoples.media/the-inca-prophecy-of-the-eagle-and-the-condor/ The ceremony takes place every four years. The next ceremony is in 2024. https://www.facebook.com/supportpdj/ There was strength in this prophecy.

The "Eagle and the Condor" are the words that came to me when one of the book authors asked me how I came the idea for this book. Ceremony. Some of us run. Some of us write.

Compilation of References

Agyekum, K. (1999). The Pragmatics of Duabo "Grievance Imprecation" Taboo among the Akan. *Pragmatic, 9*(3), 357–382.

Ahmad, J., Khan, N., & Mozumdar, A. (2021). Spousal violence against women in India: A social–ecological analysis using data from the National Family Health Survey 2015 to 2016. *Journal of Interpersonal Violence, 36*(21-22), 10147–10181. doi:10.1177/0886260519881530 PMID:31642354

Al-e-Ahmad, J. (1968). Triennial Memoir [Kār-nāma-ye se sāla]. Tehran.

Allendorf, K. E. E. (2009). *The quality of family relationships, women's agency, and maternal and child health in India* [Doctoral dissertation]. University of Wisconsin-Madison.

Allendorf, K. (2012). Like daughter, like son? Fertility decline and the transformation of gender systems in the family. *Demographic Research, 27*(16), 429–454. doi:10.4054/DemRes.2012.27.16 PMID:27147902

Anderson, A. M. (2003). Restorative justice, the African philosophy of Ubuntu and the diversion of criminal prosecution. In *17th International Conference of the International Society for the Reform of Criminal Law* (pp. 24-28). Academic Press.

ArafaM. A. (2018). Islamic Criminal Law: The Divine Criminal Justice System between Lacuna and Possible Routes. *Journal of Forensic and Crime Studies, 102*. https://ssrn.com/abstract=3189521

Arjmandi, G., & Noroozi, A. (2010). Conflict Resolution among the Bakhtiaris of Izeh: 'Khoon-bori' or 'Khoon-bas' as a Custom. *Iranian Journal of Social Problems in Iran, 1*(1), 1–44. https://journals.ut.ac.ir/article_20744.html

Asadullah, M., Kashyap, R., Tiwari, R., & Sakafi, N. (2021). Community and Restorative Justice Practices in India, Nepal, and Bangladesh: A Comparative Overview. In T. Gavrielides (Ed.), *Comparative Restorative Justice*. Springer. doi:10.1007/978-3-030-74874-6_11

Asati, G. (2019). The Correlative Notion of Dharma as Duties in Hindu Law. *Supremo Amicus, 10*, 106.

Assmann, J. (1992). When Justice Fails: Jurisdiction and Imprecation in Ancient Egypt and the Near East. *The Journal of Egyptian Archaeology, 78*(1), 149–162. doi:10.1177/030751339207800108

Atmasasmita, R. (2018). *Integrative Law Theory, Reconstruction of Development Law Theory and Progressive Law Theory*. Genta Publishing.

Bajpai, G. S. (2002). Towards Restorative Justice. Development Without Disorders.

Bakhtiarnejad, P. (2009). *Faaje'eye Khamush: ghatlhaye namusi* [The Silent Tragedy: Honor Killing]. https://engare.net/honor-killing/

Baldwin, G. B. (1973). The Legal System of Iran. *International Lawyer, 7*(2), 492-504. https://scholar.smu.edu/til/vol7/iss2/19

Barton, C. K. (2003). *Restorative justice: The empowerment model*. Hawkins Press.

Batley, M., & Dodd, J. (2005). International Experiences and Trends. In Beyond Retribution: Prospects for Restorative Justice in South Africa. Pretoria: Monograph Series No 111.

Bazelon, L. (2018). *Rectify: The Power of Restorative Justice After Wrongful Conviction*. Beacon.

Bazemore, G. (1998). Restorative justice and earned redemption communities, victims, and offender reintegration. *The American Behavioral Scientist, 41*(6), 768–813. doi:10.1177/0002764298041006003

Bazemore, G. (2005). Whom and How Do We Reintegrate? Finding Community in Restorative Justice. *Criminology & Public Policy, 4*(1), 131–148. doi:10.1111/j.1745-9133.2005.00011.x

Bazemore, S. G., & Walgrave, L. (1999). *Restorative juvenile justice: Repairing the harm of youth crime*. Criminal Justice Press.

Beckwith, M. W. (1929). *Black Roadways: A Study of Jamaican Folk Life*. University of North Carolina Press.

Bell, H. H. J. (1889). *Obeah: Witchcraft in The West Indies*. Sampson Low.

Bezuidenhout, C., & Joubert, S. (2003). *Child and Youth Misbehavior in South Africa: A Holistic View*. Van Schaik.

Bhadra, C., & Shah, M. T. (2007). *Nepal: Country gender profile*. Report prepared for JICA.

Bigdelou. (2020). Houses of Equity; judicial modernization or a return to procedural traditions. *Journal of Iran History, 13*(1), 101–120. doi:10.52547/irhj.13.1.101

Bilby, K. (1997). Swearing by the Past, Swearing to the Future: Sacred Oaths, Alliances, and Treaties among the Guianese and Jamaican Maroons. *Ethnohistory (Columbus, Ohio), 44*(4), 655–689. doi:10.2307/482884

Bolivar, D. (2010). Conceptualizing Victims 'Restoration' in Restorative Justice. *International Review of Victimology, 17*(3), 237–265. doi:10.1177/026975801001700301

Braithwaite, J. (2007). Encourage restorative justice. *Criminology & Public Policy, 6*(4), 689–696. doi:10.1111/j.1745-9133.2007.00459.x

Compilation of References

Brathwaite, K. (1972). *The Development of Creole Society in Jamaica, 1770-1820*. Clarendon Press.

Bridgens, R. (1836). *West India scenery with illustrations of Negro character, the process of making sugar, &c. From sketches taken during a voyage to and residence of seven years in, the island of Trinidad*. R. Jennings.

Britannica. The Editors of Encyclopaedia. (2010). Mechanical and Organic Solidarity. *Encyclopedia Britannica.* https://www.britannica.com/topic/mechanical-and-organic-solidarity

Britannica. The Editors of Encyclopaedia. (2013). Victim-offender reconciliation. In *Encyclopedia Britannica.* https://www.britannica.com/topic/workhouse

Britannica. The Editors of Encyclopaedia. (n.d.). People of Iran. *Encyclopedia Britannica.* (https://www.britannica.com/place/Iran/The-Abbasid-caliphate-750-821

Burton, J. (1990). *Conflict: Resolution and Prevention* (1st ed.). St. Martin's Press.

Cabinet Decision. (2016). *The Regulation of Mediation in Criminal Matters 2016*, no. 52773/95749. https://rrk.ir/Laws/ShowLaw.aspx?Code=12750

Cayley, D. (1998). *The expanding prison: The crisis in crime and punishment and the search for alternatives*. Toronto: House of Anansi.

Chakraborty, N. (2021). The Role of Nyaya Panchayat in Delivery of Rural Justice in India: A Critical Analysis. *VIPS Student Law Review, 3*(1), 83–93.

Charles, C. (2020). Therapeutic jurisprudence in India and its scope in cases of domestic violence and sexual harassment. In *International Academic Conference on Access to Justice to End Violence*. UNODC & TISS.

Christie, N. (2007). *Limits to Pain: The Role of Punishment in Penal Policy*. Wipf and Stock Publication.

Cole, R. (2010). Juvenile offenders and the criminal justice system in Botswana: Exploring the restorative approach. *Reflections on Children in Botswana, 2010*, 54.

Collins, R. (2004). Interaction Ritual Chains. Princeton University Press.

Cominelli, L. (2018). *Cognition of the Law: Toward a Cognitive Sociology of Law and Behavior*. Springer. doi:10.1007/978-3-319-89348-8

Conners, R. (2003). Oppression Theory Critique. *Racial issues in criminal justice: The case of African Americans*, 255.

Cooper, C. (2019). Evaluating the Application of TJ Principles: Lessons from the Drug Court Experience. In *The Methodology and Practice of Therapeutic Jurisprudence*. Carolina Academic Press.

Cremini, H. (2007). *Peer Mediation: Citizenship And Social Inclusion Revisited: Citizenship and Social Inclusion in Action*. McGraw-Hill International.

Creswell, J. W., Plano Clark, V. L., Gutman, L. M., & Hanson, E. W. (2003). Advanced Mixed Methods Research. In *Handbook of Mixed Methods in Social & Behavioral Research*. Sage Publications.

Daicoff, S. (2000). The Role of Therapeutic Jurisprudence within the Comprehensive Law Movement. In *Practicing Therapeutic Jurisprudence: Law as a Helping Profession*. Carolina Academic Press.

Daicoff, S. (2013). Apology, Forgiveness, Reconciliation & Therapeutic Jurisprudence. *Pepperdine Dispute Resolution Law Journal*, *13*(1), 131–180.

Daly, K. (2000). Revisiting the relationship between retributive and restorative justice. *Restorative justice: Philosophy to practice*, 33-54.

Daly, K. (2002). Restorative justice: The real story. *Punishment & Society*, *4*(1), 55–79. doi:10.1177/14624740222228464

Daly, K., & Immarigeon, R. (1998). The Past, Present, and Future of Restorative Justice: Some Critical Reflections. *Contemporary Justice Review*, *1*(1).

Dargahi, H. & Beiranvand, A. (2021). *Macroeconomics and Social Harms/Problems: Investigating the Interaction between Divorce, Crime and Drug Addiction with Economic Growth in Iran*. Donya-ye-Eqtesad Publications.

Davis, F. (2017). *Restorative Justice: Spiritual Resources for Sustainable Peace in Communities*. Harvard Divinity School News Archive. https://news-archive.hds.harvard.edu/news/2017/10/03/restorative-justice-spiritual-resources-sustainable-peace-communities

DebaratiH. (2015). Cyber Stalking Victimisation of Women: Evaluating the Effectiveness of Current Laws in India from Restorative Justice and Therapeutic, in Jurisprudential Perspectives. *TEMIDA*, 103-130. doi:10.2298/TEM1504103H

Dey, A., & Orton, B. (2016). Gender and caste intersectionality in India: An analysis of the Nirbhaya case, 16 December 2012. In *Gender and race matter: Global perspectives on being a woman*. Emerald Group Publishing Limited. doi:10.1108/S1529-212620160000021006

Dignan, J. (2005). Understanding Victims and Restorative Justice. In Crime and Justice. Open University Press.

Dijk, J. J., Zebel, S., Classen, J., & Nelen, H. (2020). Victim-Offender Mediation and Reduced Reoffending: Gauging Self-Selection Bias. *Crime and Delinquency*, *66*(6-7), 949–972. doi:10.1177/0011128719854348

Dressler, J., Murphy, J. G., & Hampton, J. (1990). Hating Criminals: How Can Something That Feels So Good Be Wrong? *Michigan Law Review*, *88*(6), 1448–1473. doi:10.2307/1289323

Ebrahimi, M. (2020). *Khoon-bas* [Cease-Blood]. Center for the Great Islamic Encyclopedia. https://www.cgie.org.ir/fa/article/246533/%D8%AE%D9%88%D9%86-%D8%A8%D8%B3

Compilation of References

Ebrahimi, S. (Ed.). (2011). *Issues of Criminal Sciences: A Series of Lectures of Professor Ali-Hossein Nadjafi Abranabadi*. http://adminshop.mizanlaw.ir/Content/upload/Tblbooklet/be55ab6b2fb54c62a1999d5aa383b85d.pdf

Eglash, A. (1959). Creative restitution: Its roots in psychiatry, religion and law. *Brit. J. Delinq.*, *10*, 114.

Elechi, O., Morris, S. V., & Schauer, E. J. (2010). Restoring justice (ubuntu): An African perspective. *International Criminal Justice Review*, *20*(1), 73–85. doi:10.1177/1057567710361719

Ellis, A. B. (1887). *The Tshi-Speaking Peoples of Gold Coast of West Africa: Their Religion, Manners, Customs, Laws, Language, Etc*. Chapman and Hall.

Elmangoush, N. (2015). *Customary Practice and Restorative Justice in Libya*. United States Institute of Peace.

Emmanuel, K. (2015, September 6). *Angry youth of Nkoranza community revoke curses on Central Bank*. Pulse.Com.Gh. https://www.pulse.com.gh/ece-frontpage/illegal-microfinance-angry-youth-of-nkoranza-community-revoke-curses-on-central-bank/nje9d0d

Erbe, C. (2004). What is the Role of Professionals in Restorative Justice? In H. Zehr & B. Toews (Eds.), Critical Issues in Restorative Justice (pp. 289–297). Academic Press.

Erez, E., & Hartley, C. C. (2003). Battered Immigrant Women and the Legal System: A Therapeutic Jurisprudence Perspective. *Western Criminology Review*, 155–169.

Esposito, J. L. (Ed.). (1931). Qisas. In *The Oxford Dictionary of Islam*. Oxford Islamic Studies Online. https://www.oxfordislamicstudies.com/article/opr/t125/e1931) (https://www.oxfordislamicstudies.com/article/opr/t125/e1931

Evans, A., & Evans, A. (1977). An Examination of the Concept 'Social Solidarity.'. *Mid-American Review of Sociology*, *2*(1), 29–46. https://www.jstor.org/stable/23254926

Fathi, H. (2005). Dispute Resolution Councils: A Critic and Evaluation. *Islamic Law (Figh and Law)*, *1*(4), 85-108. http://hoquq.iict.ac.ir/article_22698.html?lang=fa

Foley, E. A. (2014). It still 'takes a village to raise a child'-an overview of the restorative justice mechanism under the Children's Protection and Welfare Act, 2011 of Lesotho. *Article 40, 16*(1), 15-19.

Fombad, C. M. (2004). Customary courts and traditional justice in Botswana: Present challenges and future perspectives. *Stellenbosch Law Review*, *15*(1), 166–192.

Freeman, M. B. (2008). Love Means Always Having to Say You're Sorry: Applying the Realities of Therapeutic Jurisprudence to Family Law. *UCLA Women's Law Journal*, *17*(2), 215. doi:10.5070/L3172017812

Fulcher, L. (2001). Cultural Wisdom: Lessons from Maori Wisdom. *Reclaiming Children and Youth*, *10*(3), 153–157.

Gade, C. B. (2013). Restorative justice and the South African truth and reconciliation process. *South African Journal of Philosophy= Suid-Afrikaanse Tydskrif vir Wysbegeerte, 32*(1), 10-35.

Gal, T., & Shidlo-Hezroni, V. (2011). Restorative Justice as Therapeutic Jurisprudence: The Case of Child Victims. In *Therapeutic Jurisprudence and Victim Participation in Justice: International Perspectives*. Carolina Academic Press.

Gaspar, D. B. (1999). *Bondmen and Rebels: A Study of Master-Slave Relations in Antigua*. Duke University Press.

Gavrielides, T., & Artinopoulou, V. (2016). *Reconstructing restorative justice philosophy*. Routledge. doi:10.4324/9781315604053

GhoshP. (2014). Restorative Justice: The New Paradigm in the Province of Justice in India? doi:10.2139/ssrn.2467373

Gilroy, P. (1993). *The Black Atlantic: Modernity and Double Consciousness*. Harvard University Press.

Gomda, A. R. (2015, August 29). Juju Hits EC. *Daily Guide*. https://www.modernghana.com/news/639445/juju-hits-ec.html

Goyal, S. (2020). Prostitution: Legalising the White Slavery Abode. *Supremo Amicus, 22,* 64.

Gray, N. (2000). *The Legal History of Witchcraft in Colonial Ghana: Akyem Abuakwa, 1913-1943* [Unpublished: Doctoral dissertation]. Columbia University.

Gray, N. (2001). Witches, Oracles, and Colonial Law: Evolving Anti-Witchcraft Practices in Ghana, 1927-1932. *The International Journal of African Historical Studies, 34*(2), 339–363. doi:10.2307/3097485 PMID:18198526

Gromet, D. M. (2012). Restoring the Victim: Emotional Reactions, Justice Beliefs, and Support for Reparation and Punishment. *Critical Criminology, 20*(1), 9–23. doi:10.100710612-011-9146-8

Grover, S. (2009). Lived experiences Marriage, notions of love, and kinship support amongst poor women in Delhi. *Contributions to Indian Sociology, 43*(1), 1–33. doi:10.1177/006996670904300101

Gupta, H., & Singh, Y. (2019). *Emerging trends of Hindu marriage and their impact*. Retrieved from https://www.researchgate.net/profile/Yogendra-Singh-57/publication/359002312_EMERGING_TRENDS_OF_HINDU_MARRIAGE_AND_THEIR_IMPACT/links/6221ba5a97401151d2fab5ef/EMERGING-TRENDS-OF-HINDU-MARRIAGE-AND-THEIR-IMPACT.pdf

Halder, D. (2015). *Cyber Stalking Victimisation of Women: Evaluating the Effectiveness of Current Laws in India from Restorative Justice and Therapeutic Jurisprudential Perspectives*. Academic Press.

Hamshahri. (n.d.). Combatting with Street Crime. *Weekly Annex of Hamshahri Newspaper, 175.*

Compilation of References

Hamshahri-Online. (n.d.). A *Narration of the National Register of a Traditional Ritual: Khuzestan laid claim to Cease-Blood (Khoon-bass)*. https://www.hamshahrionline.ir/news/541113/

Handler, J. S., & Bilby, K. M. (2012). *Enacting Power: The Criminization of Obeah in the Anglophone Caribbean 1760-2011*. University of the West Indies Press.

Harris, M. K. (1996). Key differences among community corrections acts in the United States: An overview. *The Prison Journal*, *76*(2), 192–238. doi:10.1177/0032855596076002006

Heaner, G. (2008). Religion, law and human rights in post-conflict Liberia. *African Human Rights Law Journal*, *8*(2), 458–485.

Hinz, M. O. (2008). *Traditional courts in Namibia–part of the judiciary? Jurisprudential challenges of traditional justice*. Academic Press.

Horn, N., & Bösl, A. (2008). *The independence of the judiciary in Namibia*. Macmillan Education.

Hubble, M. A., Duncan, B. L., & Miller, S. D. (Eds.). (1999). *The heart and soul of change: What works in therapy*. American Psychological Association. doi:10.1037/11132-000

Hurston, Z. N. (1931). Bahamian Obeah. *Journal of American Folklore*, 320–326.

Islamic Parliament Research Center of the Islamic Republic of Iran. (2000). *The Third Program of Economic, Social and Cultural Development Act*. https://rc.majlis.ir/fa/law/show/93301

Islamic Parliament Research Center of the Islamic Republic of Iran. (2002). *The Administrative Regulation of Article 189 of The Third Program of Economic, Social and Cultural Development Act*. https://rc.majlis.ir/fa/law/show/121958

ISNA. (2017). *Social Problems and the Danger of Insecurity in Society*. https://www.irna.ir/news/83054077/

Jassal, N. (2020). Gender, law enforcement, and access to justice: Evidence from all-women police stations in India. *The American Political Science Review*, *114*(4), 1035–1054. doi:10.1017/S0003055420000684

Johnson, S. (2014). Developing First Nations courts in Canada: Elders as foundational to Indigenous therapeutic jurisprudence +. *Journal of Indigenous Social Development*, *3*(2). http://hdl.handle.net/10125/34473

Johnstone, G., & Van Ness, D. W. (2007). The idea of restorative justice. Handbook of restorative justice, 1-23.

Johnstone, G., & Van Ness, D. W. (2013). The meaning of restorative justice. In *Handbook of restorative justice* (pp. 27–45). Willan. doi:10.4324/9781843926191-8

Jones, E., & Kawalek, A. (2019). Dissolving the Stiff Upper Lip: Opportunities and Challenges for the Mainstreaming of Therapeutic Jurisprudence in the United Kingdom. *International Journal of Law and Psychiatry*, *63*, 76–84. doi:10.1016/j.ijlp.2018.06.007 PMID:29996972

Kalita, S (2022). Introducing goddesses as role models: a selective examination of some sahadharmini ideals in goddesses. *Women and Nation Building*, 23.

Karlekar, M. (1995). Reflections on Kulin Polygamy—Nistarini Debi's Sekeley Katha. *Contributions to Indian Sociology, 29*(1-2), 135-155. Retrieved from https://www.cwds.ac.in/wp-content/uploads/2016/09/ReflectionsonKulinPolygamy.pdf

Khanmohammadi, K., & Ehsani, H. (2019). Anthropological Study of the Phenomenon of "Khunbas" in the Seydun Region of Khuzestan. *Islam and Social Studies, 1*(21), 140–169. doi:10.22081/JISS.2018.66171

Kierstead, S. (2012). Therapeutic Jurisprudence and Child Protection. *Comparative Research in Law & Political Economy*, 31-44.

King, M. S. (2008). Non-adversarial Justice and the Coroner's Court: A Proposed Therapeutic, Restorative, Problem-solving Model. *Journal of Law and Medicine, 16*(3), 442–457. PMID:19205307

King, M. S. (2008). Restorative Justice, Therapeutic Jurisprudence and the Rise of Emotionally Intelligent Justice. *Melbourne University Law Review, 32*(3).

Konadu, K. (2010). *The Akan Diaspora in the Americas*. Oxford University Press. doi:10.1093/acprof:oso/9780195390643.001.0001

Koss, M. P. (2000). Blame, shame, and community: Justice responses to violence against women. *The American Psychologist, 55*(11), 1332–1343. doi:10.1037/0003-066X.55.11.1332 PMID:11280942

Krishnamurthy, V. (2017). The concept of dharma in Indian jurisprudence. *VIDHIGYA: The Journal of Legal Awareness, 12*(2), 31–37. doi:10.5958/0974-4533.2017.00011.2

Kumar & Associates. vs State of UP & Another CRIMINAL REVISION No. - 1092 of 2022. https://www.livelaw.in/pdf_upload/sushil-kumar-and-6-others-v-state-of-up-and-another-criminal-revision-no-1092-of-2022-allahabad-hc-416420.pdf

Kumar, V. (2017). Bigamy and Hindu marriage. *Journal of the Indian Law Institute, 59*(4), 356–382.

Kuokkanen, R. (2000). Towards an "Indigenous paradigm" from a Sami perspective. *The Canadian Journal of Native Studies, 20*(2), 411–436.

Laing, J. & Frost, W. (Eds.). (2017). Rituals and Traditional Events in the Modern World. Routledge.

Latimer, J., Dowden, C., & Muise, D. (2005). The effectiveness of restorative justice practices: A meta-analysis. *The Prison Journal, 85*(2), 127–144. doi:10.1177/0032885505276969

Laub, J. H., & Frisch, N. E. (2016). Translational criminology: A new path forward. In *Advancing Criminology and Criminal Justice Policy* (1st ed.). Routledge. doi:10.4324/9781315737874

Leebaw, P. (2003). Legitimation or Judgment? South Africa's Restorative Approach to Transitional Justice. *Polity, 36*(1), 23–51. doi:10.1086/POLv36n1ms3235422

Lemons, K. (2010). *At the margins of law: Adjudicating Muslim families in contemporary Delhi.* UC Berkeley: Anthropology. Retrieved from https://escholarship.org/uc/item/6f66n4dn

Llewellyn, J. (2013). Truth commissions and restorative justice. In *Handbook of restorative justice* (pp. 373–393). Willan. doi:10.4324/9781843926191.ch19

Llewellyn, J. J., & Howse, R. (1999). Institutions for restorative justice: The South African truth and reconciliation commission. *University of Toronto Law Journal*, *49*(3), 355–388. doi:10.2307/826003

Lord, V., Shekhar, B., & Stokes, T. (2015, March 4). *Juvenile Victim-Offender Restorative Justice Program: Process Evaluation.* Academy of Criminal Justice Sciences, American Society of Criminology.

Mackey, V. (1981). *Punishment: In the scripture and tradition of Judaism, Christianity and Islam.* Paper presented to the National Religious Leaders Consultation of Criminal Justice, Claremont, CA.

Maghsoodi, M. (2018). Assessment of Iranian Collective Identity, Emphasizing Social Solidarity. *National Studies Quarterly.*, *19*(75), 23–46. 20.1001.1.1735059.1397.19.75.2.5

Makhari, M. R. (2021). *Legal history of the reform of traditional courts in South Africa: insights from Botswana and the Kingdom of eSwatini* (Doctoral dissertation). North-West University.

Mangena, F. (2015). Restorative justice's deep roots in Africa. *South African Journal of Philosophy=Suid-Afrikaanse Tydskrif vir Wysbegeerte, 34*(1), 1-12.

Manoharan, A. (2021). *Handbook for Facilitation of Restorative Practices in Child Care Institutions.* Enfold Proactive Health Trust.

Marshall, T. F. (1992). Restorative Justice on Trial in Britain. In H. Messmer & H.-U. Otto (Eds.), *Restorative Justice on Trial* (pp. 15–28). Kluwer Academic Publishers. doi:10.1007/978-94-015-8064-9_2

Marshall, T. F. (1999). *Restorative justice: An overview.* Home Office.

Matory, J. L. (2005). *Black Atlantic Religion: Tradition, Transnationalism, and Matriarchy in the Afro-Brazilian Candomblé.* Princeton University Press.

Mavundla, S. D., Strode, A., & Essack, Z. (2022). Access to Justice for Women in Eswatini: HIV- Positive Women as a Vulnerable Population. In Violence Against Women and Criminal Justice in Africa: Volume II (pp. 339-370). Palgrave Macmillan.

Mbiti, J. S. (1989). *African Religions and Philosophy* (2nd ed.). Heinemann Education Botswana Publishers.

McCold, P. (1999). Restorative Justice: The state of the field 1999. *Building Strong Partnerships for Restorative Practices Conference.*

McCold, P. (2004). Paradigm muddle: The threat to restorative justice posed by its merger with community justice. *Contemporary Justice Review*, *7*(1), 13–35. doi:10.1080/1028258042000211987

Meschievitz, C. S., & Galanter, M. (1982). In search of Nyaya Panchayats: The politics of a moribund institution. In *Comparative Studies* (pp. 47–77). Academic Press. doi:10.1016/B978-0-12-041502-1.50007-3

Mika, H. (1992). Mediation interventions and restorative justice: responding to the astructural bias. In *Restorative Justice on Trial* (pp. 559–567). Springer. doi:10.1007/978-94-015-8064-9_40

Mintz, S. W., & Price, R. (1976). *An Anthropological Approach to the Afro-American Past: A Caribbean Perspective*. Institute for the Study of Human Issues.

Mirsky, L. (2004, April 27). *Restorative justice practices of Native American, First Nation and other Indigenous People of North America*. International Institute of Restorative Practices. https://www.iirp.edu/news/restorative-justice-practices-of-native-american-first-nation-and-other-indigenous-people-of-north-america-part-one

Mitra, S. K., & Fischer, A. (2002). Sacred laws and the secular state: An analytical narrative of the controversy over personal laws in India. *India Review*, *1*(3), 99–130. doi:10.1080/14736480208404635

Mo'in, M. (2002). *Mo'in Persian Encyclopedic Dictionary* (19th ed.). Amirkabir Publisher.

Modernghana. (2022, January 6). *Asamankese: Five policemen interdicted for allegedly assaulting and planting 'weed' on driver*. https://www.modernghana.com/news/1130045/asamankese-five-policemen-interdicted-for-alleged.html

Modo, I. V. O. (2002). Dual legal system, Basotho culture and marital stability. *Journal of Comparative Family Studies*, *33*(3), 377–386. doi:10.3138/jcfs.33.3.377

Moore, E. P. (1993). Gender, power, and legal pluralism: Rajasthan, India. *American Ethnologist*, *20*(3), 522–542. doi:10.1525/ae.1993.20.3.02a00040

Moran, F. (2017). Restorative Justice: A Look at Victim Offender Mediation Programs. *21st Century Social Justice*, *4*(1), 1–5. https://fordham.bepress.com/swjournal/vol4/iss1/4

Morgan, S. P., & Niraula, B. B. (1995). Gender inequality and fertility in two Nepali villages. *Population and Development Review*, *21*(3), 541–561. doi:10.2307/2137749

Moumakwa, P. C. (2011). *The Botswana Kgotla system: a mechanism for traditional conflict resolution in modern Botswana: case study of the Kanye Kgotla* (Master's thesis). Universitetet i Tromsø.

Mousourakis, G. (2021). Restorative justice, criminal justice, and the community: fostering a collaborative approach to addressing conflict and crime. *A continental de R Atura Jurídica*, *2*(2), 88.

Munshi, S., & Lama, U. (1978). The Tamangs of Darjeeling: Organized Expression of the Ethnic Identity-Part II. *Journal of the Indian Anthropological Society*, *13*(3), 265–286.

Murhula, P. B., & Tolla, A. D. (2021). The Effectiveness of Restorative Justice Practices on Victims of Crime: Evidence from South Africa. *International Journal for Crime, Justice and Social Democracy*, *10*(1), 98–110.

Mutsvara, S. (2020). *Inhuman sentencing of children: A foucus on Zimbabwe and Botswana* (Doctoral dissertation). University of the Western Cape.

MyJoyOnline. (2022, January 6). *Police interdict 5 officers over alleged extortion while on patrol duty*. MyJoyOnline.

Nadjafi Abrand Abadi, A. H. (2003). "Penal Mediation: A Manifestation of Restorative Justice" (Preface). In *Abbasi, M. New Horizon of Criminal Justice: Penal Mediation* (1st ed.). Daneshvar Publications.

Natarajan, M. (2005). Women police stations as a dispute processing system. *Women & Criminal Justice*, *16*(1-2), 87–106. doi:10.1300/J012v16n01_04

Nozarpoor, A. (1991). The Mechanism of Social Control (Resolution as a Ritual) in Tribal Community of Arabs of Khuzestan. *Development of Education of Social Sciences, 8*, 44-51. http://ensani.ir/fa/article/213346/

O'Brien, M., & Yar, M. (2008). *Criminology: The Key Concepts*. Routledge.

O'Connell, T. (2019). The Best Is Yet to Come: Unlocking the True Potential of Restorative Practice. In Routledge International Handbook of Restorative Justice. Theo Gavrielides.

O'Mahony, D., & Doak, J. (2009). Restorative Justice and Youth Justice: Bringing Theory and Practice Closer Together in Europe. In *JReforming Juvenile Justice*. Springer. doi:10.1007/978-0-387-89295-5_10

Oba, A. A. (2008). Juju Oaths in Customary Law Arbitration and Their Legal Validity in Nigerian Courts. *Journal of African Law*, *52*(1), 139–158. doi:10.1017/S0021855308000065

Omale, J. O. (2011). Restorative justice and alternative dispute resolution: An analytical discourse for African professionals. *Int'l J. Advanced Legal Stud. & Governance: An International Journal of Policy, Administration and Institutions*, 2, 102.

Osanloo, A. (2020). Forgiveness Work: Mercy, Law, and Victims' Rights in Iran. Princeton University Press.

Osanloo, A. (2012). When Blood Has Spilled: Gender, Honor, and Compensation in Iranian Criminal Sanctioning. *Political and Legal Anthropology Review*, *35*(2), 308–326. doi:10.1111/j.1555-2934.2012.01205.x

Palmié, S. (2013). *The Cooking of History: How Not to Study Afro-Cuban Religion*. Chicago University Press. doi:10.7208/chicago/9780226019734.001.0001

Pandey, M. (2018). *"My mother is a goddess","I am an inmate here": Male prisoners' attitudes towards women and their perceptions of culpability from Delhi Prison* [Doctoral dissertation]. Anglia Ruskin University.

Parker, J. (2021). *In My Time of Dying: A History of Death and the Dead in West Africa*. Princeton University Press.

Paton, D. (2015). *The Cultural Politics of Obeah: Religion, colonialism and modernity in the Caribbean world*. Cambridge University Press. doi:10.1017/CBO9781139198417

Peachey, D. E. (1992). Restitution, reconciliation, retribution: Identifying the forms of justice people desire. In *Restorative justice on trial* (pp. 551–557). Springer. doi:10.1007/978-94-015-8064-9_39

Penner, H. H. (2016). Ritual. In *Encyclopedia Britannica*. https://www.britannica.com/topic/ritual

Perlin, M. L., & Lynch, A. J. (2016). Therapeutic Jurisprudence. In Sexuality, Disability, and the Law (pp. 145-157). Palgrave Macmillan. doi:10.1057/9781137481085_6

Perlin, M. L., & Lynch, A. J. (2015). Love is just a four-letter word: Sexuality, international human rights, and therapeutic jurisprudence. *Canadian Journal of Comparative and Contemporary Law*, *1*, 9.

Pogodin, A. V., & Krasnov, E. V. (2018). Integrative Law Understanding as Basis for the Lawyer. *The Journal of Social Sciences Research*, *5*(5), 400–403. doi:10.32861/jssr.spi5.400.403

Pothen, S. (1989). Divorce in Hindu society. *Journal of Comparative Family Studies*, *20*(3), 377–392. doi:10.3138/jcfs.20.3.377

Pranis, K. (2001). Restorative justice, social justice, and the empowerment of marginalized populations. In G. Bazemore & M. Schiff (Eds.), *Restorative community justice: Repairing harm and transforming communities* (p. 287). Anderson Press.

Putman, L. (2012). Rites of Power and Rumors of Race: The Circulation of Supernatural Knowledge in the Greater Caribbean, 1890–1940. In D. Paton & M. Forde (Eds.), *Obeah and Other Powers: The Politics of Caribbean Religion and Healing* (pp. 249–254). Duke University Press.

Raha, S. (2019). Treatment of Children as Adults under India's Juvenile Justice (Care and Protection of Children) Act, 2015: A Retreat from International Human Rights Law. *International Journal of Children's Rights*, *27*(4), 757–795. doi:10.1163/15718182-02704004

Ramsey, K. (2013). Vodouyizan Protest: An Amendment to the Constitution of Haiti. *Journal of Haitian Studies*, *19*(1), 272–281. doi:10.1353/jhs.2013.0019

Ranjani, R. (2021). Victims in Post-Conflict Sri Lanka seeking Transitional Justice on the Road to Peace and Reconciliation. In B. Shekhar & S. P. Sahni (Eds.), *Victims of Crime and Victim Assistance - A Global Perspective*. Bloomsbury.

Rattray, R. S. (1927). *Religion & Art in Ashanti*. Clarendon Press.

Compilation of References

Rattray, R. S. (1929). *Ashanti Law and Constitution*. Oxford University Press.

Rautenbach, C. (2015). Legal Reform of Traditional Courts in South Africa: Exploring the Links Between Ubuntu, Restorative Justice and Therapeutic Jurisprudence. *Journal of International and Comparative Law*, 275.

Rautenbach, C. (2016). A family home, five sisters and the rule of ultimogeniture: Comparing notes on judicial approaches to customary law in South Africa and Botswana. *African Human Rights Law Journal*, *16*(1), 145–174. doi:10.17159/1996-2096/2016/v16n1a7

Rautenbach, C. (Ed.). (2018). *Introduction to legal pluralism in South Africa*. LexisNexis.

Rayejian Asli, M. (2021). Incorporating the United Nations Norms into Iranian Post-Revolution Criminal Policy: A Criminological-Victimological Approach. In H. Kury & S. Redo (Eds.), *Crime Prevention and Justice in 2030* (pp. 69–82). Springer Nature Switzerland. doi:10.1007/978-3-030-56227-4

Rayejian Asli, M., & Amrollahi Byouki, M. (2016). Forced Marriage in Islamic Countries: The Role of Violence in Family Relationships. In *Women and Children as Victims and Offenders: Background, Prevention, Reintegration* (pp. 729–753). Springer International Publishing Switzerland. doi:10.1007/978-3-319-08398-8_26

Rayejian Asli, M., & Daneshnejad, A. (2015). Informal Settlement of Criminal Conflicts without Police Intervention. *Journal of Research Police Sciences*, *17*(2), 83–100.

Ray, S. N. (1908). Sources of Hindu Law. *Allahabad LJ*, *5*, 249.

Rigoni, C. (2016). Restorative justice and mediation in penal matters. A stock-taking of legal issues, implementation strategies and outcomes in 36 European countries. *Restorative Justice*, *4*(2), 276–279. doi:10.1080/20504721.2016.1197539

Robins, S. (2009). Restorative approaches to criminal justice in Africa - The case of Uganda. In *The theory and practice of criminal justice in Africa*. African Human Security Initiative.

Ross, R. (1996). Leaving our White eyes behind: The sentencing of Native accused. In M. O. Nielsen & R. A. Silverman (Eds.), *Native Americans, crime, and justice*. Westview.

Rugge, T., & Scott, T.-L. (2009). *Restorative Justice's Impact on Participants' Psychological and Physical Health*. Public Safety Canada.

Rush, G. E. (2003). *The Dictionary of Criminal Justice* (6th ed.). Dushkin/Mc-Graw-Hill.

Sekaran, U. (2003). *Research Methods for Business: A Skill Building Approach*. John Wiley & Sons.

Shekhar, B. (2021, September 2). *Restorative Justice – A New Lens for Holistic Justice*. Dr. Harisingh Gour Central University.

Shekhar, B. (2002). Restorative Justice System - An Alternative to the Existing Retributive Justice System. *Social Defence*, *53*(152), 56–74.

Shekhar, B. (2020). From the Frying Pan into the Fire? Victim Turned Offender. In B. Shekhar & S. P. Sahni (Eds.), *A Global Perspective of Victimology & Criminology – Yesterday, Today and Tomorrow*. Bloomsbury.

Shoradad. (n.d.). https://shoradad.eadl.ir/

Simpson, L. (2001). Aboriginal peoples and knowledge: Decolonizing our processes. *The Canadian Journal of Native Studies, 21*(1), 137–147.

Sinha, K. (2014). Be It Manu, Be It Macaulay: Indian Law and the Problem of the Female Body. *J. Indian L. & Soc'y, 5*, 61.

Skelton, A., & Batley, M. (2021). A Comparative Review of the Incorporation of African traditional justice processes in Restorative Child Justice Systems in Uganda, Lesotho and Eswatini. *Comparative Restorative Justice*, 245-264.

Stark, R. (1996). Deviant places: A theory of the ecology of crime. *Criminology, 25*(4), 893–910. doi:10.1111/j.1745-9125.1987.tb00824.x

Strang, H. K. (2002). *Repair or Revenge: Victims and Restorative Justice*. Clarendon Press.

Subba, T. K. (1989). *Dynamics of a Hill Society. Mittal Publications*.

Sullivan, D., & Tifft, L. (2007). *Handbook of restorative justice: A global perspective*. Routledge. doi:10.4324/9780203346822

T., L. P., & Coyne, C. J. (2012). Sassywood. *Journal of Comparative Economics, 40*(4), 608–620.

Tamang, G. M. (2015). *Indigenous Methods of Conflict Resolution in Sikkim: A Study of Dzumsa*. Sikkim University.

Tamarit, J., & Luque, E. (2016). Can Restorative Justice Satisfy Victims' Needs? Evaluation of the Catalan Victim-Offender Mediation Programme. *Restorative Justice, 4*(1), 68–85. doi:10.1 080/20504721.2015.1110887

Tanha, A. (2021). The Economy of Crime. *Tejarat-e-Farda Magazine., 435*, 40–41.

Tavassoli, G. A. (1996). Urban Sociology. Payam-e-Noor University Press.

Thapa, S. (1989). The ethnic factor in the timing of family formation in Nepal. *Asia-Pacific Population Journal, 4*(1), 3–34. doi:10.18356/a0ff19ee-en PMID:12315769

The Government Gazette. (2014, Apr. 23). *Criminal Procedure Code 2014*, no. 20135. https://dotic.ir/news/5584/

The Government Gazette. (2016, Jan. 27). *Dispute Resolution Councils Act 2015*, no. 20652. https://rrk.ir/Laws/ShowLaw.aspx?Code=9094

The Ministry of Justice . (2021). Retrieved from https://www.moj.go.jp/ENGLISH/m_hisho06_00046.html

Thilagaraj, R. (2017). Nyaya Panchayat. In *Restorative Justice in India* (pp. 3–12). Springer. doi:10.1007/978-3-319-47659-9_1

Thornton, J. K. (1992). *Africa and Africans in the Making of the Atlantic World, 1400-1680.* Cambridge University Press.

Towhidian, Y. (2018). Exploring Threatening Factors of Social Solidarity within Neighborhoods. *Urban Sociological Studies (Journal of Islamic Azad University, Dehaghan Branch), 8*(28), 165-188.

Traguetto, J., & Guimaraes, T. (2019). Therapeutic Jurisprudence and Restorative Justice in the United States: The Process of Institutionalization and the Roles of Judges. *International Journal of Offender Therapy and Comparative Criminology, 63*(11), 1971–1989. doi:10.1177/0306624X19833528 PMID:30829089

Tripp, T. M. (2001). The Rationality and Morality of Revenge. *Justice in the workplace: From theory to practice, 2,* 197.

Tweneboah, S. (2014). The Culture of Duabɔ (Imprecation), Legal Dysfunction and the Challenge of Human Rights Development in Ghana. *Human Rights Research, 9,* 1–10.

Tweneboah, S. (2020). *Religion, Law, Politics and the State in Africa: Applying Legal Pluralism in Ghana.* Routledge.

Tweneboah, S. (2021a). Akan Deities as Agents of Conflict Resolution Mechanism in Ghana: Promises and Pitfalls. In E. T. Yin & N. F. Kofie (Eds.), *Advancing Civil Justice Reform and Conflict Resolution in Africa and Asia: Comparative Analyses and Case Studies.* IGI Global. doi:10.4018/978-1-7998-7898-8.ch001

Tweneboah, S. (2021b). Religion, Law, and Politics in Ghana: Duabɔ (Imprecation) as Spiritual Justice in the Public Sphere. *African Journal of Legal Studies, 14*(2), 209–229. doi:10.1163/17087384-12340081

Ubink, J. M. (2011). Gender Equality on the Horizon: The Case of Uukwambi Traditional Authority, Northern Namibia. *Northern Namibia,* (3), 51–71.

Umashankar, P. (2022). Study of the Judiciary and Administration in Ancient India with Special Reference to Manusmriti and Arthashastra and Its Relevance in Present Indian System. *Issue 2 Int'l JL Mgmt. &. Human., 5,* 534.

Umbreit, M. S., Vos, B., & Coates, R. B. (2006). *Restorative Justice Dialogue: Evidence-based practice.* Center for Restorative justice Peacemaking, University of Minnesota.

Umbreit, M. S. (1995). Holding juvenile offenders accountable: A restorative justice perspective. *Juvenile & Family Court Journal, 46*(2), 31–42. doi:10.1111/j.1755-6988.1995.tb00815.x

USAID. (2019). Non-State Justice System Programming: A Practitioners' Guide (AID-OAA-I-13-00034/7200AA18F00003). United States Agency for International Development.

Van Ness, D., & Strong, K. (2006). Restoring Justice (3rd ed.). Lexis Nexis Publishing.

Van Ness, D., & Strong, K. H. (2014). *Restoring justice: An introduction to restorative justice.* Routledge. doi:10.4324/9781315721330

Vatuk, S. (2013). The "women's court" in India: An alternative dispute resolution body for women in distress. *Journal of Legal Pluralism and Unofficial Law*, *45*(1), 76–103. doi:10.1080/07329113.2013.774836

Volpe, M. R., & Strobl, S. (2005). *Restorative justice responses to post–September 11 hate.* Academic Press.

Wachtel, T., & McCold, P. (2004). Building a Global Alliance for Restorative Practices and Family Empowerment. In *The IIRP's Fifth International Conference on Conferencing, Circles, and Other Restorative Practices.* International Institute for Restorative Practices.

Walgrave, L. (2013). Integrating criminal justice and restorative justice. In *Handbook of restorative justice* (pp. 581–601). Willan. doi:10.4324/9781843926191.ch26

Warner-Lewis, M. (1999). *Trinidad Yoruba: From Mother-Tongue to Memory.* University of the West Indies Press.

Warren, C. S. (2019). Islamic Criminal Law. *Oxford Bibliographies.* (https://www.oxfordbibliographies.com/view/document/obo-9780195390155/obo-9780195390155-0035.xml)

Wessels, J. W. (2013). *History of the Roman-Dutch law.* Read Books Ltd.

Wexler, D. B. (2012). New Wine in New Bottles: The Need to Sketch a Therapeutic Jurisprudence 'Code' of Proposed Criminal Processes and Practices. SSRN *Electronic Journal*, *14*(7). doi:10.2139/ssrn.2065454

Wexler, D. B. (2015). Moving Forward on Mainstreaming Therapeutic Jurisprudence: An Ongoing Process to Facilitate the Therapeutic Design and Application of the Law. In Therapeutic Jurisprudence: New Zealand Perspectives. Warren Brookbanks.

Wexler, D. (2000). Therapeutic jurisprudence: An overview. *TM Cooley L. Rev.*, *17*, 125.

Wexler, D. B. (2000). Therapeutic Jurisprudence: An Overview. *Thomas M. Cooley Law Review*, *17*, 125–134.

Wexler, D. B. (2014). Two Decades of Therapeutic Jurisprudence. *Touro Law Review*, 1–14.

White Hat, L. (2003, November 26). Seeking Our Wellness workshop offers positive resources to public. *Tribune/News.*

Worden, N. (2011). *The making of modern South Africa: Conquest, apartheid, democracy.* John Wiley & Sons.

World Justice Project. (2013). *Customary Justice: Challenges, Innovations and the Role of the UN.* International Development Law Organization (IDLO). https://worldjusticeproject.org/news/customary-justice-challenges-innovations-and-role-un

Compilation of References

Wright, J. K. (2016). *Lawyers as Changemakers: The Global Integrative Law Movement*. ABA Book Publishing.

Wright, J. K. (n.d.). Integrative Law. *University of Western Australia Law Review*, *46*(2), 237–252.

YarAhmadi, Q. (2010). The Ritual of Resolution (*Fasl*) in Besri Village of Borujerd City. *Najvaa-ye Farhang*, *14*, 57-60. https://www.magiran.com/paper/742430

Zakeri. (2021). Social Solidarity and Its Enemies. Nashr-e-Nay.

Zehr, H. (1995). Justice paradigm shift? Values and visions in the reform process. *Mediation Quarterly*, *12*(3), 207–216. doi:10.1002/crq.3900120303

Zehr, H. (1997). *Restorative Justice: When Justice and Healing Go Together*. Track Two.

Zehr, H. (2002). *The little book of restorative justice*. Good Books.

Zehr, H. (2015). *The little book of restorative justice: Revised and updated*. Simon and Schuster.

226

Related References

To continue our tradition of advancing information science and technology research, we have compiled a list of recommended IGI Global readings. These references will provide additional information and guidance to further enrich your knowledge and assist you with your own research and future publications.

Abdel-Hameid, S. O., & Wilson, E. (2018). Gender, Organization, and Change in Sudan. In N. Mahtab, T. Haque, I. Khan, M. Islam, & I. Wahid (Eds.), *Handbook of Research on Women's Issues and Rights in the Developing World* (pp. 107–120). Hershey, PA: IGI Global. doi:10.4018/978-1-5225-3018-3.ch007

Abdullahi, R. B. (2018). Volunteerism in Urban Development the Case of Non-Cash, Non-Digital Crowdfunding Growth in Nigeria. In U. Benna & A. Benna (Eds.), *Crowdfunding and Sustainable Urban Development in Emerging Economies* (pp. 188–210). Hershey, PA: IGI Global. doi:10.4018/978-1-5225-3952-0.ch010

Abioye, T. O., Oyesomi, K., Ajiboye, E., Omidiora, S., & Oyero, O. (2017). Education, Gender, and Child-Rights: Salient Issues in SDGS Years in ADO-ODO/OTA Local Government Area of Ogun State, Nigeria. In O. Nelson, B. Ojebuyi, & A. Salawu (Eds.), *Impacts of the Media on African Socio-Economic Development* (pp. 141–154). Hershey, PA: IGI Global. doi:10.4018/978-1-5225-1859-4.ch009

Adalı, G. K. (2022). Measuring the Attitudes of Governmental Policies and the Public Towards the COVID-19 Pandemic. In Ş. Omeraki Çekirdekci, Ö. İngün Karkış, & S. Gönültaş (Eds.), *Handbook of Research on Interdisciplinary Perspectives on the Threats and Impacts of Pandemics* (pp. 163–187). IGI Global. https://doi.org/10.4018/978-1-7998-8674-7.ch009

Related References

Adisa, W. B. (2018). Land Use Policy and Urban Sprawl in Nigeria: Land Use and the Emergence of Urban Sprawl. In A. Eneanya (Ed.), *Handbook of Research on Environmental Policies for Emergency Management and Public Safety* (pp. 256–274). Hershey, PA: IGI Global. doi:10.4018/978-1-5225-3194-4.ch014

Afolabi, O. S., Amao-Kolawole, T. G., Shittu, A. K., & Oguntokun, O. O. (2018). Rule of Law, Governance, and Sustainable Development: The Nigerian Perspective. In K. Teshager Alemu & M. Abebe Alebachew (Eds.), *Handbook of Research on Sustainable Development and Governance Strategies for Economic Growth in Africa* (pp. 273–290). Hershey, PA: IGI Global. doi:10.4018/978-1-5225-3247-7.ch015

Agyemang, O. S. (2018). Institutional Structures and the Prevalence of Foreign Ownership of Firms: Empirical Evidence From Africa. In K. Teshager Alemu & M. Abebe Alebachew (Eds.), *Handbook of Research on Sustainable Development and Governance Strategies for Economic Growth in Africa* (pp. 455–479). Hershey, PA: IGI Global. doi:10.4018/978-1-5225-3247-7.ch024

Aham-Anyanwu, N. M., & Li, H. (2017). E-State: Realistic or Utopian? *International Journal of Public Administration in the Digital Age*, *4*(2), 56–76. doi:10.4018/IJPADA.2017040105

Al Balushi, T., & Ali, S. (2020). Theoretical Approach for Instrument Development in Measuring User-Perceived E-Government Service Quality: A Case of Oman E-Government Services. *International Journal of Electronic Government Research*, *16*(1), 40–58. doi:10.4018/IJEGR.2020010103

Al-Jamal, M., & Abu-Shanab, E. (2018). Open Government: The Line between Privacy and Transparency. *International Journal of Public Administration in the Digital Age*, *5*(2), 64–75. doi:10.4018/IJPADA.2018040106

Alsaç, U. (2017). EKAP: Turkey's Centralized E-Procurement System. In R. Shakya (Ed.), *Digital Governance and E-Government Principles Applied to Public Procurement* (pp. 126–150). Hershey, PA: IGI Global. doi:10.4018/978-1-5225-2203-4.ch006

Amadi, L. A., & Igwe, P. (2018). Open Government and Bureaucratic Secrecy in the Developing Democracies: Africa in Perspective. In A. Kok (Ed.), *Proliferation of Open Government Initiatives and Systems* (pp. 1–28). Hershey, PA: IGI Global. doi:10.4018/978-1-5225-4987-1.ch001

Arble, E., & Arnetz, B. B. (2021). Four Fundamental Principles to Enhance Police Performance and Community Safety. In E. Arble & B. Arnetz (Eds.), *Interventions, Training, and Technologies for Improved Police Well-Being and Performance* (pp. 231–245). IGI Global. https://doi.org/10.4018/978-1-7998-6820-0.ch015

Arora, G. C. (2020). The Problem of Climate-Induced Displacement: Analyzing the International Framework on Protection of Rights of Climate Migrants. In R. Das & N. Mandal (Eds.), *Interdisciplinary Approaches to Public Policy and Sustainability* (pp. 67–82). IGI Global. https://doi.org/10.4018/978-1-7998-0315-7.ch004

Arora, T., & Mehra, N. (2021). Administration of Civil Justice in India: Ancient and Modern Perspectives. In E. Yin & N. Kofie (Eds.), *Advancing Civil Justice Reform and Conflict Resolution in Africa and Asia: Comparative Analyses and Case Studies* (pp. 17–45). IGI Global. https://doi.org/10.4018/978-1-7998-7898-8.ch002

Arteta, A. (2019). *Democracy and Government: Making Decisions*. IGI Global. doi:10.4018/978-1-5225-7558-0.ch001

Asante, M., & Botchway, T. P. (2021). Shielding Members of Parliament Against Court Summons: Interrogating the Question of Parliamentary Immunity. In E. Yin & N. Kofie (Eds.), *Advancing Civil Justice Reform and Conflict Resolution in Africa and Asia: Comparative Analyses and Case Studies* (pp. 210–229). IGI Global. https://doi.org/10.4018/978-1-7998-7898-8.ch012

Ateş, V. (2021). Critical Antecedents of Trust in E-Government Services in Turkey. In C. Babaoğlu, E. Akman, & O. Kulaç (Eds.), *Handbook of Research on Global Challenges for Improving Public Services and Government Operations* (pp. 94–116). IGI Global. https://doi.org/10.4018/978-1-7998-4978-0.ch006

Ayeni, A. O. (2018). Environmental Policies for Emergency Management and Public Safety: Implementing Green Policy and Community Participation. In A. Eneanya (Ed.), *Handbook of Research on Environmental Policies for Emergency Management and Public Safety* (pp. 40–59). Hershey, PA: IGI Global. doi:10.4018/978-1-5225-3194-4.ch003

Ayodele, J. O. (2017). The Influence of Migration and Crime on Development in Lagos, Nigeria. In G. Afolayan & A. Akinwale (Eds.), *Global Perspectives on Development Administration and Cultural Change* (pp. 192–230). Hershey, PA: IGI Global. doi:10.4018/978-1-5225-0629-4.ch009

Baarda, R. (2017). Digital Democracy in Authoritarian Russia: Opportunity for Participation, or Site of Kremlin Control? In R. Luppicini & R. Baarda (Eds.), *Digital Media Integration for Participatory Democracy* (pp. 87–100). Hershey, PA: IGI Global. doi:10.4018/978-1-5225-2463-2.ch005

Balakrishnan, K. (2017). The Rationale for Offsets in Defence Acquisition from a Theoretical Perspective. In K. Burgess & P. Antill (Eds.), *Emerging Strategies in Defense Acquisitions and Military Procurement* (pp. 263–276). Hershey, PA: IGI Global. doi:10.4018/978-1-5225-0599-0.ch015

Related References

Banerjee, S. (2017). Globalization and Human Rights: How Globalization Can Be a Tool to Protect the Human Rights. In C. Akrivopoulou (Ed.), *Defending Human Rights and Democracy in the Era of Globalization* (pp. 1–16). Hershey, PA: IGI Global. doi:10.4018/978-1-5225-0723-9.ch001

Bessant, J. (2017). Digital Humour, Gag Laws, and the Liberal Security State. In R. Luppicini & R. Baarda (Eds.), *Digital Media Integration for Participatory Democracy* (pp. 204–221). Hershey, PA: IGI Global. doi:10.4018/978-1-5225-2463-2.ch010

Bhat, M. Y. (2020). Environmental Problems of Delhi and Governmental Concern. In M. Merviö (Ed.), *Global Issues and Innovative Solutions in Healthcare, Culture, and the Environment* (pp. 133–167). IGI Global. https://doi.org/10.4018/978-1-7998-3576-9.ch008

Bhat, R. A. (2021). Identification of Various Dimensions and Indicators of Immigrant Integration Into Global Scenarios. In M. Mafukata (Ed.), *Impact of Immigration and Xenophobia on Development in Africa* (pp. 247–260). IGI Global. https://doi.org/10.4018/978-1-7998-7099-9.ch014

Boachie, C. (2017). Public Financial Management and Systems of Accountability in Sub-National Governance in Developing Economies. In E. Schoburgh & R. Ryan (Eds.), *Handbook of Research on Sub-National Governance and Development* (pp. 193–217). Hershey, PA: IGI Global. doi:10.4018/978-1-5225-1645-3.ch009

Boachie, C., & Adu-Darko, E. (2018). Socio-Economic Impact of Foreign Direct Investment in Developing Countries. In V. Malepati & C. Gowri (Eds.), *Foreign Direct Investments (FDIs) and Opportunities for Developing Economies in the World Market* (pp. 66–81). Hershey, PA: IGI Global. doi:10.4018/978-1-5225-3026-8.ch004

Bogdanoski, M., Stoilkovski, M., & Risteski, A. (2020). Novel First Responder Digital Forensics Tool as a Support to Law Enforcement. In I. Management Association (Ed.), *Improving the Safety and Efficiency of Emergency Services: Emerging Tools and Technologies for First Responders* (pp. 239-270). IGI Global. https://doi.org/10.4018/978-1-7998-2535-7.ch011

Borràs, S. (2017). Rights of Nature to Protect Human Rights in Times of Environmental Crisis. In C. Akrivopoulou (Ed.), *Defending Human Rights and Democracy in the Era of Globalization* (pp. 225–261). Hershey, PA: IGI Global. doi:10.4018/978-1-5225-0723-9.ch010

Bouaziz, F. (2021). E-Government and Digital Transformation: A Conceptual Framework for Risk Factors Identification. In K. Sandhu (Ed.), *Disruptive Technology and Digital Transformation for Business and Government* (pp. 67–90). IGI Global. https://doi.org/10.4018/978-1-7998-8583-2.ch004

Bradford, A. C., McElroy, H. K., & Rosenblatt, R. (2019). Social Climate Change and the Modern Police Department: Millennials, Marijuana, and Mass Media. In I. Management Association (Ed.), *Police Science: Breakthroughs in Research and Practice* (pp. 34-51). IGI Global. https://doi.org/10.4018/978-1-5225-7672-3.ch003

Brusca, I., Olmo, J., & Labrador, M. (2018). Characterizing the Risk Factors for Financial Sustainability in Spanish Local Governments. In M. Rodríguez Bolívar & M. López Subires (Eds.), *Financial Sustainability and Intergenerational Equity in Local Governments* (pp. 206–223). Hershey, PA: IGI Global. doi:10.4018/978-1-5225-3713-7.ch009

Budd, J. R., & Littrell, M. W. (2021). Law Enforcement Challenges to Gathering Intelligence in the Street: The Fourth Amendment. In E. de Silva & A. Abeyagoonesekera (Eds.), *Intelligence and Law Enforcement in the 21st Century* (pp. 18–40). IGI Global. https://doi.org/10.4018/978-1-7998-7904-6.ch002

Bush, C. L. (2021). Policing Strategies and Approaches to Improving Community Relations: Black Citizens' Perceptions of Law Enforcement Efforts to Intentionally Strengthen Relationships. In M. Pittaro (Ed.), *Global Perspectives on Reforming the Criminal Justice System* (pp. 56–75). IGI Global. https://doi.org/10.4018/978-1-7998-6884-2.ch004

Canto Moniz, G. (2020). Is There Anything Left of the Portuguese Law Implementing the GDPR?: The Decision of the Portuguese Supervisory Authority. In M. Tzanou (Ed.), *Personal Data Protection and Legal Developments in the European Union* (pp. 125–139). IGI Global. https://doi.org/10.4018/978-1-5225-9489-5.ch007

Casoria, M., & AlSarraf, E. M. (2020). The Impact of the GDPR on Extra-EU Legal Systems: The Case of the Kingdom of Bahrain. In M. Tzanou (Ed.), *Personal Data Protection and Legal Developments in the European Union* (pp. 224–237). IGI Global. https://doi.org/10.4018/978-1-5225-9489-5.ch011

Chaves, A. (2022). Government Response Capacity to the COVID-19 Pandemic: Estimating the Impact of Lockdown Measures in Colombia. In G. Antošová (Ed.), *Innovative Strategic Planning and International Collaboration for the Mitigation of Global Crises* (pp. 114–137). IGI Global. https://doi.org/10.4018/978-1-7998-8339-5.ch008

Chen, M., & Su, F. (2017). Global Civic Engagement as an Empowering Device for Cross-Ethnic and Cross-Cultural Understanding in Taiwan. In R. Shin (Ed.), *Convergence of Contemporary Art, Visual Culture, and Global Civic Engagement* (pp. 24–45). Hershey, PA: IGI Global. doi:10.4018/978-1-5225-1665-1.ch002

Related References

Chigwata, T. C. (2017). Fiscal Decentralization: Constraints to Revenue-Raising by Local Government in Zimbabwe. In E. Schoburgh & R. Ryan (Eds.), *Handbook of Research on Sub-National Governance and Development* (pp. 218–240). Hershey, PA: IGI Global. doi:10.4018/978-1-5225-1645-3.ch010

Chowdhury, M. A. (2017). The Nexus Between Institutional Quality and Foreign Direct Investments (FDI) in South Asia: Dynamic Heterogeneous Panel Approach. In T. Dorożyński & A. Kuna-Marszałek (Eds.), *Outward Foreign Direct Investment (FDI) in Emerging Market Economies* (pp. 293–310). Hershey, PA: IGI Global. doi:10.4018/978-1-5225-2345-1.ch015

Christopher, M. E., & Tsushima, V. G. (2017). Police Interactions with Persons-in-Crisis: Emergency Psychological Services and Jail Diversion. In C. Mitchell & E. Dorian (Eds.), *Police Psychology and Its Growing Impact on Modern Law Enforcement* (pp. 274–294). Hershey, PA: IGI Global. doi:10.4018/978-1-5225-0813-7.ch014

Ciftci, D. (2022). Digital Citizenship and E-Government Integration: The Case of North Cyprus. In E. Öngün, N. Pembecioğlu, & U. Gündüz (Eds.), *Handbook of Research on Digital Citizenship and Management During Crises* (pp. 34–55). IGI Global. https://doi.org/10.4018/978-1-7998-8421-7.ch003

Citro, F., Lucianelli, G., & Santis, S. (2018). Financial Conditions, Financial Sustainability, and Intergenerational Equity in Local Governments: A Literature Review. In M. Rodríguez Bolívar & M. López Subires (Eds.), *Financial Sustainability and Intergenerational Equity in Local Governments* (pp. 101–124). Hershey, PA: IGI Global. doi:10.4018/978-1-5225-3713-7.ch005

Correa de Mello, M. B. (2019). The Information Access Law as a Full Constitutional Citizenship Instrument. In A. Melro & L. Oliveira (Eds.), *Constitutional Knowledge and Its Impact on Citizenship Exercise in a Networked Society* (pp. 55–72). IGI Global. https://doi.org/10.4018/978-1-5225-8350-9.ch003

Covell, C. E. (2018). Theoretical Application of Public Sector Planning and Budgeting. In M. Rodríguez Bolívar & M. López Subires (Eds.), *Financial Sustainability and Intergenerational Equity in Local Governments* (pp. 248–279). Hershey, PA: IGI Global. doi:10.4018/978-1-5225-3713-7.ch011

Cunha, A. M., Ferreira, A. D., & Fernandes, M. J. (2018). The Impact of Accounting Information and Socioeconomic Factors in the Re-Election of Portuguese Mayors. In G. Azevedo, J. da Silva Oliveira, R. Marques, & A. Ferreira (Eds.), *Handbook of Research on Modernization and Accountability in Public Sector Management* (pp. 406–432). Hershey, PA: IGI Global. doi:10.4018/978-1-5225-3731-1.ch019 da Rosa, I., & de Almeida, J. (2017). Digital Transformation in the Public Sector: Electronic Procurement in Portugal. In R. Shakya (Ed.), *Digital Governance and E-Government Principles Applied to Public Procurement* (pp. 99–125). Hershey, PA: IGI Global. doi:10.4018/978-1-5225-2203-4.ch005

Daramola, O. (2018). Revisiting the Legal Framework of Urban Planning in the Global South: An Explanatory Example of Nigeria. In K. Teshager Alemu & M. Abebe Alebachew (Eds.), *Handbook of Research on Sustainable Development and Governance Strategies for Economic Growth in Africa* (pp. 258–271). Hershey, PA: IGI Global. doi:10.4018/978-1-5225-3247-7.ch014

Dau, L. A., Moore, E. M., Soto, M. A., & LeBlanc, C. R. (2017). How Globalization Sparked Entrepreneurship in the Developing World: The Impact of Formal Economic and Political Linkages. In B. Christiansen & F. Kasarcı (Eds.), *Corporate Espionage, Geopolitics, and Diplomacy Issues in International Business* (pp. 72–91). Hershey, PA: IGI Global. doi:10.4018/978-1-5225-1031-4.ch005

De Man, P. (2019). In-Situ Resource Utilization: Legal Aspects. In A. Nakarada Pecujlic & M. Tugnoli (Eds.), *Promoting Productive Cooperation Between Space Lawyers and Engineers* (pp. 211–224). IGI Global. https://doi.org/10.4018/978-1-5225-7256-5.ch013

Drenner, K. (2017). Introduction to Faith in State Legislatures: Land of the Brave and the Home of the Free – The Star-Spangled Banner. In *Impacts of Faith-Based Decision Making on the Individual-Level Legislative Process: Emerging Research and Opportunities* (pp. 1–25). Hershey, PA: IGI Global. doi:10.4018/978-1-5225-2388-8.ch001

Drenner, K. (2017). The Holy Wars of Marriage. In *Impacts of Faith-Based Decision Making on the Individual-Level Legislative Process: Emerging Research and Opportunities* (pp. 92–116). Hershey, PA: IGI Global. doi:10.4018/978-1-5225-2388-8.ch004

Drenner, K. (2017). The Implications of Religious Liberty. In *Impacts of Faith-Based Decision Making on the Individual-Level Legislative Process: Emerging Research and Opportunities* (pp. 143–162). Hershey, PA: IGI Global. doi:10.4018/978-1-5225-2388-8.ch006

Duncan, S. T., & Geczi, H. (2021). Body-Worn Cameras: Panacea or Distraction for Increased Police Use of Force Accountability? In M. Pittaro (Ed.), *Global Perspectives on Reforming the Criminal Justice System* (pp. 1–25). IGI Global. https://doi.org/10.4018/978-1-7998-6884-2.ch001

Related References

Duran, D. Ş. (2019). Reflections of the Multi-Level Governance Approach on the Turkish Metropolitan Municipality System: Evaluations on the Metropolitan Law No 6360. In T. Uysal & C. Aldemir (Eds.), *Multi-Level Governance in Developing Economies* (pp. 52–91). IGI Global. https://doi.org/10.4018/978-1-5225-5547-6. ch003

Durnalı, M., & Eriçok, B. (2019). Legal Challenges on Developing Education Policy for Immigrants in Turkey. In I. Management Association (Ed.), *Immigration and Refugee Policy: Breakthroughs in Research and Practice* (pp. 223-237). IGI Global. https://doi.org/10.4018/978-1-5225-8909-9.ch013

Ehalaiye, D., Redmayne, N. B., & Laswad, F. (2020). The Case of Accounting Information for Infrastructural Assets Reporting: Local Government Borrowings and Investment Choices in the Context of Moral Hazard and Local Government Politics. In A. Cunha, A. Ferreira, M. Fernandes, & P. Gomes (Eds.), *Financial Determinants in Local Re-Election Rates: Emerging Research and Opportunities* (pp. 176–201). IGI Global. https://doi.org/10.4018/978-1-5225-7820-8.ch007

Elena, S., & van Schalkwyk, F. (2017). Open Data for Open Justice in Seven Latin American Countries. In C. Jiménez-Gómez & M. Gascó-Hernández (Eds.), *Achieving Open Justice through Citizen Participation and Transparency* (pp. 210–231). Hershey, PA: IGI Global. doi:10.4018/978-1-5225-0717-8.ch011

Eneanya, A. N. (2018). Integrating Ecosystem Management and Environmental Media for Public Policy on Public Health and Safety. In A. Eneanya (Ed.), *Handbook of Research on Environmental Policies for Emergency Management and Public Safety* (pp. 321–338). Hershey, PA: IGI Global. doi:10.4018/978-1-5225-3194-4.ch017

Erickson, G. S. (2019). Sharing Knowledge With the Government: Implications of FOIA Requests. In Y. Albastaki, A. Al-Alawi, & S. Abdulrahman Al-Bassam (Eds.), *Handbook of Research on Implementing Knowledge Management Strategy in the Public Sector* (pp. 143–158). IGI Global. https://doi.org/10.4018/978-1-5225-9639-4.ch007

Essien, E. D. (2018). Strengthening Performance of Civil Society Through Dialogue and Critical Thinking in Nigeria: Its Ethical Implications. In S. Chhabra (Ed.), *Handbook of Research on Civic Engagement and Social Change in Contemporary Society* (pp. 82–102). Hershey, PA: IGI Global. doi:10.4018/978-1-5225-4197-4. ch005

Eweida, A. M. (2021). Urban Laws in Harmony or at Odds With Knowledge-Based Urban Policies: A Case Study on Egypt. In A. Galaby & A. Abdrabo (Eds.), *Handbook of Research on Creative Cities and Advanced Models for Knowledge-Based Urban Development* (pp. 23–40). IGI Global. https://doi.org/10.4018/978-1-7998-4948-3.ch002

Fanaian, T. (2017). The Theocratic Deception Trap: Khomeini's Persuasion Techniques and Communication Patterns in His Books, Guardianship of the Jurist 1979 and Testament 1989. In E. Lewin, E. Bick, & D. Naor (Eds.), *Comparative Perspectives on Civil Religion, Nationalism, and Political Influence* (pp. 62–105). Hershey, PA: IGI Global. doi:10.4018/978-1-5225-0516-7.ch003

Faura-Martínez, U., & Cifuentes-Faura, J. (2020). Does E-Government Promote Transparency and the Fight Against Corruption in the European Union? *International Journal of Electronic Government Research*, *16*(4), 42–57. https://doi.org/10.4018/IJEGR.2020100103

Fawsitt, J. (2020). Government Policy and the Disintegration of Village Community Life and Individual Identity in Urbanising Japan. In M. Merviö (Ed.), *Recent Social, Environmental, and Cultural Issues in East Asian Societies* (pp. 76–94). IGI Global. https://doi.org/10.4018/978-1-7998-1807-6.ch005

Fidanoski, F., Sergi, B. S., Simeonovski, K., Naumovski, V., & Sazdovski, I. (2018). Effects of Foreign Capital Entry on the Macedonian Banking Industry: Two-Edged Sword. In B. Sergi, F. Fidanoski, M. Ziolo, & V. Naumovski (Eds.), *Regaining Global Stability After the Financial Crisis* (pp. 308–338). Hershey, PA: IGI Global. doi:10.4018/978-1-5225-4026-7.ch015

Franconi, A. I. (2018). Economic Variations and Their Impact on Labor Legislation Throughout History in Argentina. In S. Amine (Ed.), *Employment Protection Legislation in Emerging Economies* (pp. 77–98). Hershey, PA: IGI Global. doi:10.4018/978-1-5225-4134-9.ch004

Friedrich, P., & Chebotareva, M. (2017). Options for Applying Functional Overlapping Competing Jurisdictions (FOCJs) for Municipal Cooperation in Russia. In M. Lewandowski & B. Kożuch (Eds.), *Public Sector Entrepreneurship and the Integration of Innovative Business Models* (pp. 73–107). Hershey, PA: IGI Global. doi:10.4018/978-1-5225-2215-7.ch004

Garad, A., & Qamari, I. N. (2021). Determining Factors Influencing Establishing E-Service Quality in Developing Countries: A Case Study of Yemen E-Government. *International Journal of Electronic Government Research*, *17*(1), 15–30. https://doi.org/10.4018/IJEGR.2021010102

Garita, M. (2018). The Negotiation and Effects of Fiscal Privileges in Guatemala. In M. Garita & C. Bregni (Eds.), *Economic Growth in Latin America and the Impact of the Global Financial Crisis* (pp. 119–137). Hershey, PA: IGI Global. doi:10.4018/978-1-5225-4981-9.ch008

Gascó-Hernández, M. (2017). Digitalizing Police Requirements: Opening up Justice through Collaborative Initiatives. In C. Jiménez-Gómez & M. Gascó-Hernández (Eds.), *Achieving Open Justice through Citizen Participation and Transparency* (pp. 157–172). Hershey, PA: IGI Global. doi:10.4018/978-1-5225-0717-8.ch008

Gáspár-Szilágyi, S. (2017). Human Rights Conditionality in the EU's Newly Concluded Association Agreements with the Eastern Partners. In C. Akrivopoulou (Ed.), *Defending Human Rights and Democracy in the Era of Globalization* (pp. 50–79). Hershey, PA: IGI Global. doi:10.4018/978-1-5225-0723-9.ch003

Gavrielides, T. (2017). Reconciling Restorative Justice with the Law for Violence Against Women in Europe: A Scheme of Structured and Unstructured Models. In D. Halder & K. Jaishankar (Eds.), *Therapeutic Jurisprudence and Overcoming Violence Against Women* (pp. 106–120). Hershey, PA: IGI Global. doi:10.4018/978-1-5225-2472-4.ch007

Gechlik, M., Dai, D., & Beck, J. C. (2017). Open Judiciary in a Closed Society: A Paradox in China? In C. Jiménez-Gómez & M. Gascó-Hernández (Eds.), *Achieving Open Justice through Citizen Participation and Transparency* (pp. 56–92). Hershey, PA: IGI Global. doi:10.4018/978-1-5225-0717-8.ch004

Gerger, A. (2021). Technologies for Connected Government Implementation: Success Factors and Best Practices. In Z. Mahmood (Ed.), *Web 2.0 and Cloud Technologies for Implementing Connected Government* (pp. 36–66). IGI Global. https://doi.org/10.4018/978-1-7998-4570-6.ch003

Germann, S. K. (2019). The International Space Station: Legal Aspects. In A. Nakarada Pecujlic & M. Tugnoli (Eds.), *Promoting Productive Cooperation Between Space Lawyers and Engineers* (pp. 96–113). IGI Global. doi:10.4018/978-1-5225-7256-5.ch007

Gillath, N. (2017). Avoiding Conscription in Israel: Were Women Pawns in the Political Game? In E. Lewin, E. Bick, & D. Naor (Eds.), *Comparative Perspectives on Civil Religion, Nationalism, and Political Influence* (pp. 226–256). Hershey, PA: IGI Global. doi:10.4018/978-1-5225-0516-7.ch009

Górski, J. (2019). Northern Sea Route: International Law Perspectives. In V. Erokhin, T. Gao, & X. Zhang (Eds.), *Handbook of Research on International Collaboration, Economic Development, and Sustainability in the Arctic* (pp. 292–313). IGI Global. https://doi.org/10.4018/978-1-5225-6954-1.ch014

Grant, B., Woods, R., & Tan, S. F. (2017). Subnational Finance in Australia and China: The Case for Municipal Bond Banks. In E. Schoburgh & R. Ryan (Eds.), *Handbook of Research on Sub-National Governance and Development* (pp. 150–166). Hershey, PA: IGI Global. doi:10.4018/978-1-5225-1645-3.ch007

Gurpinar, B. (2018). Supporter, Activist, Rebel, Terrorist: Children in Syria. In C. Akrivopoulou (Ed.), *Global Perspectives on Human Migration, Asylum, and Security* (pp. 97–114). Hershey, PA: IGI Global. doi:10.4018/978-1-5225-2817-3.ch005

Gussen, B. F. (2018). The United States. In *Ranking Economic Performance and Efficiency in the Global Market: Emerging Research and Opportunities* (pp. 109–136). Hershey, PA: IGI Global. doi:10.4018/978-1-5225-2756-5.ch005

Halder, D., & Bhati, D. (2021). Culture, Ethnicity, and Hate Crimes: A Comparative Analysis of Preventive Laws Between India and the USA. In M. Pittaro (Ed.), *Global Perspectives on Reforming the Criminal Justice System* (pp. 236–245). IGI Global. https://doi.org/10.4018/978-1-7998-6884-2.ch013

Haque, T. (2018). Women-Friendly Working Environment in Bangladesh: Critical Analysis. In N. Mahtab, T. Haque, I. Khan, M. Islam, & I. Wahid (Eds.), *Handbook of Research on Women's Issues and Rights in the Developing World* (pp. 52–68). Hershey, PA: IGI Global. doi:10.4018/978-1-5225-3018-3.ch004

Heuva, W. E. (2017). Deferring Citizens' "Right to Know" in an Information Age: The Information Deficit in Namibia. In N. Mhiripiri & T. Chari (Eds.), *Media Law, Ethics, and Policy in the Digital Age* (pp. 245–267). Hershey, PA: IGI Global. doi:10.4018/978-1-5225-2095-5.ch014

Hwangbo, Y. (2022). Government Challenges Over Global Electronic Commerce Using FinTech: Design of Consumer Payment Tax (CPT) System. In M. Anshari, M. Almunawar, & M. Masri (Eds.), *FinTech Development for Financial Inclusiveness* (pp. 197–213). IGI Global. https://doi.org/10.4018/978-1-7998-8447-7.ch011

Ibrahim, F., Suhip, H., Kura, K. M., & Noor, H. M. L. (2022). Exploratory Study on User Satisfaction of E-HRM: Evidence From Brunei Government Employee Management System (GEMS). In P. Ordóñez de Pablos (Eds.), *Handbook of Research on Developing Circular, Digital, and Green Economies in Asia* (pp. 243-271). IGI Global. https://doi.org/10.4018/978-1-7998-8678-5.ch014

Related References

Islam, M. R. (2018). Abuse Among Child Domestic Workers in Bangladesh. In I. Tshabangu (Ed.), *Global Ideologies Surrounding Children's Rights and Social Justice* (pp. 1–21). Hershey, PA: IGI Global. doi:10.4018/978-1-5225-2578-3.ch001

Jankovic-Milic, V., & Džunić, M. (2017). Measuring Governance: The Application of Grey Relational Analysis on World Governance Indicators. In J. Stanković, P. Delias, S. Marinković, & S. Rochhia (Eds.), *Tools and Techniques for Economic Decision Analysis* (pp. 104–128). Hershey, PA: IGI Global. doi:10.4018/978-1-5225-0959-2.ch005

Jenkins, B., Semple, T., Quail, J., & Bennell, C. (2021). Optimizing Scenario-Based Training for Law Enforcement. In E. Arble & B. Arnetz (Eds.), *Interventions, Training, and Technologies for Improved Police Well-Being and Performance* (pp. 18–37). IGI Global. https://doi.org/10.4018/978-1-7998-6820-0.ch002

Jiménez-Gómez, C. E. (2017). Open Judiciary Worldwide: Best Practices and Lessons Learnt. In C. Jiménez-Gómez & M. Gascó-Hernández (Eds.), *Achieving Open Justice through Citizen Participation and Transparency* (pp. 1–15). Hershey, PA: IGI Global. doi:10.4018/978-1-5225-0717-8.ch001

Karatzimas, S., & Miquela, C. G. (2018). Two Approaches on Local Governments' Financial Sustainability: Law vs. Practice in Catalan Municipalities. In M. Rodríguez Bolívar & M. López Subires (Eds.), *Financial Sustainability and Intergenerational Equity in Local Governments* (pp. 58–81). Hershey, PA: IGI Global. doi:10.4018/978-1-5225-3713-7.ch003

Khachaturyan, M., & Klicheva, E. (2021). Risks of Introducing E-Governance Into Strategic Management Systems of Russian Companies in the Context of the Pandemic. *International Journal of Electronic Government Research*, *17*(4), 84–102. https://doi.org/10.4018/IJEGR.2021100105

Khan, S. A., & Alag, A. (2020). Arbitration in Patent Disputes: To What Extent Is It Possible? In N. Dewani & A. Gurtu (Eds.), *Intellectual Property Rights and the Protection of Traditional Knowledge* (pp. 76–102). IGI Global. https://doi.org/10.4018/978-1-7998-1835-9.ch004

Kirsanov, S., Safonov, E., Tuzcuoglu, F., & Mammadov, Z. (2022). Modern Problems of Staff Training for State and Municipal Services in Russia. In O. Kulaç, C. Babaoğlu, & E. Akman (Eds.), *Public Affairs Education and Training in the 21st Century* (pp. 325–337). IGI Global. https://doi.org/10.4018/978-1-7998-8243-5.ch021

Kita, Y. (2017). An Analysis of a Lay Adjudication System and Open Judiciary: The New Japanese Lay Adjudication System. In C. Jiménez-Gómez & M. Gascó-Hernández (Eds.), *Achieving Open Justice through Citizen Participation and Transparency* (pp. 93–109). Hershey, PA: IGI Global. doi:10.4018/978-1-5225-0717-8.ch005

Kuatova, A., Bekbasarova, T., & Abdrashev, R. (2020). Introducing E-Government in Kazakhstan: The Concept of E-Democracy for the State-Public Interaction. In G. Tazhina & J. Parker (Eds.), *Toward Sustainability Through Digital Technologies and Practices in the Eurasian Region* (pp. 1–16). IGI Global. https://doi.org/10.4018/978-1-7998-2551-7.ch001

Kumari, S., Patil, Y., & Rao, P. (2017). An Approach to Sustainable Watershed Management: Case Studies on Enhancing Sustainability with Challenges of Water in Western Maharashtra. In P. Rao & Y. Patil (Eds.), *Reconsidering the Impact of Climate Change on Global Water Supply, Use, and Management* (pp. 252–271). Hershey, PA: IGI Global. doi:10.4018/978-1-5225-1046-8.ch014

Kumburu, N. P., & Pande, V. S. (2018). Decentralization and Local Governance in Tanzania: Theories and Practice on Sustainable Development. In K. Teshager Alemu & M. Abebe Alebachew (Eds.), *Handbook of Research on Sustainable Development and Governance Strategies for Economic Growth in Africa* (pp. 131–148). Hershey, PA: IGI Global. doi:10.4018/978-1-5225-3247-7.ch007

Kunock, A. I. (2017). Boko Haram Insurgency in Cameroon: Role of Mass Media in Conflict Management. In N. Mhiripiri & T. Chari (Eds.), *Media Law, Ethics, and Policy in the Digital Age* (pp. 226–244). Hershey, PA: IGI Global. doi:10.4018/978-1-5225-2095-5.ch013

Kurebwa, J. (2019). Young People-Sensitive and Participatory Governance Approaches: Lessons for the Zimbabwean Government. In J. Kurebwa & O. Dodo (Eds.), *Participation of Young People in Governance Processes in Africa* (pp. 80–99). IGI Global. https://doi.org/10.4018/978-1-5225-9388-1.ch005

Lawrie, A. (2017). The Subnational Region: A Utopia? The Challenge of Governing Through Soft Power. In E. Schoburgh & R. Ryan (Eds.), *Handbook of Research on Sub-National Governance and Development* (pp. 96–115). Hershey, PA: IGI Global. doi:10.4018/978-1-5225-1645-3.ch005

Lentzis, D. (2020). Revisiting the Basics of EU Data Protection Law: On the Material and Territorial Scope of the GDPR. In M. Tzanou (Ed.), *Personal Data Protection and Legal Developments in the European Union* (pp. 19–33). IGI Global. https://doi.org/10.4018/978-1-5225-9489-5.ch002

Related References

Leote, F. J., Teixeira, N. M., & Galvão, R. (2021). Entrepreneurship and Unemployment: Government Grants and Challenges in a Pandemic Context. In N. Teixeira, & I. Lisboa (Eds.), *Handbook of Research on Financial Management During Economic Downturn and Recovery* (pp. 20-40). IGI Global. https://doi.org/10.4018/978-1-7998-6643-5.ch002

Lewin, E., & Bick, E. (2017). Introduction: Civil Religion and Nationalism on a Godly-Civil Continuum. In E. Lewin, E. Bick, & D. Naor (Eds.), *Comparative Perspectives on Civil Religion, Nationalism, and Political Influence* (pp. 1–31). Hershey, PA: IGI Global. doi:10.4018/978-1-5225-0516-7.ch001

Luyombya, D. (2018). Management of Records and Archives in Uganda's Public Sector. In P. Ngulube (Ed.), *Handbook of Research on Heritage Management and Preservation* (pp. 275–297). Hershey, PA: IGI Global. doi:10.4018/978-1-5225-3137-1.ch014

Mabe, M., & Ashley, E. A. (2017). The Local Command Structure and How the Library Fits. In *In The Developing Role of Public Libraries in Emergency Management: Emerging Research and Opportunities* (pp. 44–60). Hershey, PA: IGI Global. doi:10.4018/978-1-5225-2196-9.ch004

Macilotti, G. (2020). Online Child Pornography: Conceptual Issues and Law Enforcement Challenges. In A. Balloni & R. Sette (Eds.), *Handbook of Research on Trends and Issues in Crime Prevention, Rehabilitation, and Victim Support* (pp. 226–247). IGI Global. https://doi.org/10.4018/978-1-7998-1286-9.ch013

Maher, C. (2018). Legal Framework, Funding, and Procurement Polices to Accelerate the Growth of the Social Enterprise Ecosystem. In *Influence of Public Policy on Small Social Enterprises: Emerging Research and Opportunities* (pp. 52–83). Hershey, PA: IGI Global. doi:10.4018/978-1-5225-2770-1.ch003

Mahmood, M. (2019). Transformation of Government and Citizen Trust in Government: A Conceptual Model. In A. Molnar (Ed.), *Strategic Management and Innovative Applications of E-Government* (pp. 107–122). IGI Global. https://doi.org/10.4018/978-1-5225-6204-7.ch005

Mahmood, Z. (2021). Cloud Computing Technologies for Connected Digital Government. In Z. Mahmood (Ed.), *Web 2.0 and Cloud Technologies for Implementing Connected Government* (pp. 19–35). IGI Global. https://doi.org/10.4018/978-1-7998-4570-6.ch002

Malik, I., Putera, V. S., & Putra, I. E. (2018). Traditional Leaders in the Reconciliation of Muslim-Christian Conflicts in Moluccas. In A. Campbell (Ed.), *Global Leadership Initiatives for Conflict Resolution and Peacebuilding* (pp. 235–248). Hershey, PA: IGI Global. doi:10.4018/978-1-5225-4993-2.ch011

Martin, S. M. (2017). Transnational Crime and the American Policing System. In M. Dawson, D. Kisku, P. Gupta, J. Sing, & W. Li (Eds.), Developing Next-Generation Countermeasures for Homeland Security Threat Prevention (pp. 72-92). Hershey, PA: IGI Global. https://doi.org/ doi:10.4018/978-1-5225-0703-1.ch004

Mekonnen, G. A., & Kassie, W. A. (2020). Fiscal Decentralization at Local Government of Ethiopia: Theory vs Practices. In S. Chhabra & M. Kumar (Eds.), *Civic Engagement Frameworks and Strategic Leadership Practices for Organization Development* (pp. 171–197). IGI Global. https://doi.org/10.4018/978-1-7998-2372-8.ch008

Mensah, I. K., Luo, C., & Abu-Shanab, E. (2021). Citizen Use of E-Government Services Websites: A Proposed E-Government Adoption Recommendation Model (EGARM). *International Journal of Electronic Government Research*, *17*(2), 19–42. https://doi.org/10.4018/IJEGR.2021040102

Mhiripiri, N. A., & Chikakano, J. (2017). Criminal Defamation, the Criminalisation of Expression, Media and Information Dissemination in the Digital Age: A Legal and Ethical Perspective. In N. Mhiripiri & T. Chari (Eds.), *Media Law, Ethics, and Policy in the Digital Age* (pp. 1–24). Hershey, PA: IGI Global. doi:10.4018/978-1-5225-2095-5.ch001

Mishaal, D. A., & Abu-Shanab, E. A. (2017). Utilizing Facebook by the Arab World Governments: The Communication Success Factor. *International Journal of Public Administration in the Digital Age*, *4*(3), 53–78. doi:10.4018/IJPADA.2017070105

Morim, A. C., Inácio, H., & Vieira, E. (2018). Internal Control in a Public Hospital: The Case of Financial Services Expenditure Department. In G. Azevedo, J. da Silva Oliveira, R. Marques, & A. Ferreira (Eds.), *Handbook of Research on Modernization and Accountability in Public Sector Management* (pp. 77–102). Hershey, PA: IGI Global. doi:10.4018/978-1-5225-3731-1.ch005

Mupepi, M. G. (2017). Developing Democratic Paradigms to Effectively Manage Business, Government, and Civil Society: The African Spring. In E. Schoburgh & R. Ryan (Eds.), *Handbook of Research on Sub-National Governance and Development* (pp. 432–462). Hershey, PA: IGI Global. doi:10.4018/978-1-5225-1645-3.ch020

Related References

Mwakisisya, H. J., Rugeiyamu, R., & Cyprian, S. (2021). Blending Local Government Authorities and Grassroots for Industrial Economy Through Participatory Development Communication in Tanzania. In F. Nafukho & A. Boniface Makulilo (Eds.), *Handbook of Research on Nurturing Industrial Economy for Africa's Development* (pp. 74–98). IGI Global. https://doi.org/10.4018/978-1-7998-6471-4.ch005

Naidoo, V., & Nzimakwe, T. I. (2019). M-Government and Its Application on Public Service Delivery. In R. Abassi & A. Ben Chehida Douss (Eds.), *Security Frameworks in Contemporary Electronic Government* (pp. 1–14). IGI Global. https://doi.org/10.4018/978-1-5225-5984-9.ch001

Navaratnam, R., & Lee, I. Y. (2017). Globalization as a New Framework for Human Rights Protection. In C. Akrivopoulou (Ed.), *Defending Human Rights and Democracy in the Era of Globalization* (pp. 17–49). Hershey, PA: IGI Global. doi:10.4018/978-1-5225-0723-9.ch002

Nemec, J., Meričková, B. M., Svidroňová, M. M., & Klimovský, D. (2017). Co-Creation as a Social Innovation in Delivery of Public Services at Local Government Level: The Slovak Experience. In E. Schoburgh & R. Ryan (Eds.), *Handbook of Research on Sub-National Governance and Development* (pp. 281–303). Hershey, PA: IGI Global. doi:10.4018/978-1-5225-1645-3.ch013

Neupane, A., Soar, J., Vaidya, K., & Aryal, S. (2017). Application of E-Government Principles in Anti-Corruption Framework. In R. Shakya (Ed.), *Digital Governance and E-Government Principles Applied to Public Procurement* (pp. 56–74). Hershey, PA: IGI Global. doi:10.4018/978-1-5225-2203-4.ch003

Njie, S. N., Wogu, I. A., Ogbuehi, U. K., Misra, S., & Udoh, O. D. (2021). Rising Global Challenges in Energy Demand and the Politics of Climate Change in Government Operations: Policy and Economic Development Implications. In C. Babaoğlu, E. Akman, & O. Kulaç (Eds.), *Handbook of Research on Global Challenges for Improving Public Services and Government Operations* (pp. 242–263). IGI Global. https://doi.org/10.4018/978-1-7998-4978-0.ch013

Ogunde, O. (2017). Democracy and Child Rights Protection: The Problem of the Nigerian Constitution. In C. Akrivopoulou (Ed.), *Defending Human Rights and Democracy in the Era of Globalization* (pp. 123–144). Hershey, PA: IGI Global. doi:10.4018/978-1-5225-0723-9.ch006

Ojedokun, U. A. (2017). Crime Witnesses' Non-Cooperation in Police Investigations: Causes and Consequences in Nigeria. In S. Egharevba (Ed.), *Police Brutality, Racial Profiling, and Discrimination in the Criminal Justice System* (pp. 89–99). Hershey, PA: IGI Global. doi:10.4018/978-1-5225-1088-8.ch005

Okeke, G. S. (2018). The Politics of Environmental Pollution in Nigeria: Emerging Trends, Issues, and Challenges. In A. Eneanya (Ed.), *Handbook of Research on Environmental Policies for Emergency Management and Public Safety* (pp. 300–320). Hershey, PA: IGI Global. doi:10.4018/978-1-5225-3194-4.ch016

Ökten, S., Akman, E., & Akman, Ç. (2018). Modernization and Accountability in Public-Sector Administration: Turkey Example. In G. Azevedo, J. da Silva Oliveira, R. Marques, & A. Ferreira (Eds.), *Handbook of Research on Modernization and Accountability in Public Sector Management* (pp. 18–39). Hershey, PA: IGI Global. doi:10.4018/978-1-5225-3731-1.ch002

Oladapo, O. A., & Ojebuyi, B. R. (2017). Nature and Outcome of Nigeria's #NoToSocialMediaBill Twitter Protest against the Frivolous Petitions Bill 2015. In O. Nelson, B. Ojebuyi, & A. Salawu (Eds.), *Impacts of the Media on African Socio-Economic Development* (pp. 106–124). Hershey, PA: IGI Global. doi:10.4018/978-1-5225-1859-4.ch007

Olmos, S., & Nares, J. J. (2020). Applying Fault Trees to the Analysis at the Minimum Age for Sexual Consent in the Criminal Law of México. In A. Balloni & R. Sette (Eds.), *Handbook of Research on Trends and Issues in Crime Prevention, Rehabilitation, and Victim Support* (pp. 60–78). IGI Global. https://doi.org/10.4018/978-1-7998-1286-9.ch005

Olukolu, Y. R. (2017). Harmful Traditional Practices, Laws, and Reproductive Rights of Women in Nigeria: A Therapeutic Jurisprudence Approach. In D. Halder & K. Jaishankar (Eds.), *Therapeutic Jurisprudence and Overcoming Violence Against Women* (pp. 1–14). Hershey, PA: IGI Global. doi:10.4018/978-1-5225-2472-4.ch001

Onyebadi, U., & Mbunyuza-Memani, L. (2017). Women and South Africa's Anti-Apartheid Struggle: Evaluating the Political Messages in the Music of Miriam Makeba. In U. Onyebadi (Ed.), *Music as a Platform for Political Communication* (pp. 31–51). Hershey, PA: IGI Global. doi:10.4018/978-1-5225-1986-7.ch002

Osmani, A. R. (2017). Tipaimukh Multipurpose Hydroelectric Project: A Policy Perspective – Indo-Bangla Priorities, Indigenous Peoples' Rights, and Environmental Concerns. In P. Rao & Y. Patil (Eds.), *Reconsidering the Impact of Climate Change on Global Water Supply, Use, and Management* (pp. 227–251). Hershey, PA: IGI Global. doi:10.4018/978-1-5225-1046-8.ch013

Related References

Owolabi, T. O. (2018). Free Media and Bank Reforms in West Africa: Implications for Sustainable Development. In A. Salawu & T. Owolabi (Eds.), *Exploring Journalism Practice and Perception in Developing Countries* (pp. 18–39). Hershey, PA: IGI Global. doi:10.4018/978-1-5225-3376-4.ch002

Öztürk, N. K. (2021). Government Systems and Control of Bureaucracy. In C. Babaoğlu, E. Akman, & O. Kulaç (Eds.), *Handbook of Research on Global Challenges for Improving Public Services and Government Operations* (pp. 133–150). IGI Global. https://doi.org/10.4018/978-1-7998-4978-0.ch008

Pacheco, F. M., & Alves, D. R. (2019). The New Paths of Fundamental Rights in the 21st Century: Globalization and Knowledge in a Digital Age as a Proposal. In A. Melro & L. Oliveira (Eds.), *Constitutional Knowledge and Its Impact on Citizenship Exercise in a Networked Society* (pp. 1–26). IGI Global. https://doi.org/10.4018/978-1-5225-8350-9.ch001

Panda, P., & Sahu, G. P. (2017). Public Procurement Framework in India: An Overview. In R. Shakya (Ed.), *Digital Governance and E-Government Principles Applied to Public Procurement* (pp. 229–248). Hershey, PA: IGI Global. doi:10.4018/978-1-5225-2203-4.ch010

Pande, V. S., & Kumburu, N. P. (2018). An Overview of Population Growth and Sustainable Development in Sub-Saharan Africa. In K. Teshager Alemu & M. Abebe Alebachew (Eds.), *Handbook of Research on Sustainable Development and Governance Strategies for Economic Growth in Africa* (pp. 480–499). Hershey, PA: IGI Global. doi:10.4018/978-1-5225-3247-7.ch025

Parikh, M., & Krishna, V. S. (2021). Recent Trends and Repercussions in Civil and Criminal Justice Systems: A Comparative Analysis of England, Singapore, and India. In E. Yin, & N. Kofie (Ed.), *Advancing Civil Justice Reform and Conflict Resolution in Africa and Asia: Comparative Analyses and Case Studies* (pp. 230-242). IGI Global. https://doi.org/10.4018/978-1-7998-7898-8.ch013

Pattnaik, P. N., & Shukla, M. K. (2020). Understanding Indian Political Parties Through the Lens of Marketing Management: Towards a Conceptual Political Marketing Model. In S. Kavoğlu & M. Salar (Eds.), *Political Propaganda, Advertising, and Public Relations: Emerging Research and Opportunities* (pp. 170–190). IGI Global. https://doi.org/10.4018/978-1-7998-1734-5.ch008

Paulin, A. A. (2017). Informating Public Governance: Towards a Basis for a Digital Ecosystem. *International Journal of Public Administration in the Digital Age*, 4(2), 14–32. doi:10.4018/IJPADA.2017040102

Perelló-Sobrepere, M. (2017). Building a New State from Outrage: The Case of Catalonia. In M. Adria & Y. Mao (Eds.), *Handbook of Research on Citizen Engagement and Public Participation in the Era of New Media* (pp. 344–359). Hershey, PA: IGI Global. doi:10.4018/978-1-5225-1081-9.ch019

Pohl, G. M. (2017). The Role of Social Media in Enforcing Environmental Justice around the World. In K. Demirhan & D. Çakır-Demirhan (Eds.), *Political Scandal, Corruption, and Legitimacy in the Age of Social Media* (pp. 123–156). Hershey, PA: IGI Global. doi:10.4018/978-1-5225-2019-1.ch006

Popescu, C. R. (2022). Environmental, Social, and Corporate Governance by Avoiding Management Bias and Tax Minimization: Reaching a General Consensus Regarding a Minimum Global Tax Rate. In C. Popescu (Ed.), *COVID-19 Pandemic Impact on New Economy Development and Societal Change* (pp. 94–132). IGI Global. https://doi.org/10.4018/978-1-6684-3374-4.ch006

Popoola, T. (2017). Ethical and Legal Challenges of Election Reporting in Nigeria: A Study of Four General Elections, 1999-2011. In N. Mhiripiri & T. Chari (Eds.), *Media Law, Ethics, and Policy in the Digital Age* (pp. 78–100). Hershey, PA: IGI Global. doi:10.4018/978-1-5225-2095-5.ch005

Prakash, O. (2020). History, Policy Making, and Sustainability. In R. Das & N. Mandal (Eds.), *Interdisciplinary Approaches to Public Policy and Sustainability* (pp. 1–17). IGI Global. https://doi.org/10.4018/978-1-7998-0315-7.ch001

Provazníková, R., Sobotková, L., & Sobotka, M. (2021). Local Government Development in the Czech Republic: Dilemmas and Challenges. In C. Babaoğlu, E. Akman, & O. Kulaç (Eds.), *Handbook of Research on Global Challenges for Improving Public Services and Government Operations* (pp. 151–171). IGI Global. https://doi.org/10.4018/978-1-7998-4978-0.ch009

Qawasmeh, F. A. (2022). Understanding the Field of Public Policy in the Context of Public Administration Evolution. In O. Kulaç, C. Babaoğlu, & E. Akman (Eds.), *Public Affairs Education and Training in the 21st Century* (pp. 22–44). IGI Global. https://doi.org/10.4018/978-1-7998-8243-5.ch002

Rahman, M. S. (2017). Politics-Administration Relations and the Effect on Local Governance and Development: The Case of Bangladesh. In E. Schoburgh & R. Ryan (Eds.), *Handbook of Research on Sub-National Governance and Development* (pp. 256–279). Hershey, PA: IGI Global. doi:10.4018/978-1-5225-1645-3.ch012

Related References

Ramachandran, M., Chelliah, P. R., & Soundarabai, P. B. (2021). Towards Connected Government Services: A Cloud Software Engineering Framework. In Z. Mahmood (Ed.), *Web 2.0 and Cloud Technologies for Implementing Connected Government* (pp. 113–135). IGI Global. https://doi.org/10.4018/978-1-7998-4570-6.ch006

Ravotti, N. (2020). In the [Source] C\ode of the Conquerors: On the Need for Culturally-Minded Tribal Law Research Databases. In S. Edwards III, & D. Santos (Eds.), *Digital Transformation and Its Role in Progressing the Relationship Between States and Their Citizens* (pp. 124-137). IGI Global. https://doi.org/10.4018/978-1-7998-3152-5.ch006

Razzante, R. (2020). The Fight Against Corruption. In A. Balloni & R. Sette (Eds.), *Handbook of Research on Trends and Issues in Crime Prevention, Rehabilitation, and Victim Support* (pp. 167–186). IGI Global. doi:10.4018/978-1-7998-1286-9.ch010

Reddy, P. S. (2017). Political-Administrative Interface at the Local Sphere of Government with Particular Reference to South Africa. In E. Schoburgh & R. Ryan (Eds.), *Handbook of Research on Sub-National Governance and Development* (pp. 242–255). Hershey, PA: IGI Global. doi:10.4018/978-1-5225-1645-3.ch011

Rombo, D. O., & Lutomia, A. N. (2018). Tracing the Rights of Domestic and International Kenyan House Helps: Profiles, Policy, and Consequences. In N. Mahtab, T. Haque, I. Khan, M. Islam, & I. Wahid (Eds.), *Handbook of Research on Women's Issues and Rights in the Developing World* (pp. 1–18). Hershey, PA: IGI Global. doi:10.4018/978-1-5225-3018-3.ch001

Rouzbehani, K. (2017). Health Policy Implementation: Moving Beyond Its Barriers in United States. In N. Wickramasinghe (Ed.), *Handbook of Research on Healthcare Administration and Management* (pp. 541–552). Hershey, PA: IGI Global. doi:10.4018/978-1-5225-0920-2.ch032

Ryan, R., & Woods, R. (2017). Decentralization and Subnational Governance: Theory and Praxis. In E. Schoburgh & R. Ryan (Eds.), *Handbook of Research on Sub-National Governance and Development* (pp. 1–33). Hershey, PA: IGI Global. doi:10.4018/978-1-5225-1645-3.ch001

Sabao, C., & Chingwaramusee, V. R. (2017). Citizen Journalism on Facebook and the Challenges of Media Regulation in Zimbabwe: Baba Jukwa. In N. Mhiripiri & T. Chari (Eds.), *Media Law, Ethics, and Policy in the Digital Age* (pp. 193–206). Hershey, PA: IGI Global. doi:10.4018/978-1-5225-2095-5.ch011

Saidane, A., & Al-Sharieh, S. (2019). A Compliance-Driven Framework for Privacy and Security in Highly Regulated Socio-Technical Environments: An E-Government Case Study. In R. Abassi & A. Ben Chehida Douss (Eds.), *Security Frameworks in Contemporary Electronic Government* (pp. 15–50). IGI Global. https://doi.org/10.4018/978-1-5225-5984-9.ch002

Sandill, S. (2020). Law, Equality, and Entrepreneurship Through a Gendered Lens: Bridging the Gap Between Academia, Legislature, and Politics. In T. Moeke-Pickering, S. Cote-Meek, & A. Pegoraro (Eds.), *Critical Reflections and Politics on Advancing Women in the Academy* (pp. 124–149). IGI Global. https://doi.org/10.4018/978-1-7998-3618-6.ch008

Santos, H. R., & Tonelli, D. F. (2019). Smart Government and the Maturity Levels of Sociopolitical Digital Interactions: Analysing Temporal Changes in Brazilian E-Government Portals. In A. Molnar (Ed.), *Strategic Management and Innovative Applications of E-Government* (pp. 176–199). IGI Global. https://doi.org/10.4018/978-1-5225-6204-7.ch008

Saponaro, A. (2021). "Visible" and "Invisible" Victims in the Criminal Justice System: Victim-Oriented Paradigms and Models. In R. Blasdell, L. Krieger-Sample, & M. Kilburn (Eds.), *Invisible Victims and the Pursuit of Justice: Analyzing Frequently Victimized Yet Rarely Discussed Populations* (pp. 1–23). IGI Global. doi:10.4018/978-1-7998-7348-8.ch001

Shaikh, A. K., Ahmad, N., Khan, I., & Ali, S. (2021). E-Participation Within E-Government: A Bibliometric-Based Systematic Literature Review. *International Journal of Electronic Government Research*, *17*(4), 15–39. https://doi.org/10.4018/IJEGR.2021100102

Shakya, R. K., & Schapper, P. R. (2017). Digital Governance and E-Government Principles: E-Procurement as Transformative. In R. Shakya (Ed.), *Digital Governance and E-Government Principles Applied to Public Procurement* (pp. 1–28). Hershey, PA: IGI Global. doi:10.4018/978-1-5225-2203-4.ch001

Shambare, R. (2019). Facilitating Consumers' Adoption of E-Government in South Africa: Supply Side-Driven Virtuous Cycles. In A. Gbadamosi (Ed.), *Exploring the Dynamics of Consumerism in Developing Nations* (pp. 243–265). IGI Global. https://doi.org/10.4018/978-1-5225-7906-9.ch011

Siphambe, H., Kolobe, M., & Oageng, I. P. (2018). Employment Protection Legislation and Unemployment in Botswana. In S. Amine (Ed.), *Employment Protection Legislation in Emerging Economies* (pp. 157–191). Hershey, PA: IGI Global. doi:10.4018/978-1-5225-4134-9.ch008

Song, M. Y., & Abelson, J. (2017). Public Engagement and Policy Entrepreneurship on Social Media in the Time of Anti-Vaccination Movements. In M. Adria & Y. Mao (Eds.), *Handbook of Research on Citizen Engagement and Public Participation in the Era of New Media* (pp. 38–56). Hershey, PA: IGI Global. doi:10.4018/978-1-5225-1081-9.ch003

Sood, P., Malhotra, M., & Nijjer, S. (2021). Government Policies During Lockdown: Indian vs. International Perspective. In V. Kumar & G. Malhotra (Eds.), *Stakeholder Strategies for Reducing the Impact of Global Health Crises* (pp. 18–39). IGI Global. https://doi.org/10.4018/978-1-7998-7495-9.ch002

Stacey, E. (2018). Networked Protests: A Review of Social Movement Literature and the Hong Kong Umbrella Movement (2017). In S. Chhabra (Ed.), *Handbook of Research on Civic Engagement and Social Change in Contemporary Society* (pp. 347–363). Hershey, PA: IGI Global. doi:10.4018/978-1-5225-4197-4.ch020

Stamatakis, N. (2017). Authority and Legitimacy: A Quantitative Study of Youth's Perceptions on the Brazilian Police. In S. Egharevba (Ed.), *Police Brutality, Racial Profiling, and Discrimination in the Criminal Justice System* (pp. 151–213). Hershey, PA: IGI Global. doi:10.4018/978-1-5225-1088-8.ch009

Steinert, S. W. (2021). An Interview With Chief Sargent of the Worcester, MA Police Department. In E. Arble & B. Arnetz (Eds.), *Interventions, Training, and Technologies for Improved Police Well-Being and Performance* (pp. 185–197). IGI Global. https://doi.org/10.4018/978-1-7998-6820-0.ch011

Sugars, J. M. (2017). Refoulement and Refugees. In C. Akrivopoulou (Ed.), *Defending Human Rights and Democracy in the Era of Globalization* (pp. 181–197). Hershey, PA: IGI Global. doi:10.4018/978-1-5225-0723-9.ch008

Takaya-Umehara, Y. (2019). Suborbital Spaceflight: Legal Aspects. In A. Nakarada Pecujlic & M. Tugnoli (Eds.), *Promoting Productive Cooperation Between Space Lawyers and Engineers* (pp. 64–78). IGI Global. https://doi.org/10.4018/978-1-5225-7256-5.ch005

Tan, S. F. (2017). Local Representation in Australia: Preliminary Findings of a National Survey. In E. Schoburgh & R. Ryan (Eds.), *Handbook of Research on Sub-National Governance and Development* (pp. 368–384). Hershey, PA: IGI Global. doi:10.4018/978-1-5225-1645-3.ch017

Tavares, M. D., & Rodrigues, L. L. (2018). Strategic Responses of Public Sector Entities to GRI Sustainability Reports. In G. Azevedo, J. da Silva Oliveira, R. Marques, & A. Ferreira (Eds.), *Handbook of Research on Modernization and Accountability in Public Sector Management* (pp. 159–188). Hershey, PA: IGI Global. doi:10.4018/978-1-5225-3731-1.ch008

Thakre, A. G. (2017). Sexual Harassment of Women in Workplace in India: An Assessment of Implementation of Preventive Laws and Practicing of Therapeutic Jurisprudence in New Delhi. In D. Halder & K. Jaishankar (Eds.), *Therapeutic Jurisprudence and Overcoming Violence Against Women* (pp. 135–146). Hershey, PA: IGI Global. doi:10.4018/978-1-5225-2472-4.ch009

Tiwary, A. (2017). Key Elements of CEAF. In *Driving Efficiency in Local Government Using a Collaborative Enterprise Architecture Framework: Emerging Research and Opportunities* (pp. 25–61). Hershey, PA: IGI Global. doi:10.4018/978-1-5225-2407-6.ch002

Toscano, J. P. (2017). Social Media and Public Participation: Opportunities, Barriers, and a New Framework. In M. Adria & Y. Mao (Eds.), *Handbook of Research on Citizen Engagement and Public Participation in the Era of New Media* (pp. 73–89). Hershey, PA: IGI Global. doi:10.4018/978-1-5225-1081-9.ch005

Trompetter, P. S. (2019). A History of Police Psychology. In I. Management Association (Eds.), *Police Science: Breakthroughs in Research and Practice* (pp. 377-402). IGI Global. https://doi.org/10.4018/978-1-5225-7672-3.ch019

Tryma, K., & Salnikova, N. (2021). The Influence of Religion on Political Parties of the European Union. In E. Alaverdov & M. Bari (Eds.), *Global Development of Religious Tourism* (pp. 98-112). IGI Global. https://doi.org/10.4018/978-1-7998-5792-1.ch007

Tsabedze, V. W. (2020). Strategies for Managing E-Records for Good Governance: Reflection on E-Government in the Kingdom of Eswatini. In M. Rodríguez Bolívar & M. Cortés Cediel (Eds.), *Digital Government and Achieving E-Public Participation: Emerging Research and Opportunities* (pp. 63–86). IGI Global. https://doi.org/10.4018/978-1-7998-1526-6.ch004

Tshishonga, N. (2017). Operation Sukuma-Sakhe: A New Social Contract for Decentralized Service Delivery and Responsive Governance in KwaZulu-Natal. In E. Schoburgh & R. Ryan (Eds.), *Handbook of Research on Sub-National Governance and Development* (pp. 304–323). Hershey, PA: IGI Global. doi:10.4018/978-1-5225-1645-3.ch014

Related References

Tsygankov, S., & Gasanova, E. (2017). Electronification of the Public Procurement System: A Comparative Analysis of the Experience of the Russian Federation and Ukraine. In R. Shakya (Ed.), *Digital Governance and E-Government Principles Applied to Public Procurement* (pp. 267–277). Hershey, PA: IGI Global. doi:10.4018/978-1-5225-2203-4.ch013

Tüzünkan, D. (2018). The International Migration Movements and Immigrant Policies From the Ottoman Empire 1299 to Republican Turkey 2016. In Ş. Erçetin (Ed.), *Social Considerations of Migration Movements and Immigration Policies* (pp. 13–45). Hershey, PA: IGI Global. doi:10.4018/978-1-5225-3322-1.ch002

Ullah, Z. (2022). Violent Extremism and the Politics of Education in Pakistan: An Analysis of the Links Between Anti-Terror Laws, the Curriculum, and the Islamised Public Sphere. In O. Kulaç, C. Babaoğlu, & E. Akman (Eds.), *Public Affairs Education and Training in the 21st Century* (pp. 256–275). IGI Global. https://doi.org/10.4018/978-1-7998-8243-5.ch017

Valenzuela, R., & Ochoa, A. (2018). Open Mexico Network in the Implementation of National Open Data Policy. In A. Kok (Ed.), *Proliferation of Open Government Initiatives and Systems* (pp. 50–67). Hershey, PA: IGI Global. doi:10.4018/978-1-5225-4987-1.ch003

Valera-Ordaz, L., & Humanes, M. L. (2022). What Drives Selective Exposure to Political Information in Spain? Comparing Political Interest and Ideology. In D. Palau-Sampio, G. López García, & L. Iannelli (Eds.), *Contemporary Politics, Communication, and the Impact on Democracy* (pp. 93–112). IGI Global. https://doi.org/10.4018/978-1-7998-8057-8.ch006

van der Vliet-Bakker, J. M. (2019). Environmentally Forced Migration and Human Rights. In I. Management Association (Eds.), *Immigration and Refugee Policy: Breakthroughs in Research and Practice* (pp. 336-362). IGI Global. https://doi.org/10.4018/978-1-5225-8909-9.ch019

Waller, P. (2017). Co-Production and Co-Creation in Public Services: Resolving Confusion and Contradictions. *International Journal of Electronic Government Research, 13*(2), 1–17. doi:10.4018/IJEGR.2017040101

Wodecka-Hyjek, A. (2017). Co-Operation between the Public Administration and Non-Profit Organisations as a Condition of the Development of Public Entrepreneurship: On the Example of the Selected World Solutions. In V. Potocan, M. Üngan, & Z. Nedelko (Eds.), *Handbook of Research on Managerial Solutions in Non-Profit Organizations* (pp. 253–275). Hershey, PA: IGI Global. doi:10.4018/978-1-5225-0731-4.ch012

Yang, K. C., & Kang, Y. (2017). Social Media, Political Mobilization, and Citizen Engagement: A Case Study of the March 18, 2014, Sunflower Student Movement in Taiwan. In M. Adria & Y. Mao (Eds.), *Handbook of Research on Citizen Engagement and Public Participation in the Era of New Media* (pp. 360–388). Hershey, PA: IGI Global. doi:10.4018/978-1-5225-1081-9.ch020

Yang, K. C., & Kang, Y. (2020). Will Microblogs Shape China's Civil Society Under President's Xi's Surveillance State?: The Case of Anti-Extradition Law Protests in Hong Kong. In V. Kumar & G. Malhotra (Eds.), *Examining the Roles of IT and Social Media in Democratic Development and Social Change* (pp. 156–184). IGI Global. https://doi.org/10.4018/978-1-7998-1791-8.ch007

Yasmeen, H., Wang, Y., Zameer, H., & Ismail, H. (2020). Modeling the Role of Government, Firm, and Civil Society for Environmental Sustainability. In I. Management Association (Ed.), *Developing Eco-Cities Through Policy, Planning, and Innovation: Can It Really Work?* (pp. 62-83). IGI Global. https://doi.org/10.4018/978-1-7998-0441-3.ch003

Yavuz, N., Karkın, N., & Sevinç Çubuk, E. B. (2020). Explaining Government Crowdsourcing Decisions: A Theoretical Model. In M. Rodríguez Bolívar & M. Cortés Cediel (Eds.), *Digital Government and Achieving E-Public Participation: Emerging Research and Opportunities* (pp. 159–183). IGI Global. https://doi.org/10.4018/978-1-7998-1526-6.ch008

Zhaleleva, S., Zhaleleva, R., & Pasternak, A. (2020). Evolution of Business-Government Interaction Models: Their Use and Management. In G. Tazhina & J. Parker (Eds.), *Toward Sustainability Through Digital Technologies and Practices in the Eurasian Region* (pp. 17–35). IGI Global. https://doi.org/10.4018/978-1-7998-2551-7.ch002

Zhao, B. (2018). A Privacy Perspective of Open Government: Sex, Wealth, and Transparency in China. In A. Kok (Ed.), *Proliferation of Open Government Initiatives and Systems* (pp. 29–48). Hershey, PA: IGI Global. doi:10.4018/978-1-5225-4987-1.ch002

About the Contributors

Marta Vides Saade has served as an Associate Professor, Philosophy, Ramapo College of New Jersey (RCNJ) USA since 2004. She also serves as Program Manager, Course Enrichment, Maharishi Univeristy of Enlightenment (MUE), USA. Her formal education includes: J.D. Santa Clara University School of Law, 1981. M.Div. Jesuit School of Theology at Berkeley, 1994. Ph.D. Ethics and Social Theory, Graduate Theological Union, 2003. Dr. Vides Saade is Pueblo Nahua Sihuatehuacan, and a member of Xiuhcoatl Danza Azteca Bajo La Palabra Real Del Santo Niño De Atocha. She is a Certified Teacher of Transcendental Meditation. Her writing includes various articles and encyclopedia entries on restorative justice, therapeutic jurisprudence, indigenous traditions, cultural traditions, and transformative spirituality.

Debarati Halder is a practitioner and is presently working in Parul Institute of Law, Parul university, Gujarat, India as a Full Professor. Prof(Dr.)Debarati Halder is the Honorary managing director of Centre for Cyber Victim Counselling (CCVC) (www.cybervictims.org), an online not for profit organization and a think-tank meant for helping and counselling the victims of internet and digital communication crime victims. Dr. Halder had been awarded prestigious 2022 EqualityNow Public Voices Fellow (https://www.equalitynow.org/news_and_insights/public-voices-fellowship-on-advancing-the-rights-of-women-and-girls/) . She has won two awards in 2019 for her work on cyber laws, gender rights, Therapeutic Jurisprudence, criminal laws and creating awareness on cyber crimes against women: these are "Webwonderwomen Award" by Ministry of Women & Children Affairs, Government of India & Twitter on 6th March, 2019 and "TechNext India 2019 Best Faculty of the year" award by Computer Society of India, Mumbai Chapter on 28th September, 2019Dr. Debarati Halder has developed a theory called "Irrational coping theory for online victimisation" which is published as a book chapter titled Irrational Coping Theory and Positive Criminology: A Frame Work to Protect Victims of Cyber Crime in the book titled "Positive Criminology", (2015) edited by Natti Ronel and Dana Segav, Routledge, Taylor & Francis group, UK. Dr. Debarati Halder, also works closely with intermediaries like Facebook etc, government stakeholders like National Commission for women, State Commissions for women and Commissions for protection of child rights etc, to help them shape new policy guidelines towards protection of women and children from online offences. She has also been invited by government stakeholders like the Bihar, Kerala, West Bengal, Tamil Nadu, Gujarat, Assam State commissions for protection of child rights, Maharastra commission for protection of women's rights etc, for imparting training to stakeholders committed for protection of child rights. Dr.Halder has also assisted UNICEF India in creating child online safety related materials including Child Online Protection in India (https://www. icmec.org/wp-content/uploads/2016/09/UNICEF-Child-Protection-Online-India-pub_doc115-1.pdf). Dr.Debarati Halder is also the founding secretary of South Asian Society of Criminology and Victimology (SASCV)(www.SASCV.org). She is also a member of Board of trustees of International society of Therapeutic Jurisprudence (https://www.intltj.com/). Dr. Halder is an independent legal researcher. She has authored six books and edited one book including "Cyber Victimology"(ISBN: 9781032107523) by Routledge Taylor & Francis group (in print, expected date of publication is October, 2021), "Child sexual abuse and protection laws in India" (ISBN: 9789352806843) by Sage publications (2018)"Cyber crime against women in India"(2016) by SAGE Publications and "Cyber Crime and victimisation of women: Laws, rights and regulation" (2011), published by IGI Global, Hershey, P.A., . Dr.Halder has also edited a book titled "Therapeutic Jurisprudence and Overcoming Violence against Women" (2017) published by IGI Global, US in 2017. Her book "Cyber crime against women in India"(2016) by SAGE Publications has also been published in Hindi and Marathi by Sage Bhasha in 2019. Dr. Halder is also the founder-Associate editor -Book review of two Scopus-UGC listed journals namely, International Journal of Cyber Criminology (http://www.cybercrimejournal.com/) and International Journal of criminal justice sciences (www.http://www.sascv.org/ijcjs/index.html) Apart from this, Dr.Debarati Halder has also published many scholarly articles on online victimisation of women, cyber law, Child rights, Therapeutic Jurisprudence, Human rights, Prison rights of women etc in many national as well as international peer reviewed journals and edited book chapters including Routledge legal pedagogy series, British Journal of Criminology, International Annals of Criminology, National Law School Journal, Journal of Law and religion and many edited books including "Cyber criminology", "Social networking as a criminal enterprise", published by CRC press, Taylor & Francis Group. Dr. Debarati Halder was also an invited speaker in the Stockholm Criminology Symposium, 2012. Dr.Debarati Halder, is an expert resource person on cyber law, cyber security, cybercrimes against women and laws, online child protection, Criminal laws, Victimology and Penology etc for many national and international policy making bodies, including UNICEF, Facebook, National Commission for Women, West Bengal, Kerala and Assam State commission for protection of child rights,

Maharastra state commission for women etc. She is also invited as expert resource person by Courts and institutes including Manipur High court, North Eastern Police academy, Meghalaya, KIIT Law School, Bhubaneswar, Rajiv Gandhi Institute for Youth Development, Kancheepuram, Tamil Nadu etc. She is also invited as resource person in many UGC assisted workshops and seminars. Dr.Debarati Halder also served as Vice president for kids and Teens division and internet safety advocate for Working to Halt Online Abuse (WHOA)(www.haltabuse.org) from 2008-2015.

* * *

Jane Adebusuyi is a sociologist/anthropologist by academic background. She is currently an Associate Professor of Medical Social Work at the Lead City University, Ibadan, Oyo State, Nigeria. She practiced as a Medical Social Worker for 35 years and has handled various psychosocial problems of patients at the University College Hospital Ibadan. Similarly, she has handled several cases of domestic violence and interpersonal conflict and played an advocacy role on behalf of her clients. She is a Fellow of the Institute of Policy Management Development of Nigeria. She has participated in academic discourses on "Social Problems and Social Work", Conflict Resolution and Family Therapy. She is the author of 32 published academic papers, and has presented 83 papers at conferences and scientific workshops.

Johnson Ayodele is an Associate Professor of Criminology and Security Studies at the Lead City University, Ibadan, Oyo State, Nigeria. He is a specialist in Criminology, Victimology, Social Problems, and Social Works, with a special interest in victims' crime reporting to the police. He has done extensive work in the states of Nigeria. His latest interest is on Victimology in south-western Nigeria where he intends to interrogate the cultural value-driven praxis within the framework of Yoruba beliefs. His work has focused on social responses to victimization, police attitudes to victims, women as victims of widowhood, subsidy withdrawal injustice, and marital rape. Ayodele has some of his works published in local and reputable and scholarly international journals. He is the editor of Global Perspectives on Victimisation Prevention and Analysis.

Angelo Brown is an assistant professor of criminology with a Ph.D. from Washington State University in criminal justice and criminology.

Ranjani Castro is a Research Scholar, Department of Criminology, Karunya Institute of Technology and Sciences (KITS), Tamil Nadu, India. She has recently completed her Master's in Criminology with specialization in Forensic Psychology at National Forensic Sciences University (NFSU), Gujarat, India. She also holds a

Bachelor's degree in Psychology, a diploma course on Criminology and Applications in Forensic Psychology, and a Post Graduate certificate course on Victimology, Victim Assistance, and Criminal Justice. Her research interests on criminal psychology, international humanitarian crimes and laws, transitional justice, restorative justice, therapeutic jurisprudence, and victimology.

Hitesh Goyal is a Criminologist and working as a Teaching & Research Assistant (TRA) in Criminology at School of Forensic Psychology, Criminology Program, National Forensic Sciences, University(NFSU) Delhi Campus, (An Institution of National Importance) Ministry of Home Affairs (MHA), Government of India, Mr. Goyal is also currently pursuing his PhD from Tata Institute of Social Sciences, Mumbai.

Swikar Lama is the Associate Dean, Faculty of Criminal Justice and Police Studies at Sardar Patel University of Police, Security & Criminal Justice, Jodhpur, where he has served since 1st January 2014. He received his Ph.D. from IIT Delhi and M.Sc. in Criminology from LNJN National Institute of Criminology and Forensic Science, Ministry of Home Affairs, India, where he was awarded the 2007 University Topper and Gold Medal in M.Sc. Criminology. He served as 'Junior Research Officer' at International Institute for Non-Aligned Studies, during which he represented the International Institute for Peace at the 6th Session UN Human Rights Council at Geneva (2007-2008). He was awarded the Fellow of Indian Society of Criminology for the year 2017 for his contribution in criminology. He received the 2nd Best Research Paper Award at the XXII Annual Convention of the National Academy of Psychology Conference at Christ University, Bangalore, Karnataka, 10-12 December 2012. Grants awarded include Travel Grant from Ministry of Foreign Affairs, Netherlands to attend the 14th International Symposium of World Society of Victimology, 20-24 May 2012, and Indian Council for Social Science Research (ICSSR) Travel Grant (partial assistance to present paper at International Conference, January, 2012) at 'Women, crime and criminal justice practice' at University of Cambridge, 10-12 January, 2012.

Mehrdad Rayejian Asli is an Iranian Criminologist and Victimologist. Under the title "Criminalization of Abuse of Power in the Light of Interaction between Human Rights and Criminal Law", he received a PhD in Criminal Law and Criminology from Shahid Beheshti University (SBU), Tehran, Iran in 2006. Rayejian is Assistant Professor of the Institute for Research & Development in Humanities (SAMT Organization). He is also served as the Deputy of Research of UNESCO Chair for Human Rights, Peace and Democracy. Rayejian began his international career with visiting scholars in Leiden University (Netherlands) in 2002 and Max-Planck Institute

(Freiburg, Germany) in 2005. His first English article was published in European Journal of Crime, Criminal Law and Criminal Justice (Brill I Nijhoff, 2006). His another English article entitled "Introducing a General Theory of Victimology in Criminal Sciences" (International Journal of Humanities, 20 (3), 2013) is a high ranking one at the international social networking platforms, including ResearchGate and GoogleScholar. His coauthor chapter "Forced Marriage in Islamic Countries" has been published by international publisher Springer in 2016. He also published a paper about victims of terrorism in the UNESCO Chair's Journal of Islamic Studies on Human Rights and Democracy (ISHRD) in 2018-2019. Recently, his chapter has been published in "Crime Prevention and Justice in 2030" (Springer, 2021) for the 14th United Nations Congress of Crime Prevention and Criminal Justice in Kyoto, Japan (March 2021). "Protecting Victims of Terrorism in the Light of Global Criminology: International Experiences and Developments in the Early Third Millennium" is one of his latest article, which has been published in the International Annals of Criminology by the Cambridge University Press on April 2021.

Anthony Richards is a biochemist with an interest in the ethnobotany of the african diaspora. He received a BSc in Biological Sciences, University of the West Indies, and PhD in Microbiology, Kings College (Lond.) He has served as Vice President of the Society for Economic Botany (Caribbean Chapter).

Rod Robinson is an enrolled member of the Northern Cheyenne tribe from Montana. He is the grateful father of 4 beautiful children, several adopted children, nieces, nephews and a new grand-daughter. He is a Master's level licensed therapist and has practiced in his field of healing and recovery from addictions for over 40 years. In this time, he has served the People as a ceremony man, a mentor, a clinician, administrator, educator, policy maker and innovator. He is eternally grateful that the Creator has called him to serve in this manner. Aho!

Beulah Shekhar is the Chair Professor of Criminology, Loknayak Jayprakash Narayan (LNJN) & National Institute of Criminology & Forensic Science (NICFS). She also visits the Karunya Institute of Technology & Sciences, Coimbatore, India, as Emeritus Professor of Criminology. Her responsibilities include teaching research & Extension activities with a special focus on collaborative research. She was formerly Professor & Head of the Department of Criminology and Criminal Justice Sciences, Manonmaniam Sundaranar University, and also Co-coordinator of the UGC sponsored programs, Victimology & Victim Assistance and The Human rights & Duties Education. She was the Director, Center for Empowerment & Women's Studies at MSU and the Special Officer, RTI/ CM Cell / Local Fund Audit. She has also served as the Juvenile Justice board member for the three southern districts of Tirunelveli, Tuticorin & Kanyakumari, was the Director of the Childline Nodal agency, and the Sahodari Family Counselling Center Project at Tirunelveli The thrust area of all her work is public affairs and social issues. Her research concentrates on the inequalities in various areas increasing the vulnerabilities and denying access to justice to excluded groups like women, Dalits, children, transgender persons, victims of crime, and abuse of power. She significantly focuses on developing partnerships between researchers, policymakers, program developers, agency personnel, and other community groups. Through these partnerships, she conducts basic and applied research and evaluation in issues of sociological concerns and the many different facets of Victimology, Crime, Criminology, Law, and Justice. She holds degrees in Womens' Studies, Psychology, Education Management, Human rights, Victimology, Counseling, Law, and Christian Studies, She serves as a research guide and examiner in various Universities and guides M.Sc., M.A. M.Phil & Ph.D. Scholars. She is involved in the training of the police & and the judiciary in the concepts of Victimology to fill the gaps in services to victims of crime in the Criminal Justice System in India She has completed five major projects funded by the University Grants Commission (UGC), Indian Council of Social Science Research (ICSSR), Bureau of Police Research And Development (BPR&D) and United Kingdom-India Educational Research Initiative (UKIERI) and coordinated funded skill-based training programs for the Criminal Justice Professionals all over the country. She was the first to introduce a standalone Victimology course in India, in 2008, to bring the Victimological courses in Post Graduate Diploma (PG Diploma) and Master of Philosophy (M.Phil) in India through UGC – Innovative Program. She has published her research work widely in national and international journals and has been invited to present her research findings in Australia, Hong Kong, Kenya, Japan, U K, Portugal, Switzerland, Indonesia, Taiwan, Canada, Netherlands, Sweden, to mention a few. She was on deputation from the University to the YWCA of India as the National General Secretary, heading 85 local associations all over India. She has served as a member of National Consultations in various reforms and evaluations of the legislation and the working of the Criminal Justice Systems. She was invited as an individual expert at the 12th United Nations Congress on Crime Prevention and Criminal Justice, in Brazil and part of the Delegation of the World Society of Victimology in the Crime Commission at Vienna in May 2011 and the UN preparatory meeting at San Jose, Costa Rica in February 2014. She was awarded the prestigious Indo-Hungarian fellowship in 2010 and was a visiting researcher at the University of Montreal in 2011. She was also the recipient of the Commonwealth Academic Staff Fellowship 2013- 2014. She is the recipient of the Fulbright Fellowship 2014-2015 has worked in the John Jay College of Criminal Justice, New York from November 2014. She is the recipient of prestigious awards from the Indian Society of Victimology in 2014 and the Indian Society of Criminology in 2018. She has been invited to organize a panel discussion at the 14th United Nations Congress on Crime Prevention and Criminal Justice held in Kyoto, Japan in March 2021, on the topic, Access to Justice- Initiatives, Involvement, Innovations, and Institutional frameworks in India.

Seth Tweneboah (PhD) is a lecturer at the Centre for African Studies of the University of Education, Winneba, Ghana. He received his PhD in Religious Studies (with specialization in law and politics) from the Victoria University of Wellington, New Zealand. Seth has an MPhil from the University of Ghana, Legon and an MA from the Florida International University, Miami. His research focuses on the religious human rights and the religion-law interrelationships in Africa. He is the author of Religion, Law, Politics, and the State in Africa: Applying Legal Pluralism in Ghana.

Rosemary White Shield leads initiatives focused on centering equity, culture, and community values in policymaking. She is a member of the national team providing strategic planning, project development and management, and training and technical assistance. She also collaboratively leads the development and provision of technical assistance in service to Tribal Nations. She has worked with Tribal Nations and others across the U.S. in the behavioral health fields.

Index

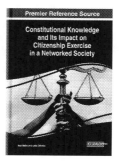
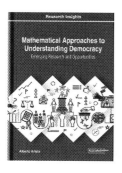

 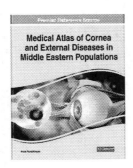 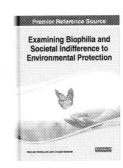 

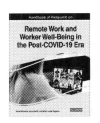

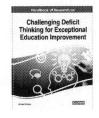